About the Author

Albert Hamilton is Kent Professor of Project Management at the University of Limerick, Ireland. A graduate in civil and mechanical engineering, he has managed projects as far afield as Malawi, South Africa, Zambia, Canada, Nicaragua and Pakistan, in water resources, mining operations, heavy industry and energy generation.

A native of County Antrim in Northern Ireland, Professor Hamilton set up his own consultancy practice in England, specialising in the management of overseas projects. In 1990, he returned to Ireland as visiting professor in project management at the Queen's University, Belfast, before taking up his current post at the University of Limerick in 1991.

Albert Hamilton is a Fellow of the Institution of Engineers of Ireland, the Institution of Civil Engineers, the Institution of Mechanical Engineers and the Association of Project Managers. He is also a Member of the Project Management Institute, the American Society of Civil Engineers, the Society of American Value Engineers and the American Association of Cost Engineers.

Management by Projects

Achieving Success in a Changing World

Albert Hamilton

 Thomas Telford, London

Published by Thomas Telford Services Ltd., Thomas Telford House,
1 Heron Quay, London E14 4JD.

First published 1997
Published in the Republic of Ireland and Northern Ireland by Oak Tree
Press, Dublin.

Distributors for Thomas Telford Books are:
USA: American Society of Civil Engineers, Publications Sales
Department, 345 East 47th Street, New York, NY 10017-2398
Japan: Maruzen Co. Ltd., Book Department, 3-10 Nihonbashi 2-chome,
Chuoku, Tokyo 103
Australia: DA Books and Journals, 648 Whitehorse Road, Mitcham 3132,
Victoria

A catalogue record of this book is available from the British Library

ISBN 0 7277 2632 3

Typeset in the Republic of Ireland by Oak Tree Press, Dublin.
Printed in the Republic of Ireland by Colour Books, Dublin.

CONTENTS

LIST OF FIGURES

PART 4: PROBLEM SOLVING AND DECISION-MAKING

PART 5: ORGANISATIONAL THEORIES, ORGANISATIONS AND PEOPLE

PART 6: CONCEPTION AND DEFINITION PHASES

PART 7: PLANNING, SCHEDULING AND TIME–COST OPTIMISATION

PART 8: IMPLEMENTATION AND COMPLETION PHASES

FOREWORD

Professor Albert Hamilton's book *Management by Projects: Achieving Success in a Changing World* is a refreshing treatment of an important subject.

The author takes time at the beginning of his book to set the stage for change and the importance of the management of that change in contemporary organisations. As a further preparatory strategy, Professor Hamilton introduces the importance of understanding and representing systems as a prelude to the project management process. The theory and means for better problem solving and decision-making are then presented as a further prelude to an overview of organisation theories, organisational design, and the human side of project management. The life cycle of projects is then introduced within the context of budget estimating, value assessment, and project risk. The key elements of project planning, scheduling, and time-cost optimisation are then presented. Finally, the author provides a theoretical and practical model for the implementation and completion of projects as elements of organisational strategy.

The Project Management Institute's Body of Knowledge (PMBOK) is given its due recognition in this book through placing it in the overall context of the theory and practice of project management. The author has provided an ample inventory of excellent figures that are valuable in modelling the concept and process of project management. The manuscript is further complemented by appropriate bibliographies and a glossary of terms which strengthen the textual material.

This is a first rate primer on project management. It will prove valuable for project management users as well as for those students who seek to learn the important basics of project management. It will be recognised as a meaningful contribution to the basics of project management — and how that discipline fits into the management discipline. A careful perusal of this book will provide the reader with a deep appreciation of how project management contributes to the management of change in contemporary organisations.

Professor Hamilton's book will occupy an important position in my project management library!

David I. Cleland

Holder of the Ernest E. Roth Chair,
Professor of Engineering Management,
University of Pittsburgh.

DEDICATION

To my late mother, Sarah, who gave me encouragement in the early part of my working life and to my wife, Jalyn, who has faithfully provided me with continuous support throughout my career.

PREFACE

This book has been written in response to a growing need for recognising the "world of projects" and for the better management of projects.

The changing and chaotic environment within which we work and live throws up ever-demanding problems that need innovative and creative solutions in increasingly shorter response times. Business is beginning to recognise that what most people in organisations have to deal with can be classified as projects. Many people are also recognising that they are "managers", and are often involved in certain aspects of many types of projects. Individuals are beginning to see their life as a project consisting of a series of problems that, to be solved, need discipline.

This book is for all who work within contemporary organisations and who seek knowledge of the something extra, the missing link, that is needed to better manage what they do. The book will be of benefit and interest to everyone who works within a projects environment. The book will also be of importance to many people because it deals with how to handle many of the "change issues" found in daily life.

Once it is recognised that fairly common change issues — a family wedding, a motor-car rally, the preparation of a report, an in-company seminar, developing a new product within a company, designing and building a new transportation route, minting and circulating new coinage — are all projects, then perhaps it will start a thought train in most people's minds that they are regularly engaged in some aspect of many different projects.

Projects can be managed by a single person or by a team of people. The human resources that are needed are usually a function of the size and complexity of the project. The management of a family wedding is the sort of project that could be handled by one person. Presenting an in-company seminar may require a team of two or three people. The design and construction of a major project, such as the Channel Tunnel between Britain and France, requires a multi-national team of several thousand people.

Business management and academic wisdom have, over the past decades, been inextricably linked to what is referred to as "traditional" management. This linkage has been so well-institutionalised that it has been difficult to establish a different form of management.

Traditional management is very suitable for handling continuous operations, but it has been found wanting when dealing with something that is "unique" and a "once-off" endeavour. It is these, and other, characteristics that distinguish projects from operations. This book sets out to demonstrate that projects by their nature cannot be dealt with adequately and comprehensively through using traditional management.

Project management uses most of the tools of traditional management, but it also uses many other techniques that are not used by traditional management.

The traditional management tools that are used include personnel management and administration, cost budgeting, accountancy practices, financial management, etc. The project management tools that traditional management ordinarily doesn't use include value analysis, risk analysis, critical path method planning, life-cycle costing, concurrency, configuration management, time and cost integrated control, and so on. These and other project management tools form the basis of this book.

The intention of this book is to present clearly many of the significant procedures and methods that are considered to be the modern project management process. The book also deals with other important aspects that impact on the management of projects. It introduces "systems thinking" and how the systems approach provides us with a better understanding for solving problems. The book emphasises the types of organisational structures, and the importance of people, that are traditionally found in projects. The book throughout deals with problem solving and decision-making, and the reader will soon appreciate the statement *"project management is a process; it is a way of thinking and acting"*.

The book has been structured into eight Parts.

In Part 1 a view is presented of the complexity of our living and working environment and how we can handle that complexity more effectively by recognising the importance and complementary nature of the holistic approach to the more traditional analytical approach. The importance of the systems approach to the well-being of business and management is also contained within Part 1.

The importance of being able to think "systemically" and how mapping helps in this process is dealt with in Part 2. The reader will be provided with the tools to be able to "map" and in so doing will be able to add to their ability to develop detailed strategies for conceptualising actions and for problem solving.

The next part, Part 3, gives an overview of the project management process, the project management body of knowledge, and the significant factors that have been identified as impacting on project success or failure.

Decision analysis has a major role to play in helping managers of projects gain a greater understanding of the problems they face. Many decision problems are complicated by the need to consider a range of issues, such as the environment, divergent views of project stakeholders, etc. To reflect this, Part 4 includes extensive coverage of problems involving multiple objectives and methods which are designed to assist groups of decision-makers in tackling problems.

Organisation structures and people factors that impact on projects are described in Part 5 of the book. They are considered to be as important as the procedures and methods used in project management. My involvement with the management of projects has demonstrated continually that, even using the best and most modern procedures and methods, effectiveness and project success will not be assured without the right organisation structure and the right people.

The conception and definition phases, perhaps the most important period in the life-cycle of projects, are dealt with in the next part of the book. Generally, it is recognised that if these phases are not undertaken with consistency, and with the correct depth of analysis, then there is the potential for many problems to surface later in the life cycle of projects. The key procedures and methods during these phases, such as financial appraisal methods, the value process, risk identification and its analysis, the make-up of a project's master plan, etc., are all described in Part 6 of the book.

Time and cost planning are other important aspects for establishing a framework from which related problems can be identified and solutions generated. The use of network planning and scheduling techniques, such as the critical path method (CPM) and programme evaluation review technique (PERT), provide some of the most powerful procedures for project management decision-making. These procedures and other methods are described in Part 7 of the book.

Part 8 describes the implementation and completion phases of a project which are perhaps the most exciting, in that it is during this time that the project can be seen in its developing physical form. As the project nears the end of implementation, it enters the completion stage. It is at this point, the end of the close-out stage, that the project is no longer considered a project and becomes known as "a facility". This Part also describes the important elements of work status, trending, forecasting and other methods used in the control of projects. Control is unquestionably important, because without control it will not matter how well the concept has been developed, how diligent the definition and constraints for the project requirements have been obtained, or how pedantically the planning has been carried out.

In the book each Part is divided into suitably titled Sections. At the beginning of each Section there are "Aims and Objectives" which introduce you to the content. The main text of each Section deals with the planned transfer of knowledge. This is undertaken using suitable illustrations, learning aids and, where necessary, worked examples.

Each Part begins with an overview of the issues dealt with, alongside a "systems map", showing the place of the Part within the overall scheme of the book. At the end of each Part there is a summary of key points.

Like most projects, writing a book involves using the inspiration and work of other people. The publications which have provided me with the greatest inspiration and interest in what they had to say about our living and working environment, the general systems theory, project management and the many associated elements are listed at the end of each Part. To these authors, I wish to extend a grateful acknowledgement for their indirect help.

I am indebted to the College of Business and the University of Limerick for providing me, by virtue of my role as Director of the Centre for Project Management, with the opportunity that made this project possible.

My special thanks goes to my wife Jalyn. She read the entire text and provided an invaluable proofreading input as well as numerous helpful suggestions. If this book is readable it is largely because of her devoted enthusiasm to "get it right".

Despite the help and my own efforts to get it right there are likely to be mistakes or omissions. As I was the "project manager" on this project I accept full responsibility for such errors.

Albert Hamilton

Kent Professor of Project Management,
University of Limerick, Ireland.

PART 1

CHANGE AND THE IMPORTANCE OF MANAGEMENT

This Part of the book sets out a view on some of the changes that we are experiencing daily and the impact technology is having on such changes.

The connection between change and technology is presented and a theory offered on why innovation is a direct result of how we have been taught to think.

Section 1 concludes with a comparison of two fundamental ways of thinking: analysis and synthesis. The historical development of analytical thinking is provided. The inadequacy of the analytical approach alone in understanding problems is explained.

The need for a complementary approach — the systems approach — for a better understanding of the complex world in which we live, and, as "managers", for the solving of real life problems in organisations, is described.

The relationship between science and the systems approach is explained. A brief explanation is offered on why management needs to be structured differently in order to address the everyday chaos faced by most organisations.

This Part of the book is in two Sections. At the beginning of each Section the contents and the objectives of the Section are displayed. At the end of Part 1 there is a summary of key points.

A list of references that were, in part, the inspiration for this Part of the book are to be found after the summary of key points.

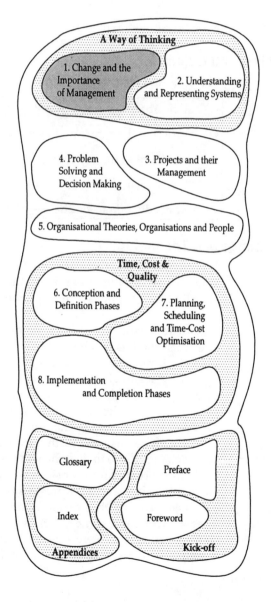

SECTION 1: THE DILEMMA OF CHANGE

Contents

- Aims and Objectives
- Change and Technology
- Expectation for Further Change
- Machine Age Thinking
- Systems Age Thinking
- Analysis and Synthesis

Aims and Objectives

The aims and objectives of Section 1 are to provide:

- An insight into what is meant by "change";
- A vision of the future and its effect on our lives and work;
- An account of history that gave us our analytical way of thinking;
- What is meant by the "systems age";
- An introduction to synthesis — "thinking differently".

Change and Technology

It is often said that there are only two things in life that we can predict and be absolutely certain about: one is death, the other is change. Generally we are very reluctant in our endeavours to understand, or to come to terms with, both certainties.

Our reluctance to address the meaning of death until the individual is of an age when there is less life to be lived than has been lived is perhaps understandable. Such reluctance is not really defensible since the individual would be best served by acknowledging death and planning for its consequences. Similarly, as change is inevitable and has a major impact on our lives, we should not be afraid of it but try to understand the process and use it for our own benefit.

You might be asking the question: "but what is meant by change?" Change and what it means need further explanation. A good example for introducing the term "change" is to look at the way we work.

In the period of little, or slow, work and business change prior to the Industrial Revolution, bureaucracies mistrusted change and were happy to maintain the *status quo*. During that period, change occurred at a rate that was almost unnoticeable; work and work practices were relatively unchanged between successive generations. There were indeed work changes but the relative practices of, for example, successive generations of lawyers, doctors, stone-masons, and many others remained virtually unchanged for a long period of time. This was the case until the end of the nineteenth century or, in some occupations, well into the twentieth century.

We are now witnessing phenomenal rates of change in our lives and this can, in some cases, be observed over periods of as little as a month or a few weeks. During this century the rate of change pattern has shifted; the rate of change is rapidly increasing. Change is all around, change is happening all the time. The business and living environments are becoming more and more affected by this ever-increasing rate of change. The changes are complex, they are volatile, and in many instances they are chaotic. A successful service, product or process strategy that is continued without constant improvement will become vulnerable to competitive alternatives. It is incumbent upon us all that we recognise what has been happening and try to understand what is meant by change.

To reach a fuller understanding of change, let us look at the growth of the world's human population (Vickers, 1970). From Figure 1-1, we can observe that, until about the seventeenth century, the rate of change was relatively slow and insignificant in comparison with the change, for instance, over the last 150 years. Between the birth of Christ and the middle of the seventeenth century — a period of approximately 1,650 years — the population grew from an estimated 250 million to 500 million people. In other words, it doubled in just over 1,500 years; since then, change has accelerated. There was a doubling of the earth's population from 1650 to 1850 (200 years). It doubled again from 1850 to 1925 (75 years). And it doubled yet again from 1925–1970 (45 years). The world's population is expected to exceed 8 billion within 30 years. It is obvious that in relatively recent times, the numbers of human beings have exploded.

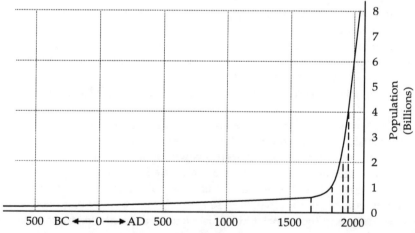

Figure 1-1: Earth's Human Population Change

By about 2050, it is expected that the population will peak at 10 or 11 billion — that is, twice the present level. Although the increase has been dramatic in the past 50 years, there are signs that the rate of increase is slowing.

There are no such parallels in the growth patterns of other earthly non-human populations, with perhaps the exception of certain bird colonies and lemmings, the arctic rodent. It is clear from the study of nature's "systems" that no trend can be expected to continue in the same direction indefinitely.

The way lemmings deal with an increasing population is fairly well known: they rush headlong into the sea and drown. Other non-human species have their populations controlled through changes in disease patterns, ecosystem changes, and other natural causes. The major difference between human population patterns as observed in western societies and that of other species springs from the increased rate of change of technology. Based on this premise, it can be concluded that the explosion of humans has been accommodated by improved technology.

This conclusion helps to explain the exponential increase in technology since the industrial revolution and particularly during this century. If it was possible to plot technology's impact against time then we would possibly see a very similar trend to that shown in Figure 1-1. If we consider for a moment such everyday activities as how we travel, calculate, communicate, produce, consume, etc. the significant changes within our, albeit limited, lifetime will in most cases be viewed as impressive. When compared with change during the Middle Ages or the Renaissance period, the changes that we are currently witnessing are astronomical.

Some of the changes are unique. Until recently technological and social change have been slow enough to allow us to adapt to such changes. It therefore can be said that change did not really press people in the past. Because human beings seek stability and don't like change, there was a general ignorance of, and reluctance to confront, the demand for change. However, the rapid change in technology is altering people's position on confrontation. Most of today's adults have lived through a period which has been witness to a relatively high rate of change. These same people know the "world" they are living in today is different to the one they were born into, and they are also aware of the world being increasingly dynamic and unstable.

Another unique aspect of accelerating change is the increasing complexity of the problems that we face. The more complex these problems are the more time it takes to solve them. By the time we find solutions to many problems, the problems have so changed that our solutions to them are no longer relevant or effective.

What are the agents that are creating this change? Does it start with people and their ability to use their intelligence? Are governments the agents of change? Do we look at the various organisations within society as creating the impetus? Is change brought about simply through improved technology?

Technology has to be, and is certainly, a major factor. Technology has brought us supersonic air travel, hydrofoil sea travel, high quality engineered road transport vehicles and the associated infrastructure to shrink distances to hours even if the journey is halfway round the world or from one end of a country to the other.

In the 1950s the north Atlantic Ocean could take five to six days to traverse by sea; the same journey can now be carried out in half that time by passenger ship. High-powered boats have completed the journey in less than half the time that it takes passenger ships to cross. Today's airliners can complete the crossing in seven hours or less. Tomorrow's means of transporting people will probably be capable of completing the journey in an hour or less.

The rising popularity of personal and private transportation through the motor car has created a different world in most developed countries. Motorways, flyovers, tunnels, multi-storey carparking, underground parking, garages, quick-fit component workshops, drive-in restaurants and cinemas, etc. have all changed the urban and to some extent the rural landscape. The population of cars in many developed countries is challenging the human population in the "numbers game". For example, the United Kingdom currently (1996) has a licensed vehicle population of 25 million; this to be compared with its human population of about 57 million. A visitor from a foreign planet might be excused for believing that this was a planet for "motorised vehicles" as much as it was for humans. The point is that transportation and its associated infrastructure have changed remarkably during this century.

Thirty years ago, a student at an education establishment was likely to carry out calculations using a slide rule; hand held calculators were just beginning to appear. The establishment of centralised electronic computers and their subsequent transformation into decentralised desktop computers has totally revolutionised the way the individual now carries out calculations. Decision-making software is available for most scientific disciplines allowing the user to carry out technological solutions to problems in a fraction of the time that it took in the 1960s. Similar advances can also be recorded for the non-scientific disciplines.

How we communicate has been one area that has seen perhaps some of the greatest changes. In the 1960s the telephone and the telex machine were at the forefront of technology; mobile hand-held devices were limited to field radios. Today we can communicate with people almost irrespective of where they are; be they sitting in their cars, in trains, in their bath, etc., or while sitting in front of their computers.

Communications now includes access to information. Through computers and associated technology we now have access to more data than we know what to do with or how to handle. Although change in communications has been impressive, the Internet and its associated system developments will create future communications change during the twenty-first century that will make previous changes seem as if little past progress was actually achieved.

In the last forty years or so technology has revolutionised the way we produce and consume. A good example of this is the food industry. The range of food products, the levels of quality, the different packaging, the ready-mixed items for home cooking, and so on have spoiled us with choice and convenience. Shopping, although made easier through the design of supermarkets, is also now made more difficult because of availability and choice. Consumption has changed with the change in our lifestyle. Eating, to an increasing extent, is being satisfied through quick cook meals, fast food outlets, and other convenience facilities.

There are many, many, more examples of the impact that change has made in our lives. It can be concluded that technology has to a very large extent countered, and is balancing, the impact of change in the way we live and work. Technology is in itself neutral. It is the impact which technology has, and will have, on our lives that is important. What we need to recognise is that technology's response to change is all around us; we can either use it to enrich our lives or it can be let loose, unmanaged, to dwindle all its impact for good.

Expectation for Further Change

If current knowledge indicates that technology is the balancing factor to the earth's population explosion then it is clear that future actions will also need to be made with an understanding of not only past changes but also with some understanding of future predictions of change. When we view what has happened in, for instance, the last 100 years it is difficult to get a picture of life 100 years from now — in the year 2097.

Charles Handy (1989; 1990; 1994) contemplates many possible or probable changes in the next five years, by the early years of the twenty-first century. Work and work-related activities will be possible from almost anywhere through the use of cordless telephones which are linked to lap-top computers that, through modems, allow the receiving and the sending of electronic data. We will not need offices but if we work for organisations we will require "work stations".

Having work stations means that you would be one of many users of a station consisting of desk, chair, PC, communications equipment, etc. As you and your colleagues camp and decamp for, more than likely, short periods of time there will not be the need for the same floor space. Many buildings will either have their use reassigned or will become redundant and hence be removed for the next generation of more useful land utilisation.

Westernised societies are becoming profiled as what is termed "30-30-40". This indicates that of the available working population thirty percent do not work, thirty percent work but are untenured, and forty percent are full-time tenured employees. In other words, it is anticipated that in less than ten years a minority of people will have full-time jobs, the rest will be self-employed, part-time, temporary or without a job. The British Isles is already at the stage where less than half of male workers remain in employment until the age of 65.

It is anticipated that the whole concept of work will change because of the way we will be forced to think. We will stop thinking naturally of employers and employees. Work will be an activity, some of which is paid for. Some expert workers would be rewarded for not using their skills. For instance, dentists and doctors could be paid for decreasing numbers attending their surgeries. By paying these experts on the number of treatments, as is the current procedure, there is a temptation to diagnose the need for treatment.

The normal 2,000 hours per year of work activity that we will be engaged in is likely to be distributed in a variety of ways; 40 hours for 5 days per week will be only one of many variants; 50 or 60 hours, or more, per week will not be unusual for some people. Under such a scenario the person may only work for six months or so in a year. Paying more money, or providing more time off for more effort are changes that we are likely to experience. The concept of having more than one career, so that you could switch from one to the other as the years go by, will also become a possibility.

Technological changes will make these or other work practices a reality. Life will likely be prolonged through preventing particular diseases by developing genetically engineered bacteria. Scavenger proteins will be designed that will locate and devour undesirable substances in the blood stream. Cures will probably be found for senile dementia and maybe for such modern killers as cancer and AIDS.

People will be able to shop without leaving their home. Telecatalogues will bring personal shopping to the home television screen. The television will be linked to voice- and vision-sensitive systems that will permit two-way exchanges for carrying out business between the "all goods store" and the home. Pick-up centres will be located in areas that will cater for populations within defined catchments.

Smart cards will replace cash, keys, credit, debit and cash cards. The smart card will allow the holder to enter the home, their car(s), arrange purchases, obtain services and cash, update and monitor their bank balances, etc. Due to these and other predicted changes in our lives, the way we think will also change.

If these and other significant changes will be with the "developed world" by around the end of this century it is difficult to comprehend the changes that will take place during the next millennium. Life will be unrecognisable at AD 3000 in the same way as life between AD 1000 and AD 2000 simply could not have been envisaged by the people of the Middle Ages.

Machine Age Thinking

To understand the way we think it is worth examining the way our ancestors were likely to think and what we may have inherited from them.

Russell Ackoff (1981) refers to the period up to the 1940s as the "machine age". He refers to the period since then as the "systems age"; what is meant by this age is dealt with more fully in Part 2. It is necessary, before discussing what is known as "general systems theory", that we deal with and explain what is meant by analysis. For this reason, an insight into the machine age is useful.

Let us first consider what life was like for people in the Middle Ages. This is the period from the fall of the Roman Empire in the fifth century to the start of the Renaissance period in the fourteenth century. Infant and child mortality was very high. Imagine the infant and child diseases and malnutrition which we in the West witness today as part of the normal life pattern in many of the world's under-developed countries. This devastation of early life in the Middle Ages was of an extent that surpasses even the worst effects of famine and disease that we have seen or read about in recent modern times.

The adolescent and adult populations were frequently devastated through war as well as disease. Poverty and deprivation were rife. People lived in family and tribe groups and there was little personal freedom. They seldom travelled more than a few miles beyond their birth place. The life span was relatively short and was within the general range of 20 to 35 years. You had little chance of reaching what is today considered "middle life" — 40–60 years — and you had no chance of reaching the stage of the elderly as we recognise it today.

For these and other reasons, the intellectual life of the time focused on the inner spiritual life and the afterlife. This sort of focus is evident in the art of the age, which largely reflects a desire to win salvation in heaven. Paintings of that period primarily depict Christ and the angels. Because life on earth was of little consequence, the spiritual and afterlife was considered to be something more desirable, albeit speculative. All in all, the people of the Middle Ages were severely restricted in many ways. It was a period of little progress and great probation.

The Renaissance of the fourteenth and fifteenth centuries was a reawakening for people because they re-entered the world of nature. Nature was approached with awe and wonder and people began to study its mysteries. The science of the day was not unsophisticated, but the people were naïve in their approach and understanding. Analysis became the process for trying to unravel nature's wonders.

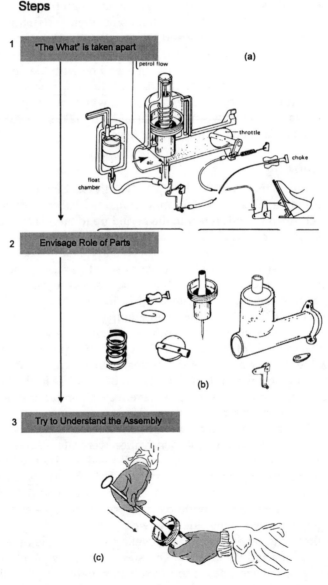

Steps

1   "The What" is taken apart   (a)

2   Envisage Role of Parts   (b)

3   Try to Understand the Assembly   (c)

Figure 1-2: Analytical Process

Since the Renaissance, analysis has been the basic method of enquiry. Analysis, which has not changed much, is a three step process; the three steps are described pictorially in Figure 1-2. The example that has been selected is a car's carburettor which is the part of the engine that mixes petrol and air before it enters the cylinders.

View (a) shows a cut-away of a the particular carburettor type being analysed. The carburettor is taken apart (step 1) and the parts placed at random on a flat surface, view (b). At this point the parts are viewed and the "analyst" tries to envisage the role of the separate parts (step 2). In viewing the separate parts, the analyst tries to understand the assembly of the parts, see view (c). This attempt to understand becomes the final step (step 3) in the analytical process. The success of the analysis is determined by the "understanding" matching the original "something" that has been analysed.

As human beings we are naturally adept at analysis. Other modern words that are used as alternatives to analysis are "reductionism", or "segmentalism".

The concept of mechanisation and the important characteristics of the Industrial Revolution were derived from the machine age. In other words, science was all about analysis. So what confronted man right through to the nineteenth century was the view that if you wanted to understand something then you had to take it apart to understand its parts. And in turn you had to take the parts apart, etc. down to their basic elements. Leading scientists had the belief, until relatively recently, that in this way a complete understanding of the world was possible.

Scientists believed that in physics all objects were reducible to particles of matter and in this way "mass and energy" could be explained. Likewise in chemistry everything was reducible to cells, in psychology it was reducible to psychic atoms, in linguistics to sound units called phonemes, and so on. From nineteenth century physics it was believed that even the most complex behaviours could be reduced to the interaction of a few simple laws.

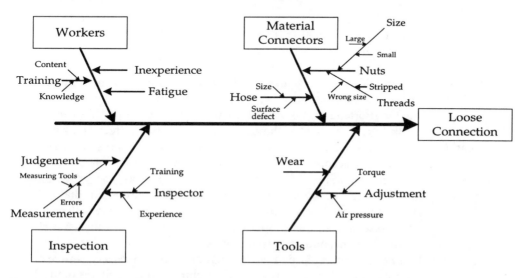

Figure 1-3: Cause and Effect Diagram
Source: Schroeder and Roberts, *Operations Management*

It was also believed that from such interactions the exact future behaviour of any physical system could be predicted. It was believed that almost everything could be explained by using the technique known as "cause and effect". Such analysis could be shown in diagrammatic format, as in Figure 1-3.

The cause and effect type of diagram is today synonymously referred to as a fishbone diagram or Ishikawa diagram but the traditional terminology is retained within this book's text.

In analysing a problem the use of the cause–effect diagram required the selection of the "effect" and placing that at the right side of the diagram. The "causes", which would create or lead to the effect, are developed on the left side of the diagram and drawn in a relational format. Cause and effect can be explained by examining the diagram in Figure 1-3. It can be seen that the principal causes for, say, "loose connections", an effect that is observed within the assembly shop of a manufacturing facility can be separated into groupings.

The principal groupings that are used in explaining an effect are found to generally fall under the acronym PEMPEM; this stands for people, environs, methods, plant, equipment, and materials. Not all of these groupings are to be found as the cause of all effects. Which groupings apply will depend upon the effect.

There are other causes, such as communication, that are the result of modern life and associated modern technology. By constructing a cause–effect diagram the potential causes of a problem become readily apparent. Each of these would then be evaluated, one by one, in order to find the true cause of the problem. In acceptance of a cause as being sufficient for its effect we inherited what is known as "causal thinking".

The cause–effect methodology states:

- One thing is said to be the cause of another (the effect)

- One thing is necessary for another if the other cannot occur unless the first occurs

- One thing is sufficient for another if the occurrence of the first assures the occurrence of the second.

A "cause" was, and still is, taken to explain its "effect" completely; nothing else outside of its immediate connections was required to explain it.

To appreciate the shortcomings of such thinking, take the example of an acorn, the seed of an oak tree. The acorn is the cause of the oak tree (effect). However this can only be the case when the surrounding geography and greater outside environment is taken into account. In other words, the Earth has to provide fertile ground, sunshine and rainfall in order for the acorn to take root and grow. An acorn falling into the water of a pond or stream is another environment that will not have the same impact. Such an environment would not support the "effect" of an oak tree. It can be seen from this simple example that the use of cause and effect ignores the outside environment as an influence.

The Industrial Revolution replaced man by man-made machines as a source of work; the two central concepts were work and machines. The mechanisation of work was greatly facilitated by reducing it to a set of simple tasks. Work was analysed to reduce it to its elements. The nature of the workplace today, as the twentieth century comes to a close, can be seen to have resulted from the analytical approach.

Systems Age Thinking

Since the turn of this century, investigators have been aware that dilemmas confronting one field of enquiry also arose in others. Awareness intensified during the 1940s, particularly as a result of certain problems that the allied powers had to grapple with. The interaction of the solutions of the disassembled parts were of greater importance than the solutions considered separately.

By the 1950s interdisciplinary scientific activities included management science, decision science, computer science, etc. It was recognised that the source of similarity of the interdisciplines was their shared preoccupation with the behaviour of systems. The word "systems" introduced a term whose meaning, not being clear, required definition.

A system was defined as a set of two or more elements that satisfy the following conditions:

- The behaviour of each element has an effect on the behaviour of the whole

- The behaviour of the elements and their effects on the whole are interdependent

- However subgroups of the elements are formed, each has an effect on the behaviour of the whole and none has an independent effect on it.

From this definition it therefore can be said that a system is a whole that cannot be divided into independent parts. From this fact derives the two most important properties of a system:

- Every part of a system has properties that it loses when separated from the system

- Every system has some essential properties that none of its parts do.

The essential properties of a system taken as a whole derive from the interactions. When a system is taken apart it loses its essential properties. Because of this, *a system is a whole that cannot be understood by analysis.*

So, as the analysis process focuses on the structure of things and tries to reveal how they work, the synthesis process focuses on function and why things operate as they do. Analysis is about knowledge and the ability to describe. Synthesis is about understanding and the ability to explain.

From the Middle Ages we inherited the process of analytical thinking and from the Industrial Revolution we inherited work structure, and the ways of doing things which included management and work practices. Generation after generation tried to further understand the new issues they had to deal with. They were doing this at a time when change was not all that spectacular; they were therefore able, to some degree, to improve efficiency and effectiveness. As change accelerated in the twentieth century, we can now reflect that the ability to counter and address dilemmas was severely restricted by the inherited cause and effect approach.

Analysis on its own is inadequate as a methodology in a systems environment because it does not help to explain the dilemmas or issues that need explaining during this world experience of chaos.

As members of modern society all, or most, of us should have the ability to synthesise as well as analyse. In other words, in the same way as people from the Middle Ages either knowingly or unknowingly used analysis as the methodology for furthering knowledge and the ability to describe, so today we now require the added ability for understanding and the ability to explain. This is necessary because of our understanding that *"most things are connected to other things"*.

Analysis and Synthesis

In the analytical process the thing to be explained is treated as a whole to be taken apart. In the synthesis process the thing to be explained is treated as a part of a containing whole. The former reduces the focus of the investigator; the latter expands it.

Let's compare each of the three steps of the two processes:

- In the analytical process the steps are:

    ◊   take apart the thing to be understood

    ◊   try to understand the behaviour of the parts taken separately

    ◊   try to assemble this understanding into an understanding of the whole.

- In the synthesis process the steps are:

    ◊   identify a containing whole (system) of which the thing to be explained is a part

    ◊   explain the behaviour, or properties, of the containing whole

    ◊   explain the behaviour, or properties, of the thing to be explained in terms of its roles or functions within its containing whole.

As an example of what the steps in the process means, let us look at a sparking plug which is part of a petrol-fuelled engine; see (a) in Figure 1-4.

Step 1 of the analytical process would provide us with the knowledge of the parts that together make a spark plug. There is the core which takes in electric current through the terminal nut [1] and passes it along the terminal stud [6], through the special conductive glass seal [5] to the centre electrode [10]. The spark is created by the current "arcing" between the centre electrode and the ground electrode [11]. The core is surrounded by an insulator [4] and leakage-current barrier [3], and towards the electrode end is a heat shrunk fitting [7] and gasket [9] which secures the spark plug in position on the engine head.

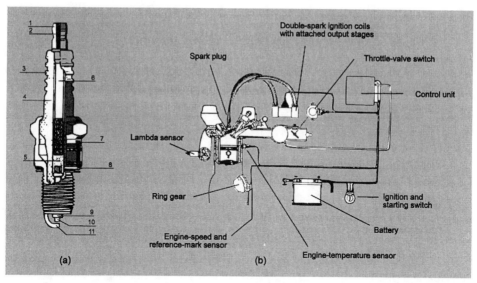

Figure 1-4: Systems Process

Having identified the parts, step 2 of the analytical process would be to understand the behaviour of the separate parts. In other words, to understand the action of the core, the insulator, the threaded section.

Step 3 of the process would require us to assemble the *separate understandings*
of *the behaviour, or actions, of the parts* into an overall action of all the parts when
placed together as required.

There is nothing new to us in this process; we do it all or most of the time
when we analyse something. But let us look now at the synthesis process.

Step 1 requires us to identify what the spark plug will be fitted to; this is
known as the system, and let us assume that it will be a car engine.

Step 2 of the synthesis process requires an explanation of the actions of the
engine. This would cover, but not be limited to, such matters as: the cylinder fir-
ing order, the rotational speed, the fuel usage, the power transmitted, and the
engine temperature. Step 3 would require us to explain the actions of the spark
plug within the overall actions of the engine's performance. View (b) in Figure 1-4
is helpful in providing the understanding to explain.

So, from this simple example, the comparison can be summarised simply:
analysis looks into things, synthesis looks out of things.

Early thinking, as explained in the previous sub-Section, "Machine Age
Thinking", was concerned only with the interactions of the parts of the thing to be
explained. Systems thinking is similarly concerned, but it is additionally occupied
with the interactions of that thing with other things within its environment, and
with its environment.

Systems thinking is also concerned with the functional interaction of the parts
of a system. This orientation derives from the preoccupation of systems thinking
with the design and redesign of systems. In systems design, parts identified by
analysis of the function(s) to be performed by the whole are designed to fit each
other so as to work together harmoniously as well as efficiently and effectively.

Harmony concerns:

- The effect of the interactions of the parts on the whole

- The effects of the functioning of the whole

- The interactions of the parts on the parts themselves

- The effects of the functioning of the parts and the whole on the containing system and other systems in its environment.

As Mitchell Waldrop (1992) says, scientists finally seem to be understanding that dissecting everything into molecules and atoms and nuclei and quarks is inadequate in helping us to understand. Instead of, or in addition to, looking for the simplest pieces possible, scientists are starting to look at how these pieces go together into complex wholes. Elegant equations and fancy mathematics are no more than tools. The crucial skill is the ability to see connections.

This aspect of harmony is central to the application of the systems approach to management.

By the early 1980s physicists began to realise that a lot of messy, complicated systems could be described by a powerful theory known as "non-linear dynamics". In the process they have been forced to face up to the disconcerting fact that *the whole really can be greater than the sum of the parts*. This was hardly a revelation, as Aristotle was of this view three to four hundred years before the birth of Christ, (see Part 2, Section 1, sub-Section "Scientific Revolution").

Everything is connected, often with considerable sensitivity. Tiny perturbances won't always remain tiny. Under the right circumstances the slightest uncertainty can grow until the system's future becomes unpredictable or chaotic. Tiny molecular motions can grow into cells. Seeds and embryos can grow into fully developed living creatures. Mild tropical winds can grow into hurricanes. A slight change in temperature in one location can create extreme weather conditions at other locations many hundreds, or thousands, of kilometres away.

So traditionally our way of solving problems has been through the reductionist approach: the dissection of the world into the smallest and simplest pieces. We look for the solution of some more-or-less idealised set of problems, somewhat divorced from the real world and constrained sufficiently so that a solution can be found. This approach breeds upon itself and it leads to greater and greater fragmentation of science.

The real world demands a more holistic approach. As everything affects everything else it is incumbent upon us earthlings to understand the whole web of connections.

SECTION 2: MANAGEMENT — REGULATING THE TRANSFORMATION PROCESS

Contents

- Aims and Objectives

- Segmentalism versus Wholeness

- Business Response

- Profitability and Jobs

- What is Management?

- Randomness and Chance

- Learning Organisations

- Summary of Key Points

- References

Aims and Objectives

The aims and objectives of Section 2 are to provide:

- An introduction to reductionist and holistic organisational approaches;

- A view on how people and organisations must address daily dilemmas;

- A hypothesis on high, and low, performing organisations;

- A definition of management;

- An outline of traditional management limitations;

- The ingredients of a "learning" organisation.

Segmentalism versus Wholeness

The contrasting style of thought and action which prevents change has been referred to as "segmentalism" by Rosabeth Moss Kanter (1983).

Traditionally, management has undertaken its role through using an analytical approach — taking apart the thing to be understood, trying to understand the behaviour of the parts taken separately, and then trying to assemble this understanding into an understanding of the whole. This approach is "segmentalism".

Many, if not most, organisations practice this form of thought and action. They see problems as narrowly as possible, independent of their connection to any other area or problem — the actions, events and problems are compartmentalised. Segmentalism assumes that problems can only be solved when they are carved into pieces and assigned to specialists who work in isolation.

Figure 1-5 shows a typical regional organisation responsible for law and order. The Figure focuses on only part of such an organisation, namely, the north-west subdivision, as part of the north division of "operations". It can be seen how a constable engaged on shift work is likely to be far removed from a detective constable even within the same subdivision, such as north west. If the organisation was expanded to show all the other divisions, i.e. west, south, and east, the isolation and compartmentalisation of people and the actions, events, and problems that they have to deal with become even more thought provoking.

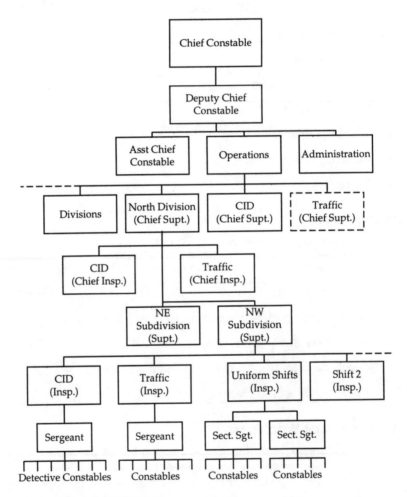

Figure 1-5: Segmented Organisation Structure

This raises the issue of whether the problems that are faced by the officers of the law can be adequately tackled by a segmentalised structure. It is contended that any organisational structure similar to that shown in Figure 1-5 would be a significant factor in an organisation being less successful as they could be in solving problems.

The executives of companies in which segmentalism is the dominant culture usually cannot innovate or handle change. Many executives are not willing to accept change and are inflexible when it comes to adopting a different approach to the way their organisation undertakes its operations. These same people appear to focus their attention and resources on controlling what they already know rather than developing what they do not yet know.

Much managerial and academic wisdom about organisational problem-solving stems from the study of segmented structures and segmentalist cultures. It is therefore no surprise that this is not very helpful in understanding innovation and change.

It is for this reason — that is, to better handle change — that *the current high interest in the discipline of "project management"* can be explained.

"Wholeness" is practised by those organisations who carry out their business by thinking about and seeing what they do as an integrated whole instead of segmented from mainstream operations. This is also referred to as the "holistic approach". This integrative thinking actively embraces change. It is more likely to be found within organisations whose structures and cultures are also integrative and where the wider implications of actions are the focus for consideration (see Figure 1-4).

Such organisations create mechanisms for exchange of information and problem-solving across organisational boundaries. These organisations ensure that many perspectives are included within the decision-making process. Conflict and animosity can be reduced between units within the same organisation. Direction and focus is given to the whole organisation. In these team environments, where the culture is co-operation, change can be better handled and innovation is given the opportunity to grow.

Innovation, which is needed to create change, flourishes, or should flourish, in team orientated co-operative environments. It is fairly clear that people matter in such environments. People don't need to matter when an organisation exists in stable circumstances, where everything operates like clockwork and the work practices do not vary.

Creating teams that horizontally span traditional vertical organisational units is a strong method for solving isolation and addressing conflict. This aspect is dealt with more fully in Part 5, "People and Project Organisation Structures". Through this structural arrangement the boundaries that are a feature of segmentalised organisations are removed, and this provides an environment for open transfer of information and idea generation. Decision-making is then undertaken with the benefit of all vertical segments or disciplines being brought together; the multi-perspective approach of such decisions being taken with the whole in mind. The experiences of the people within these teams along with the greater perception they obtain of the organisation and its resources, offer the whole organisation an opportunity for creating loyalty, better working practices and directional focus.

Business Response

In addition to our personal life experiences, political, social, economic and technological changes in global circumstances have recently been awesome. Countries, organisations and people are scrambling to develop and implement strategies for dealing with and institutionalising these changes. The successful organisation and manager, the successful entity of the future will be those which have the flexibility, the right attitude, to respond to change.

Prior to the 1960s, society simply demanded that products should be available. As we know, industry's answer to this demand was largely to turn to mass production techniques.

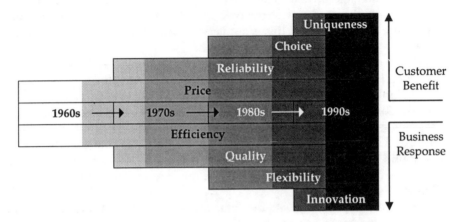

Figure 1-6: Changing Emphasis of Business

Thirty years ago (1960s) the "customer benefit" that society sought was price. The successful company or organisation concentrated on efficiency. Twenty years ago (1970s) the additional benefit that was demanded was reliability; the successful company concentrated on quality. Ten years ago the additional benefit that customers demanded was choice. The successful company concentrated on flexibility. In this current decade the additional customer-sought benefit is uniqueness. What should companies that want to be successful be doing? They should be concentrating on innovation. In fact, today the really successful organisations are those that are concentrating on all four customer benefits of price, reliability, choice and uniqueness through, respectively: efficiency, quality, flexibility, innovation.

Assuming that a company is efficient, concentrates on quality and provides customer choice through being flexible, what does that company need to do to be innovative. What does it take to be innovative? Companies that have succeeded, and are succeeding, have recognised what their clients, or customers, want. They have recognised what has been referred to earlier as "customer benefit" within their industries.

In general, it can be said that the 1980s brought about something of a revolution in management practices in the private sector and, to a certain extent, in the public sector. New emphasis has been placed upon leaner, more effective organisational forms, and on measuring the performance of individuals, groups and organisations at work.

The revolution in management practices in the 1980s has to be paralleled by a new revolution in the 1990s and into the next century, which emphasises accountability and goal setting/achievement for the development and implementation of new and improved ways of doing things. In this current environment, and in most future business environments, all managers must have the ability to understand change and develop responses to it.

To envisage work, or most work, as belonging to the projects model, a look at how the management of these projects are undertaken will demonstrate the effectiveness of the organisation in handling change, introducing innovation, and providing value for money. What is referred to as "project management" is a process, a people behaviour, a way of thinking, a set of procedures. Project management has the necessary elements to handle today's work in a way in which the traditional form of management has not been able to demonstrate.

Profitability and Jobs

If a company has survived the latest recession it will typically already have cut costs and reduced overheads. But, such businesses are increasingly faced with exceptional demands from customers; this usually means further price cuts. Recession-ending, rather than reducing price pressure, actually adds to the problems (Peters, 1989).

Chasing after "market share" isn't the solution. The solution is to target profitability. Profitability and its achievement will determine the survival of companies. Profitability determines that jobs are created. Profit is something we all have to strive for — for ourselves, our families and the organisations we work for. This is required whether we are from the public or private sector, working in a limited liability company, a partnership or operating as a sole trader.

Jobs are only created when the business climate allows organisations to make a profit. Profit ensures that organisations survive. The on-going generation of profits ensures the well-being of complete industries. Obviously without this recognition of the importance of profitability, complete industries will be depleted, organisations will disappear, and many individual's will lose their jobs. Many of us have been witness to this process all too often in our life-time.

Since profitability is a necessity in most management activity it is worth starting with identifying differences between high producing (performance) and low performance groups (Flippo and Munsinger, 1978). The hypothesis is that many differences are attributable to the way the groups are supervised.

In high performance groups the supervisor assumes a leadership role, feels secure with higher level supervision and is equally concerned with employees and with production. There is full up, down, and sideways undistorted communication; flexibility and adaptability prevail.

In low performance groups there is usually great pressure on the supervisor from above. The supervisor is largely production oriented, and the closer the supervision the lower the production. Working groups are seldom kept informed and the supervisor is inconsistent in giving orders.

Let this comparison be our starting point to begin a discussion on management.

What is Management?

"Traditional management" is a broad subject that includes topics such as:

- Finance and accounting, sales and marketing, research and development

- Manufacturing and distribution

- Strategic planning, tactical planning and operational planning

- Organisational structures, organisational behaviour, personnel administration

- Compensation, benefits and career paths

- Managing work relationships (delegation and supervision) and

- Managing yourself (stress, personal time).

The traditional management process attempts to emphasise parts (departments/divisions) of the organisation and separate activities into tasks for the organisational parts to deal with. It does not effectively consider inter-relationships or the integration of activities.

Traditional management does not normally provide the basis for an integrated, systematic organisation model. Traditional management cannot therefore work when the target is change; it cannot handle the introduction of change or its management.

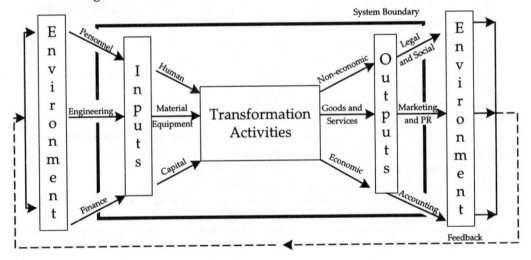

Figure 1-7: A System and its Management

Management is the regulation of the transformation of certain inputs, taken from the environment, converting them into a usable form as outputs, which are then put back into the environment. Management, in its regulation of the transformation activities, generally undertakes four functions: planning, organising, directing and controlling. These functions can be briefly explained as follows:

- *Planning* is the specification of goals and means

- *Organising* is the creation of an organisation to implement the plan

- *Directing* is stimulating the organisation to take action along the lines of the plan, and

- *Controlling* is the means of regulating actions resulting from the process of directing.

In a "process company", that is, one which is engaged in repetitive work operations (see "Segmentalism versus Wholeness" in this Section), the central core within which the prime business of the organisation is contained is normally what is called a closed system. What goes on within the core is self-contained, hence "closed". *Within the core*, the activities are not chaotic and are usually repetitive in nature; *within the core*, the traditional form of management is therefore likely to work extremely well.

Although the core is working in an inner atmosphere that is non-chaotic and repetitive, both middle management and top management, who are *outside the core*, are more than likely to be working with chaos and with non-repetitive activities. Top management is likely to be more exposed to chaos and non-repetition than middle management. Yet what do we find in most organisations at top and middle management? They are established along traditional management lines! Is it any wonder that these organisations can't handle change?

Management pervades virtually every aspect of our society which includes the individual, the family unit, the corporation, the government, the United Nations and other international agencies. Virtually everyone is a manager at some phase of their daily life. Everyone knows something about management; for example managing our time and our financial resources. Although we all have preconceived ideas about what management is, we are not management experts.

David Cleland and William King (1972) talk about the operational definition of management. Operational definitions are important in science because everything must be defined in terms of what would be observed if certain operations were performed. There are five observable criteria which, if satisfied, indicate that a management environment exists. The five operational criteria that define management are given as:

- Organised activity

- Objectives

- Relationships among resources

- Working through others

- Decisions.

The manager is the person who works toward objectives, through others, in an organised environment by establishing relationships among resources and making decisions.

Concepts of management are applicable to one's own management of personal resources. However the most significant area of application is in organisations. Increasingly within our society we see large organisations as being the prime movers in management knowledge. Because of the size and complexity of society and the increasing rate of change within that society, good management is more important today than it ever has been.

Organised activity can be understood as people working towards a common goal. The group can take a variety of forms, ranging from a multinational army such as that assembled for "Desert Storm", to a network of two people (it can even be one person) brought together to produce and present a training course.

The goal will be some form of *deliverable* or achievement. The activities organised are those needed to plan, define and produce the deliverable. The process of management serves to provide the co-ordinated effort that is needed to organise the activities.

The *objective* is the goal(s) towards which group activity is directed. Objectives may be explicit, as in completing the manuscript for this book by a set date, or implicit, as in this book being of interest to project managers.

Objectives can be fully defined or rather loosely defined. An objective that states: the report should be spiral bound, of not more than 5,000 words, be double-side printed, flush left with font Arial 11 point, and three copies should be submitted by a particular time on a particular date is a fully defined requirement, or objective. A very loosely defined objective would state that a report has to be prepared and submitted as soon as possible.

"Resources" is a general term which includes material, supplies, equipment, money or financing, and people. The goal-oriented organised activity needs to be brought about by establishing certain *relationships with the resources*.

Relationships among material, supplies and equipment resources tend to be physical in nature. An example of the relationship in material resources could be that between a new door and the existing opening in the brickwork wall at home. An example of the relationship in supplies could be the use of a particular ink cartridge for a computer printer in the office. An example of an equipment relationship could be that which the photocopier maintenance company has in maintaining the office copier. In the case of finance, an example could be the petty cash that is used for the everyday purchase of minor miscellaneous items.

There are both formal and informal human resource relationships that can challenge the operational criteria for management. Human resources perhaps provide the greatest relationship challenge. The relationships can be both formal, such as the requirement by the organisation for the person to conform with organisational procedures, and informal, such as that which arises daily as people relate to one another.

Within the informal relationships, personal inter-relationships are evolved into responsibility and authority patterns; responsibility being the obligation to respond to directions from other people; and authority being the legal right to command or direct the efforts of others.

Working through others is interpreted as being the delegation of responsibility to others to accomplish the goal(s) through organised activity that needs to be brought about by establishing certain relationships among the resources. A human tendency is to "do the thing yourself". The idea of working through others can be interpreted as assigning tasks to others within a group or to subordinates.

An active involvement with problems and decision-making is the final criterion of management. Decision-making means the evaluation and selection of the preferred option from a range of alternatives. The quality of the *decisions* determine the performance of the system, project, component or element being considered and whether or not the objective(s) will be achieved.

In summary, meaningful management is being practised when these criteria are observed as being present in a work situation.

Humans organise to accomplish some goal collectively that none can achieve alone. An organisation can be thought of as an agreement among people to co-operate in some endeavour. Its essential elements are the five operational criteria; these five elements are common to management.

Each of us is associated with many different organisations. The roles we play in organisations are varied and often interdependent. Organisations are purposeful systems, the purpose being the achievement of goals. In modern society, the various goals sought by different organisations are interdependent, thus ensuring that the organisations are themselves interdependent.

Randomness and Chance

New technologies are transforming the way people do things in organisations. The more "hard" technology becomes a factor in competition and survival, the more managerial and academic wisdom appears to concentrate on such "soft" arts as employee motivation, leadership, and change management. In other words, as David Freedman (1992) puts it, "the more science and technology reshape the very essence of business, the less useful the concept of management itself as a science seems to be".

It is contended that one of the principal reasons why many businesses are in a poor state is because they use traditional (general) management techniques, and traditional management is not capable of dealing with the dynamics of change. Bureaucracies, in particular, are being seriously tested because they cannot respond to this rapid change.

Traditional management, which was borne out of nineteenth century military usage, was designed for hierarchical structures to deal with continuity and repetition. Traditional management was subsequently adopted to assist industry to handle processes. Processes, or work operations, are continuations of something. In other words, doing the same task each day, and the day after, and the days after that, etc. is a process.

This form of "continuity" management is incapable of dealing with chaotic, non-repetitive situations — in fact this form of management cannot deal with change. Change by inference is almost everything we are confronted with in our working and living environment today.

Where today the demands on organisations are focused on price, reliability, choice and the uniqueness of what they do, so the response of these organisations must include innovation as a principal feature. Traditional academic and managerial wisdom can tend to stifle innovation.

The traditional scientific approach to management finds it roots in Frederick Winslow Taylor's work (1911) at the turn of the century. Taylor, born in the USA in 1856, was trained as an engineer and worked in industry for most of his life. Taylor's experience in the steel industry led him to believe that all was not well in modern industry. Managers approached their jobs in arbitrary rule-of-thumb ways. Workers were casual and lackadaisical in meeting their work commitments. Taylor recommended making management a science, resting on fixed principles instead of more or less hazy ideas. In particular, he set himself the task of devising methods of job study, control of work flow and incentives, and succeeded brilliantly.

In modern parlance, Taylor preached the doctrine of cost effectiveness, and that implied control. In other words the traditional scientific approach which has been the basis of management for most of this century was based on analysis, prediction and control. As we approach the end of the century the world of management has to deal with unpredictability and uncertainty. Our business world is a world of chaos and complexity and it is questionable whether it can be controlled.

Scientific management appears to be less relevant to the practical concerns of modern managers; indeed, it would seem to be counterproductive. The problems may lie less in the shortcomings of the scientific approach than in an understanding of science. Management may indeed be a science but not the science that most managers think.

Taylor wrote:

> the best management is a true science resting upon clearly defined laws, rules, and principles as a foundation. In the past man has been first; in the future the system must be first.

Taylor's ideas contributed to massive increases in productivity and people's living standards. Taylor and his ideas were without question right for their time. Taylor's methods can be referred to as reductionism where problems under consideration were broken down into isolated parts in order to better control them. He suggested the use of planning departments, time and motion study, standardisation of methods and tools, etc.

Taylor's principles contributed to massive increases in productivity and the standard of living. During the last 20 years or so, the scientific principles have been shown to be a recipe for disaster.

In fast-changing markets the fragmentation of work, the separation of planning from execution, and the isolation of workers from each other create rigid organisations that cannot adapt quickly to change. As a result managers must now rethink the fundamental elements of Taylor's system: work organisations, employee motivation, and the task of management.

The majority of new managerial ideas — such as cross-functional teams, self-managed work groups, and the networked organisation — are either direct or indirect responses to the inadequacies of Taylor's original model. Yet for all of the proliferation of specific techniques, the fundamental principles of a new managerial paradigm are far from clear.

During the past few decades more and more scientists conclude that many of science's traditional assumptions about the way nature operates are fundamentally wrong. Far from being predictable, nature appears as random as a throw of the dice.

Current thinking from one source, the Santa Fe Institute, is referred to in Waldrop's publication on complexity (1992). The concept of "chaos theory", where an infinitesimal change in initial conditions could have a profound effect on the evolution of the entire system, applies to the vast majority of physical systems. At Sante Fe, scientists believe that minute changes can lead to radical deviations in the behaviour of a natural system (refer to "Analysis and Synthesis" in Section 1). Randomness and chance in the late twentieth century has taken over from the emphasis on predictability and control in the nineteenth century. The current belief is that behaviour of even relatively simple physical systems is fundamentally unpredictable.

There are, however, patterns beneath the seemingly random behaviour of these systems. Certain paths apparently make more sense, or at least occur more frequently, and chaos theorists call such paths "strange attractors". Strange attractors allow scientists to determine within broad statistical parameters what a system is likely to do but never exactly when a system is likely to do it. The cause–effect precision of traditional physics has been replaced by the statistical estimate of probabilities.

Scientists in predicting patterns in a system don't turn to reductionism but to the holistic approach. Instead of attempting to explain how order is designed into the parts of a system, scientists now emphasis how order emerges from the interaction of those parts as a whole.

Some of the most successful complex adaptive systems in nature have several characteristics in common (Carter, 1988). They are self-managed, show co-operative behaviour and produce feedback. The systems have a network of agents that act independently from one another and without guidance from any central control. Such systems form groups or "communities" that co-operate in producing higher order behaviours that no single agent could accomplish on its own. Feedback makes self-management possible. As external conditions change, the structure of the system automatically changes.

In general, complex adaptive systems found in nature contain individual agents that network to create self-managed but highly organised behaviour. Such systems respond to feedback from the environment and adjust their behaviour accordingly. These characteristics may sound familiar because they closely match the new kind of organisation that many people are trying to create in order to cope with a more uncertain, complex, business environment.

Learning Organisations

Our western education has taught us to break apart something to better understand and manage it. However, the real world that we live in presents us with complex tasks and subjects, and when analysing these it becomes difficult to try to reassemble the fragments in our mind in order to see the whole, or to see what is sometimes referred to as the "big picture". In fact we begin to feel that the task of trying to recreate the complexity is quite futile and after a while we give up trying to see the whole.

The idea that the world is created of separate, unrelated forces is an illusion. As Peter Senge (1990) points out, once we give up this illusion we can build what he refers to as *learning organisations*. These will be organisations where people can continually expand their capacity to create the results they desire, where new and expansive patterns of thinking will be nurtured, where collective aspiration will be set free, and where people will be continually learning "how to learn together".

According to Peter Senge, business is the only institution that has a chance to fundamentally improve the injustice of the way we think and solve problems. To do this he says it is necessary to move through the barriers that are keeping us from being truly vision-led and capable of learning.

To create learning organisations requires five new "component technologies" which are referred to as:

- Systems thinking

- Personal mastery

- Mental models

- Building shared vision

• Team learning.

Team learning is vital because teams, not individuals, are the fundamental learning unit in organisations. Teams and team learning are the basis of Part 5 which has been devoted to (project) organisation structures and the members who make up the organisation.

Building shared vision is the capacity to hold a shared picture of the future that we seek to create. Such vision involves the skills of unearthing shared "pictures of the future" that foster genuine commitment and enrolment rather than compliance.

Mental models is what influences how we understand the world and how we undertake action. Working with mental models starts with "turning the mirror inwards", thus exposing our own thinking. This creates a needed opportunity of opening our thinking to the influence to others. Thinking and the use of mapping to create these *mental models* are the subject of Part 2.

Personal mastery is the discipline of continually clarifying and deepening our personal vision. It is a fact that, over time, people lose their sense of mission and commitment. An organisation's commitment to and capacity for learning can be no greater than that of its members.

The fifth discipline, *systems thinking*, is an essential aspect of all learning organisations because business and human endeavours are systems. They are bound by the inter-related actions which may take years to play out their useful connections. *Systems thinking* is a conceptual framework, a body of knowledge that will help to make patterns and change clearer. The subject of systems thinking is discussed in detail in Part 2.

The five disciplines differ from more familiar management disciplines in that they are "personal disciplines". To practise a discipline is to be a lifelong learner. It is questionable whether you ever arrive; you spend your life mastering disciplines. Practising a discipline is different from emulating a model. Senge says that he does not believe that great organisations have ever been built on trying to emulate another organisation, any more than individual greatness is achieved by trying to copy another "great person".

Vision without systems thinking is "painting lovely pictures of the future" with no deep understanding of the forces that must be mustered to move from here to there. If non-systemic thinking predominates, the first condition for nurturing vision is not met. This condition is *a genuine belief that we can make our vision real in the future.*

Of ten companies established today, only three or four will last three years and only one or two will still be around in five years' time. It is estimated that the average lifetime of the largest industrial enterprise is less than forty years; this is roughly half the lifetime of human beings. Individuals are therefore likely to have to change their job at least once in their lifetime and most individuals will be required to change jobs many times. Most organisations do not learn very well. The way they are designed and managed, the way people's jobs are defined and the way they have been taught to think and interact create fundamental learning disabilities.

Learning has lost its central meaning in contemporary usage. It has come to be synonymous with "taking in information". Real learning gets to the heart of what it means to be human. Through learning we recreate ourselves.

Let's examine some of the learning disabilities that are fairly common. When a person is asked what they do for a living they will mostly *describe the tasks* they perform each day and not the *purpose of the greater enterprise* in which they take part. When people in organisations focus only on their position, they have little sense of responsibility for the results obtained when all positions interact. They don't see how their actions extend beyond the boundary of their position. When these actions have consequences that come back to affect our position or our tasks we misconceive these new problems as being externally caused.

In taking charge, all too often people create an illusion of proactiveness which is really reactiveness in disguise. True proactiveness comes from seeing how we contribute to our own problems.

Some people focus on events. Such focus distracts us from seeing the longer term patterns of change. Primary threats to the survival of organisations and societies come not from sudden events but from slow gradual processes.

The most powerful learning comes from direct experience. Although we learn best from experience, we never directly experience the consequences of many of our most important decisions. Traditionally, organisations attempt to surmount the difficulty of coping with the breadth of impact from decisions by breaking the organisation into components.

And finally there is the myth of the management team. Teams in business tend to spend their time fighting for "territory" and avoiding anything that will make them look bad personally. Because school trains us to admit that we do not know the answer, most managers and many people find collective enquiry inherently threatening. Most corporations reinforce this lesson by rewarding people who excel in advocating their views, not enquiring into complex issues.

Enthusiasm for creating our future is not enough. For most people the deepest insight usually comes when they realise that their problems and their hopes for improvement are inextricably tied to how they think. Generative learning cannot be sustained in an organisation where event thinking predominates. It requires a conceptual framework of structured or systemic thinking, which provides the ability to discover structural causes of behaviour and effectively solve problems.

Summary of Key Points

- Business and living environments are becoming more and more affected by the ever-increasing rate of change. A successful service, product or strategy that is continued without constant improvement will become vulnerable to competitive advantage.

- Technology has revolutionised the way we do things. To ensure our lives are enriched technology's response to change will have to be managed.

- Science as a subject is unique in having, since the early nineteenth century, developed organised human activity in western civilisations by adopting the analytical process to explain and attempt to solve complex issues. Science has been a strong influence in the way westerners have been educated and in the universal use of analytical thinking.

- Analysis on its own is an inadequate methodology in understanding and explaining the real life problems of today. Systemic thinking and the systems approach are, respectively, an ability and a methodology for all members of society to use in better understanding the structure, the function, and how things operate as they do.

- The real skill in problem-solving in the ever complex and dynamic world where we live and work is in understanding and being able to explain the interconnections between components within a system and between systems.

- The response of business and management in dealing with ever-increasing demands of society, which are as we know continually changing, is to be innovative. Innovation is best brought about by management that is able to both analyse and synthesise.

- Organisations that practise systemic thinking and use the systems approach are more capable in handling change than those organisations that don't. In these team environments where the culture is co-operation, change can be better handled and innovation given the opportunity to grow.

- Work in the organisation of the future has to be seen as project work in which work is seen as an integrated whole instead of segmented from other operations. The management of these projects will demonstrate the effectiveness for handling change, introducing innovation, and providing value for money.

- Meaningful management is being practised when there is organised activity, the group has objectives, there is established relationships among resources, the work is achieved by working through others, and in deciding on action there is a means for evaluating and selecting preferred options.

- "Continuity" or traditional management is incapable of dealing with chaotic, non-repetitive situations which is what we refer to as "change".

- Businesses of the future must improve the way they think and solve problems they must become learning organisations based on systems thinking, personal mastery, mental models, building shared vision, and team learning.

References

References used in the development of Part 1:

Ackoff, Russell L. (1981), *Creating the Corporate Future*, John Wiley and Sons Ltd.

Carter, Ruth et al. (1988), *Systems, Management and Change*, Paul Chapman Publishing Ltd.

Cleland, David I. and King, William R. (1972), *Management: A Systems Approach*, McGraw-Hill Inc.

Flippo, Edwin B. and Munsinger, Gary M. (1978), *Management*, 4th edition, Allyn and Bacon.

Freedman, David (1992), "Is Management Still a Science?" *Harvard Business Review*, Nov–Dec.

Handy, Charles B. (1989), *The Age of Unreason*, Business Books Limited.

Handy, Charles B. (1990), *Inside Organisations*, BBC Books.

Handy, Charles B. (1994), *The Empty Raincoat*, Hutchinson.

Kanter, Rosabeth Moss (1983), *The Change Masters*, Unwin Hyman Limited.

Peters, Tom (1989), *Thriving on Chaos*, Pan Books Ltd.

Senge, Peter M. (1990), *The Fifth Discipline*, Century Business.

Vickers G. (1970), *Freedom in a Rocking Boat*, Allen Lane.

Taylor, Frederick Winslow (1911), *The Principles of Scientific Management*, Harper.

Waldrop, M. Mitchell (1992), *Complexity: The Emerging Science at the Edge of Order and Chaos*, Penguin Books.

PART 2

UNDERSTANDING AND REPRESENTING SYSTEMS

This Part of the book examines the importance of systemic, or holistic, thinking and the techniques that can be used to allow us to think in a different way.

What is meant by Systems Age thinking was introduced in Part 1. Part 2 further refines what is meant by and how to understand systems. The theory, approach, typology, and practice are all contained within Section 1 of the two Sections that constitute Part 2.

The sub-systems of the human body and how they interrelate are used to demonstrate the structure and processes of a "perfect" system.

The relationship between the systems approach and the project management process will be presented and the differences and advantages/disadvantages of synthesis and analysis will be explained.

Systems, or holistic thinking, is compared with other ways of thinking, and the need for such thinking in understanding wholes is explained.

Techniques used in representing systems are introduced and the use of diagramming, or mapping, is explained in some detail. Mapping techniques include: multiple cause diagrams, systems maps, influence diagrams, sign-graphs, and rich pictures.

A brief "Glossary of Terms" used when dealing with systems is presented after the "Summary of Key Points".

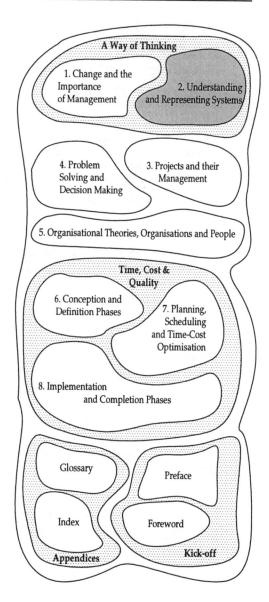

SECTION 1: THE NEED FOR UNDERSTANDING SYSTEMS

Contents

- Aims and Objectives
- Scientific Revolution
- Systems Theory
- Systems Approach
- A Systems Typology
- Systems Practice
- A Model System: The Human Body

Aims and Objectives

The aims and objectives of Section 1 are to provide:

- A brief explanation of the reductionism of scientific thinking;

- An explanation of the components of a system and the systems approach;

- The names and characteristics of the four types of systems;

- An explanation of the terms and processes that are found in systems;

- A description of how the human body can be used as a means for describing a perfect system and the inter-relationships between the body's sub-systems.

Scientific Revolution

Western civilisation is characterised by a unique combination of art and culture derived from the Judaeo-Christian tradition and technologies which reach beyond those developed in any previous civilisation. In fact, western civilisation is unique in having developed its particular organised human activity: what became known as science. Our world in the twentieth century is essentially the world created by the activity of science. The initiation of the process which led to the development of modern science we owe to the Greeks.

History has shown that the importance of different subjects has varied over time. With these changes in intellectual fashion new concerns emerge; at other times, old situations are newly perceived as a set of problems that are worthy of study. Early in the nineteenth century Auguste Comte conceived of a new science of society as the apex of the hierarchy of sciences; this was first called "social physics" then later became known as "sociology". By the 1880s many of the science subjects that we know today had been named. One of the last was the combination of experimental physiology and mental philosophy; these led to the development of psychology.

Science has been powerful enough to create the modern outlook. The exploitation of science in western technology has largely created the modern world in a physical sense. This lofty position of science is due to the potent combination of rational thinking and experimentation.

Peter Checkland (1993) sets out an interesting analysis of the history of the systems movement and its close links with science. He points out that western civilisation, in particular, has in the last 300 years provided us with a powerful means of observing the world, thinking about it and acquiring well-tested knowledge of its regularities; this means is the method of science.

Copernicus	1473–1543	Suggested a heliocentric model of the universe which reduced the complications of earlier earth-centred models.
Gilbert	1540–1603	An important emphasis on an experimental approach to practical problems (e.g. navigation).
Bacon	1561–1626	Declaimed the power of experimental science to give power over the material conditions of life and urged the method of experimentation.
Galileo	1564–1642	A major challenge to the Aristotelian world picture through work on mechanics. Experimental demonstrations expressed in the language of mathematics.
Kepler	1571–1630	Brahe's astronomical observations reduced to three mathematical laws. Number seen as nature's language.
Harvey	1578–1657	Experimentation and practical observation in medical research yields the theory of the circulation of the blood; the conclusion backed by calculation.
Descartes	1596–1650	The methodology of rationalism established; reductionism as the aim of scientific explanation.
Newton	1642–1727	The culmination of the move to experiment and mathematical expression started by Galileo. The method unites terrestrial and celestial mechanics and finally demolishes the Aristotelian picture of the world. Principles of experimentation established.
Einstein	1879–1955	Establishes a new world picture which explains observations more completely than Newton's and which survives stringent tests.

Figure 2-1: The Scientific Revolution and Beyond
Source: Checkland (1993)

Scientific work can, according to Checkland, be summarised in three crucial characteristics, each of which can be traced back to the development of science. The three characteristics which define the pattern of activity are reductionism, repeatability, and refutation. Human activity in dealing with the variety of real problems *reduces* their complexity through experiments whose results are validated by their *repeatability*, and knowledge is acquired by *refuting* hypotheses. Clearly, because scientific work is based on reductionism, scientific thinking is synonymous with analytical thinking.

Rene Descartes (1596–1650) was one of a long line of scientists, stretching from Copernicus in the fifteenth and sixteenth centuries to Einstein in the twentieth century, who were part of what is called the "scientific revolution". Descartes taught western civilisation that the thing to do with complexity was to break it into component parts and tackle them separately. Anyone who has a western-style education has learned this lesson well. Figure 2-1 contains the names, life span, and significant contributions made to science by certain important scientists.

The reductionist ideal can be seen in virtually all science of the eighteenth and nineteenth centuries. The scientific approach emphasises reducing the situation observed in order to increase the chance that experimentally reproducible observations will be obtained. To what extent can the method of science cope with complexity?

An interesting snapshot of early history tells us that Aristotle (384–322 BC) argued "that a whole was more than the sum of its parts". The scientific revolution whose principle was reductionism, which deeply permeated science for nearly 400 years, could be seen as having misdirected our development and understanding of real world problems.

The world is a giant complex with dense connections between its parts. We cannot cope with it in that form and are forced to reduce it to elements which we can examine separately. Thus our knowledge of the world becomes divided into different "subjects" or "disciplines" and in the course of history these change as our knowledge changes.

Nature does not consist of physics, chemistry, and biology, etc., these are arbitrary man-made divisions and are merely a convenient way of carving up the task of investigating nature's mysteries. Because from the start our education is conducted in terms of this division into distinct subjects, it is not easy to remind ourselves continually that the divisions are man-made and arbitrary.

Not until the twentieth century have significant challenges to reductionism been made. The most serious challenge to the reductionist movement is likely to be the systems movement. The reason for this is that although the reductionist method of science can cope with problems that are defined in the laboratory it cannot cope with the problems of the real world.

What other subjects are comparable to systems? Only science is! Professional scientists work in one of the many branches of the subject. If science is studied as a whole then we refer to the people who do so as philosophers. Science provides us with the phrase "scientific approach" just as systems provides a "systems approach". Science deals with the so-called "laws of nature", the regularities; systems deal with the irregularities, the chaos.

Systems Theory

General systems theory has been attributed to the German philosopher Georg Wilhelm Freidrich Hegel (1770–1831). The general systems theory was originally conceived to solve a specific problem; the problem being that there was no analytical "systems map" to fully explain organic biology. Biology is concerned with subparts and subsystems affecting each other and the overall organism.

Hegel's postulation of that time can be summarised:

- The whole is more than the sum of the parts

- The whole determines the nature of the parts

- The parts cannot be understood if considered in isolation from the whole

- The parts are dynamically interrelated and interdependent.

The problems associated with the general systems theory is that it initially takes from us the comfort of handling detail and encourages us to consider a broader view. To understand systems we must be content to understand relationships instead of absolute fact. General systems theory introduces dual objectives, e.g. optimisation *versus* sub optimisation; idealism *versus* realism; incrementalism *versus* innovation; agreement *versus* consensus.

On the other hand, the strengths of the general systems theory are that it provides a single language and a single set of laws for many studies. In addition it gives us the potential to understand functioning organisations of matter, people, events, ideas, and happenings.

For example, let us consider the designer. All designers expect to learn their chosen fields of study. For business designers, among others, the immediate field they should expect to learn — organisational systems and their broader environments — can be mastered only with the help of general systems theory.

Systems theory is a set of related concepts, or body of knowledge, which underlies:

- The philosophy — the way of thinking

- The management — the design and operations of organisations as systems

- Analysis — the techniques of problem solving

- The idea of systematic (i.e. logical, thorough and regular) thinking.

Philosophical reasoning provides the following principles for the general theory:

- The whole is primary and the parts are secondary

- Integration is the condition of the inter-relatedness of the many parts within one

- The parts so constitute an indissoluble whole that no part can be affected without affecting all other parts

- Parts play their role in light of the purpose for which the whole exists

- The nature of the part and its function is derived from its position in the whole and its behaviour is regulated by the whole-to-part relationship

- The whole is any system or complex or configuration of energy which, no matter how complex, behaves like a single piece

- Everything should start with the whole as a premise and the parts and their relationship should evolve.

Systems Approach

The study of systems is not readily recognised as a legitimate subject because it is different in kind from most other disciplines. Its concern is not a particular set of phenomena such as we find in chemistry, physics, etc., nor does it overlap existing subjects, such as biochemistry, nor is it a subject which brings together a number of different streams of knowledge such as town planning and social administration, etc. What distinguishes systems is that it is a subject which can illuminate many other subjects. It is a meta-discipline whose subject matter can be applied within virtually any other discipline. It is for these reasons that we refer to "the systems approach".

The word system is abused in much the same way as such words as model, engineer, manager, executive and so on. It is a word which people tend to slip into conversations. "You have to understand the system" is often heard when really what is meant is you have to enlighten yourself, become more knowledgeable, about something or other that is being referred to. However the word system has a legitimate academic use in describing a useful set of concepts associated with a particular approach to practical analysis and action.

A system is made up of an assembly of components which may be called "elements" or "subsystems". The distinction is important. If a component is considered to be an *element* it has been assumed that there will be no need to try to subdivide that component any further. Conversely, for a component of a system to be considered as a *subsystem* it will have all the qualities and characteristics of a system, including the fact that it can be broken down into a number of components which will also be elements or subsystems. This distinction is shown in Figure 2-2.

The system is designated by everything within the border (1); there is one subsystem (2); and six elements (aaa, bbb, 2 x ccc, and 2 x ddd). There are also components or elements (5) outside the system boundary and these are positioned within the systems environment. This Figure will be referred to in Section 2 of this Part which provides further detailed explanation of the components.

To reiterate what was stated in Part 1 (p. 11): a system is a set of two or more elements that satisfy the following three conditions:

- The behaviour of each element has an effect on the behaviour of the whole

- The behaviour of the elements and their effects on the whole are interdependent

- However the subgroups of the elements are formed, each has an effect on the behaviour of the whole and none has an independent effect on it.

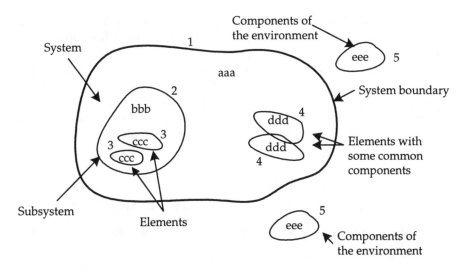

Figure 2-2: System, Subsystems, Elements

A system is a whole that cannot be divided into independent parts. The essential properties of a system taken as a whole derive from the interactions between the parts. These interactions are lost when the system is taken apart. To restate the maxim introduced in Part 1, Section 1, sub-Section "Systems Age Thinking": *a system is a whole that cannot be understood by analysis.*

The systems approach is an approach to a problem which takes a broad view, tries to take all aspects into account, and concentrates on the interactions between the different parts of the problem (Cleland and King, 1983).

The systems approach implies particular attitudes to analysis and suggests broad programmes for structuring the analytical process and for choosing if and when it might be useful to incorporate specific techniques.

Basically there are three approaches that can be used (Carter, 1988):

- Failure approach

- Hard systems approach

- Soft systems approach.

The *failure approach* is particularly relevant when confronted with a situation that seems to have gone wrong. Perhaps an obvious disaster of some sort (the water tank in your house roof space has just sprung a leak) or perhaps just a general dissatisfaction with the way things are going (you cannot get the resources you need to do what you planned). You often learn much more about something when it goes wrong than when it functions correctly, and the failures approach regards the alleged failure merely as one output from a systemic complex. The attempt to understand the failure is a useful way of understanding the systemic complex.

The *hard systems approach* is particularly relevant when the situation is not too confusing and you can get an acceptably clear, quantitative or at least logical picture of what is involved. In this case it makes sense to use more formalised techniques for simulation modelling. Hard systems are precise, well-defined and quantitative. Hard systems are used in situations where it makes sense to measure them, make models of them, and expect them to behave with a predictable degree of regularity.

The *soft systems approach* is particularly relevant when the situation is very confusing so that the top priority is to find out how one can begin to begin think about it, and to work with others towards some form of shared view of what is going on. Soft systems do not attempt to represent the original situation precisely and unambiguously because they involve emotional reactions, personal values and attitudes and shifting expectations. Soft systems are "personal" rather than "technical".

The systems approach should :

- Help you to take a balanced view of your problems

- Make you more alert to the possibility of unexpected side effects of your actions

- Make you less likely to "home-in" prematurely on particular superficial aspects of your problems before you understand their deeper roots

- Give you a language and set of skills suited to dealing with the effects of complexity which is a general property of many practical problems.

Although these are the benefits of the approach they are no substitute for the specialised knowledge and skills that are also necessary to deal with practical problems.

A Systems Typology

Systems can be classified (Open University, 1993) into four types: natural, designed physical, designed abstract, and human activity.

Natural systems are those whose origins are in the origin of the universe and which are as they are as a result of the forces and processes which characterise the universe. They are systems which could not be other than they are, given a universe whose patterns and laws are not erratic. These patterns and laws give us a profound belief in its orderliness.

Natural systems, although consisting of atoms and molecules, can be further classified into the "non-living" world of inorganic crystals, rocks, minerals, etc. and the "living things" world of single-celled creatures, the plant and animal kingdoms, and the systems of ecology. Living things include human beings and human behaviour systems.

Other characteristics of natural systems are that they are wholes with irreducible properties, they maintain themselves in a changing environment, they create themselves in response to the challenge of the environment and they are co-ordinating interfaces in nature's hierarchy.

These systems range from atomic nuclei to galactic systems, and include the living systems observed on earth. Examples would include the world tectonic plate movement system, the edible vegetables system, the human being system, etc.

Designed physical systems are the result of conscious design and man's ability to make what has been designed. These systems are designed as a result of some human purpose and they exist to serve a purpose. Examples would include household equipment, telecommunications, space travel, etc.

Designed abstract systems are the ordered conscious product of the human mind. Examples include, poems, theories, etc.

Human activity systems are less tangible systems than either the natural or the designed systems. They are sets of human activities more or less consciously ordered in wholes as a result of some underlying purpose or mission. Examples would include the soccer team playing together against an opposing team, the individual driving a nail with a hammer, etc.

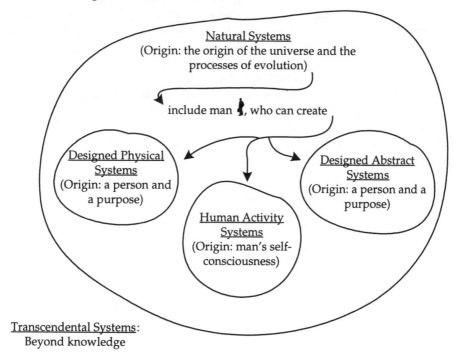

Figure 2-3: Systems Classes

A simple "systems classes" map of the universe is shown in Figure 2-3. In addition to the four classes shown there is one other system which includes the systems that are beyond knowledge; these are referred to as *transcendental systems*. Any whole entity which we may observe as a system may be described as a system of any one of these five classes, or it may be observed as any combination of two or more of the five classes.

Pursuing systems thinking becomes a matter of ascertaining the properties of systems of each class, and the way in which they combine and interact to form wider systems showing emergent properties. The systems movement is the search for conditions governing the existence of emergent properties, and a spelling out of the relation between such properties and the wholes which exhibit them.

The natural world is very orderly; we know the sun will always set in the west, that the day will be 24 hours; in other words, the patterns are predictable. This predictability provides scientific investigation with meaning. The orderly patterns of natural systems also mean that all members of a group will have similar properties, and will remain members of that group.

Systems Practice

The central concept "system" embodies the idea of a set of parts connected together to form a whole. This shows properties of the whole rather than properties of the component parts. For example, the smell of car fumes is a property of the combustion gases from a running engine; this gas is carbon monoxide and consists of carbon molecules and oxygen molecules. The smell does not come from either of the constituents carbon or oxygen because they do not have any smell.

Five or six interdependent components in a system are probably something that most people could get to grips with but a system having, say twenty-five components is likely to be beyond even intuitive judgement. Because ultimately everything tends to be connected to everything else the world can be perceived as an immensely complicated place. However to be able to see the situation as a whole is to understand and to be able to explain.

To assist us in talking about systems we need to have common definitions on the primary terms:

- **Elements**: The relatively fixed parts of the situation (system), at the finest level of analysis that we want to reach.

- **Sub-system**: Elements may be grouped together into sub-systems to give a picture of the structure of the system.

- **Connecting links**: These indicate the changing flows, influences and causal connections that bring the structure to life.

- **Boundary**: A means of delineating those components that are to be treated as part of the system and those that are not.

- **Open system**: One in which the environment is so important that the system merges into it, has an arbitrary boundary, has no stable identity and is very hard to manage or plan for.

- **Closed system**: Self-contained with no environment at all. It could not be influenced by external events, you could not intervene in it and it could not serve any useful external purpose.

- **Negative feedback**: Information about the outcome of a process is fed back to the beginning to control it through balancing and compensation, e.g. shower, body temperature, population of pests (see example below).

- **Positive feedback**: Information about the outcome of a process is fed back to the beginning to control it through exaggerating and reinforcing the process, e.g. arms race, mistakes in TV interviews (see example below).

- **Adaptive control**: Closed loop control (same as negative feedback).

- **Non-adaptive control**: Effort goes into setting the system up correctly and reliably in advance so that subsequent checking is not needed (open loop).

- **Multiple feedback**: Must look at each interconnection and see how they affect one another.

There is a more comprehensive glossary of terms (Carter, 1988) at the end of this Part.

A system is an arrangement and set of relationships among multiple parts operating as a whole. All social systems are composed of:

- Inputs (human, materials, money, etc.)

- Throughputs or processor

- Outputs (intended and unintended)

- Management (standards, feedback, initiator).

Ours is an organisational society; our lives are spent within boundaries of a variety of formal organisations such as, hospitals, schools, churches, business organisations, military units, universities, government agencies, etc. Organisations are systems that take inputs and transform them (Wilson, 1990). Regulation of this transformation process is what we know as management.

In Figure 2-4, the primary elements of the organisation system are the inputs, the outputs, what is referred to as the processor, and feedback. Inputs to the system normally consist of human or non-human energy, materials and information. Outputs can be almost anything that the organisation is expected to produce and these are generally referred to as objectives. The processor, also referred to as the transformation system, utilises the inputs within the organisation to form the desired outputs.

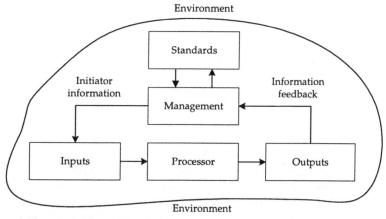

Figure 2-4: Model of an Organisation System

Subsystems of the organisation can include production, marketing, finance, personnel, research and development, etc. The individual is a subsystem of the organisation, but at the same time it needs to be acknowledged that the individual is a system composed of multiple physical and psychological subsystems.

Systems are characterised by a high degree of interconnectedness between the parts. A further kind of interconnection is called feedback.

Feedback is a control mechanism which concerns such system outputs as quality, quantity, cost, and time. The feedback control can be either positive or negative. Negative feedback control utilises information about the outcome and feeds back into controlling the inputs through balancing and compensation. An example of negative feedback control is a person taking a shower. While standing under the shower the water temperature is found to be too cold so the water mixer control is adjusted to allow more warm water to enter the mix and hence the person feels the temperature change through the skin nerve-endings. The temperature will then either be just right or may require some fine adjustment to the shower water mixer to satisfy the user's "input" (temperature) needs.

Positive feedback control is the same in that it uses information about the outcome of a process and feeds it back to the input end of the system but this time the control does not balance but exaggerates and reinforces the effect of the outcome. An example would be a mistake made in the output of a TV interview which is then recirculated to the input and requires the person who made the mistake to address a further related aspect of the mistake.

Management is the regulation of the transformation subsystem (or processor) within a system. Management, as we will see later, consists of the functions of planning, organising, directing and controlling. Other functions can include staffing, etc.

The environment is one other aspect that is dealt with in Figure 2-4. Most social systems are open systems; within the environment outside the system boundary will be such entities as competitors, unions, government, etc.

Systems thinking (see Section 2 in this Part, sub-Section, "Ways of Thinking") makes conscious use of the particular concept of wholeness captured in the word "system". Systems practice then implies using the product of this thinking to initiate and guide actions we take in the world.

A Model System: The Human Body

One way of trying to understand the model introduced in the previous two sub-Sections is to consider a well known system, the human body, because its components and their operation are understood by most people. The human body is the most perfect system known and it is worth examining certain aspects of the body's physiology and functioning as a way of understanding most aspects of the systems approach (see Figure 2-5)

Lauralee Sherwood's *Human Physiology* (1993) is an easy-to-understand and well-presented description of human physiology from cells to systems.

She recounts that during the minute that it will take you to read this paragraph and the following two paragraphs, your eyes will convert the image from this part of the page into nerve impulses and your nervous system will transmit the information to your brain for processing. Besides receiving and processing such visual input, your brain will also provide output to your muscles to help maintain your posture and move your eyes across the page as you read. Chemical messages will carry signals between your nerves and muscles to trigger appropriate muscle contraction.

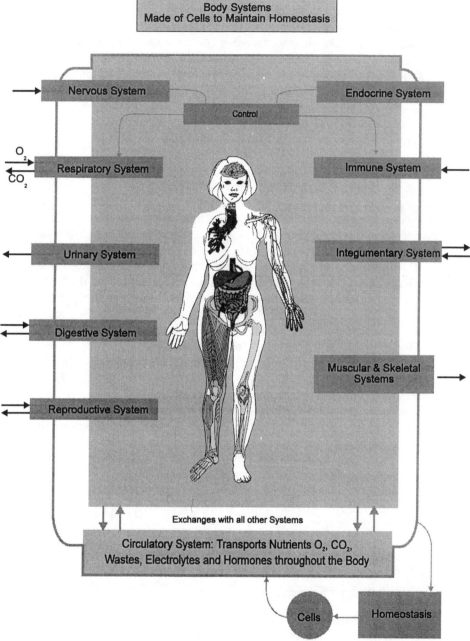

Figure 2-5: The Human Body's Subsystems

Your heart will beat seventy times, pumping 5 litres of blood to your lungs and another 5 litres to the rest of your body. More than 1 litre of blood will flow through your kidneys, which will act on the blood to conserve the "wanted" materials and eliminate the "unwanted" materials in the urine. Your kidneys will produce about a thimbleful of urine during this minute.

You will breathe in and out about 12 times, exchanging 6 litres of air between the atmosphere and your lungs. Your cells will consume about a cupful (250 ml) of oxygen and produce 200 ml of carbon dioxide. Your digestive system will be processing your last meal for transfer into your bloodstream for delivery to your cells. You will use about 2 calories of energy derived from food to support your body's "cost of living" plus your contracting muscles will burn additional calories.

In the past minute your nervous, respiratory, urinary, digestive, endocrine, muscular and skeletal systems have all been at work. In addition, your circulatory system which has exchanges with all other systems in the body has been maintaining what is called "homeostasis". This term will be defined and explained later in this Section.

No machine has been constructed that can take over even a portion of a natural body function as effectively. Physiologists view the body as a machine whose mechanisms or actions can be explained in terms of cause and effect sequences of physical and chemical processes — the same type of processes that occur in other components of the universe.

The human body has being used as an example of a system because we are familiar with our bodies; to some extent we understand how the body works, and it is relatively easy to describe it in terms of systems. It is also worth recalling the advice of Francis Bacon (1561–1626 — see Figure 2-1), when he argued that to understand we must consult nature and not books.

Physiology is closely interrelated with anatomy, the study of the structure of the body. Just as the functioning of an automobile depends on the shapes, organisation and interactions of its various parts, the same is true of the human body. Therefore structure and function are inseparable.

The basic unit of the human body is the cell. In the human body there are about 75 trillion of them. They are very tiny in size: 100 of them set touching side-by-side in a line would measure only 1 millimetre. The cell is also the first level of a four level "body organisation"; the others are tissues, organs, and systems. Cells of similar structure and function are organised into tissues, of which there are four primary types: muscle, nervous, epithelial, and connective tissue. Each tissue consists of cells of a single specialised type, along with varying amounts of "outside of the cell" material.

The tissue types are relatively easily explained. Muscle tissue is composed of cells specialised in contraction and force generation. This includes muscles which relate to movement of the skeleton, around the heart for pumping blood, and around hollow tubes and organs for the control and movement of the enclosed contents.

Nervous tissue consists of cells specialised for initiation and transmission of electrical impulses, sometimes over long distances. Nervous tissue is found in the brain and the spinal cord. It is also the medium that signals information about the external environment and about the status of various internal factors in the body that are subject to regulation, such as blood pressure. Nervous tissue also compose the nerves that influence muscle contraction or gland secretion.

Epithelial tissue is made up of cells specialised in the exchange of materials between the cell and its environment. For example, the outer layer of the skin is epithelial tissue.

Connective tissue is distinguished by having relatively few cells dispersed within an abundance of extracellular material. Connective tissue serves to connect, support and anchor various body parts. It includes such diverse structures as the loose connective tissue that attaches epithelial tissue to underlying structures, tendons that attach skeletal muscles to bones, bone, which gives the body shape, support and protection, and blood which transports between one part of the body and another.

Organs are composed of two or more types of primary tissue organised to perform a particular function or functions. The stomach is an example of an organ made up of all four primary tissue types:

- It is lined with epithelial tissue that restricts the transfer of harsh digestive chemicals and undigested food from the stomach lumen (cavity within the interior of organs) into the blood

- Smooth muscle tissue whose contraction mixes ingested food with the digestive juices and propels the mixture into the intestine

- Within the walls is nervous tissue which controls muscle contraction and gland secretion

- These various tissues are bound together by connective tissue.

Organs are further organised into body systems, each of which is a collection of organs that perform related functions and interact to accomplish a common activity that is essential for the survival of the whole body. For example, the digestive system consists, in addition to the stomach, of the mouth, pharynx (throat), oesophagus, small intestine, large intestine, salivary glands, pancreas, liver, and gall bladder. These digestive organs co-operate to accomplish the breakdown of dietary food into small nutrient molecules that can be absorbed into the blood.

The total body — a single independently living individual — is composed of the various organ systems structurally and functionally linked together as an entity that is separate from the external (outside of the body) environment.

The functions performed by each of the eleven body systems are directed toward maintaining homeostasis. The body's systems functions ultimately depend on the specialised activities of the cells composing each system.

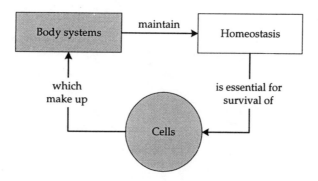

Figure 2-6: The Body's Interdependent Relationships

The body converts food into stores of energy. This begins when food is broken down by digestive processes in the stomach and intestines to release nutrients such as glucose, fatty and amino acids. Nutrients from the food are absorbed directly into the bloodstream and distributed to cells throughout the body. The cells then use glucose and fatty acids to fuel chemical reactions that lead to the release of energy stored as adenosine triphosphate (ATP). The contraction of muscle, for example, breaks ATP down to ADP (adenosine diphosphate), freeing the stored energy.

The body cells can live and function only when they are bathed by extracellular fluid that is compatible with their survival; thus, the chemical composition and physical state of the internal environment can be allowed to deviate only within narrow limits. As cells remove nutrients and oxygen from the internal environment, these essential materials must constantly be replenished in order for the cells' ongoing maintenance of life processes to continue. Likewise, wastes must constantly be removed from the internal environment so that they do not reach toxic levels. Other elements in the internal environment that are important for the maintenance of life also must be kept relatively constant. Maintenance of a relatively stable internal environment is termed homeostasis.

This account of the human body as a system is presented as a model for the better explanation of what, in business and management terms, is meant by systems, interrelationships between systems, open and closed systems, and the term "feedback".

In summary, *no part of a human being is human; only the whole is.*

SECTION 2: REPRESENTING SYSTEMS

Contents

- Aims and Objectives
- Ways of Thinking
- Techniques Used in Representing Systems
- Main Types of Diagrams
- Multiple Cause Diagrams
- Systems Maps
- Influence Diagrams
- Sign-graph Diagrams
- Summary of Key Points
- Glossary of Terms
- References

Aims and Objectives

The aims and objectives of Section 2 are to:

- Name the three ways of thinking and the significance of holistic thinking
- Describe the techniques that can be used to convert an issue into a diagram
- Define the different types of diagramming that can be used to describe systems
- Provide the rules and guidelines for mapping systems by using a range of diagramming techniques
- Offer a limited glossary of systems terms and definitions.

Ways of Thinking

Einstein once wrote:

> What precisely is thinking? When at the reception of sense impressions, memory pictures emerge, this is not yet "thinking". When such pictures form a series each member of which calls forth another, this too is not yet "thinking". When however, a certain picture turns up in many such series then precisely through such return it becomes an orderly element for such series, such an element becomes an instrument . . . a concept. I think that the transition from free association or "dreaming" to thinking is characterised by the more or less dominating role which the concept plays.

There are three main ways of thinking:

- **Logical**: This is a way of linking ideas together. This form of thinking has three properties: it is objective, it is necessary, and it is sequential. In other words *if* a, *then* b. An example of logical thinking is "if all bicycles are a means of transport, and this is a bicycle, then this is a means of transport".

- **Causal**: This is a way of linking events together; the same three properties that categorise logical thinking also characterise causal thinking. An example of causal thinking is "at my home last night there were too many electrical appliances operating at the same time. This caused an overload which activated a trip-switch, the result being a power failure."

  These two ways of thinking do not help us to think about systems. Systems are characterised by interconnectedness and feedback, so a way of thinking that is structured along a sequence (linear arrangement) is not helpful in considering the many different interacting factors and feedback loops. Hence there is a need for a way of thinking about systems; a way which has been developed to take account of their particular characteristics.

- **Holistic**: Deals with thinking about the whole rather than the parts. It takes multiple partial views of reality, each of which is a simplification, but which together help us to understand the whole. Holistic thinking allows us to look at nature and behaviour of the whole; if this doesn't yield results the next step will be to look at a larger whole.

Holistic thinking makes conscious use of the particular concept of wholeness, captured in the word "systems", to order our thoughts. "Systems pictures" then implies using the product of this thinking to initiate and guide actions we take in the world.

What are the main features shared by logical and causal thinking which distinguish them from holistic thinking? Which of the following statements about holistic thinking are true, and which are false?

Holistic thinking:

- Separates causes and effects (False)

- Always considers the motives of the people involved (False — but only sometimes)

- Simplifies the ideas and information in a given situation (True)

- Takes wholes as its unit of analysis (True)

- Examines each aspect of a problem separately (False — without the word *separately* the statement would be true).

Holistic thinking reverses the three-stage order of Machine Age thinking of:

1) Decomposition of that which is to be explained

2) Explanation of the behaviour or properties of the parts taken separately

3) Aggregating these explanations into an explanation of the whole.

It is worth noting that the third step is synthesis.
In holistic thinking the three steps are:

1) Identify a containing whole (system) of which the thing to be explained is a part

2) Explain the behaviour or properties of the containing whole

3) Then explain the behaviour or properties of the thing to be explained in terms of its role(s) or function(s) within its containing whole.

It is important to note that within holistic thinking synthesis precedes analysis.

If we want to work with systems we have to think about them in a certain way, and that way will mean concentrating on their interconnections.

Techniques Used in Representing Systems

There are three ways to represent systems: language, diagrams and quantitative models (Open University, 1991).

Attempting to describe a system using words is not easy. The advantages of diagrams over words is that they can show the interconnections visually. They make you think hard about what to include and what to leave out, i.e. what is important and what isn't. The diagram itself will be useful once it is drawn, but far more useful is the understanding gained in drawing it.

Why convert perfectly clear text into a map? There are three good reasons:

• You can learn a lot more from reading the map than you can from reading the text

• Drawing a map to represent someone else's thoughts can give you ideas and insights you'd never get from conventional notes

• Comparing the maps of different people concerned with the same problem or issue can be an invaluable tool for discussion and negotiation.

The process itself forces you to be clear and specific about your view of a system. As you draw a line or add a phrase, you will be thinking to yourself — "does that really work like that?" or "what else is affected by that?". Sometimes it may require six or seven attempts at a diagram before it is as clear and coherent as you can make it.

The advantages of quantitative models over physical models are that they are quicker and easier to build and can ask the question "what would happen if . . ." over and over again simply by changing the numbers in the model.

If you want to be able to work with systems then you need to be able to draw diagrams of them. Let us look at what is meant by systems diagrams.

As an example the hierarchy of a system which describes a "story B" in a newspaper is shown in view (a) in Figure 2-7. This type of tree presentation is reasonably well known and used. However, view (b) shows the same information presented in the form of another type of diagram. The diagram in view (b) is called a systems map. By examination it can be seen that all the relationships and levels that were in the tree are clearly within the nesting of boundaries.

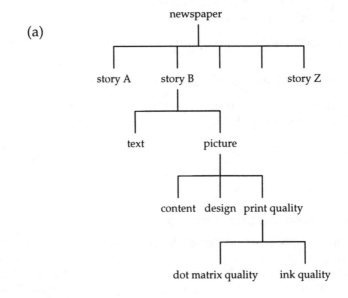

(a)

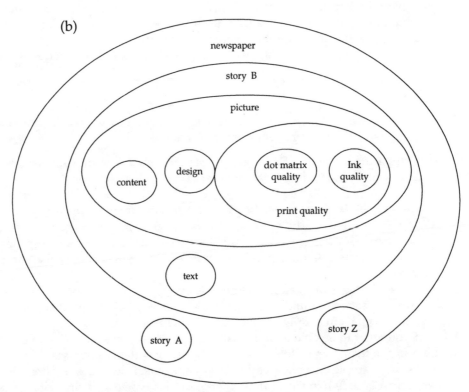

(b)

Figure 2-7: From Tree Diagram to Systems Diagram

If you wish to attempt drawing this type of diagram then the following will give you just that opportunity. If you don't wish to test yourself continue to the next sub-Section.

- Consider an issue that you are concerned about; one that puzzles or worries you and seems complicated.

- Take a piece of paper and write on it a brief title to the puzzle or problem you face.

- Turn over the paper and on the other side jot down the first ten or so thoughts you have about the key features of the issue. Don't write them down as a list, but write them as if they were in small boxes scattered at random on the page.

- See which of your thoughts have something in common, i.e. seem to be about the same point or problem, and draw a boundary around them. You may end up with two or three boundaries. Don't include all your ideas just for the sake of it; if one or more seem(s) to have no strong connection with any of the others, leave it without a boundary around it.

- For each set of thoughts enclosed in a boundary, write down the point or problem they have in common, then jot down any ideas you may have for dealing with that problem.

- Look at the brief title on the other side of the paper, and see if what you have done has helped you to take a new view of the issue.

It is advisable that a boundary should be placed around things that have something "in common". On most occasions this allows you to determine the boundaries instinctively. If in need of help try drawing the boundaries first and reflecting on them afterwards. If this doesn't generate new views then try the following:

- Interest and concern: the boundary separates those aspects which are vital to you and those of secondary importance.

- Influence and control: separates those aspects of the issue which are under the control of, or are strongly influenced by, separate people or groups.

The following sub-Sections provide further detail on diagrams and the primary types of maps that are used in systems.

Main Diagram Types

As mentioned earlier, we use diagrams because of their many advantages over text. The range of diagrams are assigned to three groups, namely: pre-analysis diagrams, structure and relationship diagrams, and process diagrams.

The names of the diagram types, what they show, their elements and some comments on each are shown in Figure 2-8 (Open University, 1993).

Name	Shows	Elements	Notes
Spray diagram*	Relationship of ideas	Ideas as twigs, branches, trunk	Complexity allowed. Loops allowed if necessary.
Relationship diagrams*	Structure of relationship	Words in blobs, lines	Blobs are preferably components, not other things. Lines mean "is related to" or "affects". Avoid crossing lines. Short lines show closeness.
Multiple cause diagram	Causality	Words, arrows	Arrows mean "cause", "contribute to", "enable", "permit", "authorise".
Rich picture**, situation summary	Depiction of a complicated situation	Pictorial symbols, key words, cartoons, sketches	Captures richness, structure and process evident; thumbnail sketches connected together. Systems not delineated.
Systems map*	Components of system and environment	Words in blobs. No arrows.	Irregular shapes preferred. Sparing on overlaps. Restrict multiple overlaps. Component nature consistent.
Influence diagrams*	Structure of influence	Words in blobs. Arrows, varying thickness with words maybe.	Based on systems map. Arrows don't show flows. Arrows denote capacity to influence. Arrows terminate at a component, not at a system boundary.
Input–output diagrams	Inputs to a process, outputs	One system box	Inputs and outputs correspond. Labelled arrows.
Flow-block diagrams	Actual flows between components (nouns)	Words in blocks, labelled arrows, clouds	Arrows do not show influence or sequence directly but a particular flow. Boxes are components. A box's outputs are transformed inputs. Flows of different things may be differentiated.
Flow-process diagram	Actual flows between processes (-ing verbs)	Words in blocks, labelled arrows, clouds	Arrows represent flows, not influence or sequence directly. Flow of items are transformed by the processes shown.

* Structure and relationship diagrams
** Pre-analysis diagrams
(the rest of the diagrams are "process diagrams")

Figure 2-8: Diagram Types

Four diagram types studied in greater detail are: multiple cause diagrams, systems maps, influence diagrams and sign-graph diagrams.

Multiple Cause Diagrams

These are used to explore why a given event happened or why a certain class of event tends to occur. It is not intended to predict behaviour, but may be used to develop a list of factors to bear in mind when considering comparable circumstances in the future.

In constructing such a diagram you normally begin at the factor/event to be explained and work backwards. A diagram should include more than one such end factor *only* if the contributory factors were related, and explaining both events is important. Because the arrows may represent different kinds of contribution/cause, it may be helpful to label them. It is not necessary to put blobs around phrases, although if it improves clarity you can. Boxes, with their "designed system" implications are best avoided. It helps in checking a draft to ensure that each individual relationship is clear. For example, in Figure 2-9, aaa and bbb may both be necessary if ccc is to occur; or either may be sufficient to cause ccc. Insert any necessary intermediate variables/factors if not. This type of diagram does not distinguish between necessary and/or sufficient causes. If the distinction is important for your purpose you will need to annotate your diagram to indicate this. It is not necessary to indicate a system boundary on a multiple-cause diagram. Drawing such a diagram may well, however, develop your ideas about where to draw a boundary. It is important to remember that this diagram type, while superficially resembling an influence diagram, is different in that it is read *sequentially*, rather than as a snapshot representation.

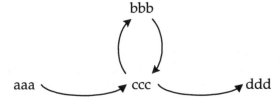

Figure 2-9: Multiple Cause Diagram

Some useful rules associated with drawing this type of diagram are:

- The phrases may be physical "things" (e.g. a building). But as the diagram is developed, it is preferable to describe the relevant variables associated with those things (e.g. number of users of building). Phrases may also represent events (e.g. failure of buildings ventilation system).

- Arrows do not necessarily mean causes. They may be read as meaning "contributes to", "is followed by", "enables", or similar terms.

- The diagram may be entirely sequential, or it may contain loops.

Systems Maps

A systems map is essentially a snapshot. It shows components of a system and environment at a point in time. Unless some components are grouped into subsystems and/or there are significant overlaps, a map conveys no more information than a list of components but it carries much more impact, and is easier to grasp.

The main uses of systems maps are to help you to decide how you are going to structure a situation and to communicate to others just what system you have chosen to study. In particular, system maps are used for the following purposes:

- To clarify thoughts at an early stage of analysis

- To decide upon structural elements for a more detailed programme

- To experiment with trial boundaries

- To decide upon the level of your system of interest ("focusing")

- To communicate to others the basic structure of the system you are describing.

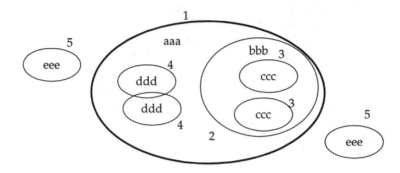

Figure 2-10: Systems Map

In constructing systems maps it should be clear which is the "system boundary". The system boundary can be emphasised by the use of colour, or a thicker line. A dashed line can be used to emphasise that the boundary is subjective and tentative.

Irregular blobs are normally preferable to regular boxes. Boxes imply that (sub)systems are clearly defined, which seldom is the case, and have the practical disadvantage that the eye finds it hard to distinguish between a series of parallel lines. Use overlaps sparingly, they tend to reduce the impact and clarity of the map. Overlap only when the sharing of components is important from your particular viewpoint. This applies equally to components within and spanning the boundary. Multiple overlaps should be avoided at all costs. It is virtually impossible to interpret overlaps on more than three sub-systems.

Aim for consistency between components. For example, avoid representing system properties as elements. Although the size of the blob used is not determined by size, importance, or other characteristics of the component that it represents, it makes sense to show important sub-systems at a reasonable size, and less important ones somewhat smaller, as this is the way relative importance is likely to be interpreted by a reader. Similarly, although there are no firm rules on the positioning of components (other than nesting and overlapping) it makes sense to put important components close together. This will facilitate subsequent additions of sub-system boundaries.

It is a good idea to leave some space within your map. Not only does this allow components to stand out clearly, but it leaves room for any components you may wish to add later.

Some useful rules associated with drawing this type of diagram are:

- The blob lines, (1) to (5) in Figure 2-10, represent boundaries of system components

- Words are used to name each system or component

- Blobs (5) outside the main system boundary (1) represent components of the *environment*

- Blobs (2), (3) and (4) *inside* the system boundary (1) represent components of the *system*. Components, e.g. (3) can be shown as grouped into systems (2). Undifferentiated components may themselves be subsystems

- Blobs may overlap only if some components (which need not be depicted) are clearly common to both.

Influence Diagrams

An influence diagram represents the main structural features of a situation and the important relationships that exist among them. It presents an overview of areas of activity or organisational and other groupings and their main interrelationships. It is used either to explore those relationships, perhaps leading to a regrouping and redefinition of the system and its components, or to express a broad view of how things actually are within the situational territory being considered.

In constructing influence diagrams avoid using arrows from features in the environment to the system boundary. By definition factors in the environment affect the system, so such arrows are superfluous. Arrows from environmental factors should terminate at a specific system component where possible. Arrows to the system boundary carry information only if they distinguish different types of influence. Different thickness of lines can indicate different strengths of influence. It is possible to distinguish different types of influence (e.g. influence via finance, information, supply of materials). Do so only if such distinctions are important and not self-evident, by the use of different lines (colour, dashing) to show this, and a key to explain them. Resist the temptation to overload the diagram with information. It may be helpful to you to put down all influences you can think of at first, but for communication to others, select the significant ones. Space and relative distance can also be used to suggest things about the nature of the relationships shown — e.g. an important but remote relationship.

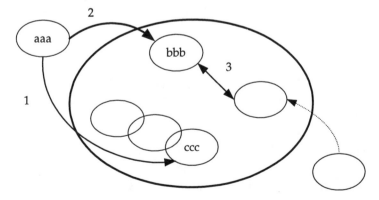

Figure 2-11: Influence Diagram

Some useful rules associated with drawing this type of diagram are:

- As in systems maps, blob lines represent component boundaries. Inclusion of a system boundary is optional

- An arrow, e.g. (1) or (2) in Figure 2-11 joining component aaa to component bbb or ccc respectively, shows that aaa can or does influence bbb or ccc

- A double-headed arrow, e.g. (3) denotes a two-way influence

- Words label components and system (if shown). They may also label arrows, if the nature of the influence is not obvious from the context.

- Arrows do *not* show material flows

- An influence diagram, like a systems map, is a snap shot. Arrows denote capacity to influence, *not* a sequence in time.

Sign-graph Diagrams

A sign-graph diagram is a development of a multi-cause diagram in order to represent and investigate the relationships between variables in a given situation. Hence it is good for thinking about the likely effects of changes, and in particular, of interventions in systems. A sign-graph diagram can be thought of as a model of a system, and such diagrams are often drawn to establish the structure of planned quantitative models.

In constructing sign graphs, start off with the simplest diagram you can, and then elaborate it as necessary. In that way you can be sure that you understand the meaning and implications of your diagram before it becomes too complex. When checking that you've got the signs right on your arrows, it helps to read through the diagram by asking "Does more of (*first variable*) lead to more of (*second variable*)? The diagram can be built up by working backwards from the factor/event to be explained, as with a multiple-cause diagram, or from a variable which you imagine to be very important — following through its ramifications.

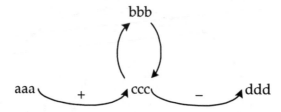

Figure 2-12: Sign-graph Diagram

Some useful rules associated with drawing this type of diagram are:

- The phrases should refer to variables (so phrases like "number of . . .", "cost of . . .", "speed of . . . " are often found in these diagrams

- The phrases should not themselves refer to variations (so do not use "more/less" or "increase/decrease" in the phrases).

- Use a "minus" sign by an arrow where a change in the variable at the tail produces an *opposite* change in the variable at the arrowhead. So, in Figure 2-12, an increase in bbb will lead to a decrease in ccc, and a decrease in bbb will lead to an increase in ccc.

- Use a "plus" sign by an arrow where a change in the variable at the tail produces a similar change in the variable at the arrowhead. So, in Figure 2-12, an increase in aaa leads to an increase in ccc. Equally, a decrease in aaa will lead to a decrease in ccc; that is also a *similar* change.

Summary of Key Points

- Aristotle (384–322 BC) argued "that a whole was more than the sum of its parts". The scientific revolution whose principle was reductionism, which deeply permeated science for nearly 400 years, could be seen as having misdirected our development and understanding of real world problems.

- The whole is more than the sum of the parts, the whole determines the nature of the parts, the parts cannot be understood if considered in isolation from the whole, and the parts are dynamically interrelated and interdependent.

- A system is a whole that cannot be divided into independent parts. The essential properties of a system taken as a whole derive from the interactions between the parts. These interactions are lost when the system is taken apart. Therefore a system is a whole that cannot be understood by analysis alone.

- The systems approach should help you to take a balanced view of your problems, make you more alert to the possibility of unexpected side effects of your actions, make you less likely to "home-in" prematurely on particular superficial aspects of your problems before you understand their deeper roots, and give you a language and set of skills suited to dealing with the effects of complexity, which is a general property of many practical problems.

- A system is an arrangement and set of relationships among multiple parts operating as a whole. All social systems are composed of inputs, throughputs or processor, outputs, and management.

- Management is the regulation of the transformation subsystem (or processor) within a system. Management consists of the functions of planning, organising, directing and controlling; other functions can include staffing, etc.

- The human body is the most perfect system known and it is worth examining certain aspects of the body's physiology and functioning as a way of understanding most aspects of the systems approach. No part of a human being is human; only the whole is.

- Ways of thinking that are structured along a sequence, such as logical and causal thinking, are not helpful in considering the many different interacting factors and feedback loops. Hence there is a need for holistic thinking, a way of thinking about systems developed to take account of their particular characteristics.

- Multiple cause diagrams are used to explore why a given event happened or why a certain class of events tends to occur. They are not intended to predict behaviour, but may be used to develop a list of factors to bear in mind when considering comparable circumstances in the future.

- The main uses of systems maps are to help you to decide how you are going to structure a situation and to communicate to others just what system you have chosen to study. In particular, systems maps are used to clarify thoughts at an early stage of analysis, to decide upon structural elements for a more detailed programme, to experiment with trial boundaries, to decide upon the level of your system of interest, and to communicate to others the basic structure of the system you are describing.

- An influence diagram represents the main structural features of a situation and the important relationships that exist among them. It presents an overview of areas of activity or organisational and other groupings and their main inter-relationships.

- A sign-graph diagram is a development of a multi-cause diagram in order to represent and investigate the relationships between variables in a given situation. Hence it is good for thinking about the likely effects of changes, and in particular, of interventions in systems. A sign-graph diagram can be thought of as a model of a system, and such diagrams are often drawn to establish the structure of planned quantitative models.

Glossary of Terms

action — something that somebody does knowingly, consciously, and deliberately. For example to open a door is action but snoring while asleep is behaviour.

adaptive control — a closed loop control mechanism, that is, one involving feedback. The continuous or intermittent adjustment of some activity so that it matches changing conditions.

agent — the person (or group of people) who initiate, carry out, or mediate action.

analysis — a phase of the agent's activity which concentrates on trying to understand a situation.

boundary — the notional demarcation line used by an analyst or observer to separate a system from its environment. It acts as a rule which indicates whether or not some entity is inside the system.

closed loop control — a control mechanism where part of the output of a system is returned to the input in such a way as to affect the input or some of the operating characteristics of the system (also called adaptive control).

closed system — a system which has no interaction with its environment. In their "pure" form such systems exist only as theoretical concepts.

component — a recognisable part of a system which may be a sub-system or an element.

control — the mechanisms which act to preserve the relationship between the structure and process of a system.

element — a system component which, at the current level of analysis, is not subdivided further.

environment — this is the set of elements that affect the system, but are not controlled by it. Though clearly relevant to the system, they are regarded as falling outside its boundary.

goal — target for medium to long-term strategies. A direction to move in, rather than a detailed quantitative objective.

hard system — a system which is designed and quantifiable, with well-defined objectives.

heuristic approach — tackling a problem on the basis of learning by experience, trial and error, and intuition.

implementation — a phase of the agent's activity which concentrates on the actual execution of changes that have important consequences and cannot easily be reversed.

iteration — the repeated application of a set of procedures, or stages of a method, to the same material, with the intention that each pass will produce some further progress towards a full solution.

model — description of a real or hypothetical situation, usually formal and simplified, which is used to develop understanding.

objective — short-term practical and specific target. Much more detailed than a goal.

open system — a system which interacts with an environment, i.e. there is an exchange of energy , information, materials across a boundary.

process — change. The events, actions, communications, and changing relationships in a situation.

relationship — A is said to have a relationship to B when A's behaviour is affected by the presence of B.

resolution — because of limitations in our capacity to process information, analyses cannot be both detailed and broad. Any analysis must be conducted at an appropriate compromise between breadth and depth. This is its level of resolution.

soft system — a system depending largely on non-routinised human actions, so that the human capacity for free choice, and the agent's limited access to the subjective values, beliefs and wishes of the participants means that wholly objective descriptions or quantitative modelling are not appropriate.

strategy — a medium or long-term programme of activities related to particular goals. A strategic programme usually leaves flexibility for later adjustments and choice of detailed tactics, but it will probably set broad directions, outer limits, and general guidelines.

sub-system — a system component above the chosen limits of resolution so that it may contain within it sub-sub-systems, or elements.

synergy — the effect produced when the operation of a whole appears to be greater than the sum of the operation of each of its parts.

system — a recognisable whole which consists of a set of interdependent parts. More specifically:

- A system is an assembly of components connected together in an organised way.
- The components are affected by being in the system and the behaviour of the system is changed if they leave it.
- This organised assembly of components does something.
- This assembly as whole has been identified by someone who is interested in it.

systematic — carried out in a planned and orderly fashion.

systemic — using systems ideas; treating things as systems or from a systems viewpoint.

tactic — a short-term local plan of specific activities in connection with a particular project.

Weltanschauung — the particular image of the world, outlook or world-view which colours and characterises the perception of a person regarding any situation.

References

References used in the development of Part 2:

Carter, Ruth et al. (1988), *Systems, Management and Change*, Paul Chapman Publishing Ltd.

Checkland, Peter (1993), *Systems Thinking, Systems Practice*, John Wiley and Sons Ltd.

Checkland, Peter & Scholes, Jim (1990), *Soft Systems Methodology in Action*, John Wiley and Sons Ltd.

Cleland, David I. and King, William R. (1983), *Systems Analysis and Project Management*, McGraw-Hill Book Company.

Open University (1993), *Applying a Systems Approach:* (T301, a third level course), Open University Press.

Open University (1991), *Working with Systems:* (T247, a second level course), Open University Press.

Sherwood, Lauralee (1993), *Human Physiology: From Cells to Systems*, 2nd edition, West Publishing Company.

Wilson, Brian (1990), *Systems: Concepts, Methodologies, and Applications*, 2nd edition, John Wiley and Sons Ltd.

PART 3

PROJECTS AND THEIR MANAGEMENT

This Part of the book explains what is meant by projects and their management. Project management is described as a continuous process within the limited life of a project. To help to understand this description the organisation of work through projects or its alternative, operations, is illustrated. Project stakeholders, life cycle, project phases, deliverables, and many more terms are identified and clarified.

A brief overview of the historical development of project management is also given in Section 1.

The integrative process of project management, the sub-processes of project management, and the sub-process interactions between phases are identified and defined.

The framework and structure of project management used in this Part of the book are modelled on that developed by the Project Management Institute in their guide called "Project Management Body of Knowledge" (PMBOK).

The PMBOK organises the project management practices into nine knowledge areas. These knowledge areas are: scope, time, cost, quality, human resources, communications, risk, procurement and integration.

Within each of these knowledge areas the relative processes are described by exploring their inputs, the mechanisms that are used to create outputs, and the outputs.

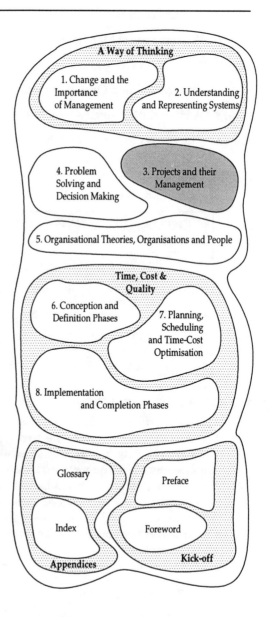

SECTION 1: THE PROJECT MANAGEMENT PROCESS

Contents

- Aims and Objectives
- "Projects" versus "Operations"
- Projects Defined
- What is Project Management?
- Project Life Cycle and Deliverables
- Stakeholder and Organisational Influences
- A Historical Overview — Old to Modern
- The Project Management Process

Aims and Objectives

The aims and objectives of Section 1 are to:

- Recognise the differences between projects and operations — the two common types of work;
- Explain what is meant by projects and project management;
- Name the life cycle phases and stages;
- Explain the role of the stakeholders;
- Name and describe the project management process and sub-processes;
- Explain the interactions that are the project management process.

"Projects" versus "Operations"

Work is performed within organisations. Work can generally be classified as either *operations* or *projects*. The two types of work differ primarily in that operations are ongoing and repetitive while projects have characteristics that include impermanence, uniqueness and uncertainty. An example of "operations" would be a production line within a manufacturing plant that has large batch production of a standard product, such as cartons of milk produced by a dairy. An example of "projects" would be the design and installation of a new computerised IS (information system) to handle customers' accounts for the many branches of a "high street bank".

Both classifications of work share many characteristics. For example, they are:

- Performed by people
- Constrained by limited resources

- Describable as processes and sub-processes

- Planned, executed and controlled.

Both "operations" and "projects" require the mental and physical skills of people to undertake what needs to be carried out. Producing cartons of milk, and designing and installing the bank's information system will have one or more of the following constraints: time, cost, quality and "scope". Other resource constraints include people, materials, equipment, etc. Both examples require processes and sub-processes to achieve whatever is to be produced, which is called the "deliverable" or the product.

Deliverables are also produced at the end of each phase of the project life cycle. Deliverables will be discussed further in the sub-Section "Project Life Cycle and Deliverables", later within this Section. The activities needed to produce all the deliverable(s) have to be planned in detail, the associated work has to be executed and there must be a procedure that controls the work to ensure that it satisfies the initial requirements.

To further explain what is meant by projects and operations it is worth comparing the list of characteristics presented in Figure 3-1.

Projects	*Operations*
Revolutionary change	Evolutionary change
Disequilibrium	Equilibrium
Limit in time and scope	Eternal
Unbalanced objectives	Balanced objectives
Unique	Repetitive
Transient resources	Stable resources
Goal oriented	Role oriented
Effectiveness	Efficiency

Figure 3-1: Project Work versus Operations

In the increasingly complex environment of change that we currently have to deal with, the environment is one of *revolutionary change*. It is within, and because of, this change environment that we learn, more and more, that chaotic change can only be accommodated by thinking and taking action in terms of projects. On the other hand, it is generally accepted that operations can handle change through the more sedate state of *evolution*. This is possible because the type of change that is associated with operations is gradual and non-chaotic.

Due to the change environment within which projects are managed, projects are undertaken within a state of *disequilibrium* where nothing stays the same. This means that the starting position today on a project will be quite different to the starting position yesterday. Typically in the management of operations, operations are generally in *equilibrium* because the starting position today is not radically different to the starting position yesterday, or the day before, or for that matter the first day when operations started.

Because of their impermanence projects are *limited in time and scope*. In operations there are no such restrictions; time and scope will be determined by such things as "when we have produced enough". In other words, operations are *eternal*.

Within the projects' environment there is a continuous need to deal with *unbalanced objectives* (also sometimes referred to as constraints). These objectives are:

- Performance

- Time schedule

- Overall budget cost.

Project management continually has to deal with playing off one objective against the others in an attempt to balance the overall effect. In the operations environment the three variables generally remain fixed, hence operations have *balanced objectives*.

A primary characteristic of projects, not shared by operations, is that they are *unique*. In other words, whatever the project, it has never before been undertaken in its current form. Something similar may have been undertaken but not exactly the same as now being contemplated. On the other hand operations are *repetitive*. That is, what was produced yesterday is identical, or very similar to, what was produced the day before, and so on. Human endeavours range from totally repetitive to totally unique; project-based endeavours are at the unique end of the range.

People resources on a project are required for limited time periods and when their contribution to a project is completed they will either return to their "home base" or will be transferred to another project; this is referred to as *transient resources*. The management of operations utilises people that "do not move" and because of little change, a repetitive process, and other reasons, operations and *stable resources* are axiomatic.

Project management personnel have the fixed purpose of achieving project objectives. The objectives of a project were mentioned earlier; they are performance, time schedule, and overall budget cost. Therefore it is concluded that the personnel in projects' are *goal oriented*. In operations, people fulfil roles defined by precedent, and so often lose sight of the objectives. In the operations environment personnel undertake functions by performing roles; they are therefore *role oriented*.

Within the projects' environment, where there is no precedent for having undertaken a project because each project is unique, the emphasis is on *effectiveness*. Effectiveness is recognised as "doing the right things". In the operations environment, where the learning process, continually recycled through repetition, uses the same work activities, the emphasis is on *efficiency*. Efficiency is defined as "doing things right".

Projects Defined

Now we have seen that the traditional management approach is based on, amongst other things, evolutionary change, equilibrium, balanced objectives, repetition, roles, stability and efficiency. On the other hand, we have seen that the projects approach is based on revolutionary change, disequilibrium, unbalanced objectives, uniqueness, goal orientation, transience and effectiveness.

Most top and middle management are handling projects every day of the week, but they don't generally recognise that fact. More significantly they perform their work within their organisations using the traditional management approach. They are, in many cases, working within a system that cannot respond to the dynamics of a change management environment. It almost appears that they are unaware of any alternative management approach. Substantial opportunities exist in contemporary organisations for using the projects approach. There is evidence to suggest that this is beginning to be recognised.

The previous sub-Section, "'Projects' versus 'Operations'", helped to differentiate the characteristics of the two types of work that we commonly experience. Projects, however, can be identified by using a "three word" test. If the work of an organisation, or within a part of an organisation, is *unique, uncertain* and *impermanent* then such work would be classified as consisting of projects. Such classification cannot be applied to operations. As we have seen operations are anything but unique, uncertain and impermanent.

Unique means the work needed to produce the product, or service, or whatever, is different in some distinguishing way from other products, or services, or whatever. *Uncertain* signifies that because of unknowns and degrees of complexity there are degrees of risk associated with the work of the project. *Impermanence*, which implies some sort of temporary nature, indicates that a project has a definite ending point.

Traditional management, in handling operations, deals with matters that are neither unique, uncertain or temporary. In fact operations have characteristics that are, to a large extent, the exact opposite of project characteristics.

Projects are undertaken at all levels within organisations. Within project-based organisations, projects will be the norm at all management levels. Projects can be found within the work activity of top management and middle management in most organisations. Within contemporary organisations, traditional management will normally be used, and will continue to be used, to perform the core business of such organisations.

One way of categorising projects is by their "source of sponsorship". Projects can be categorised under one of the following:

- Personal/family

- Organisation (for the organisation)

- Customer (by your organisation)

- Sub-contracted (for your organisation)

- Government sponsored

Sponsorship can include the individual, the family (or extended family), by or for an organisation, an entrepreneur, such as a developer, financier, etc., local or central government entity, and so on. Projects may involve a single person or many thousands of people. Projects can be large or small, technical or non-technical, undertaken by an individual or by teams. It may require less than 100 hours of input or effort, or require over 10 million hours of effort to complete a particular project. Some examples of projects are shown in Figure 3-2.

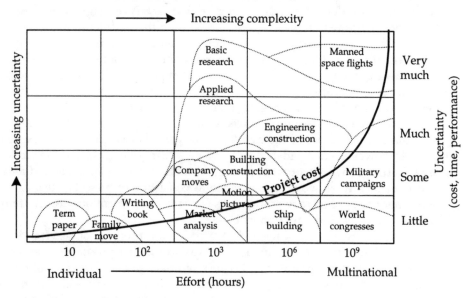

Figure 3-2: Complexity–Uncertainty Relationship

It can be seen that projects can be categorised by their "level of uncertainty" in knowing the final out-turn cost, project time period, and the scope of the project work. Projects can also be categorised by their "degree of complexity" which is also closely linked with sponsorship.

The Figure shows the "level of effort" as the abscissa plotted against the ordinate, "level of uncertainty". A positive concave curve from bottom left to top right reflects a "cost of project" trend curve which is minimum when there is little uncertainty and complexity and the source is personal, and maximum when the source is multinational and there is a very high level of uncertainty and complexity. The project examples shown on the Figure range from an individual's production of a "term paper", which is low cost, to the high-cost exploration and use of outer space such as "manned space missions".

Other examples of projects, some of which have been indicated on Figure 3-2, include:

- Developing a new product or service

- Effecting a change in structure, staffing, or style of an organisation

- Designing a new transportation vehicle

- Developing a new or modified information system

- Constructing a building or facility

- Running a campaign for political office

- Implementing a new business procedure or process.

Based on the foregoing it can be concluded that most things that we experience in life that require mental and/or physical effort are likely to be classified as projects. But we really need a definition of projects so that we can be more discerning in their identification and categorisation.

A project can be defined (Turner, 1993) as *something that has a beginning and an end*. This definition, which has been credited to Martin Barnes, is not really sufficient as many things satisfy this definition but could not be classified as projects. For instance, cleaning your teeth, reading the newspaper, having a telephone conversation, attending a meeting, etc., are all things that have a beginning and an end but they cannot be defined as projects.

Anderson et al. (see Turner, 1993) have defined a project as a human endeavour which creates change; is limited in time and scope; has mixed goals and objectives; involves a variety of resources; and is unique. This is a much more comprehensive definition and could be accepted but it will be noted that no mention of money in the form of the anticipated cost of the project is given. Cleland and King (1983) provide an acceptable definition of the term project by stating that it is a complex effort to achieve a specific objective within a schedule and budget target, which typically cuts across organisational lines, is unique, and is usually not repetitive within the organisation.

However if we are looking for a more succinct definition, that provided by Smith (Turner, 1993) — *a one-time, unique endeavour by people to do something that has not been done that way before* — might appear to have some merit.

The author's preferred definition of a project is: *any series of activities and tasks that together achieve predetermined deliverables in accordance with a quality definition, have defined start and end dates, intermediate milestones, funding limits, and utilise resources such as equipment, materials, people, etc.*

In dealing with projects it is also important to differentiate between what is meant by schemes, projects, facilities, and products. A project goes through a form of change as it develops from an idea and eventually is transformed into something else. So as all biological organisms go through change we can visualise projects as similarly going through phases in a lifetime. An organism's phases are referred to as birth, maturity, decline and death. The equivalent terms used relative to projects are conception, definition, implementation and completion. During the conception phase, also called the "pre-investment period" the term scheme shall be used. During the conception phase it is normal for a number of options, or schemes, to be considered. One of these schemes, or sometimes some other scheme, may become the project.

"To do nothing" is always one of the options and should that option result in being the most attractive option then there will be no project. The best scheme only becomes "the project" when a decision has been taken to "invest" and the work of defining and, thereafter, implementing the project starts. Once a project has been completed and closed-out, which means the finalisation of all "deliverables", it is usual for the project to be identified as either a "facility" or a "product".

Let us interpret what this means by looking at two example projects that were illustrated earlier in Figure 3-2. The design, implementation, and commissioning of an "engineering construction" project will be the result of having analysed a number of scheme options during the conception phase before deciding on the most attractive scheme which then becomes the project. Once the project — say, a nuclear power plant — has been commissioned and handed over to its owner for operating, the power plant becomes a facility producing electrical energy. On the other hand a "motion picture" project, which is likely to have been the result of analysing a number ideas or schemes, will require a writing, acting, directing and production team(s) to produce the movie. When the movie has been completed, edited and verified it will become a product that as a film will be shown in theatres or as a video in the home.

What is Project Management?

Everyone is to some extent a manager. Even if "manager" is not our job title we are all confronted with the need to manage our time, our income, our behaviour, our health, family activities, and so on.

Today, as "managers" of one sort or another, we are faced with significant challenges such as high cost escalation, demands from stockholders, unions, etc., high rates of inflation, recession and downturns in demand, and so on. Our normal response as managers has been to introduce cost-reduction measures which usually means redundancies, early retirement, etc. The result of this response is that organisations now have less people doing the same amount of work and this has usually necessitated the approval of increased expenditures on capital equipment. This response has worked but there is a limit to how far this process can go; it is not a long-term solution to the challenges faced by "managers".

One of the important elements of project management is the planning and control process. Better planning and control of resources is perceived to be the solution to better management, whether a downsized large organisation, a small group or any size of organisation between is being considered. Project management is also designed to make better use of resources by getting work to flow horizontally as well as vertically. It utilises the systems approach to management by having functional personnel, referred to as "the vertical hierarchy", assigned to a specific project, referred to as "the horizontal hierarchy". Project management is a new way of thinking about problems and how to identify solutions. Project management presents a systematic and logical approach to achieving project objectives. As will be explained, the project management process has been identified as a strong source of better management within most organisations.

Because project management is an outgrowth of systems management, it is essential that the underlying principles of the general systems approach should be understood (refer to Part 2). The aim of the systems approach is to facilitate better understanding in a complex environment. In other words, if the system within which managers make decisions can be given a more explicit framework, then such decision-making should be easier to handle.

The term project management is also used to describe an organisational approach, e.g. "our company has recently implemented project management". This approach is called *management by projects* and treats many aspects of ongoing operations as projects in order to apply the project management process to them.

Project management has certain essential features that, if used, will provide a strong basis for many organisations which, being prepared to accept change, will achieve greater success in their operations. These features are:

- Total accountability assumed by a single person

- Project dedication rather than functional dedication

- Requirement for co-ordination across functional lines

- Proper utilisation of integrated planning and control.

The successful management of projects is linked directly to the appointment of an individual called "the project manager" and the responsibility and authority assigned to that position. There is a direct correlation between accountability for the project being in the hands of the project's manager and the successful outcome of the project.

When the organisation identifies its projects from its operations then the focus of those involved in projects has to be the projects and not their functional alliances. The significance of this feature is understood more clearly when, as mentioned in the sub-Section "'Projects' versus 'Operations'", we remind ourselves that within the projects' environment the personnel need to be goal-oriented while within the "functional environment", the personnel are generally role-oriented.

As mentioned in the third paragraph of this sub-Section the organisation structure of the entity that is performing the project work and providing its management is required to make better use of resources by getting work to flow horizontally as well as vertically. Project management offers greater success by having functional personnel (the vertical hierarchy) assigned to a specific project (the horizontal hierarchy).

It is not possible to control anything unless it has been satisfactorily planned. Planning and control are therefore inter-related elements of the project management process that if not undertaken will create a greater degree of uncertainty regarding the eventual outcome of projects.

It can be seen that project management is characterised by methods of restructuring management and adopting special management techniques. The project management process provides the basis for innovation and the tools and techniques that permit the solving of problems. Project-based management has become the "new traditional management" through which many contemporary organisations are responding to change to develop and exploit markets ahead of their competitors. Project management is clearly a management option whose time has come. It is the principal strategy by which organisations can accommodate and institutionalise change.

Using the project management process will lead to our ability to commercialise technology sooner, at lower cost and with higher product and process quality and value. The objectives of any project can then be stated to be: "time", "cost", and "performance".

Where perhaps the time and cost objectives are self-explanatory, the performance function needs some further explanation. Performance concerns other targets that do not include either time or cost. In other words it will deal with the what, the how, the who, etc.; the other functions that are applicable. Performance, for convenience, can be interpreted as being constituted from two functions, namely "scope" (the what) and "quality" (the how, the who, etc.).

The objectives are shown in Figure 3-3 related to one another in the form of a mathematical vector.

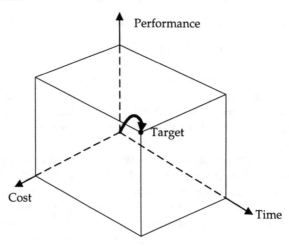

Figure 3-3: Project Objectives

These three objectives are sometimes known as the triple constraints. It is project management's job to ensure that the triple constraints are continually balanced and that at completion the project achieves or betters the predetermined target values of the triple constraints. It is highly likely throughout the life cycle of a project that, in order to meet the "cost" objective at any time in a project, it may be necessary to relax on the requirements of the other two objectives.

The process of project management is an integrative one. An action, or a failure to take action, in one area will usually affect other areas. The interactions may be straightforward and well understood, for example, a lower budget for defining the project often means a higher cost for implementation and vice-versa. The interactions may be subtle, for example, a scope (performance) change may affect factors as diverse as team morale and product quality.

According to the Project Management Institute, *project management* is the application of knowledge, skills, tools, and techniques in order to meet or exceed the requirements of the intended project sponsor or owner. Meeting or exceeding these requirements means balancing competing demands among:

- The scope, time, cost, quality functions and any other applicable project functions

- The involved parties who are likely to have different requirements

- The identified requirements (needs) and the unidentified requirements (expectations).

In North America, more and more organisations are moving over to using the project management process. They are restructuring because the size and complexity of their activities have grown to a point where they are unmanageable within their current structural framework.

How is the need for project management within an organisation determined? How do know whether your organisation should be using project management? The following five questions normally give some insight as to whether or not project management is necessary:

- Are the jobs complex?

- Are there dynamic environmental considerations?

- Are the constraints tight?

- Are there several activities to be integrated?

- Are there several functional boundaries to be crossed?

If any of these questions are answered yes, then some form of project management is likely to assist your organisation. It is worth noting that it is possible for project management to exist in only one area, department or division, or to exist perhaps for just certain types of project within a organisation's range of outputs. In other words an organisation may manufacture large batches of a consumer product and need traditional management to manage the associated operation. New products, which let's assume are handled through a department of that name, will be engaged in "research and development projects" and therefore would be a candidate for using project management.

Not all organisations need project management. Organisations engaged in simple tasks, whether in a static or dynamic environment, do not need project management. Manufacturers with slowly changing technology do not need project management, unless, of course, they have a requirement for special projects, such as, capital equipment activities, which would interrupt the flow of their normal production. Organisations whose objectives are not tightly constrained, or whose activities are uni-functional, or whose projects require one or two activities to undertake the project will not need project management.

Project Life Cycle and Deliverables

As we have seen under the sub-Section "Projects Defined", projects are unique undertakings that involve a degree of uncertainty about the probability of successful completion. Because of this and as means of controlling uncertainty, organisations performing projects will divide each project's overall time period into several phases. Each phase is likely to be further sub-divided into a number of stages. Collectively, these phases and stages are known as the *project life cycle*.

Each project is marked by the achievement of one or more *deliverable*. The end of each phase, and also each stage, is marked by a deliverable or deliverables. A deliverable is a tangible, verifiable work product such as a feasibility study, a detail design, or a working prototype. The deliverables, and hence the phases, are part of a generally sequential logic designed to ensure proper definition of the outcomes of the project.

Organisations are required to divide each project into several project phases. Although many project life cycles are similar, few are identical. Most have four or five phases, but some have nine or more. Even within a single application area, there can be significant variations — one organisation's software development life cycle may have a single design phase while another may have separate phases for functional and detail design.

Project life cycles vary greatly in their overall time period. For instance, insurance projects will likely last for just a few weeks, software development projects may last a few months to a year or so, engineering projects can last between six months and two years, construction projects may take three to five years although it can be greater or less than this range, nuclear power projects can take ten years or more from conception to commissioning.

There is great diversity in the terms used to describe the phases of a project life cycle. This is shown by some typical examples in Figure 3-4. These terms are samples; they are not necessarily recommended or preferred.

Most project life cycles share a common staffing and cost pattern. They tend to progress slowly at the start, quicken their momentum towards the middle, and then again drop their momentum as the project draws to a conclusion. The staffing and cost build-up are relatively slow at the beginning, during the time when the project is being established and trying to develop a momentum for the future. Having passed this period of slow growth the project enters a period of rapid growth in its "middle age" and continues at this maximum growth rate until towards the end of its life when it again slows down.

Software development is a type of project likely to have a large number of phases. Software development phases are given names such as feasibility, requirements, product design, detail design, coding, integration, and implementation. On the other hand a construction-type project is likely to have fewer phases and will likely call its phases something like: feasibility investigation, conceptualisation, design, procurement, and construction.

In this book, a four-phase life cycle will be used and the phases will be referred to as conception, definition, implementation, and completion. This is shown on Figure 3-4 and is referred to as the generic life cycle.

Deliverables from a preceding phase are usually approved before work can start on the next phase. When a later phase is commenced before the completion of a preceding phase, and when the risks involved are deemed to be acceptable, this procedure is called *fast-tracking*.

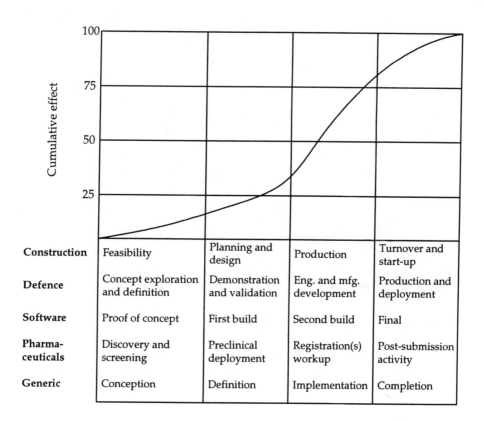

Construction	Feasibility	Planning and design	Production	Turnover and start-up
Defence	Concept exploration and definition	Demonstration and validation	Eng. and mfg. development	Production and deployment
Software	Proof of concept	First build	Second build	Final
Pharma-ceuticals	Discovery and screening	Preclinical deployment	Registration(s) workup	Post-submission activity
Generic	Conception	Definition	Implementation	Completion

Figure 3-4: Project Life Cycles

Finally let's look at the level of effort versus the phases of the life cycle of projects.

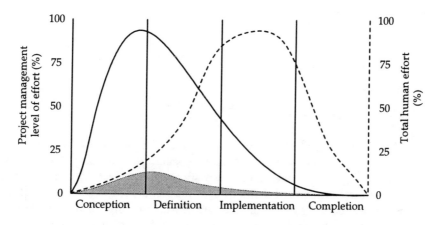

Figure 3-5: Levels of Effort

Figure 3-5 shows the normal distribution of effort expended during the life of a project. The broken line on the graph shows the overall effort from all project stakeholders on the project which is read against the scale on the right ordinate. Figure 3-5 shows a refinement of the "slow-quick-slow" characteristics of project life cycles, as mentioned earlier. The level of total project effort is low in the conception phase, increases in the definition phase, reaches a maximum in the implementation phase, and drops off rapidly in the completion phase.

On the other hand, an examination of the project management effort, which is the heavier line on Figure 3-5, shows the trend of effort to be quite different. This effort is read from a different scale to the total project effort and this is shown as the left ordinate. The project management effort has considerable impact during the conception and definition phases and can utilise much of the total effort used on the project (see the shaded area on the Figure). The effort drops off significantly during the completion phase.

Many believe that the management effort during the life of a project takes place during the implementation phase; this is just another misconception about the project management process. It comes as quite a surprise to some people to learn that the management effort takes place during the early phases of a project.

Stakeholders and Organisational Influences

Project stakeholders are those individuals and organisations who are involved in the project, or whose interests may be affected by it. There are many different categories of stakeholders, some or all of whom could be engaged in a project. They include:

- Customers and sponsors

- Internal and external entities

- Owners and funders

- Suppliers and contractors

- Team members and their families

- Government agencies

- Media outlets

- Individual citizens

- Society at large.

One of the early activities in the management of projects is to identify the stakeholders, identify what their needs and expectations are, and then manage and influence those expectations to ensure a successful project. Identifying stakeholders is not a straightforward action. For example, an assembly line worker whose future employment depends on the successful outcome of a "new product design" project is a stakeholder in that project. As the project is about a new product it can be seen that it requires lateral thinking to identify the significance of the assembly line worker in question.

One way of visualising stakeholders is given by Rodney Turner (1993) and is shown in Figure 3-6. Stakeholders can be categorised as primary, secondary or tertiary in accordance with their position relative to the project under consideration. Primary, or core, stakeholders are those that make a direct contribution to the project and may include the sponsor, the owner, the funder, the "doing" team, and the customer. The secondary group may be those individuals or organisations that act as vendors (suppliers) to the project, external entities, support to the "doing" team, and other similar parties. The tertiary group are the rest; the statutory authorities, the media, society, individual citizens, etc.

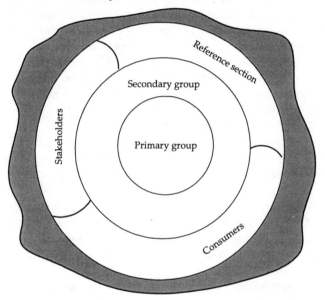

Figure 3-6: Project Stakeholders
Source: Turner (1993)

Having identified the stakeholders the next part of the process is to manage them. Managing stakeholder expectations may be difficult because stakeholders often have very different objectives. This matter is dealt with throughout Parts 5 to 8.

Projects are typically part of an organisation which is larger than the project. Even if the project is the organisation, the project will still be influenced by the organisation that set it up. Project-based organisations are of two types:

- Those that derive their revenue primarily from performing projects for others

- Those that have adopted management by projects.

Project-based organisations tend to have management systems in place to facilitate project management. Non-project based organisations (manufacturing companies, service-type companies, healthcare, etc.) seldom have management systems to support project needs. There is a need to be acutely aware of how the performing organisation's systems are likely to affect the project. But what is perhaps at least equally important is the organisational type of the project performing organisation and the organisational structure used in undertaking projects.

There are numerous organisational types that can be used when dealing with projects". The types range from the traditional functional, or vertical, hierarchy to the projectised, or project team arrangement; the range spans from the "army" chain of command to the multi-relational, respectively. The matter of organisational structure and its influence within a project's environment is dealt with in Part 5.

A Historical Overview — Old to Modern

Mankind has been involved in project activities for a long time (Nicholas, 1990). The buildings and structures of the Egyptians, the Romans, the Chinese are testament to this involvement. Designing and building the pyramids in 2500 BC is an example of what could be called "a large scale project". However it was not the first large scale project. The Bible describes projects which required the organisation and management of thousands of people; an example is the exodus of the Hebrews from the bondage of the Egyptians. Since these early records, obviously the nature of projects and the environment has changed but as long as mankind does things, there will be projects.

What is referred to as Modern Project Management (MPM) has it beginnings in the United States in the mid- to late 1950s. Two organisations were wrestling with the development of solution systems that would provide them with the means to reduce risk in the undertaking of certain projects. The two organisations were the United States Navy, and Dupont, the US chemical company.

The US Navy was engaged in the Polaris nuclear submarine programme and was having difficulty in finding a way to manage the thousands of procurement packages to ensure that they could control the huge time risk that was becoming apparent.

They engaged the help of the management consultant, Booz Allen Hamilton, and by 1958 a mathematical technique had been developed that would prove to be of enormous help to the Navy in managing their projects. The system became known as Program Evaluation Review Technique (PERT). PERT was based on using a statistical approach to determine activity durations and using network diagrams to analyse the integration of activities, to be able to establish the overall project duration and the probability of achieving it.

Simultaneously, but quite independently, Dupont was investigating ways in which they could reduce the outage time when undertaking major maintenance operations of their chemical plants. They developed a mathematical technique that became known as the Critical Path Method (CPM). CPM was based on single values for activity duration and, like PERT, used network diagrams to analyse the integration of activities and the overall duration of projects. These two techniques, PERT and CPM, will be described in more detail later, in the sub-Section "Time Management".

These events in 1958 are considered to be the birth of MPM. So even modern project management is not new, but it is a new management technique when compared with the scientific, humanistic and other management approaches that were developed during the nineteenth and early part of the twentieth centuries. In almost 40 years both CPM and PERT have been refined and further developed but the basis of all of today's network planning and scheduling tools can be traced back to these significant achievements in 1958.

There is another misconception held by some people that project management consists of the planning and scheduling of activities. Project management certainly does include the planning and scheduling of activities but, as a management process, it is much more than just planning and scheduling.

The complete "body of knowledge" of project management covers a wide range of management areas, such as project scope, time, cost, quality, human resources, communications, risk, procurement, etc. Since 1958 those engaged in the development of the art and science of project management have introduced an impressive array of techniques that support all of the required management skills. As mentioned in an earlier sub-Section, "What is Project Management?", project management's time has arrived as a method of management. More and more organisations are recognising the benefits of a different approach and are turning to and using the techniques of MPM.

Project management has been developing in the USA over the past 40 years. Much insight can be gained by briefly looking at this development process. During the first ten years (the decade of the 1960s) project organisational structures were experimented with and adopted. The next ten years saw the period of formal adoption of the people side of projects, i.e. the people characteristics needed to better undertake and manage projects. During the 1980s, organisations concentrated on the right procedures and techniques to ensure that the people within the organisational structures function more effectively. The current decade, the 1990s, is being referred to as the period of maturity.

An analysis of project management within Europe clearly demonstrates that reaching maturity is, however, still far away. "Apparent project management" in Europe is probably no more than 15 years old and we don't seem to be learning totally from the sound experience of the USA. It seems that, as usual on this side of the Atlantic, there is a need "to reinvent the wheel". Many associated with projects in Europe have yet to understand fully the general concept, let alone the effect of various organisational structures, the importance of the people and the range of procedures and techniques available to those who initiate or work in projects.

There are, relatively speaking, few organisations within Europe that can demonstrate a real project management capability. Initially this capability was to be found mainly in the field of process engineering. More recently most of the new project management ability is to be found among the professional practices, such as architects, consulting engineers, quantity surveyors, and, sometimes, constructors. There are a few professional companies that could be referred to as "pure" project management professionals with no vested interest in the technical design functions or the implementation of the project. An exciting development in the history of project management is the interest that the subject is generating in such "new" disciplines as software development, healthcare management, pharmaceutical product development, to mention just a few.

The Project Management Process

As stated earlier the process of project management is an integrative one, i.e. an action or failure to take action in one area will usually affect other areas. These interactions often require trade-offs among project objectives. Successful project management requires active management of these interactions.

There are five basic project management sub-processes:

- Initiating
- Planning
- Executing
- Controlling
- Closing

These five sub-processes are inter-related, as shown in Figure 3-7.

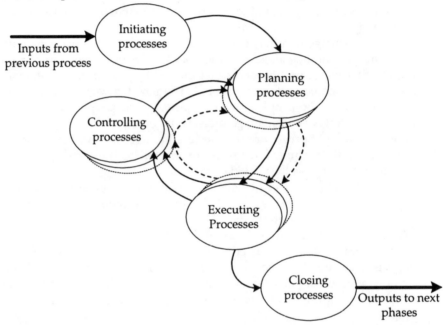

Figure 3-7: Project Management Process

Initiating refers to the process of identifying that something needs to be done and committing the organisation and its resources to do it. Planning means the devising of a work plan that will accomplish the "requirement". Executing refers to the co-ordination of the resources to achieve the "requirement". Controlling means the measurement of progress against the requirements and taking corrective action when necessary. Closing relates to the formalised acceptance that the requirements have been met and that this phase, or stage, of the project can be considered to have been concluded.

Although the planning, executing and controlling processes are also found within the traditional management approach, the sub-processes of initiating and closing are not. These two sub-processes are unique to the project management process.

These five sub-processes are not discrete one-time events; they are overlapping activities which occur at varying levels of intensity throughout each phase of the project. The output of one process becomes the input to another; the output of one phase becomes the input to initiating the next. Within each phase of a project's life cycle these sub-processes take place as a necessary sequence of actions to provide the deliverables.

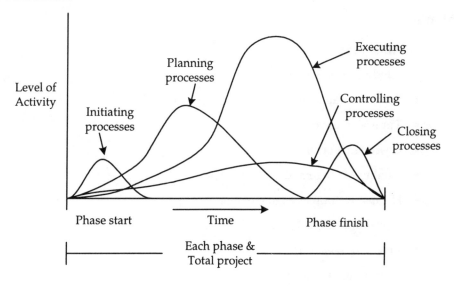

Figure 3-8: The Sub-processes within a Phase

Figure 3-8 shows the overlapping and the variation in level of effort of the five sub-processes. As can be expected, the initiating and closing sub-processes happen over relatively short periods at the beginning and end of a project's phase. The planning effort takes place over all phases except the closing period; by that time all planning will have been completed. The executing effort follows the overall effort trend (see Figure 3-5, for comparison), reaching its peak effort during the implementation, or the "doing", period. The controlling sub-process happens throughout the period of the phase and starts as soon as an initial plan has been produced.

SECTION 2: PROJECT MANAGEMENT "BODY OF KNOWLEDGE"

Contents

- Aims and Objectives
- "Body of Knowledge"
- Scope Management
- Time Management
- Cost Management
- Quality Management
- Human Resources Management
- Communications Management
- Risk Management
- Procurement management
- Integration management
- Summary of Key Points
- References

Aims and Objectives

The aims and objectives of Section 2 are to:

- List and explain the nine project management "body of knowledge" areas;
- Offer an insight into the inputs, outputs, and the mechanisms for producing the outputs of the processes within each knowledge area;
- Describe some of the more popular mechanisms used.

"Body of Knowledge"

The project management body of knowledge (PMBOK) (Project Management Institute, 1996) is an inclusive term that describes the sum of the knowledge within the profession of project management. As with other professions, the body of knowledge rests with the practitioners and academics who apply and advance it. The PMBOK includes proven, traditional practices which are widely applied, as well as innovative and advanced ones which have seen more limited use.

Generally accepted project management practices have been organised into nine knowledge areas each of which is described in terms of its components.

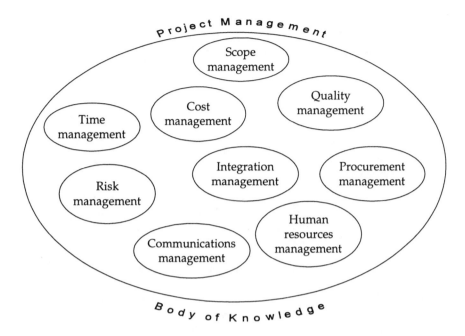

Figure 3-9: Body of Knowledge

The "project management context" describes the larger context in which projects operate. Managing the day-to-day activities of a project is necessary for success but not sufficient, as the project management team must understand the broader context. The project life cycle, the project stakeholders, the organisational influences, the key traditional management influences and the socio-economic influences are key aspects. In other words a project must be seen as a system which is a sub-system of another larger system.

The "process of project management" describes a generalised view of how various project management processes impact. For example, the process of "scope definition" produces an output called the "work breakdown structure". The WBS is then used as input to "activity definition", "activity sequencing", "resource planning", and "cost estimating".

Much of the knowledge needed to manage projects is unique or almost unique to project management (e.g. critical path analysis and work breakdown structures). However the PMBOK does overlap other management disciplines as shown.

Traditional management encompasses planning, organising, staffing, executing and controlling the operations of an on-going enterprise. The PMBOK does overlap traditional management in many areas — organisational behaviour, financial forecasting, and planning techniques to mention just a few. Traditional management skills provide much of the foundation for building project management skills.

Scope Management

According to the Project Management Institute (PMI), project scope management involves ensuring that the project does all the work that is required, and only the work required, to achieve the purpose of the project successfully.

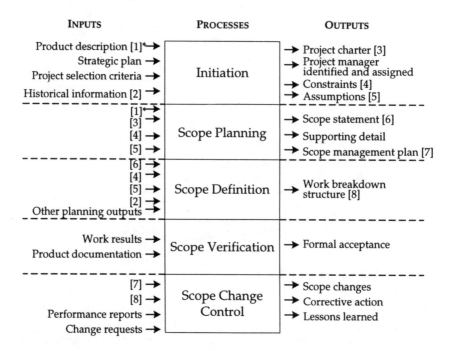

INPUTS	PROCESSES	OUTPUTS

Figure 3-10: Scope Management Processes

*Numbers in square brackets refer to previously identified inputs or outputs (e.g. [1] refers to the input "product description")

The major processes of scope management are: initiation, scope planning, scope definition, scope verification, and scope change control.

Initiation involves committing the client, or owner, organisation to the project. This is the process of formally recognising that a new project exists or that an existing project should continue into the next phase. A new project is likely to have been determined through either market demand, a business need, a customer request, a technological advance, a legal requirement, or some other need.

The inputs to *initiation* will be such matters as a product description which will be broadly based, the primary *raison d'être* for the "project", and a brief description of what is to be produced by the project. Project selection criteria will be determined and that will likely include the expected financial return, market share, public perceptions, etc.

The tools and techniques that are used in association with *initiation* include the use of decision models and the identification of subject experts. Decision models fall into two broad categories:

• Benefit measurement methods

- Constrained optimisation methods.

Benefit models are those that use "soft" systems approaches where qualitative comparisons are used, scoring models such as are used in value planning (see Part 6), and ranking of scheme options using such techniques as cost/benefit analysis. Constrained optimisation methods, where mathematical models are used, are the "hard" systems approach to making decisions. At the *initiation* stage the data available to undertake such modelling is normally of a type that will facilitate only a broad-based analysis. *Initiation* usually forms part of and succeeds a feasibility study. A properly handled project should always be authorised. The outputs from project initiation (authorisation) will include identifying and assigning a "project manager" and developing the "project charter" document.

The assignment of the project manager is one of the very early project tasks. The reason for this is that the project management effort must be applied early in the life of a project and it is essential that the project manager's assignment precedes all such effort. The skills of the appointed project manager should match the requirements of the project. Skills categories and the testing of individuals are contained within Part 5.

The project charter is the document that commits the organisation to the project once the project has been recognised officially. The project charter normally sets out the responsibility and authority of the project manager, as well as the organisation's commitment to the project through undertaking to provide the needed resources.

Scope planning includes the activities required to develop a written scope statement. A scope statement document will define the boundaries of the project work and this will include the project objectives, and the major phase (and project) deliverables. To undertake the *scope planning* exercise the product description, the project charter, and the constraints and assumptions will need to be available. The constraints will include such matters as the people available, the extent of the project's working week, the availability of funds, the importance of achieving certain project "milestone" dates (achieving crucial deliverables). If all these elements are available then the *scope planning* exercise will be limited to producing the "scope statement" document.

Some of the tools and techniques that are used in *scope planning* are: product analysis, benefit/cost analysis, alternative identification, and subject matter experts. Product analysis involves a better understanding of the product of the project; techniques that are used include systems mapping and value planning. Benefit/cost analysis involves estimating costs (outlays) and benefits (returns) and then using measures, such as, payback period and return on investment, to assess the financial viability of alternatives. The identification of alternative options will use such techniques as brainstorming, lateral thinking, and subject matter experts.

The output of *scope planning* is the "scope statement" and the "scope management plan" which will form the basis for making future project decisions. As mentioned earlier the scope statement document will include: project justification, project deliverables, and project objectives. The scope management plan will describe how the project scope will be managed and how changes to the project's scope will be handled.

Scope definition involves subdividing the major project deliverables as described in the scope statement. This definition into smaller, more manageable components is necessary in order to improve accuracy of resource estimates, to establish a baseline for progress measurement and control, and to provide a template that will deal with clear responsibility for project activities.

The inputs to *scope definition* will be the scope statement which will provide the project objectives and deliverables as well as the justification for the project.

The technique used in the *scope definition* process is known as decomposition. Decomposition involves dividing the major project deliverables into smaller more manageable but identifiable components and elements. The output of this decomposition is referred to as the Work Breakdown Structure, or WBS. The WBS is a logical structure of a project's activities and it defines the total scope of the project into elements or tasks that are definable and will be needed to produce the deliverables.

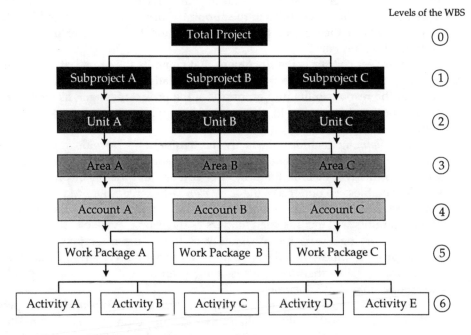

Figure 3-11: Work Breakdown Structure Template

Source: Kimmons, Robert L. (1990), *Project Management Basics*, Marcel Dekker.

Each item in the WBS consists of an activity, an identifier and the relationships between all activities and the activities within a particular grouping or "work package". The identifier is also known collectively as the "code of accounts".

Scope verification formalises acceptance of the project scope by the stakeholders (customer, client customer, etc.). It requires reviewing work products and results to ensure that all were completed correctly and satisfactorily. The inputs to *scope verification* are the documents produced to describe the product of the project (or of a phase).

The technique used in *scope verification* is inspection. Inspection includes activities such as measuring, examining, and testing to determine whether results

conform to requirements. The output of *scope verification* will be the formal acceptance of the scope documentation by the owner, or client, of the project. Such acceptance may be per phase, or for the whole project.

The *scope change control* process is concerned with influencing the factors which
create scope changes, determining that a scope change has occurred, and managing the actual changes when, and if, they occur. Where the WBS defines the scope
baseline, progress reports provide information on scope performance, and change
requests are the means, if required, for expanding the scope or shrinking it. These
items, along with the scope management plan, are the inputs to the *scope change
control* system.

The *scope change control* system is the technique that defines the procedures by
which the project scope may be changed. This technique includes the paperwork,
tracking systems, and approval levels for authorising or rejecting changes. The
outputs from the *scope change control* will be the means for handling scope
changes, the taking of corrective action, and monitoring the causes of variances
and the lessons learned from scope change control.

Time Management

Project time management includes the processes required to ensure timely completion of the project. The processes of time management are: activity definition,
activity sequencing, activity duration estimating, schedule development, and
schedule control.

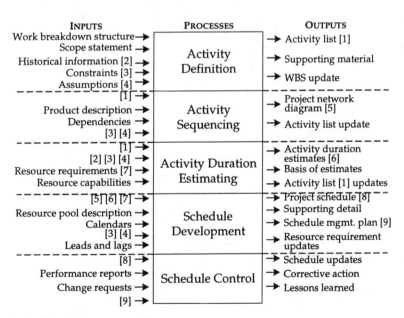

Figure 3-12: Time Management Processes

Activity definition deals with identifying and documenting the specific activities
that will be performed to produce the various project deliverables. The inputs to
activity definition include some of the outputs from scope management. These outputs are the "scope" WBS and the scope statement.

Decomposition as a technique will be used again and the intention will be to refine and add the tangible items that constitute the deliverables (the what) into the action steps needed (the how). This will transform the "scope" WBS into a "time" WBS, or "activity list". The activity list will, as per the WBS template, include a description and a code number for each activity. The description of each activity should consist of a verb-noun combination and should use a minimum number of words.

Activity sequencing is the process that identifies and documents inter-activity dependencies. The end result of this process will be a flow diagram that will show the project's activities in a sequence relative to each other.

The inputs to *activity sequencing* are the activity list, the product description, the "dependency logic" and knowledge of leads and lags between activities. The activity list will have been developed as part of "activity definition". The "product description" should be reviewed, as it is just possible that some characteristic of the product may well determine some aspect of *activity sequencing*.

Dependencies can be either mandatory (inherent in the nature of the work being undertaken), discretionary (as defined by the project management team) or external (linked to other projects or indirectly related to the current project). Leads and lags are time periods that relate to the dependencies between two activities. For instance one activity may lead, that is, be ahead of another activity. Or conversely an activity may lag, or be behind another activity.

The techniques that are used in activity sequencing are basically those used in preparing flow diagrams: a schematic method for showing logical relationships between activities. Flow diagrams were developed primarily for use in understanding processes in the chemical and manufacturing industries. A simple example of a flow diagram is shown in Figure 3-13.

The outputs of the *activity sequencing* process are the flow diagram and, if appropriate, an updated activity list which may have been produced based on the development work associated with preparing the flow diagram.

Activity duration estimating is estimating the number of work periods which will be needed to complete individual activities. The inputs to *activity duration estimating* are: the activity list, resource requirements, and resource capabilities. Each work activity that requires human, equipment, or material resources will be affected by the assignment of such resources. Durations are dependent upon the number of people, the numbers of items of plant, and the materials to be used. The resource capabilities are measured by the performance characteristics of each resource item.

Activity duration estimating has to rely more than most processes on the available historical information. Such information is often available from such sources as project files, commercial duration estimating databases, and project team knowledge. Expert knowledge and judgement should be used; if expertise is not available then estimates are inherently uncertain and risky.

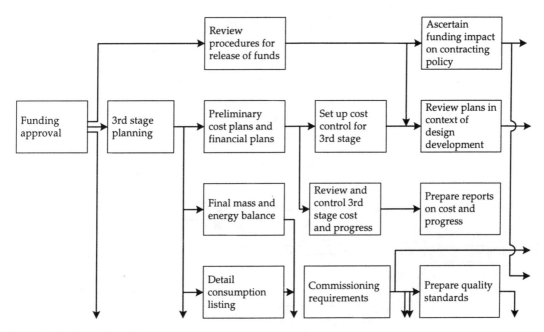

Figure 3-13: Part Flow Diagram

Schedule development means analysing the activity sequences, activity durations, and resource requirements to create the project schedule. It also means determining the start and finish dates for all the project activities. The inputs to schedule development are the flow diagram, duration estimates, resource pool description (what resources available at what times), project calendars, and constraints.

What is meant by the flow diagram and activity duration estimating has already been explained. Knowledge of what resources will be available to these inputs, at what times and in what patterns, is necessary for *schedule development*. Project and resource calendars identify periods when work is allowed. Constraints — such as imposed dates, key events or major milestones — and assumptions, are likely to impact on schedule development.

The techniques that are used are mathematical analysis, duration compression, simulation, and resource levelling heuristics.

Mathematical analysis involves calculating the hypothetical early start (ES), theoretical late start (LS), the theoretical early finish (EF), and the theoretical late finish (LF) of all project activities. The analysis techniques used are critical path method (CPM), program evaluation and review technique (PERT), and graphical evaluation and review technique (GERT).

Duration compression, a further refinement of mathematical analysis, looks for ways to shorten the project schedule without reducing the project scope. Duration compression includes techniques such as crashing and fast-tracking. Crashing means reducing the overall project time period for the least incremental cost. Fast-tracking relates to undertaking activities in parallel that would normally be done in series.

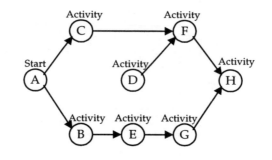

CPM Diagram

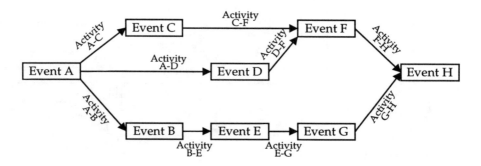

PERT Diagram

Figure 3-14: CPM and PERT Analysis Technique Templates

Simulation involves calculating many schedules with different sets of assumptions. The most common uses Monte Carlo Analysis in which a distribution of probable results is defined for each activity and used to calculate a distribution of results for the total project.

Resource levelling heuristics deals with testing the schedule with either more resources, less resources, or changes in the resource content. Resource levelling constrains schedule plans and usually results in a project duration that is longer than any preliminary schedule.

The outputs from this *schedule development* process are the project schedule, supporting detail, schedule management plan and the resource requirement updates.

Schedule control is the process concerned with:

- Influencing the factors which create schedule changes

- Determining that the schedule has changed

- Managing the actual changes when and as they occur.

Schedule control needs to be fully integrated with the overall change control system.

The inputs to *schedule control* are the project schedule, the progress reports, the change requests, and the schedule management plan.

The tools and techniques used in *schedule control* are: schedule change control system, progress measurement, additional planning, planning and scheduling software, schedule reserves. The schedule change control system defines the procedures by which the project schedule may be changed. Progress measurement techniques such as "earned value" (see the next sub-Section "Cost Management") help to evaluate the variations that occur. From these variation evaluations decisions can be taken on which activities require corrective action. Because most projects will be affected by change, new or revised activity sequencing or duration estimates will necessitate further planning and scheduling. There are numerous planning and scheduling software models available that will provide effective tracking of changes and forecasting of effects. Schedule reserves are work periods with no activities assigned to them so that these may be used as a means of time control.

The outputs from the *schedule control* process include schedule updates, corrective actions, and lessons learned. Schedule updating refers to any modification to the schedule information which is used to manage the project. Revisions, which are a special category of schedule update, are changes to the scheduled start and finish dates in the approved project schedule brought about by changes to the scope. Corrective action (expediting) is anything done to bring expected future schedule performance into line with the project plan. The causes and reasoning (lessons learned) should be documented and used as feedback to the project.

Cost Management

Project cost management incorporates the processes required to ensure that the project is completed within the approved budget.

The major processes within project cost management are: resource planning, cost estimating, cost budgeting, and cost control.

Resource planning involves determining what resources (people, equipment, materials) and what quantities of each should be used to perform project activities. The inputs to *resource planning* are the WBS, scope statement, resource pool description, and organisational policies. By resource pool description we mean the knowledge of what resources are potentially available to the project. Organisational policies refer to the performing organisation rules regarding staffing, supplies, equipment, etc.

The outputs from *resource planning* will be a description of what types of resources for addressing each activity are required and in what quantities within the WBS. The tools and techniques required for *resource planning* are usually the skills and knowledge of the project team and historical information from previous similar projects.

Cost estimating involves developing an approximation of the costs of the resources needed to complete the project's activities. The inputs to the cost estimating process are resource rates, duration estimates, and the accounting structure used by the performing organisation.

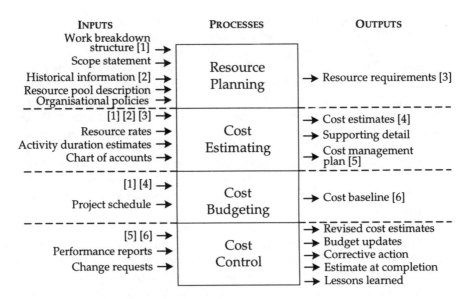

Figure 3-15: Cost Management Processes

The tools and techniques used in *cost estimating* are: historical results, parametric modelling, bottom-up estimating, analogous estimating, and computerised cost estimating software. Historical results include such matters as: file records of previous project cost, commercial cost estimating databases, and project team knowledge of similar projects. Parametric modelling will be any mathematical model that uses project characteristics to compute total project cost. Bottom-up estimating involves estimating the cost of the individual work packages and then summarising (or rolling-up) the individual estimates to get the total project cost. Analogous estimating is top-down estimating and usually means using the actual cost of a previous project to estimate the cost of the current project. Computerised estimating tools are available that can facilitate rapid consideration of many costing alternatives.

The outputs from *cost estimating* are the cost estimates, the supporting detail, and the cost management plan. The cost estimates of the likely costs of the resources required to complete the project activities must cover all resource categories which will be charged to the project. Cost estimates are usually refined during the course of the project and as additional detail becomes available. In some projects the estimating terms order-of-magnitude, budget, and definitive are used.

Figure 3-16 shows that order-of-magnitude estimates are used during the formative stages of a project during the time when initial evaluations are being carried out on one or more schemes. Their accuracy is traditionally within the range of –30 per cent to +50 per cent. Other terms used for these types of estimate are: preliminary, factored, pre-feasibility, or quickie.

Budget estimates, otherwise known as appropriation, or control estimates are used in the early stages of a project, usually in the conception phase, and before the project has been approved. Budget estimates will normally be within the accuracy range of –10 per cent to +30 per cent.

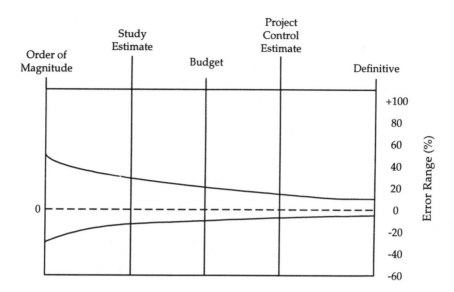

Figure 3-16: Cost Estimate Degree of Accuracy

Definitive estimates, whose accuracy range will normally be –5 per cent to +10 per cent are prepared from well defined data, specifications, drawings, etc. It is usual in engineering projects for at least 40 per cent of the detailed design to have been completed before this type of estimate is assembled. For a more detailed description of cost estimating, refer to Part 6, Section 2, sub-Section "Types of Estimating".

Cost budgeting is the allocation of the overall cost estimate to the individual work packages. The inputs to the cost budgeting are the cost estimates from the previous process, the WBS which identifies the activities to which the costs will be allocated, and the project schedule which will indicate the time periods against which the cost estimates will apply.

The relationship between the cost breakdown structure, which is the framework of the cost budget, and the work breakdown structure is shown in Figure 3-17. This shows in simple terms a WBS hierarchy for an IT project, the organisational structure for the performing organisation, and the work packages for each organisational discipline, such as project management, engineering, programming, etc. The work package for the "programming department" for preparing the "software specifications" is shown (magnified) as a "programme task" versus "calendar time" relationship.

The tools and techniques that were described under cost estimating will also apply to *cost budgeting*. The outputs from this process will be the cost baseline, the time-phased budget used to measure and monitor cost performance on the project, and spending plans, which is the cost baseline that reflects expected payments rather than expected usage.

Cost control involves controlling changes to the project budget and includes monitoring cost performance to detect variances from the plan, ensuring that all appropriate changes are recorded accurately in the cost baseline. This will prevent incorrect, inappropriate, or unauthorised changes from being included in the cost baseline, and inform appropriate stakeholders of authorised changes.

The inputs to *cost control* are the cost baseline from the previous process, the progress reports, change requests, and the cost management plan. The progress reports will provide, inter alia, information on cost performance, such as, which budgets are being met and which aren't, and issues which may cause problems. Change requests may impact on increasing or decreasing the budget. Change requests may come from many sources and they need to be fully documented.

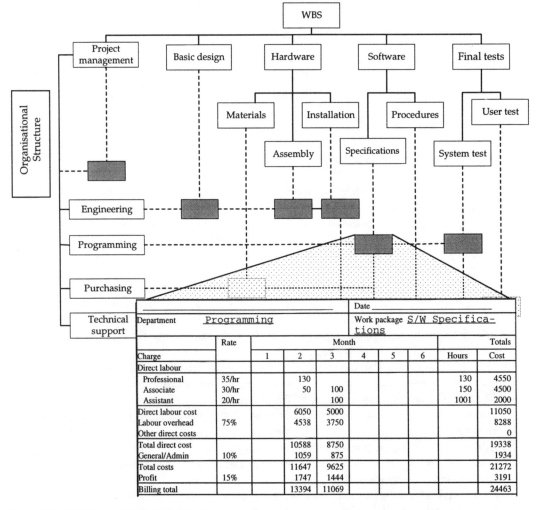

Date _____

Department Programming						Work package S/W Specifications		
	Rate				Month			Totals
Charge		1	2	3	4	5	6	Hours	Cost
Direct labour									
Professional	35/hr		130					130	4550
Associate	30/hr		50	100				150	4500
Assistant	20/hr			100				1001	2000
Direct labour cost			6050	5000					11050
Labour overhead	75%		4538	3750					8288
Other direct costs									0
Total direct cost			10588	8750					19338
General/Admin	10%		1059	875					1934
Total costs			11647	9625					21272
Profit	15%		1747	1444					3191
Billing total			13394	11069					24463

Figure 3-17: CBS and WBS Relationship

The tools and techniques that are used in *cost control* include: the cost change control system, progress measurement, additional planning, earned value, forecasting, computerised tools, and cost reserves.

The cost change control system defines the procedures by which the cost baseline may be changed. Progress measurement helps to assess the magnitude of any variations which do occur. Prospective changes may require new or revised cost estimates or analysis of alternative approaches. Earned value is a popular method for measuring project cost performance. It compares the amount of work that was planned with what was actually accomplished to determine if progress is as planned. Forecasting is used during the progress of the project to calculate an estimated cost at completion. Planned versus actual costs can be tracked using spreadsheets or planning and scheduling software. Cost reserves are budgeted amounts that are allocated but not assigned to any specific project activity.

The outputs from the *cost control* process are revised estimates, corrective action and lessons learned.

Revised estimates are any modifications to the cost information used to manage the project. Budget updates — changes to the approved cost baseline — are a special category of revised estimates. Corrective action (expediting) is anything done to bring expected future schedule performance into line with the project plan. The causes and reasoning (lessons learned) need to be documented and used as feedback to the project.

Quality Management

Project quality management covers the processes required to ensure that the project will satisfy the needs for which it is to be undertaken. It includes all activities of the overall management function that determine the quality policy, objectives, and responsibilities, and implements them by means such as quality planning, quality control, quality assurance and quality improvement, within the quality system.

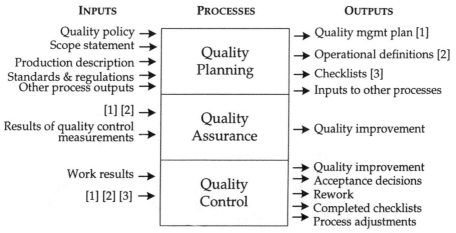

Figure 3-18: Quality Management Processes

Project quality management processes must address both the product of the project (what is produced) and the process of the project (how the other project management processes are performed).

Quality planning involves identifying which quality standards are relevant to the project and determining how to satisfy them. Quality has to be planned in, not inspected in.

The inputs to *quality planning* include quality policy, scope statement, product description, standards and regulations, and other process outputs. An organisation's overall intentions and direction with regard to quality, as expressed by top management, is what is meant by quality policy. The scope statement documents the major project deliverable as well as the project objectives. The product description, although incorporated with the scope statement, will often contain details of technical issues and other concerns that may affect quality planning. Specific standards and regulations that may affect the project have to be considered by the project management team. Other process outputs such as procurement need to be considered as they may have requirements that should be incorporated within the overall quality management plan.

The tools and techniques for *quality planning* are benefit/cost considerations, benchmarking, flowcharts, and design of experiments. The *quality planning* process must consider benefit/cost relationships. The primary benefit of meeting quality requirements is less rework which means higher productivity, lower costs, and increased stakeholder satisfaction. Through quality management it is essential that the benefits outweigh the cost.

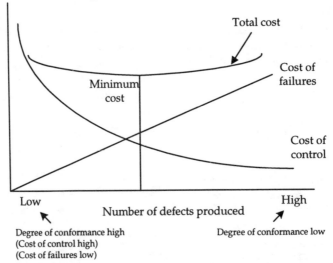

Figure 3-19: Cost of Quality

Figure 3-19 shows that the primary benefit of meeting quality requirements is less rework which means higher productivity, lower costs, and through such matters, increased stakeholder satisfaction.

Benchmarking involves comparing actual or planned project practices to those of other projects in order to generate ideas for improvement. A flowchart is any diagram which shows how components and elements relate to one another. A technique that is commonly used is the cause-and-effect diagram (Ishikawa or fishbone diagram). Design of experiments is an analytical technique which helps identify which variables have the most influence on the overall outcome.

The outputs from quality planning are the quality management plan, operational definitions, and checklists. The quality management plan will describe how the project management team will implement its quality policy. It must address quality control, quality assurance, and quality improvement for the project. Operational definitions describe what something is and how it is measured by the quality control process. Checklists are structured tools used to verify that a set of required steps have been performed.

Quality control relates to monitoring specific project results to determine if they comply with relevant quality standards and identifying ways to eliminate causes of unsatisfactory performance.

The inputs to *quality control* are work results, and the outputs from the previous process: the quality management plan, operational definitions and checklists.

The tools and techniques for quality control include inspection, control charts, and Pareto diagrams. Inspection includes activities such as measuring, examining and testing to determine whether results conform to requirements. Inspection methods include reviews, product reviews, auditing, walk-throughs, etc. Control charts are a graphical display of the results over time of a process.

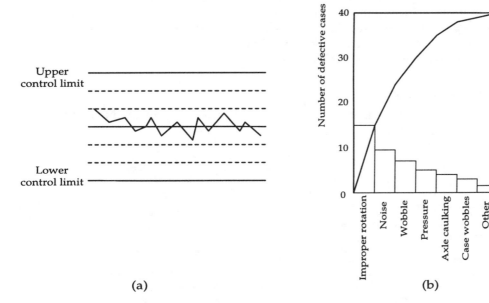

(a) (b)

Figure 3-20: Control Chart and Pareto Diagram

Control charts (a) may be used to monitor any type of output variable. They can be used to monitor cost, schedule or other process results to help determine if the project management process is in control.

A Pareto diagram (b) is a type of bar chart or histogram showing the number of defects or nonconformities ranked in order of cause. Usually it will also show the accumulated defects for a batch. This is shown as a continuous curve and is read against the right-hand scale which is registered in percentage terms. What is known as "Pareto's Law" holds that a large majority of defects are typically the result of a relatively small number of causes.

Outputs from *quality control* include quality improvements, acceptance decisions, rework, completed checklists, and process adjustments. Quality improvements will have to be handled through the change control procedures. The inspected items will be either accepted or rejected; rejected items may require rework. Checklists were discussed in the previous process "quality control". Process adjustments may need to be handled according to the defined change control procedures.

Quality assurance involves evaluating overall performance on a regular basis to provide confidence that the project will satisfy the relevant quality standards. *Quality assurance* may be provided to the project management team and to the management of the performing organisation or it may be provided to the customer and others not actively involved in the work of the project.

Inputs to *quality assurance* are the quality management plan, the results of the quality control measurements, and the operational definitions.

The tools and techniques for *quality assurance* are quality planning and inspection. When problems occur with quality control, corrective action may need to be taken. Potential corrective action is often defined in the quality management plan. Inspection includes activities such as measuring, examining, and testing quality control results to determine if the results conform to requirements.

The output from *quality assurance* is quality improvement. This includes taking action to increase the effectiveness and efficiency of the project so as to provide added benefits to the project stakeholders.

Human Resource Management

Project human resource management includes the processes required to make the most effective use of the people involved with the project.

Figure 3-21: Human Resource Management Processes

As Figure 3-21 shows project human resource management includes organisational planning, staff acquisition and team development. Organisational planning includes identifying, documenting, and assigning project roles, responsibilities, and reporting relationships. Staff acquisition relates to getting the human resources needed assigned to and working on the project. Team development includes developing individual and group skills to enhance project performance.

Organisational planning on most projects is often undertaken as part of the earliest project phases. The inputs to *organisational planning* include: project interfaces, staffing requirements, and constraints and limitations.

Project interfaces generally fall into three categories:

- Organisational interfaces which deals with reporting relationships among different organisation units

- Technical interfaces which relate to reporting relationships among different technical disciplines

- Interpersonal interfaces dealing with reporting relationships among different individuals working on the project.

Staffing requirements refers to defining what kind of skills are required, what kinds of individuals or groups, and what time frames. Constraints and limitations include such matters as organisational structure, collective bargaining agreements, preferences of the project management team, and expected staff assignments.

The tools and techniques for *organisational planning* include templates, human resource practices, and organisational theory. Although each project is unique, most projects will resemble another project to some extent; templates of other projects can help expedite the planning process. The human resource practices of the performing organisation, such as policies, guidelines, procedures, etc., can help with various aspects of *organisational planning*. Organisational theory using the available literature can help in determining how to structure the organisation. For instance a functional hierarchy is known to promote efficiency (doing the job right) while a team approach promotes effectiveness (doing the right job).

The outputs from the *organisational planning* process include role and responsibility assignments, staffing plan, organisation chart, and supporting detail.

Person / Phase	A	B	C	D	E	F	
Requirements	S	R	A	P	P		
Functional	S		A	P		P	
Design	S		R	A	I		P
Development		R		A			
Testing			S	P	I	A	P
P = Participant A = Accountable R = Review required I = Input required S = Sign-off required							

Figure 3-22: Responsibility and Accountability Matrix
Source: Project Management Institute (1996)

Figure 3-22 shows how the role and responsibility assignments set out "who does what" and "who decides what" in the project. These RAMs are directly linked to the WBS and the organisational breakdown structure of the project; they create the bridge between what has to be done on the project and who is going to do it.

The staffing plan describes, *inter alia*, when and how human resources will be brought onto and taken off the project team. An organisation chart is any graphical display of project reporting relationships both internal and external to the project. Supporting detail for organisational planning will include such matters as organisational impact assessment, job descriptions, training needs, etc.

Staff acquisition relates to getting the needed human resources assigned to and working on the project. The inputs to *staff acquisition* include the staffing plan, staffing pool description, and recruitment practices. The staffing plan is an output from the previous process. In deciding on staff assignments the project management team must consider the characteristics of potentially available staff, such as previous experience, personal interests, personal characteristics, and availability. If the performing organisations have recruitment practices then these could act as a constraint on staff assignment.

The tools and techniques for *staff acquisition* include negotiations, pre-assignment, and procurement. The project manager may need to negotiate with functional managers and other project management teams to assign scarce or specialised resources. Staff may be pre-assigned if they were included as part of a proposal that was accepted, or staff may be assigned because they were defined in the project charter. Procurement, as a means for *staff acquisition*, may be necessary if resources have to be secured from outside the organisation.

The outputs from *staff acquisition* are the assigned staff and a staff directory that lists all project team members and other stakeholders.

Team development involves developing individual and group skills to enhance project performance.

The components of *team development* are the project staff, the project plan, the staffing plan, progress reports, and the external feedback.

The tools and techniques for *team development* are team building activities, general management skills, reward and recognition systems, collocation, and training. Team building activities include management and individual actions taken specifically and primarily to improve team performance. The general management skills that should be in evidence in *team development* are those listed in the opening sub-Section, "Body of Knowledge", of this Section. Reward and recognition systems are formal management actions which promote or reinforce desired behaviour. Collocation refers to the placing of all active team members in the same physical location to enhance their ability to perform as a team. Training includes all activities designed to enhance the skills, knowledge, and capabilities of the project team members.

The outputs from *team development* will be performance improvements from individuals, the team or teams, through developing better ways of doing project work.

Communications Management

Project communications management provides the critical links among people, ideas and information necessary for success. It is the knowledge area required to ensure timely and appropriate generation, collection, dissemination, storage, and ultimate disposition of project information.

The management skill of communicating covers the broad concepts of sender–receiver models, choice of media, writing style, presentation techniques and techniques used for meetings. These concepts are not, of course, unique to the projects' environment but relate to the general management area.

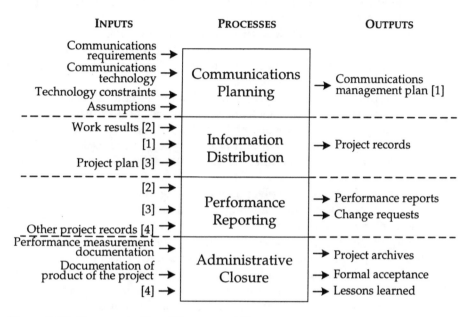

Figure 3-23: Communications Management Processes

As Figure 3-23 shows, project communications management consists of communications planning, information distribution, progress reporting, and administrative closure.

Communications planning includes determining the information and communication needs of the stakeholders. Planning will determine who needs what information, when they will need it, and how it will be given to them.

The information needs and methods of distribution will depend upon the type, size and complexity of the project. *Communications planning* will be closely linked with the needs of the stakeholder, and with organisational planning which was dealt with in "Human Resources Management" in this Section.

The inputs to *communications planning* include communications requirements, communications technology, and constraints and assumptions. Communication requirements are the total information required by the project participants. This is defined by combining the type and format of information which typically includes:

- Project organisation and stakeholder relationships

- Disciplines, departments, and specialities involved in the project

- Logistics of which specific individuals will be involved with the project and at which locations

- External information needs

Communication technology relates to the technologies or methods used to transfer information between project elements. Such transfers can vary from brief conversations to extended meetings, from simple written documents to immediately accessible on-line schedules and databases. The technology should be determined by immediacy of need for information, the availability of the technology and the expected project environment.

Constraints and assumptions are factors that limit the project management teams' options. The tool or technique used is stakeholder analysis. Stakeholder analysis should consider methods and technologies that will provide all the information needs without wasting resources.

The output from "information planning" is the communications management plan; this plan is a subsidiary element of the overall project plan. The communications management plan document provides: a collection structure, a distribution structure, a detailed description of each type of information to be handled, information production schedules, and a method for handling changes in the communications plan.

Information distribution involves implementing the communications management plan and this includes making needed information available to project stakeholders in a timely manner.

The inputs to *information distribution* include the project plan, the work results as reported from progress reporting and the communications management plan. The tools and techniques for information distribution are: communication skills, information retrieval systems, and information distribution systems. Communications skills are used to exchange information. Communicating has many dimensions:

- Written and oral, listening and speaking

- Internal (within the project) and external (to the customer, etc.)

- Formal (reports, etc.) and informal (memos, ad-hoc conversations, etc.)

- Vertical (up and down the organisation) and horizontal (with peers).

Information retrieval systems include manual filing systems, electronic text databases, project management software and systems which allow access to technical documentation (e.g. engineering drawings, etc.). Information distribution systems use a variety of methods including: project meetings, hard-copy document distribution, shared access to networked electronic databases, fax, electronic mail, and video conferencing.

Progress reporting includes collecting and disseminating progress information. This process includes status reporting (where we are), performance measurement (how well have we done), and forecasting (where will we be when we have finished).

The inputs to *progress reporting* include the project plan and the work results. The work results are the progress towards achieving the completion of the project activities.

The tools and techniques for *progress reporting* include information distribution (as described above), integrated reporting methods, schedule reporting methods, and cost reporting methods. By integrated reporting methods, the cost and schedule information will be set out within the same report to provide a fuller picture of project status. The method called "earned value", which was described in the sub-Section "Cost Management", is the most widely used integrated reporting method.

Schedule reporting methods most commonly used are the Gantt chart, CPM progress chart and milestone completion lists (which can be prepared comprehensively or on an exception basis). Cost reporting methods are expenditure tables, histograms, and S-curves, and any of these can be prepared comprehensively or on an exception basis.

The outputs from *progress reporting* include the progress reports and change requests.

Administrative closure includes generating, gathering, and disseminating information to formalise project completion. Inputs to "administrative closure" are progress measuring documents and documentation of the product of the project.

The mechanism for creating the outputs for *administrative closure* is the post-implementation review. This is a structured review and analysis of administrative closure inputs by project team members. The project management team is responsible for identifying project successes and failures, any methods or technologies developed, and transferring, or feeding back, such knowledge to other projects. The outputs from *administrative closure* are the project records and formal acceptance of the project deliverables, or project phase deliverables, by the owner.

Risk Management

Project risk management includes the processes concerned with identifying, analysing, and responding to uncertainty. The word risk can have two separate and distinct meanings. It can mean uncertainty (negative or positive outcome) or it can mean a threat (negative outcome).

As shown in Figure 3-24, project risk management consists of the processes of risk identification, risk quantification, response development, and risk control.

There is no universal definition of these terms; for example, risk identification and risk quantification are also called risk analysis; risk quantification and response development are also called risk assessment; response development is also called response planning and sometimes risk mitigation and response development and risk control are also referred to as risk management.

Risk identification relates to determining which risk events are likely to affect the project. The inputs to *risk identification* are product description, and constraints and assumptions.

Product description will include the nature of the product of the project and this will have a major effect on the risks identified (proven technology versus innovation). Constraints and assumptions will include factors that limit the project management team's options and these factors will be found in the knowledge areas of project scope management and project quality management. These areas should be reviewed for constraints and assumptions that may represent opportunity or threat: e.g. scope statements, WBS, staffing plan, and procurement management plan.

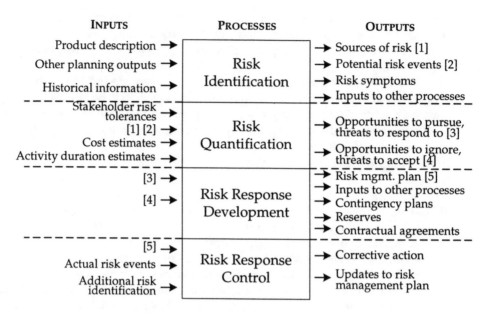

Figure 3-24: Risk Management Processes

The tools and techniques for *risk identification* include:

- Checklists organised by source of risk. Some application areas have widely used Classification schemes for sources of risk

- What actually happened on previous projects obtained from a) project files, and b) project team knowledge

- Risk-oriented interviews with various stakeholders.

The outputs from *risk identification* are: the sources of risk, the potential risk events, the risk symptoms, and the inputs to other processes, i.e. risk identification may identify a need for further activity in another area.

Potential risk events are discrete occurrences that may affect the project. Risk events should generally include estimates of the probability that the risk event will occur, the alternative possible outcomes, expected timing of the event, and anticipated frequency. Risk symptoms are indirect manifestations of actual risk events.

Risk quantification is concerned primarily with evaluating the range of possible outcomes, their likelihood of occurrence, and which risk events warrant response. *Risk quantification* is complicated by a number of factors including:

- Opportunities and threats can interact in unanticipated ways, e.g. schedule delays may force consideration of a new strategy that reduces overall project duration

- A single risk event can cause multiple effects, e.g., late delivery of a key component may produce cost overruns

- Opportunities for one stakeholder (e.g. reduced cost), may be threats to another (e.g. reduced profit)

- The mathematical techniques used can create a false impression of precision and reliability.

The inputs to *risk quantification* are: the sources of risk, the potential risk events, and the stakeholders' tolerance to risk. Different organisations and individuals have different tolerances for risk. For example, one organisation may perceive an estimate that has a 20 per cent probability of overrun as high risk while another organisation will perceive it as low risk.

The tools and techniques for *risk quantification* include: expected monetary value, statistical sums, schedule simulation, and decision trees.

Expected value, as a tool for risk quantification, is the product of two numbers: risk event probability and risk event value. These values are generally used as input to further analysis, i.e. decision trees. Statistical sums can be used to measure probability distributions of quantity estimates, cost estimates, etc.; most project cost estimates follow either a) uniform distributions, b) triangular distributions, or c) beta distributions. Schedule simulation is normally based on some form of Monte Carlo analysis of the project network and provides a statistical distribution of the calculated results, and should be used on any large or complex project, as CPM analysis tends to underestimate project durations. A decision tree is a diagram that depicts key interactions among decisions and associated chance events.

The outputs from *risk quantification* are: a list of opportunities that should be pursued and threats that require mitigation, and a document listing those risk events that the project management team has decided to accept or to ignore. These outputs become the inputs to "risk development".

Response development is the process of deciding specifically what to do. This includes defining enhancement steps for opportunities and mitigation steps for threats. Responses to opportunities are often called enhancements while responses to threats generally fall into one of three categories: avoidance, that is, eliminating the threat by eliminating the cause; mitigation, that is, reducing the expected monetary value of a risk event by reducing the probability of occurrence; and retention, that is, accepting the consequences.

The inputs to *response development* are the outputs from *risk quantification*. The mechanisms for *response development* are: contracting, contingency planning, alternative strategies, and insurance.

Contracting involves sharing downside risk by acquiring goods from outside the project organisation. Contingency planning involves defining action steps ahead of time to be taken if an identified risk event should occur. Alternative strategies are the risk events that can often be prevented or avoided by changing the planned approach. Insurance or some type of bonding is often available to deal with some categories of risk.

The outputs from *risk development* are the risk management plan, inputs to other processes, contingency plans, reserves, and contractual agreement. The risk management plan documents the procedures that will be used to manage risk throughout the project. Selected or alternative risk strategies must be fed back into the appropriate processes. Generally contingency plans are part of the risk management plan. A reserve is a provision in the project plan to mitigate cost and/or schedule risk. Contractual agreements may be entered into for insurance services, and other items, as appropriate, in order to avoid or mitigate threats.

Risk control involves responding to changes in risk over the course of the project through executing the risk management plan.

The inputs to risk control are the risk management plan, the occurrence of certain risk events, and the identification of additional risk events.

The mechanisms used for *risk control* are workarounds and additional response development. Workarounds are unplanned responses to negative risk events. Additional response development refers to a risk event that was not expected or where the effect is different to what was expected, making it necessary to repeat the response development process.

The outputs from *risk control* are corrective action, and updates of the risk management plan.

Procurement Management

Project procurement management is the knowledge area that deals with acquiring goods and services (the product) from outside the immediate project organisation. Project procurement management is discussed from the perspective of the owner, or buyer, in the buyer–seller relationship. The seller is often referred to as the contractor but is also called the vendor or supplier; the buyer is seen by the seller as the customer.

As seen from Figure 3-25, project procurement management consists of the processes of procurement planning, solicitation planning, solicitation, source selection, contract administration, and contract close-out.

Procurement planning is determining what to procure and when. *Procurement planning* is the process of identifying which project needs can best be met by procuring products or services from outside the performing organisation. *Procurement planning* will generally result in a decision to either:

- Procure all or virtually all of the goods and services through a single prime contractor

- Procure a significant portion of the goods and services required from multiple contractors

- Procure a relatively minor portion of the goods and services required

- Procure none of the goods and services.

Figure 3-25: Procurement Management Processes

The inputs to *procurement planning* include: scope statement, product description, procurement resources, market conditions, other planning outputs, and constraints and assumptions.

The scope statement describes current project boundaries, project needs and strategies. The product description, provides important information about any technical issues or concerns. The procurement resources will determine whether they are provided from the performing organisation or the project team. Market conditions consider what products are available in the market place and from whom, and under what terms and conditions. Other planning outputs, if available, must be considered. Constraints and assumptions are the factors that will limit the team's options (e.g., availability of funds).

The mechanisms for *procurement planning* are make-or-buy analysis and subject matter experts. Make-or-buy analysis can be used to determine whether a particular product can be produced cost-effectively by the performing organisation. The subject matter experts are any group, or individual, with specialised knowledge in procurement related activities.

Output from *procurement planning* consist of the procurement management plan, and statement(s) of work. The procurement management plan describes how the remaining procurement processes will be managed. The statement of work describes the procurement items in sufficient detail to allow prospective contractors to determine if they are capable of providing what the customer needs.

Solicitation planning involves preparing the documents needed to support product requirements and to identify potential sources.

The inputs to *solicitation planning* are the procurement management plan, statement of work, and other planning outputs.

The mechanisms for *solicitation planning* are what is referred to as "standard forms", and subject matter experts. Standard forms are the standard contracts, standard descriptions of procurement items, and standard versions of all needed bid documents.

The outputs from *solicitation planning* are bid documents and evaluation criteria. Bid documents are used to solicit proposals from prospective contractors. The terms "bid & quotation" are used when the decision is price-driven, the term "proposal" is used when non-financial considerations are paramount. Bid documents should be structured to facilitate accuracy and completeness and to ensure consistent comparable responses. They should include the relevant statement of work, a description of the desired form of response, and any required contractual provisions.

Evaluation criteria are used to rate or score contractor proposals; the criteria are often included as part of the bid document. The evaluation criteria may be limited to purchase price or they may include such criteria as life cycle cost, technical capability, and management approach.

Solicitation involves obtaining quotations, bids, offers or proposals as appropriate from prospective contractors on how project needs can be met. The inputs to solicitation include bid documents and prospective contractors list. The contractors' list describe the experience, finances, and organisation of prospective tenderers and if this information is not readily available the project management team will have to develop the listing.

The mechanisms for *solicitation* are bidders' conferences and advertising. Bidders' conferences are meetings with prospective contractors prior to the preparation of a bid. They are used to ensure that prospective contractors understand clearly the project's procurement process and the project's requirements. Questions and answers generated at the bidders conference are normally incorporated within the bid documents. Advertising can be used to expand existing lists of potential contractor organisations.

The outputs from *solicitation* are the contractor's proposals or contractor prepared documents that describe the contractors offer to provide the requested product.

Source selection involves the receipt of bids and proposals and the choosing from among potential contractors. The selection process may be based on price, technical merit or some other measure and is usually linked to a weighting scheme.

The inputs to *source selection* are contractors' proposals, evaluation criteria, and organisational policies that can affect the evaluation of the proposals. The mechanisms by which these inputs are converted to outputs include: contract negotiation, weighting system, screening system, and independent estimates.

Contract negotiation involves clarification and mutual agreement on the structure and requirements of the contract. The weighting system is a method for quantifying qualitative data in order to minimise the effect of personal prejudice on source selection. The screening system involves establishing minimum requirements of performance for one or more of the evaluation criteria. Independent estimates are usually those prepared by the customer to check the suppliers' proposals; these are also referred to as the "should cost" estimates.

The output from *source selection* is the contract(s). Contracts generally fall into one of three broad categories, namely:

- Fixed price or lump sum

- Cost reimbursable

- Unit price.

A fixed price contract, as its name implies, relates to the customer paying a fixed price for a well-defined product. A cost reimbursable contract involves payment to the supplier for its actual costs. Unit price contracts are those where there is a preset amount per quantity unit and the total price paid is a function of the quantities needed to complete the contract works.

Contract administration is the process of ensuring that the contractor's performance meets with contractual requirements. With multiple contractors there is a need to manage the interfaces. It also includes application of the appropriate project management processes to the contractual relationship. The project management processes which must be applied include:

- Project plan execution

- Progress reporting

- Quality control

- Change control.

The inputs to *contract administration* include the contract(s), work results, change requests, and contractor invoices. The mechanisms through which these inputs are converted into outputs are: contract change control system, progress reporting and contractor payment system.

The outputs are: contractor correspondence, contract changes, and contractor payment requests.

Contract close-out involves completion and settlement of the contract(s) including resolution of any open items. It involves both product verification and administrative close-out. The inputs are the contract documentation, the mechanism that is used is the procurement audits, and the outputs are the contract file and formal acceptance and closure.

Integration Management

Project integration management includes the processes required to ensure that the various elements of the project are properly co-ordinated. It includes the major processes of: project development plan, project plan execution, and overall change control.

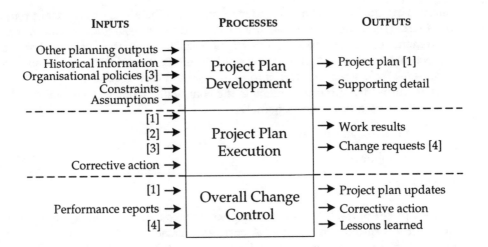

Figure 3-26: Integration Management Processes

The *project development plan* uses the outputs from all other planning processes to create a document that is used to guide project execution and project control.

Project plan execution is the primary process for carrying out the project plan.

Overall change control is concerned with influencing the factors which create beneficial changes, determining that a change has occurred, and managing the actual changes as and when they occur.

Summary of Key Points

- Work can generally be classified as either *operations* or *projects*. The two types of work differ primarily in that operations are ongoing and repetitive while projects have characteristics that include impermanence, uniqueness and uncertainty.

- A project is "any series of activities and tasks that together achieve predetermined deliverables in accordance with a quality definition, have defined start and end dates, with intermediate milestones, have funding limits, and utilise resources such as equipment, materials, people, etc."

- The process of project management is an integrative one. An action, or a failure to take action, in one area will usually affect other areas. Project management is the application of knowledge, skills, tools, and techniques in order to meet or exceed the requirements of the intended project sponsor or owner.

- Organisations engaged in simple tasks, whether in a static or dynamic environment, do not need project management. Manufacturers with slowly changing technology do not need project management. Organisations whose objectives are not tightly constrained, or whose activities are uni-functional, or require one or two activities to undertake the project will not need project management.

- Usually organisations performing projects will divide each project's overall time period into several phases. Each phase may be further sub-divided into a number of stages. Collectively, these phases and stages are known as the *project life cycle*. Each project is marked by the achievement of one, or more, *deliverables* or products. The end of each phase, and also each stage, is marked by a deliverable or deliverables.

- The project management effort should peak during either the conception phase or the definition phase, depending upon the project, and will utilise much of the total effort used on the project. The effort drops off significantly during the implementation phases and again during the final completion phase.

- Primary, or core, stakeholders are those who make a direct contribution to the project and may include the sponsor, the owner, the funder, the "doing" team, and the customer. The secondary group includes those individuals or organisations who act as vendors (suppliers) to the project, external entities, support to the "doing" team, and other similar parties. The tertiary group are the rest: the statutory authorities, the media, society, individual citizens, etc.

- Project management's time has arrived as a method of management. More and more organisations are recognising the benefits of a different approach and are turning to and using the techniques of modern project management.

- There are five basic project management sub-processes and these are: initiating, planning, executing, controlling, and closing. These sub-processes are not discrete, one-time events; they are overlapping activities which occur at varying levels of intensity throughout each phase of the project.

- The project management body of knowledge (PMBOK) is an inclusive term that describes the sum of the knowledge within the profession of project management. Generally accepted project management practices have been organised into nine knowledge areas. The PMBOK includes proven, traditional practices which are widely applied as well as innovative and advanced ones which have seen more limited use.

- Project scope management involves ensuring that the project does all the work required, and only the work required, to achieve successfully the purpose of the project. The major processes of scope management are: authorisation, scope planning, scope definition, scope change control, and scope verification.

- Project time management includes the processes required to ensure timely completion of the project. The processes of time management are: activity definition, activity sequencing, activity duration estimating, schedule development, and schedule control.

- Project cost management includes the processes required to ensure that the project is completed within the approved budget. The major processes within project cost management are: resource planning, cost estimating, cost budgeting, and cost control.

- Project quality management includes the processes required to ensure that the project will satisfy the needs for which it is to be undertaken. It includes all activities of the overall management function that determine the quality policy, objectives, and responsibilities, and implements them by means such as quality planning, quality control, quality assurance and quality improvement, within the quality system.

- Project human resource management includes the processes required to make the most effective use of the people involved with the project. Project human resource management includes organisational planning, staff acquisition, and team development.

- Project communications management provides the critical links among people, ideas and information that are necessary for success. Project communications management consists of communications planning, information distribution, progress reporting, and administrative closure.

- Project risk management includes the processes concerned with identifying, analysing, and responding to uncertainty. Project risk management consists of the processes of risk identification, risk quantification, response development, and risk control.

- Project procurement management is the knowledge area that deals with acquiring goods and services from outside the immediate project organisation. Project procurement management consists of the processes of procurement planning, solicitation planning, solicitation, source selection, contract administration, and contract close-out.

- Project integration management includes the processes required to ensure that the various elements of the project are co-ordinated properly. It includes the major processes of: project development plan, project plan execution, and overall change control.

References

References used in the development of Part 3:

Cleland, David I. and King, William R. (1983), *Systems Analysis and Project Management*, McGraw-Hill Book Company.

Nicholas, John M.(1990), *Managing Business and Engineering Projects*, Prentice-Hall Inc.

Project Management Institute (1996), *A Guide to the Project Management Body of Knowledge (PMBOK)*, PMI Publications.

Turner, J. Rodney (1993), *The Handbook of Project-Based Management*, McGraw-Hill Book Company.

PART 4

PROBLEM-SOLVING AND DECISION-MAKING

Project personnel often evaluate options and make decisions based on "seat-of-the-pants" management, where a decision has as much chance of being wrong as it has of being right. This Part of the book is concerned with the use of certain decision-making techniques.

Decision-making is the discipline for helping people make effective choices under a range of conditions. Making decisions under categories of certainty, risk, and uncertainty, are described in Section 1. The quality of most decisions can have an important impact on a project's duration, budget, and performance.

The use of a "pessimistic" strategy ("maximin"), the use of an "optimistic" strategy ("maximax") and other in-between strategies, when probabilities of uncontrollable circumstances are unknown, is also described in Section 1. The first Section also explains the use of decision trees in multi-staged decision-making. The associated concept of expected value is presented primarily through the use of worked examples.

Section 2 contains a brief introduction to probability and probability distribution. Section 3 contains useful information on the economic evaluation of project options.

Section 4 is where the reader will find guidance in the use of other decision-making techniques, such as criteria weighting, correlation, line fitting, time series, linear programming, etc.

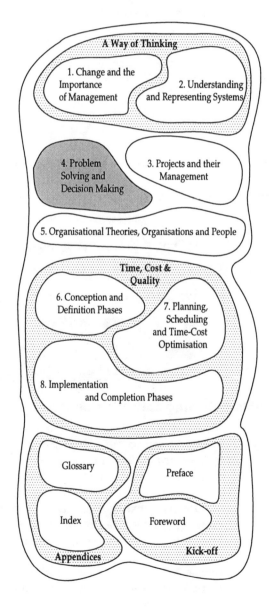

SECTION 1: INTRODUCTION TO DECISION-MAKING

Contents

- Aims and Objectives
- Problem-Solving and Decision-Making
- The Elements of a Decision
- Classification of Decisions
- Decision-Making Models
- Basic Types of Decision Problem
- A Worked Example of Types of Decision Problem
- Decision Trees
- Decision Tree Analysis
- Expected Value
- Expected Value versus Expected Utilities

Aims and Objectives

The aims and objectives of Section 1 are to:

- Explain the processes of problem-solving and decision-making;
- Describe the elements of a decision;
- Obtain a concept of decision models;
- Be aware of the basic types of decision problems;
- Understand the construction of decision trees to help with problem-solving;
- Apply and utilise the expected value concept.

Problem-Solving and Decision-Making

Management decision theory deals with the development of the means by which managers can be more productive in their principal activity — making decisions. Defined as a process rather than a single act, decision-making is characterised as a skill that can be learned and developed through practice. Good managers, it is said, are those who make good decisions.

Effective management and leadership are not based on seat-of-the-pants thinking (La Monica, 1994). These roles demand methodical thinking that draws first from theory and then intuition. The priority of a manager is to accomplish goals by activating a system. Everything that a manager does towards goal accomplishment should be based on a conscious, identified strategy that has the highest probability for success. The strategy available for doing this is referred to as the problem-solving method which is an adaptation from the scientific approach dealt with in Part 1.

The body of knowledge and methodology involving quantitative approaches to decision-making has been variously called "management science" and "operations research". F.W. Taylor (see Part 1, Section 2), is considered to have initiated the scientific revolution of the early 1900s, but the modern version of management science is generally considered to have originated during the Second World War. Teams of scientists with diverse backgrounds were formed to solve common problems through the utilisation of scientific methods.

Problem-solving can be defined as the process of identifying a difference between some actual and some desired state of affairs and then taking action to resolve the difference. The problem-solving process involves seven steps (Churchman et al., 1957):

1) identify and define the problem;

2) determine the set of alternative solutions;

3) determine the criterion or criteria that will be used to evaluate alternatives;

4) evaluate the alternatives;

5) choose an alternative;

6) implement the selected alternative;

7) evaluate the results, and determine if a satisfactory solution has been obtained.

Decision-making is the term generally associated with the first five steps of the problem-solving process.

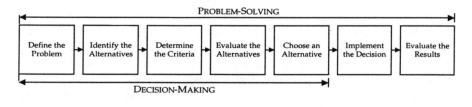

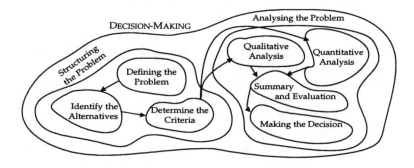

Figure 4-1: Relationship between Problem-Solving and Decision-Making

As seen from Figure 4-1 the first step in decision-making is to identify and define the problem. Decision-making ends with the choosing of an alternative *(step 5)* which is the act of making the decision. Decision-making is part of the larger process of problem-solving. Decision-making focuses on the central problem of choice between alternative courses of action.

Let us consider the following illustration of a decision-making process. The problem as identified *(step 1)* is that a business must move from its existing accommodation because the existing office site has been acquired for redevelopment. Three alternatives are available *(step 2)*, namely: Pearse Street, Constitution Hill, and Drumcondra Road. The table which follows contains criteria *(step 3)* such as annual rent, other annual costs (utilities, cleaning, etc.), image, and location; these criteria are shown above the line. Below the line each alternative has been evaluated with respect to each criterion *(step 4)*. The final step *(step 5)* of the decision-making process is to make a choice from the available alternatives.

Office Alternative	*Annual Rent (mu)**	*Other Annual Costs (mu)**	*Image*	*Location*
(a) Pearse Street	30,000	5,000	Excellent	Downtown
(b) Constitution Hill	15,000	2,800	Average	1 Mile out
(c) Drumcondra Road	12,000	3,600	Good	2½ Miles out

* mu = monetary units

While the objective is to keep costs as low as possible, other factors — such as being close to potential customers, modern layout and car-parking, etc. — need to be taken into account. Although no one alternative is best with regard to all criteria, after careful consideration let us assume that alternative (b) should be selected. Relocating the office to Constitution Hill is thus referred to as the "decision".

Missing from the list of seven steps of the problem-solving process are *step 6* and *step 7*, "implementing the decision" and "evaluating the result", respectively. As can be discerned from this and what is shown in Figure 4-1, decision-making is of more limited scope than problem-solving.

The elements of decision-making can be grouped into two sub-systems (Anderson et al., 1995) (see the systems map at the bottom of Figure 4-1). The first three elements can be combined under what is referred to as "structuring the problem"; the last two steps can be combined under the heading "analysing the problem". The analysis sub-system can be of two basic forms: qualitative and quantitative. Qualitative analysis is primarily based on the decision-maker's judgement and experience. If the decision-maker has had experience with similar problems, or if the problem is simple, then qualitative analysis may be very appropriate. If the problem is complex or the decision-maker has little experience of similar problems, then quantitative analysis is likely to be an important aspect of the decision-maker's final choice.

Although qualitative skills are, to a greater or lesser extent, inherent in the decision-maker, the skills of the quantitative approach can be learned only by studying the techniques available. A decision-maker can increase their effectiveness by learning more about quantitative methodology and by understanding better its contribution to the decision-making process. It is for this reason that project managers and all project team personnel should be knowledgeable in both the qualitative and quantitative approaches and be able to use both forms of analysis in order to make the best possible decisions.

M. Scott Peck (1990), the psychotherapist, makes the point that in life, without discipline, we can solve nothing. He is of the view that with total discipline we can solve all problems. He defines "discipline" as a system of techniques that deal constructively with (the pain of) problem-solving. Discipline is therefore a system of techniques. It can be assumed, as far as the management of projects is concerned, that these techniques refer both to the qualitative and quantitative methods of analysis.

The Elements of a Decision

The preceding sub-Section dealt with decision-making as a process, a series of linked activities, but this sub-Section will identify and describe the key elements contained within a decision. Cooke and Slack (1991) are of the view that without this identification it is difficult to understand a decision fully.

The four key elements contained within a decision are:

- the decision body

- the decision options

- the uncontrollable factors

- the consequences.

The *decision-making body* can be an individual or a team of people, or any grouping within the stated range. When more than one decision-maker carries responsibility for the decision, the decision is said to have "multi-decision-maker" involvement, but the involvement or level of responsibility need not be equal. The single "decision-maker" decision is the most easily understood, but it is the rarest, as decisions are seldom reached by a single decision-maker.

The *decision body* is the single most important element in any decision because through it the organisational objectives and criteria are determined, relevant information is perceived, options are considered, each option is evaluated and a choice is made.

The number of *decision options* can range between two and infinity. The decision options are the core of the decision-making process. Unless there is more than one way to proceed then there is no choice, although it can be said that there are always at least two options, i.e. 1) to proceed with something and 2) not to proceed.

Sometimes decision options are infinite. That is when the decision is a continuous variable. For example the purchase of stationery, say letterheads, for a Company to use in its business communications. The decision options range from zero (we don't need to order) to an infinite quantity. Even though we may set a lower limit (historically the lowest order ever placed) and an upper limit (historically the largest order ever placed), theoretically there are an infinite number of options between these limits.

Another characteristic of *decision options* is how discernible they are at the start of the decision process. The range of discernability at the start of the decision process can be found between "totally defined" to "custom made".

The third element is the *uncontrollable factors*; those parts of a decision which cannot be controlled by the decision body. These are referred to as "states of nature" because they are independent of the decision itself and are likely to influence the environment within which the decision is to be made. For instance, in the stationery example, if "demand rate" and "stationery cost" are the two uncontrollable factors in a decision and if we choose three usage rates and two levels of stationery costs, then there are six possible "states of nature" in the decision.

The possible *consequences* of a decision are a combination of the decision options and the states of nature. For instance if there are three options and six mutually exclusive "states of nature" then there will be 18 possible consequences.

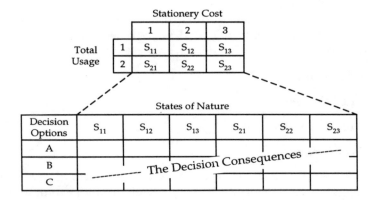

Figure 4-2: Decision Consequence Matrix

At the top of Figure 4-2 is a matrix comparing the two uncontrollable factors of demand rate and stationery cost which produce six states of nature, i.e. S_{11} to S_{23}. These states of nature (or outcomes) are then combined with the assumed three decision options to create a 3 x 6 matrix in which each of the eighteen squares of the matrix represents a possible consequence, as shown by the matrix at the bottom of the Figure.

Classification of Decisions

Decisions may be classified as being:

- structured or unstructured;

- dependent or independent;

- strategic or operational.

Some decisions are clear, well-defined, distinct, and unambiguous; these are terms that could be expected to be found in *structured* decisions. The decision body will have clear knowledge of the alternatives, the criteria, the evaluation process, all of which lead to the determination of choice. Under the "decision option" element, structured decisions are at the "totally defined" range of the scale.

Unstructured decisions would be those that could be classified as being ill-understood, unclear, and ambiguous. The decision body may not be clearly defined. The decision options, or alternatives, may not have been fully recognised because they were not immediately apparent. At the start of the decision process the decision is likely to have bordered on being "custom made".

The degree of dependency (ranging from *dependent* to *independent*) of a decision on other decisions can be measured against two variables: the decision's impact on past/present/future decisions; and the influence across other areas of the organisation. In essence decisions can be influenced by their timing, the timing of other decisions, and the degree to which a decision is isolated organisationally.

The third and perhaps most significant classification of decisions are *strategic* and *operational*. Strategic decisions differ from operational decisions in that they relate the organisation to its environment, and they involve a large part of the organisation. Strategic decisions are usually one-offs, characterised by a high degree of risk or uncertainty.

Theoretically there are an infinite number of decision types. However Cooke and Slack (1991) make a generalisation about decisions in that:

- strategic decisions tend to be unstructured and dependent;

- operational decisions tend to be structured and independent.

They then summarise this generalisation by comparing these types against each of the four decision elements described above in the sub-Section "The Elements of a Decision". The effects that each decision type has on the four decision elements are shown in Figure 4-3.

Type of Decision	Decision Body	Options	Uncontrollable Factors	Consequences
Strategic, Unstructured, Dependent	Can be single person with total authority; single decision limited, well understood, and likely to affect other decisions	Options are either difficult to generate (unstructured) or the result of compromises (dependent)	Likely to be many uncontrollable factors, some of which may not even be known, and most of which will be difficult to forecast	Likely to be several attributes of each consequence, all of which could be difficult to forecast
Operational, Structured, Independent	Decision important to whole organisation, has wide-reaching effects; hence likely to need multi-person decision body	Likely to have reasonably apparent options, but there could be many of them	Likely to be few because of bounded nature of the decision; probably well-documented	Could be several attributes of each consequence, but likely to be fairly "forecastable"

Figure 4-3: The Effects of Decision Type versus Decision Option

It is important to stress that this Figure is nothing more than informative and shows the possible, or likely, effects of operational and strategic decisions on each decision element.

Decision-Making Models

Decision-making is basically what a project manager, or any member of the project team, does. The decision maker has to decide on such matters as:

- what course of action to follow;

- what type of organisation is needed;

- how to select and motivate a member of the project team;

- when and how to correct conditions that do not measure up to the predetermined plan.

From the scientific management movement, classicists have advocated following an essentially rational and logical approach in selecting a particular decision solution. The quantitative approach is of considerable value in making this rational process more precise — not only in structuring the manager's thinking processes, but also in suggesting ways in which intuition can be combined with objective evidence to improve the chances of achieving success.

A model is an explicit statement of our image of reality. Many managers look for help in their decision-making through the use of a technique or decision model. Model building supports project management in two interrelated ways:

- by making it possible for managers to better understand the transformation systems with which they deal;

- by helping them to make decisions concerning ways and means by which systems can be made to function more productively.

In the first application, models represent the essential elements and interrelationships that describe the system. In the second application, models can be used to represent the major components of the decision-making process.

As the project manager's role is to manipulate system components in such a manner that specified organisational objectives will be met, and because this role requires decision-making, it is logical that decision-making models incorporate the results of the more general systems models. Decision-making models can serve as conduits for the understanding and knowledge gained from systems models.

As stated in the first sub-Section "Problem-solving and Decision-making", the decision-making process requires:

- *search* for opportunities to make decisions and for solutions to problems,

- *choice* of the one course of action that, upon implementation, has the best chance of satisfying the decision objective.

Although models can be and are used for the search activity, the concern is principally with those that facilitate the selection of a course of action to be implemented as the solution to the decision problem.

The process of formal model building requires us to develop an accurate reflection of our perceptions of the decision area to aid the decision process. This can be done in one of three ways:

- descriptive models;

- analogy models;

- relationship models.

These three levels of modelling can be directly linked to the conventional categories of scientific models called iconic, analogue, and symbolic, respectively.

Iconic models are those models where the scale of reality is changed, e.g. a scale layout of a river as shown on an Ordinance Survey map. Analogue models are where one set of properties are replaced by another, e.g. a graphical representation of the flow of water in the river at a particular location. A symbolic model is one which uses mathematical symbols, letters and numbers to convey the relationship between elements in the model, e.g. the water flow in the river being represented by $Q = \Sigma$ velocity (v) x area (A). This water quantity is found by summing the product of the water velocity and river cross-section area for a series of incremental vertical slices within a river cross-section between one bank of the river and the opposite river bank.

Essential prerequisites for the development of good models are:

- an understanding of the key variables within the decision;

- knowledge of the cause–effect pattern of influence between the variables;

- an appreciation of how mathematical formulation can be used to develop powerful models.

The lowest level of sophistication in modelling is to examine the variables in the traditional input–processor–output model (see Figure 1-7 in Part 1). A *variable* within a decision is some element in the decision which takes on different values. On the other hand a *parameter* is assumed to have a constant value over the range of time, or range of options, to be considered.

A variable can be either an *input*, or exogenous, variable or it can be an *output*, or endogenous, variable. Input and output variables can either be controllable or uncontrollable. Output variables are generated from the input factors and the transformation from within the decision model. Because the output variables are a consequence of the decision model and such consequences do not exist independent of the decision itself, "controllable" output variables do not exist. Controllable input variables are the inputs to the decision over which the decision body has an influence and which represent the decision options. Uncontrollable input variables are the "environmental" variables which represent the factors whose exact value cannot be determined. It is for this reason that these variables are most often represented by a probability distribution (see Section 2 of this Part) rather than by a single point.

The next level of sophistication in the modelling process is to use the likes of the cause-and-effect technique (refer to Section 1 of Part 1), thereby linking the input factors with the output factors. Cause-and-effect diagrams are a useful step in the process of understanding decision factors and the decision itself; however, they are incapable of describing the nature of the relationships. To do that it is necessary at times to use symbolic models — in other words *mathematical models*.

Basic Types of Decision Problem

A fundamental requirement for decision-making is the presence of some criterion or standard by which available alternatives can be judged against their capacity to satisfy the decision objectives.

If alternatives 1, 2, and 3 produce results x, y, and z, there must be some basis for judging alternatives according to the value of their outputs in satisfying the decision objective. If x is preferred to y and y is preferred to z, for whatever reason and by whatever standard, it follows that x is also preferred to z, that is, the preferences are transitive. Alternative 1 should be selected, because it produces an outcome preferable to those produced by alternatives 2 and 3.

The ability to rank alternatives — to judge their outcomes in terms of objectives — implies the ability to measure outcomes and to place a value on their respective capacities to satisfy objectives. To do this we can apply either nominal, ordinal, or cardinal measures. A nominal scale assigns a description to a set of elements, e.g. "a component when checked for performance may receive an acceptance or a rejection". An ordinal scale compares elements of a set according to some standard characteristic, e.g. "component batch 32 were all accepted as having passed and did better than the other 31 batches". A cardinal scale implies that some characteristic of the event is assigned a number, e.g. "each component receives a grade (an example being A $\cong$ to a score of 85–100) which indicates the level of performance achievement".

With the requirements to have the ability to specify an objective function, the capacity to measure, and the capacity to relate the interactions of alternatives and states in terms of an objective function, we can move to an investigation of the conditions under which decisions are made. These conditions make it possible for the decision-maker to adopt means by which the choice process can be effected in a rational manner.

An essential requirement of a decision problem is a "payoff" relationship between courses of action and the states (or outcomes) that can represent the post-decision environment. Assume that the alternative course of action is represented by A and identified by the subscript i. The number of alternatives "m" is represented by all A_i's. Post-decision states are represented by S and identified by subscript j. The number of states "n" is represented by all S_j's.

The "payoff" value V is the interaction between alternatives and states and is given by:

$$V_{ij} = f(A_i S_j)$$

where V_{ij} is a measure of the payoff to the decision-maker resulting from the implementation of an alternative and the occurrence of a state.

A_i = the alternatives.
S_j = the states.

A typical payoff matrix is shown in Figure 4-4.

STATES OF NATURE

Alternatives	S_1	S_2	S_3	S_j	S_n
A_1	V_{11}	V_{12}	V_{13}	V_{1j}	V_{1n}
A_2	V_{21}	V_{22}	V_{23}	V_{2j}	V_{2n}
A_i	V_{i1}	V_{i2}	V_{i3}	V_{ij}	V_{in}
A_m	V_{m1}	V_{m2}	V_{m3}	V_{mj}	V_{mn}

Figure 4-4: Typical Payoff Matrix

Decision problems can be classified according to the quantity and quality of the decision-maker's knowledge of the post-decision environment and the manner in which alternatives interact with the environment. Problems can be divided into three categories — certainty, risk, and uncertainty — which reflect the conditions under which decisions are made (Cooke and Slack, 1991).

Certainty

The decision-maker knows the outcome that will result from each alternative course of action. The exact nature of the *post-decision* environment is known or fairly well-known. Problems of this type should not be too difficult, because the element of uncertainty concerning the nature of future events is removed. These conditions can exist "as a fact", or they can be established by making limiting assumptions concerning the course of events.

In making decisions under conditions of certainty the problem is frequently more one of search than of choice. The decision maker knows the outcomes and must find the alternative that will produce the best "payoff". Linear programming, dealt with in Section 3, is a technique frequently used to identify one alternative, among a large number of alternatives, that can best satisfy the decision objective.

Risk

If the relative frequencies with which outcomes (states) will occur are, with certainty, known to the decision-maker, decisions will be made under conditions of risk.

Risk implies the applicability of the law of large numbers, which contends that as the number of recurring events considered in the development of a frequency distribution becomes larger, the probability of a deviation from the expected relative frequency of an event becomes smaller. Risk therefore implies the presence of a massive amount of objective evidence in support of the conclusion drawn with respect to the probabilities that can be attached to events occurring.

A decision to participate in a coin-tossing contest is an example of decision-making under conditions of risk, assuming that the coin is fair and is tossed fairly. The probability of "heads" on any one toss is equal to 0.5 and is demonstrable deductively, as well as inductively by tossing a fair coin an infinite number of times and recording the frequency with which "heads" occurs.

Uncertainty

In situations where the frequencies with which the specified partitions (states) of the post-decision environment occur are unknown, decisions are made under conditions of uncertainty. The majority of managerial decisions are made under these conditions. Decisions under uncertainty are perhaps the most important class of problem situations and present the greatest challenge to the decision-maker in selecting effective courses of action.

Under conditions of uncertainty it is assumed that the true probabilities underlying the possible outcomes are unknown. The decision-maker may be totally ignorant of the probability of any one outcome occurring more or less frequently than any other.

Frequently the decision-maker's knowledge of the post-decision environment will be sufficient to assign probabilities that reflect their experience and managerial intuition.

Probability assignments can also result from objective (though less compelling than in the case of risk) evidence obtained through research activities. They can also result from a combination of subjective and objective inputs from intuitive observations of the decision-maker and the results of research. Bayesian statistics provide a means by which this marriage can be consummated. The result can be the attainment of a level of understanding concerning the probable course of future events that offers the greatest hope for selection of the course of action which maximises the decision objective.

A Worked Example of Types of Decision Problem

To illustrate decision-making under the three conditions just described, consider the following problem (Cooke and Slack, 1991):

A technician working on a project with a tight deadline finds that there is ambiguity in the information available to the project's contractor. He is required to provide the contractor with what the contractor is expecting by 08.00 hours the next day, which happens to be Sunday. In order to avoid delay to the project, the contractor will need instructions so as to carry out this crucial operation on Sunday. The technician puzzles over how he can allocate the limited time available to him during Saturday to achieve the best possible result, which is how not to impact on the contractor's on-site performance. He concludes that the information to be provided will come from one of three sources:

1) detailed drawings;

2) the contract specifications; or

3) some combination of the two.

He further concludes that he has three possible courses of action:

1) study the drawings;

2) study the specifications; or

3) spend less time on each but study both drawings and specifications.

Contemplating the possible consequences of these alternatives, he concludes that by studying the drawings only, he will complete his review and get the information to the contractor on time (let's call this event an E). The contractor will be able to complete before the end of the day and do an excellent job. If he examines the specification then he is likely to do very poorly and will not complete his work until late Sunday afternoon (let's call this F). The contractor in this case will not be able to complete what is needed. If the technician's work is based on both drawings and specification then there will be a delay (G) and the contractor's performance will be directly related to the delay. Small delay (I hour) and the contractor will be able to do a very good job (VG), a delay of more than 1 and less than 3 hours will mean only a poor performance (P)

Following this reasoning, the technician develops payoff relationships between each of the other acts (A_j) and states (S_j). These relationships are presented in Figure 4-5. Payoff tables are frequently the best method for representing non-complex decisions; complex decisions can be more lucidly represented in what is referred to as a "decision tree".

| | States of Nature | | |
Alternative	S_1 Drawings only	S_2 Specification only	S_3 Drawings and Specifications
A_1 Study Drawings	E	F	P
A_2 Study Specifications	F	E	P
A_3 Study both Drawings and Specifications	G	G	VG

Key: E = Excellent   VG = Very Good   G = Good

P = Poor   F = Fail

Figure 4-5: Payoff Matrix for Worked Example

The essential elements of the problem are presented diagrammatically in Figure 4-6. Tree diagrams capture the alternatives (which is the case here) or sequence of alternatives available to the decision-maker and the consequences to which these alternatives may lead. Decision trees have alternative branches and "states of nature" branches, and they contain other information, such as conditional values of interactions between alternatives and states, which may be pertinent to the problem situation.

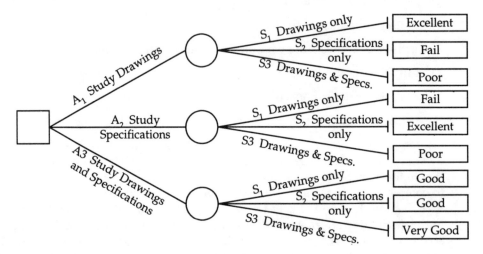

Figure 4-6: Decision Tree for Worked Example

As just mentioned, the decision tree is a different way of displaying information shown in a payoff table. A full account of preparing and using decision trees is presented later in this Section.

The tree is made of a series of nodes and branches. Each branch represents an alternative course of action or decision. The tree in Figure 4-6 shows the three alternatives — A1, A2, and A3 — making up the main limbs. At the end of each limb is a node (a chance event) and to the right of the node are the three "states of nature" or outcomes. Associated with each alternative course through the tree is a payoff and this is shown as a box at the right side of each terminal branch.

Selecting a Course of Action

Having defined our decision problem in terms of alternative courses of action, the nature of the post-decision environment, and the interaction of alternatives with these environmental conditions, we can now undertake the managerial role of selecting a particular decision.

If the decision were to be made under conditions of certainty, the manager or technician would experience little difficulty, for there are a limited number of alternatives available. For example, there would be no dilemma if the technician knew that the outcome would be based on the drawings only. Behaving rationally, he would study the drawings — the alternative that will produce the best performance. Similarly, he would study the specification if he were certain that the contractor's successful performance would be drawn from that source; he would study both drawings and specification if it were known in advance that the contractor's successful performance would be drawn from both sources.

It is not realistic, however, to assume that the technician would have sufficient information to predict with certainty the exact nature of the post-decision environment. Yet, some means must be found to rationally select only one course of action. If weights can be assigned that represent the relative frequency with which the events (states of nature) can be expected to occur — a risk situation — the decision objective may be satisfied by selecting the alternative with the highest *expected value*.

Decision under Risk

The expected value of an alternative is a weighted average of all conditional values of the alternative. That is, each conditional value is weighted by the probability of its occurrence. If the technician knows precisely the frequency with which the three states of nature will occur (perhaps from project records that indicate the frequency with which similar states have occurred in the past), the states can be assigned weights (probabilities) that reflect these frequencies. The subject of probability and probability distribution is dealt with in Section 2 of this Part.

Assume, therefore, that the technician knows the precise probability that can be associated with each state — for example, the probability that the contractor's success, drawn from studying the drawings, is equal to 0.3; the probability that it will be drawn from the specification clauses is also 0.3; and, because the states must be mutually exclusive and exhaustive of the post-decision environment, the probability that the examination will be taken from both sources is 0.4. Note that the sum of the probabilities equals unity, and that the probability assigned to each state is greater than zero but less than unity. Should any one state have a probability of occurring equal to unity, the technician would be in the previously discussed state of certainty.

Referring to the technician's payoff matrix (see Figure 4-5), we can compute the expected value of the alternative "drawings". Because it is difficult to use the letter grades, let us convert them to the usual scale of 4 for E, 3 for VG, 2 for G, 1 for P, and 0 for F. Thus, the expected value for the "drawings" alternative would be:

$$
\begin{aligned}
V &= (0.3 \times 4) + (0.3 \times 0) + (0.4 \times 1) \\
&= 1.2 + 0 + 0.4 \\
&= 1.6
\end{aligned}
$$

Expected values produced by the other two alternatives are 1.6 for "specification" and 2.4 for "both drawings and specification". These are computed in the same fashion as the first alternative illustrated above. Thus, if the technician is willing to accept the alternative that has the highest expected value, he will elect to study both the drawings and the specification.

Decision under Uncertainty

If the technician does not know with certainty what state of nature will occur, and if, in addition, he does not know the precise probability of the states occurring, his decision is obviously more difficult. In this condition of uncertainty, he can choose among a number of strategies based on his psychological state.

An adventuresome technician would choose *maximax*, selecting the alternative with the highest possible payoff, ignoring possible undesirable outcomes. The maximax decision chooses the "best of the best". In the problem under discussion, the technician would either "study drawings only" or "study specification only". Both alternatives offer the possibility of the highest possible payoff, an E (4).

If they were a pessimistic decision-maker, the technician would focus on the worst possible payoff for each alternative, and select the one that has the best of the worst possible outcomes, the *maximin*. Maximin is otherwise known as the "best of the worst". With this psychology, the technician would decide to study both drawings and specification, which produces a minimum grade of G (2), thus enabling him to scrape by regardless of what happens. Either of the other two alternatives has the possibility of failing.

A less pessimistic technician, yet also less adventuresome, might select an intermediate strategy of *minimax-regret*. In this approach, which is most closely related to the maximin, the technician focuses his attention on each individual state of nature (the columns in Figure 4-5) to determine which alternative would produce the best payoff. This act is the zero regret act for that state of nature — the perfect match of alternative and resulting state. For the first state (drawings only), it would be alternative number one (study drawings); for the second state (specification only), it would be number two (study specification clauses); and for the third (both drawings and specification), it would be the third alternative (study both).

With the zero regret alternative identified, the technician can compute the amount of regret for the other two alternatives.

The matrix of regrets is as follows:

Alternatives	S_1		S_2		S_3		Maximum Regret
			States of Nature				
A_1	4	0	0	4	1	2	4
A_2	0	4	4	0	1	2	4
A_3	2	2	2	2	3	0	2 (Minimum)

Following this strategy, the technician would select alternative 3 (study both drawings and specification), because it will minimise his maximum regret. If the technician's strategy is to be based on either the drawings only or the specification only, the maximum regret will be of the order of 2 (rather than possible maximum regret of 4 for each of the other alternatives).

The *Hurwicz* criterion, like the minimax rule, attempts to create a compromise between the cautious maximin rule and the optimistic maximax rule. However, unlike the minimax rule, weights are assigned to the best and worst payoff for each decision option and the option with the highest weighted payoff is chosen. The weighted payoff is calculated by:

$$(\alpha \times \text{worst payoff}) + ((1 - \alpha) \times \text{best payoff})$$

The value of α, a figure between 0 and 1, depends on the decision-maker's attitude to risk. The smaller the value, the bigger risk the decision-maker is prepared to take. When $\alpha = 0$ the decision will be the same as for the maximax rule. Using $\alpha = 0.6$, which represents a slightly cautious decision-maker, the weighted payoffs become:

$A_1 = (0.60 \times 0) + (0.40 \times 4) = 1.60$
$A_2 = (0.60 \times 0) + (0.40 \times 4) = 1.60$
$A_3 = (0.60 \times 2) + (0.40 \times 3) = 2.40$

So under this criterion and using $\alpha = 0.60$, the decision would be A_3 "study drawings and specifications".

The presence of complete uncertainty in the mind of a decision maker, thereby necessitating one of the above strategies would be relatively rare in most managerial decisions. The manager often has at least some information on which a calculated guess or estimate of the probability of each of the states of nature can be based.

Similarly, a technician, without benefit of past experience, might predict a probability of 0.2 for success based on drawings only, 0.2 for specification only, and 0.6 for both drawings and specifications. These can be combined with values as described previously (in the sub-sub-Section on risk) to produce expected values of 1.4 for study of drawings, 1.4 for study of specification, and 2.6 for study of both drawings and specifications. This process is known as the Bayesian approach.

To many decision theorists, this approach best combines realistic managerial reasoning with quantitative analysis to produce an effective merger of values. Most managerial problems do not have the statistical evidence necessary for the risk situation. Yet managers do have subjective estimates of probability, which, when combined with conditional values, can produce the alternative with the greatest expected value.

For our harassed but experienced technician, the highest expected value would be produced by studying both drawings and specifications.

Decision Trees

The decision tree or decision network is an alternative to the payoff table (see Section 1), as a means of presenting decision information. The tree starts at a decision point from which arrows indicating alternative actions emanate to chance event points. The arrows leaving the chance event points indicate alternative outcomes for different states of the environment. These are labelled with their assigned probabilities and terminate at the desirability measure. Lastly, the expectation corresponding to each action is shown.

The general procedure in constructing and using a decision tree is:

1) identify the decision points and alternative actions available at each decision point.

2) identify the uncertainties (chance event points) and establish the type and range of alternative outcomes at each chance event point.

3) estimate the relevant quantitative information:

- costs of the possible actions

- gains resulting from possible outcomes

- probabilities of chance events.

4) define criteria of desirability.

5) evaluate the tree to obtain expectations and position values and select appropriate course of action.

Evaluation by means of a decision tree is particularly useful for situations involving a series of sequential decisions using a "roll-back" technique. This will be explained by reference to an example in the next sub-Section.

Choosing the best alternative often requires estimating the possible outcomes and their probabilities. An organised way to cope with the situation is to use a decision tree. Decision tree analysis is both simple and powerful. If you use it often enough, it will improve your average performance in adopting alternatives.

It might seem, based upon the earlier content of Section 1, that once a decision has been made, that is the end of a particular sequence, but there are many situations where one decision leads to a series of other decisions. Decision tree analysis facilitates multi-stage decision processes where choices are faced at several consecutive stages or a big problem is broken down into smaller ones.

For example, a Roads Department within a Local Authority may have to decide: first, whether to build a proposed highway; second, the number of lanes; third, construction standards; fourth, whether to introduce a toll, and if so, at what specific charge rate; etc. At each stage in the decision process the selection of one alternative opens up a series of other choices (or sometimes events). These can best be represented by a decision tree, where the alternatives (or events) are represented by the branches of a horizontal tree as shown in Figure 4-7.

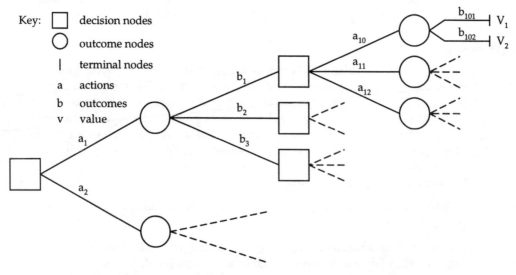

Figure 4-7: General Form of a Decision Tree

Decision tree analysis is designed primarily to present a decision problem, with the alternatives and their relative merits, in a systematic manner that helps identify and evaluate the whole problem, and helps in the selection of the "best" decision or strategy. Although most useful for tackling complex, sequential decisions, they can be used for simple ones.

In the decision tree the alternatives and events are represented by the branches, so each branch represents a different path (decision or event) which may be followed through the tree. There are three distinct types of node and these are normally annotated as shown in the key in Figure 4-7.

The decision node represents points at which decisions are made, so that all branches leaving a decision node are alternatives, the best of which should be selected. The random node represents points at which things happen, so that all branches leaving random nodes are events with known probabilities. Terminal nodes are at the right side of decisions and show the ends of all sequences of decisions and events.

To the basic structure of a decision tree has to be added the probability estimates and the payoffs.

Decision Tree Analysis

As an illustration let us consider the following issue confronting a project manager. An unsolicited request for a proposal (RFP) has been made and if successful will provide a profit of 300,000 mu (monetary units). The project manager's company and two others have received RFPs and it appears that each company has an equal chance — one in three — of being successful. The project manager's company consider that the odds will be raised to 50:50 if a working model of the project is built; it is estimated that this will cost 45,000 mu.

The decision confronting the project manager is whether or not to build a model and increase the odds of winning the competition from one-in-three to one-in-two. Figure 4-8 shows the application of a decision tree analysis.

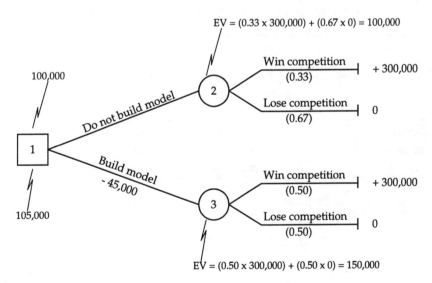

Figure 4-8: Decision Tree with Probabilities, Payoffs, and Expected Values

The tree is constructed from left to right, and annotated from left to right with actions, outcomes, and probabilities. The payoffs are then written in at the terminal nodes and the expected values (see next sub-Section) are calculated and inserted from right to left.

There are a few things that are worth drawing attention to. Firstly, the outcomes to the right of a random node must have probabilities that, when accumulated for all outcomes relative to that node, total 1.00. Secondly, the expected value (EV), of any alternative must be a weighted average of all conditional values of the alternative. For example, at node 3 the EV = (0.50 X 300,000) + (0.50 X 0) = 150,000 mu. Thirdly, the action branch (those to the right of the decision node) which has the highest EV would indicate the "best" decision.

The word "best" is used because it must be remembered that this decision will not guarantee the project manager will win the job. The project manager's company may develop the model and still lose the job. However, as was mentioned in the first paragraph of this sub-Section *use decision trees in enough cases and you will do better in making decisions over the long run.*

Expected Value

This is defined as *px* where *p* is the probability of winning x monetary units (mu). Expected value is the weighted average value of all condition values based on probabilities of occurrence.

Consider the example of a contractor trying to decide whether to bid on the construction of a dam or an airport. He does not have resources to analyse and prepare the bids for both in detail. In either case, the chance of winning the bid is one-third for the dam and one-half for the airport. The profit, on the other hand, would be 4 million mu from the dam and 2 million mu from the airport. His out-of-pocket costs for preparing the bid will be 1 million mu for the dam and 0.5 million mu for the airport. His decision is shown in the following table:

Dam			Airport		
Event	Probability	Payoff (million mu)	Event	Probability	Payoff (million mu)
Win Bid	1/3	4	Win Bid	1/2	2
Lose Bid	2/3	0	Lose Bid	1/2	0
Cost of Bid		−1	Cost of Bid		−0.5

The problem can be presented more conveniently in the form of a decision tree (see Figure 4-9).

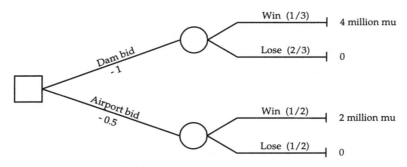

Figure 4-9: Decision Tree for Dam versus Airport Example

The EV for each alternative will be:

EV of dam bid	= 1/3 (4) + 2/3 (0) – 1	= 333,333 mu
EV or airport bid	= 1/2 (2) + 1/2 (0) – 0.5	= 500,000 mu

A decision based on maximising the EV would indicate that the contractor would bid for the airport project.

Expected Value versus Expected Utilities

A decision such as the foregoing is based on the maximisation of expected value and can be defined as risk neutral, but most decision-makers are hardly neutral with respect to risk. In fact, economic theory assumes that a decision-maker has a utility function from which the nature of the choice under risk can be predicted.

Let us analyse a situation in which an investor is willing to pay an additional 1 per cent (1 million mu) of total project costs in order to insure against an equally probable +/– 10 per cent fluctuation in such costs. Since he knows that the EV of the cost of the project would be 100 million mu, given an equal probability of this being either 90 million mu or 110 million mu, why would he pay a premium? The only possible explanation is that a cost overrun of 10 million mu is less manageable than a cost saving of an equal amount. In this instance, the disutility of loss is greater than the utility of gain of equal amount. A decision-maker with behaviour similar to the investor in our example is said to be risk-averse, or to have a *diminishing marginal utility of income*.

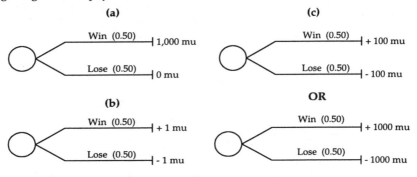

Figure 4-10: General Example Showing Concept of Expected Utility

Speaking more generally, consider the following choice between playing or not playing a game as shown by Figure 4-10 (a): the EV in this case, is 0.5 (1,000) – 0.5 (0) = 500 mu.

An individual who accepts exactly 500 mu in return for giving up the right to play the game is defined as risk-neutral. Relatively poor individuals may accept 400 or 300 mu or even 200 mu for relinquishing the right to play this game, and these amounts indicate the sacrifices they are willing to make in order to avoid risks. A very poor man may even accept a sure 100 mu rather than take a 50 per cent chance of getting nothing. A very rich man, on the other hand, could refuse the offer of 500 mu, and decide to play the game. Such behaviour indicates different attitudes toward risk.

The concept of *expected utility* (EU) presupposes that the basic attitude of a decision-maker toward risk is measurable, and EU can be defined as EV minus the risk premium. People in general are risk averse. Sooner or later, a rational man will suffer diminishing utility for each marginal increase in income. He will choose expected utility as the basis for decision-making and would prefer not to play an actuarially fair game (one where the cost of playing the game is equal to the EV of the game) except when the pleasure of playing the game (or gambling) exceeds the difference between EU and EV.

Eventually, that marginal utility diminishes and can be illustrated by taking a few simple examples. Almost anyone could decide to play the game as shown by Figure 4-10 (b) where the outcome is determined by flipping an unbiased coin. With the EV remaining zero, one might become increasingly sceptical about playing the games denoted by Figure 4-10 (c).

At a certain point an individual might refuse to play even though the game still remains actuarially fair. Although the EVs are equal to zero, EUs become negative. Expected utilities differ among individuals and depend on asset positions and marginal utilities of income. The use of EU makes the decision-making process more realistic and complements the EV criterion rather than rejecting it entirely.

SECTION 2: PROBABILITY AND PATTERNS OF PROBABILITY

Contents

- Aims and Objectives
- Elementary Probability
- An Event and its Complement
- Addition Law
- Conditional Probability
- Bayes Theorem
- Probability Distribution, Expected Value and Variance
- Normal Distribution

Aims and Objectives

The aims and objectives of Section 2 are to:

- Explain probability and how to determine it;
- Describe the important laws that are a part of probability;
- Explain probability distribution and its characteristics;
- Be able to use probability tables.

Elementary Probability

In Section 1 it was noted that the decision-maker, dealing with a problem where uncertainty is a major factor, is often not sure what will happen if a particular course of action is taken. There are a number of ways in which uncertainty can be measured and expressed. The simplest method is to use words such as: "unlikely" or "expected" or any other term between these extremes of a range. The difficulty with this method is the interpretation and meaning of the terms; different people attach very different meanings to the same term.

An explanation of probability, sufficient to understand its application to the technique of decision trees, is given in this Section. There are three methods of making assessments of chances, more properly called probabilities. These methods are called:

- subjective approach;
- empirical approach;
- *a priori* approach.

Subjective probability relates to those decisions which do not involve any measure of numerical analysis. An illustration of such an approach would be the decision of a project manager to accept a proposal from the project's contractor to work a night-shift tonight to complete a repair to a crucial outside component. The decision is made with the knowledge that it didn't rain last night and the weather forecast would appear to favour outside work.

The *empirical approach* uses measurement to estimate probabilities. In other words, based on *measurement* over the last 10 months it is known that, on average, there have been 48 hours of absenteeism per month out of a total of 4,800 hours of project team effort each month. The probability of absenteeism in future months of the project's tenure is therefore:

$$\frac{48}{4,800} \quad \text{or} \quad 0.01 \quad \text{or} \quad 1\%$$

The value of a probability can be given either as a fraction, a decimal, or a percentage.

The *a priori approach* to finding the probability of an event (see the next sub-Section for an explanation of event) is similar to the empirical approach except that it assesses the event *prior* to the actual occurrence simply by using knowledge of the situation. If the professional resource from which a project team is chosen consists of 300 individuals of which 140 are women, then the chances of choosing a woman, all other aspects being the same, will be about 47 per cent. Probability can therefore be defined as:

$$p \text{ (event)} = \frac{\text{number of ways an event occurs}}{\text{total number of outcomes}}$$

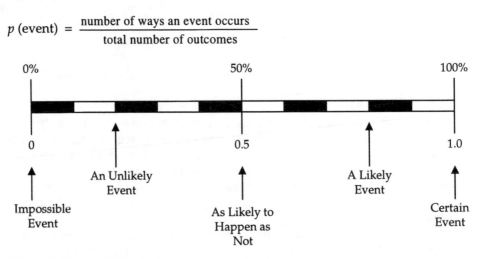

Figure 4-11: Probability Scale

Figure 4-11 shows a probability scale comparing the percentage and decimal measurements against a limited range of event. An event with a probability of zero (0 per cent) is termed "impossible" while an event with a probability of 0.5 (50 per cent) is termed "as likely to happen as not", and an event with a probability of 1.0 (100 per cent) is termed "certain". Probability is therefore measured on a scale of 0 to 1.

In computing probability there are a number of helpful relationships. These include: complement of an event, addition law, conditional probability , multiplication law and Bayes Theorem.

An Event and its Complement

An *event* is a collection of *sample points* or experimental outcomes. *Sample space* is the whole range of sample points.

For example, let us consider that the Sundays available in a project year were 52, of which 26 had even dates and 26 had odd dates, and there were seven Sundays whose even dates (2, 4, 6, 8) were a single integer, i.e. less than 10. The aim is to somehow select a Sunday with a date that is even, and one of the seven available that have a single integer. Selecting one of the seven is the *event*, the seven available dates that are single integers are the *sample points*, and the *sample space* is the 26 Sundays having even dates.

Much of the focus of probability analysis is involved with computing probabilities for various events that are of interest to a decision-maker. If the probabilities of the sample are defined, *the probability of an event is equal to the sum of the probabilities of the sample points in the event.*

For example if each of the 26 Sundays that have even dates are written on a piece of paper, folded and placed in a hat, the chances of picking a single integer date, which will be referred to as the probability of event A, would be:

$$p \text{ (event A)} = \frac{1}{26} + \frac{1}{26} + \frac{1}{26} + \frac{1}{26} + \frac{1}{26} + \frac{1}{26} + \frac{1}{26}$$

$$= \frac{7}{26} = 0.269230769$$

Considering an event A, the complement of event A is the event consisting of all sample points not in A. The complement of A is denoted by A^c. By referring to what is called a Venn Diagram in Figure 4-12, an illustration is given of the concept of complement. The rectangular area represents the sample space, and as such contains all possible sample points. The circle represents event A and therefore contains only those sample points that belong to A. The shaded area contains all sample points not in event A; by definition, this is the complement of A.

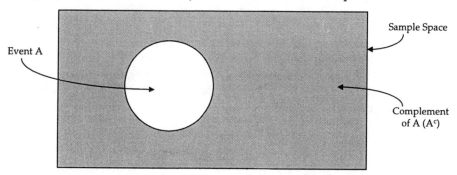

Figure 4-12: Event and Complement of Event

In any probability application, event A and its complement A^c must satisfy the following condition:

$p(A) + p(A^c) = 1$

from which:

$p(A) = 1 - p(A^c)$

This demonstrates that the probability of an event can be obtained relatively easily if the complement of the event is known. For instance if the probability that a project will not be completed on time is 65 per cent, then the probability that it will be completed on time will be 35 per cent.

Addition Law

Frequently it is necessary to find the probability of two or more events happening at the same time. For example a high-tech project has duplicated controls so that, when the project becomes operational, if one fails the other will take over control of the facility. But what is the probability that both controls will fail at the same time? Combining probabilities depends on whether the events are "independent" or whether they are "mutually exclusive".

Two or more events are independent if the occurrence of one does not affect the occurrence of the other. Two or more events are mutually exclusive if either event can occur but not both.

If we refer to the two separate events as A and B, then the probability of A *or* B happening (*mutual exclusivity*) is given by:

$$p(A \text{ } or \text{ } B) = \frac{\text{number of ways A or B can happen}}{\text{total number of possibilities}}$$

$$= \frac{\text{number of ways A can happen}}{\text{total number of possibilities}} + \frac{\text{number of ways B can happen}}{\text{total number of possibilities}}$$

$$= \text{probability of A happening} + \text{probability of B happening}$$

$$= p(A) + p(B)$$

This "or" rule says that the number of ways A or B can happen is the sum of the ways A can happen and the ways B can happen, but this is only true if A and B can't both happen at the same time. If A and B can occur simultaneously, then we will, in adding up the two sets be counting twice over those occasions on which both A and B happen. To account for this the "or" rule is modified to the "addition rule":

$p(A \cup B) = p(A) + p(B) - p(A \cap B)$

where $\cup$ means either A **or** B occurs
and $\cap$ means both A **and** B occur

The *addition law* is a useful relationship when we have two events and are interested in knowing the probability that at least one of the events occurs. Assuming event A and event B, we are interested in knowing the probability that event A or event B or both occur. For two events A and B, the "union of events" A and B is the event containing all sample points belonging to A **or** B **or** both. The union is denoted by $A \cup B$.

This is shown in Figure 4-13 (a). The shaded region is the "union of events" and contains all the sample points in event A, as well as all the sample points in event B.

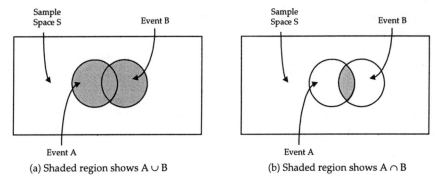

(a) Shaded region shows $A \cup B$ (b) Shaded region shows $A \cap B$

Figure 4-13: Events A and B (a) Union of Events (b) Intersection of Events

The "intersection of events" A and B is the event containing the sample points belonging to both A and B. The intersection is denoted by $A \cap B$, and is shown in Figure 4-13 (b) as the shaded area where the two circles overlap.

To apply the addition law, let us reconsider the 300 individuals who are the professional resource of an organisation (see earlier illustration). To satisfy a company's "capability profile", professionals need x years of experience at senior level or a pass level of the PMP (project manager professional) examination. Of this resource 200 have the necessary experience and 150 have achieved PMP; 140 have achieved both PMP and the necessary experience.

Let A = event of having experience, and B = event of having PMP.

$$p(A) = \frac{200}{300} = 0.67$$

$$p(B) = \frac{150}{300} = 0.50$$

$$p(A \cap B) = \frac{140}{300} = 0.47$$

$$p(A \cup B) = p(A) + p(B) - p(A \cap B) = 0.67 + 0.50 - 0.47 = 0.70.$$

So 70 per cent of the resource pool have either the required experience or have passed the professional exam.

Conditional Probability

In many probability situations it is important to be able to determine the probability of one event when another event is known to have occurred. Suppose that an event A with $p(A)$ has already occurred and that new information is obtained on A, or it is learned that another event, denoted B, has occurred. Assuming that A is related to B, then such information will be needed in computing a new or revised probability for event A. If the probability of event B occurring is dependent on whether event A has occurred we would say that "event B is conditional on event A" and this is written as $p(B|A)$. Thus, the notation $p(B|A)$ is read "the probability of B given A".

With two events A and B the general definitions of *conditional probability* is given by:

$$p(A|B) \; = \; \frac{p(A \cap B)}{p(B)}$$

and

$$p(B|A) \; = \; \frac{p(A \cap B)}{p(A)}$$

From this we can create what is referred to as the *multiplication rule* which gives:

$$p(A \cap B) \; = \; p(B) \times p(A|B) \; = \; p(A) \times p(B|A)$$

The multiplication rule is useful in situations where probabilities such as $p(A)$, $p(B)$, $p(A|B)$, and/or $p(B|A)$ are known but where $p(A \cap B)$ is not.

If two or more events are independent the rule simplifies to:

$$p(A \cap B) = p(A) \times p(B)$$

Independence is achieved when $p(B|A) = p(B)$ or whenever $p(A|B) = p(A)$. By substituting for $p(A|B)$ and $p(B|A)$ in the multiplication rule, this special case of $p(A \cap B)$ for independent events is obtained.

Bayes Theorem

Often an analysis begins with *a priori* probability estimates that needs to be revised when new information is obtained. This information can come from numerous sources such as samples, a test, a report, or other sources that provide something additional about the events. Revised probabilities, referred to as posterior probabilities, are calculated using what is known as *Bayes Theorem*.

Let's assume that a project receives parts from two suppliers. Let A_1 denote the event that a part is from supplier 1 (S1) and A_2 denote the event that a part is from supplier 2 (S2). If it is known that 60 per cent of the parts are from S1 and 40 per cent are from S2. Thus $p(A_1)$ is 0.60 and $p(A_2)$ is 0.40; these are the *a priori* probabilities. If G is used to denote the event that a part is good and acceptable, and B denotes an event that a part is bad and unacceptable then:

for supplier A$_1$ $\quad$ $p(G|A_1) = 0.95$ $\quad$ $p(B|A_1) = 0.05$

and

for supplier A$_2$ $\quad$ $p(G|A_2) = 0.97$ $\quad$ $p(B|A_2) = 0.03$

Which is derived from knowing that A$_1$'s performance provides a conditional probability of 0.98 good and 0.02 bad. Likewise A$_2$'s performance provides conditional probabilities of 0.97 that are good parts and 0.03 that are bad parts.

The process of showing these joint probabilities can be shown on a probability tree, similar to Figure 4-14.

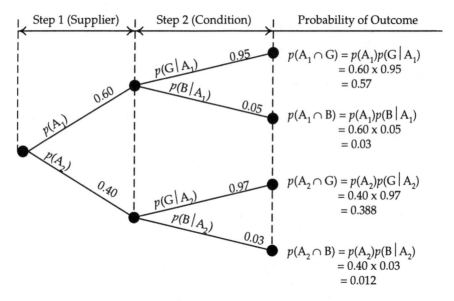

Figure 4-14: Probability Tree

The tree is constructed from left to right. The first step is to show the suppliers A$_1$ and A$_2$. The second step is to show whether the parts are good or bad. The probabilities, e.g. $p(A_1)$, $p(A_2)$, $p(G|A_1)$, etc. are then placed on each limb of the tree. The probability of an outcome is then simply found by multiplying the probabilities on the branches leading to the outcome. Let's assume that the posterior probabilities $p(A_1|B)$ and $p(A_2|B)$ represent what we are looking for then:

$$p(A_1 \cap B) = p(A_1) \times p(B|A_1)$$
and

$$p(A_2 \cap B) = p(A_2) \times p(B|A_2)$$

By substituting these equations into the conditional probability given earlier of:

$$p(A \mid B) = \frac{p(A \cap B)}{p(B)}$$

from which Bayes theorem for two stages can be derived as:

$$p(A_1 \mid B) = \frac{p(A_1)p(B \mid A_1)}{p(A_1)p(B \mid A_1) + p(A_2)p(B \mid A_2)}$$

and

$$p(A_2 \mid B) = \frac{p(A_2)p(B \mid A_2)}{p(A_1)p(B \mid A_1) + p(A_2)p(B \mid A_2)}$$

For the general case of n events:

$$p(A_j \mid B) = \frac{p(A_j)p(B \mid A_j)}{p(A_1)p(B \mid A_1) + p(A_2)p(B \mid A_2) + \ldots + p(A_n)p(B \mid A_n)}$$

Therefore, referring to the example where B denotes the bad parts: the probability of receiving bad parts from each of the two suppliers are calculated by:

$$p(A_1 \mid B) \quad = \quad \frac{0.030}{0.030 + 0.012} \quad = \quad 0.714$$

$$p(A_2 \mid B) \quad = \quad \frac{0.012}{0.030 + 0.012} \quad = \quad 0.286$$

This indicates that there is a probability of 71.4 per cent of the bad parts emanating from supplier A_1 and there is a probability of 28.6 per cent of the bad parts coming from supplier A_2.

Probability Distribution, Expected Value and Variance

We are often confronted with probability problems where there is considerable data and we need to establish if there is a pattern to the data and if it belongs to one of the well-established patterns of data. For such recurring patterns we do not need to develop the theory each time but instead can obtain the required probabilities from tables that have been calculated for such purposes. To do so firstly we need to recognise which of the established patterns the problem best conforms to, and secondly, make use of the appropriate set of tables to determine the probability needed. These standard patterns are called *probability distributions*.

Before commenting on such theoretical probability distributions as the binomial distribution, the Poisson distribution, and the normal distribution we will first examine the link between frequency distributions and probability distributions.

In estimating the time it will take to carry out a particularly complex project activity, twenty knowledgeable project personnel were asked what they thought. The results of this survey were:

Number of Days	Number of Personnel
10	1
11	3
12	8
13	6
14	2

The frequency chart for this survey is shown in Figure 4-15 (a) and it represents a histogram type of chart where the frequencies, i.e. the number of times a particular period was selected, are plotted as the ordinate (the vertical) and the abscissa (the horizontal) becomes the variable against which the frequencies are measured. In this case the variable is time and the time for the activity has been separated into classes in which each class has the same time interval of three days.

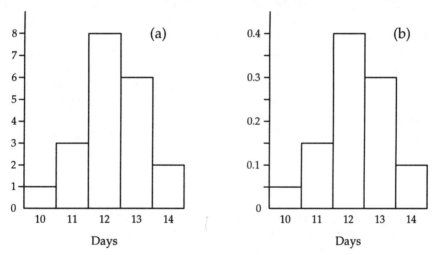

Figure 4-15: (a) Frequency Chart and (b) Probability Distribution Chart

By asking the question "what is the probability that the activity can be completed in a period of 12 days?", and assuming that the sample of 20 personnel questioned is representative, then:

$$p(\text{event}) = \frac{\text{team members estimating 12 days}}{\text{total number of personnel in survey}} = \frac{8}{20} = 0.40$$

In the same way, all other frequencies could be converted to probabilities by dividing by the $\Sigma f(x)$, which means the total number of people in the sample. In this way, the frequencies are converted into probabilities and likewise the frequency distribution can be converted into a probability distribution as shown in Figure 4-

15(b). Further explanation of converting frequencies into probabilities will be discussed after the next two paragraphs.

Apart from the vertical scale, the probability distribution is identical with the frequency chart. Whereas in the ordinary histogram (frequency chart) the area of each block represents the frequency of the corresponding class, the same histogram block (in the probability distribution chart) represents the probability that a value falls within that corresponding class. It follows from this that the overall area under the probability curve must add up to 1.0, i.e. the sum of the probabilities.

Although deriving and using this type of probability distribution has its applications, the theoretical probability distributions have application to a much wider class of problem. These theoretical probability distributions will be explained later in this Section.

In the example — determining the duration of an activity through experiment by asking the opinion of project team personnel — we are dealing with what is referred to as *discrete random variables*. A random variable is quite simply a numerical description of the outcome of an experiment. A random variable is discrete if, in representing the random variables as points on a line, then the only possible value of a variable is as given by the points. If an entire line segment between any two points also represents possible values of a random variable then the random variable is referred to as being a *continuous random variable*.

The probability function as given by the vertical axis in Figure 4-15(b) is always denoted by $f(x)$; this implies that the random variable x takes on a specific value. The graphical representation in Figure 4-15(b) can be represented by a formula that provides a corresponding $f(x)$ for every possible value of x. In developing discrete probability distributions, two conditions must be satisfied:

$$f(x) \geq 0 \qquad \text{and}$$
$$\Sigma f(x) = 1$$

After establishing a random variable and its probability distribution it is possible to develop additional probability information, depending on the needs and interests of the decision-maker.

Expected value

After constructing the probability distribution for a random variable, it is often necessary to calculate the mean or expected value. The expected value is a weighted average of all possible values of the random variable. The formula for calculating the expected value E is:

$$E(x) = \mu = \Sigma x f(x)$$

The expected value of a random variable is the mean, or average, value; it is the "long-run" average value. It is not the modal or most probable value. The expected value calculation for the example introduced on page 145 would be as follows:

x	$f(x)$	$xf(x)$
10	0.05	0.50
11	0.15	1.65
12	0.40	4.80
13	0.30	3.90
14	0.10	1.40
		$\mu = 12.25$

The expected value for the activity's duration is 12.25 days; this period could be used from both the decision-making and planning viewpoints.

Variance

The expected value gives an average or central value for the random variable. It is often necessary to know the dispersion, or variability, of the possible values of the random variable. The variance is a measure used to summarise the variability in the values of a random variable. The mathematical expression for the variance of a discrete random variable is:

$$\text{Var}(x) = \sigma^2 = \Sigma(x - \mu)^2 f(x)$$

The part of the formula $(x - \mu)$ is known as the deviation, which measures how far a particular value of the random variable is from the expected value or mean, μ. In computing the variance of a discrete random variable, the deviations are squared and then weighted by the corresponding probability. In other words the variance is a weighted average of the squared deviations. A related measure of variability is the standard deviation, σ, which is defined as the positive square root of the variance.

Referring back to the previous example of the duration of a project activity, the variance calculation is as shown below:

x	$x - \mu$	$(x - \mu)^2$	$f(x)$	$(x - \mu)^2 f(x)$
10	10 − 12.25	5.0625	0.05	0.2531
11	11 − 12.25	1.5625	0.15	0.2344
12	12 − 12.25	0.6250	0.40	0.2500
13	13 − 12.25	1.5625	0.30	0.4688
14	14 − 12.25	5.0625	0.10	0.5063
				$\sigma^2 = 1.7126$
				hence $\sigma = 1.3087$

As the standard deviation in this example is measured in days, it may be the preferred method of measuring dispersion over the variance, which is measured in days squared. Hence, for the project activity being considered, an optimistic period would be 10.94 days (12.25 − 1.31) and a pessimistic period would be 13.56 days (12.25 + 1.31).

Normal Distribution

Both Binomial and Poisson distributions are discrete probability distributions that deal with either/or situations, where the number of times a thing occurred can be counted. These two types of distribution will not be explained here, but the reader is directed to certain references (Anderson et al., 1995; Morris, 1996) at the end of this Part where a full explanation can be found.

Continuous random variables — such as weight, time, and temperature — take on any value in a certain interval or collection of intervals. For instance if a task can be done within 24 hours, then the possible values of the time to do the task would be $0 \leq x \leq 24$. In other words, x can take on any value within the interval 0 to 24.

Perhaps the most important distribution used to describe a continuous random variable is the *normal probability distribution*. This is shown in Figure 4-16 (a). What we notice about this type of distribution is its symmetry; the "bell-shaped" curve is identical on both sides of its centre peak. The characteristics of the probability distribution described in the last sub-Section apply to the normal curve: i.e. the area occupied by a frequency histogram represents probability and the total area under the distribution curve is 1. In order to distinguish one normal curve from another we need to know the mean (where the peak occurs) and the standard deviation, which demonstrates how spread out the distribution is.

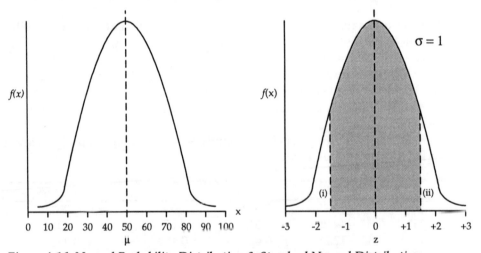

Figure 4-16: Normal Probability Distribution & Standard Normal Distribution

A random variable which has a normal distribution with a mean of 0 and a standard deviation of 1 is said to have a *standard normal distribution*; this is shown in Figure 4-16 (b). The letter z is used to designate what is called the standard normal variable. Z measures the number of standard deviations from the mean. Suppose we are required to find the probability of a random variable having a value within a specified interval which is shown by (i) and (ii) on Figure (b). This will be given by the area under the curve between (i) and (ii). To do this we have to use the Table which is included within Part 7 (Figure 7-25). The values in the Table provide the area under the curve between the mean (z = 0) and any specified positive value of z.

This method can be used to compute probabilities for any normal distribution by first converting to the standard normal distribution. Thus, when we have a normal distribution with any mean μ and any standard deviation σ, we can answer probability questions about this distribution by converting to the standard normal distribution. The z values in the Table (Figure 7-25) can be used to find the probability. The formula used to convert any normal random variable x with a mean μ and standard deviation σ to the standard normal distribution is:

$$z = \frac{x - \mu}{\sigma}$$

The process of calculating z from x is sometimes called standardisation.

Let's look at an example. An illustration is provided in Section 3 of Part 7 under the sub-Section entitled "Central Limit Theorem". The example relates to the duration of an eight-activity project (see Figure 7-26). The analysis shows that the project duration will be 14 weeks (μ) and the standard deviation (σ) is 0.9985. Based on this information, we need to know what the probability associated with completing the project in 16 days will be; the z value is:

$$z = \frac{16 - 14}{0.9985} = 2.003$$

From the Table, a z value of 2.003 gives a value of 0.977. In other words there is a 97.7 per cent chance that the project will be completed within 16 weeks.

Let us now see what the probability will be of completing the project in 13 weeks.

$$z = \frac{13 - 14}{0.9985} = -1.0015$$

From the Table at the end of this Part, a z value of –1.0015 gives a value of 0.844 for the cumulative normal distribution which, because the calculated z value is negative has to be interpreted as 1 – 0.844 = 0.156. In other words there is a 15.6 per cent chance that the project can be completed within 13 weeks.

Another calculation that can be performed would be to determine the duration equivalent to a probability of 75 per cent. The z value of a 75 per cent probability obtained from the Table is 0.68. The duration can be calculated as follows:

$$0.68 = \frac{x - 14}{0.9985}$$

from this x = 14.68 weeks; in other words by completing the project in, say, 15 weeks, there is a greater than a 75 per cent chance that it will be achieved.

SECTION 3: EVALUATING OPTIONS

Contents

- Aims and Objectives
- Introduction
- Project Cash Flow
- Pay Back Time
- Return on Investment
- Time Value of Money and Discounting
- Net Present Value (NPV)
- Discounted Cash Flow Return (DCFR)
- Comparison of NPV and DCFR in Economic Evaluation
- Quantifying Economic Uncertainty and its Implications
- Decision-Making under Conditions of Uncertainty and Risk

Aims and Objectives

The aims and objectives of Section 3 are to:

- Explain the use of cashflows to determine the economic viability of projects;
- Describe payback and return on investment techniques;
- Contrast Net Present Value and Discounted Cash Flow Return methodologies;
- Show the graphical presentation of NPV and DCFR;
- Present a method of quantifying economic risk.

Introduction

To evaluate something literally means to determine its value or worth. It means investigating, understanding and summarising the potential consequences of every option that might be considered as being a solution to a project problem.

Cooke and Slack (1991) have suggested that there are three classes of evaluation:

- feasibility
- acceptability
- vulnerability

The *feasibility* of an option when determined will indicate the degree of difficulty in satisfying the initial requirements. These requirements will have been stated in technical and monetary terms. In determining feasibility, the options will have been assessed relative to these requirements, and hence the required investment determined.

The feasibility process within a projects' environment is dealt with in Part 6, "Conception and Definition Phases".

The *acceptability* of an option will indicate whether the investment would be worthwhile. In other words the acceptability evaluation will give an indication of each option's return. This form of evaluation is described in the next sub-Sections.

The *vulnerability* of an option will indicate the extent to which things could go right, or alternatively, could go wrong if chosen. In other words the vulnerability will determine the degree of risk.

Project Cash Flow

Projects cost money. The spending of money usually has to be justified in terms of receiving a return or making a profit. The economic evaluation of projects, with which we are primarily concerned in this sub-Section, consists of comparing the costs of the resources and the effort needed to bring them about with the value of the eventual benefits which should result. In order to make this comparison, as many factors as possible are measured in the same units — usually monetary.

An economic evaluation of a project is based on estimates of the costs of the effort and resource usage, and of the monetary benefits expected. These are analysed with respect to time to find the rate of cash flow (in mu per year) and the cumulative cash flow (in mu) throughout the anticipated effective life of the project. Derek Allen (1991) provides an easy-to-understand explanation of project economic evaluation.

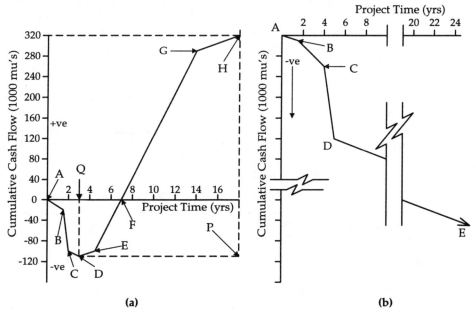

Figure 4-17: Cumulative Cash Flow Diagrams

A typical cumulative cash flow diagram for a project that has monetary benefit, such as a process plant, is shown as curve (a) in Figure 4-17. Expenditure is a negative cash outflow and income a positive cash inflow. The cash position is zero at the start of the project. For this type of evaluation, the project start is defined as the time when the first cash flow occurs. The initial costs of this type of project (one showing monetary benefit) consist of such costs as conceptual work, outline design and other preliminary work. This initial cost is shown as A to B in Figure 4-17. Traditionally this initial cost is followed by the capital investment in buildings, plant and equipment; this is shown as B to C. Working capital is spent and the plant is commissioned in readiness for commercial production, which gets under way at D, and reaches design conditions at E. The lowest point on the curve, D, represents the *maximum cumulative debt* incurred by the project.

Beyond point D, income resulting from sales of the product exceeds production and other operating costs and so the cumulative cash flow curve turns upwards. Beyond E the curve rises with a constant gradient, indicating that the net rate of cash flow (income minus costs) is positive and constant at full production capacity. At point F the cumulative cash flow is again zero.

Beyond point F is an increasingly positive net cash position. Eventually, towards the end of the project's useful life, G, the net rate of cash flow, may decrease due, for example, to increasing maintenance costs, a fall in the market place for the product or falling sales due to obsolescence of the product. Ultimately the plant will be shut down permanently, as shown by H, and this marks the end of the project. There are no further cash flows beyond H. If at shut-down any working capital is recovered or if a salvage value of the facility is realised, this would be treated as a final cash inflow.

Figure 4-17, curve (b), shows another cumulative cash flow curve; this time it represents that which would be expected from a project that has no direct monetary benefit, for example, a Local Authority's responsibility to design and construct a major county road. In other words, this Figure shows cumulative cash outflow.

The procurement of land and other up-front costs relating to planning and wayleaves is shown as A to B. The design of the road is shown as taking two years, B to C. From C to D is the Local Authority's capital investment in the road's construction. Beyond D is the associated costs, at a considerably lower rate than the capital investment, of the on-going operation, maintenance and up-keep of the road, bridges, verges, overhead lighting, etc. At E, it is considered that the useful life of the initial investment has come to an end.

Cumulative cash flows can be obtained accurately from historical data after the project is over. However, any evaluation based on this would be useless for decision-making purposes since the project decisions are also in the past. Economic evaluation as a factor in investment decision-making must be concerned with future cash flows and not past ones. Thus, for projects such as those represented by Figure 4-17 (a) or (b), the decision whether to initiate the project at point A requires an evaluation in terms of estimates or forecasts of all the future cash flows which would result from that decision. Since, at the time an economic evaluation is made, all cash flows are in the future, they are subject to varying degrees of uncertainty. The later decision at B to go ahead with the main capital investment should take account only of the estimates of cash flows beyond B and not of the actual expenditure up to B, since this is now a "sunk" cost and cannot be affected by any subsequent decision.

A major purpose of the preliminary expenditure up to B would be to provide information to enable the cash flows resulting from the major capital investment decision at B to be estimated with sufficient confidence for this decision to be made. In effect the initial decision at A would be concerned only with the preliminary expenditure up to B, since the project could be stopped at that point if necessary. This is just as well, since the estimates at A will also be of an order-of-magnitude nature.

The components of a cash flow include investment and working capital, annual fixed costs, variable costs depending on the rate of production, taxes and grants, and sales income. For an appreciation of these components and how they should be handled in deriving cash flows, both Allen (1991) and Humphreys (1991) should be consulted.

The predicted cumulative cash flow curve for a project throughout its life summarises the effects of all the relevant cash flow estimates and forecasts and forms the basis for its economic evaluation. The purpose of an evaluation is to assess the economic attractiveness or desirability of a project. The general shape of the cumulative cash flow curve itself is a qualitative guide to this.

Many quantitative measures or indices are in use. Each may be regarded as a function of the cumulative cash flow curve or as describing its properties, although in some cases additional information is used as well. Some of these indices are empirical, others have been developed more from theoretical considerations and are justified as being theoretically "correct" interpretations of the project cash flow information and the project selection situation. In each case, important features of the cumulative cash flow curve are identified and transformed into a single numerical measure as an index of the project's economic attractiveness.

Four types of such indices are:

- payback time;

- return on investment;

- net present value;

- discounted cash flow return.

The most comprehensive index, net present value, is in monetary units; the crude empirical measure, payback time, is in years; return on investment and discounted cash flow return are both rates of return. These four indices will be described since they are the ones most commonly used.

Pay Back Time

The project's break-even point occurs when the total income generated by a project just balances all the previous project expenditure. The payback time can be interpreted as the period of time from project start to the break-even point. This point can be read directly from the cumulative cash flow diagram for a project. In Figure 4-17 (a) it is given by F, which is where the rising part of the curve passes the zero line. Prior to the break-even point the project is in debt. Beyond F, the project shows a clear profit. The sooner the break-even point is reached, i.e. the shorter the payback time, the more attractive is a project.

Where long-term cash flows are difficult to forecast or where limited information is available beyond the break-even point, payback time is fairly widely used. Payback time may be used for preliminary evaluation or as a project screening device for risky projects in times of uncertainty.

Projects that have no monetary benefit, as shown by Figure 4-17 (b) do not have a payback.

Return on Investment

For the project in Figure 4-17 (a) the return on investment (ROI) is given by the following formula:

$$\text{ROI} \quad = \quad \frac{PH}{PD} \times \frac{100}{QD} \quad \% \text{ per year}$$

where PH, PD and QD are the values read from Figure 4-17.

Rate of return on investment is usually expressed as the percentage ratio of average yearly profit (net cash flow) over the productive life of the project, divided by the total initial investment.

The above definition of ROI is based solely on project cash flow information, i.e. it does not include depreciation, except insofar as this affects taxation cash flows. An alternative is to include annual depreciation as a charge against income before calculating ROI. For the project shown in Figure 4-17 (a) the ROI (including depreciation) is:

$$\text{ROI} \quad = \quad \frac{(PH - QD)}{PD} \times \frac{100}{QD} \quad \% \text{ per year}$$

The reason for including depreciation is that, since the original investment is thus paid off by the end of the project before the calculation of ROI, the ROI gives a measure of profitability above this level.

It is important that the precise method of calculating an ROI be known before interpreting it or comparing the ROIs of alternatives. For example, an ROI (excluding depreciation) of zero means that a project produces no income, whereas an ROI (including depreciation) of zero means that the income produced is just enough to pay off the initial investment by the end of the project's life.

It is worth noting that payback time and ROI select particular features of the project's cumulative cash flow and ignore others. For instance, they take no account of the pattern of cash flow during a project. The other indices to be described, net present value and discounted cash flow return, are more comprehensive because they take account of the changing pattern of project net cash flow. They also take account of the "time value" of money.

Time Value of Money and Discounting

In considering the components of project cash flows, possible charges relating to the capital used need to be considered. If the money required for the initial investment is borrowed, for example from a bank, interest would be charged until the loan is repaid out of the income from the project. This interest should therefore be included in evaluating the project cash flows. If a company invests its own funds in the project there will be no interest to pay but the company nevertheless loses the opportunity to earn a return on the money through an alternative investment, e.g. lending it to a bank. This loss of alternative earning power for funds is an opportunity cost which is also a legitimate charge on the project, since in evaluating project cash flows we are comparing the "with the project" option with "without the project" option.

When a project reaches a positive cumulative cash flow position, it generates available funds which could notionally be invested elsewhere to earn interest, which would then be a legitimate income for the project. The general idea is to regard a project as receiving capital from a pool of funds for which a "cost of capital" is incurred and as paying project profits into the pool, for which a further return at the same rate is earned. The general consideration of interest payments, which can be charged or received on a sum of money, lead to the concept that the actual value of cash is a function of time and of an interest (or discount) rate known as the cost of capital or the market rate.

The actual value of the cost of capital to use in the economic evaluation of a project depends on how the company concerned would finance the project. Frequently a company will have several alternative ways of raising capital and investing surplus funds, which may need to be pooled as far as the project is concerned.

Suppose that funds can be invested in the financial market at a compound interest rate of 10 per cent per annum. Interest is said to be simple if it is withdrawn at the end of each interest period. With compound interest the interest is added to the investment at the end of each period. Put simply, 100 mu invested now would grow to 110 mu in one year's time or, conversely, in order to have 110 mu available in a year's time only 100 mu is needed now.

Another way of interpreting this is that taking out a loan today of 100 mu, at 10 per cent interest per annum, requires 110 mu to be repaid in a year's time to clear the debt. Hence, the future value after one year of 100 mu invested now is $100 \times 1.1 = 110$ mu at an *interest* rate of 10 per cent per annum. Conversely, the present value of 110 mu existing one year from now is $110/1.1 = 100$ mu at a *discount* rate of 10 per cent per annum. Since the interest and discount rates are compounded, the future value of 100 mu after two years is $100 \times 1.1 \times 1.1 = 121$ mu, or the present value of 121 mu existing in two years' time is $121/(1.1)^2 = 100$ mu, and so on.

It is possible by means of discounting to take account of the effect of the timing of future cash flows and, for evaluation purposes, to consider their equivalent values at the same instant in time, usually the present time (the time of the evaluation). It should be noted that this effect of discounting has nothing to do with inflation. Allen (1991) should be consulted on how to handle inflation.

The other two evaluation indices to be described, net present value and discounted cash flow return, incorporate this concept of the time value of money and are the most widely used means of evaluating investment projects.

Net Present Value (NPV)

The net present value of a project is the sum of the present values of each individual constituent cash flow. In this case the "present"; is taken as the time at which the evaluation is carried out, which is usually the start of the project. It is common practice to look at the cash flows in yearly increments. The present value (PV) at year 0 of a cash flow C_t in year t at an annual discount rate of i, expressed as a decimal fraction, is:

$$PV = \frac{C_t}{(1+i)^t}$$

For a complete project, the earlier cash flows are usually negative and the later ones often positive and the project net present value (NPV) is the sum of the individual present values of the yearly cash flows, i.e. NPV = ΣPV. The life of the project is given in n years together with the estimated cash flows in each year up to n.

The use of discount tables greatly assists manual calculations of present values. Discount tables are included on pages 176–177 at the end of this Part, just before the "Summary of Key Points". Alternatively, convenient computer programs are widely available for discounted cash flow calculations.

Discounting either continuously (Table 2) or at discrete time intervals (Table 1) gives slightly different results. Continuous discounting is often more convenient when an economic discounting function is to be included in a wider mathematical model. Discounting at discrete yearly intervals is otherwise the common practice. Cumulative cash flow curves, however, are usually shown as being continuous rather than stepped; the cash flows may actually be calculated at intervals of a month, quarter, year, etc.

Returning to the cumulative cash flow curve for a project, the effect of discounting is shown in Figure 4-18 (a).

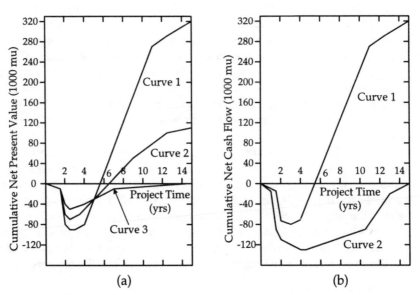

Figure 4-18: (a) NPV Diagram and (b) DCFR Diagram
Source: Allen (1991)

The ordinate is the cumulative net present value in mu. Curve 1 is the curve with no discounting, i.e., i = 0, and the project NPV is equal to the final net cash position; in this case 320,000 mu. Curve 2 shows the effect of discounting at 10 per cent per annum and the corresponding project NPV is 108,000 mu. Curve 3 shows that when the discount rate is close to 30 per cent, the NPV is zero.

It should be noted that the project NPV is given by the cumulative value at the end of the project. An intermediate point on the curve indicates the cumulative NPV of the cash flows as far as that point in time. Thus the NPV of the initial expenditures is smaller (i.e. smaller negative) than the corresponding undiscounted cumulative cash position at any time, and the positive NPV at any time after the break-even point is also smaller than its corresponding positive cumulative cash position.

The greater the positive NPV for a project, the more economically attractive it is. A project with a negative NPV is not a profitable proposition.

If, however, a project is not concerned with making a profit, but with meeting a necessary objective at the minimum overall cost, for example, investment in a road construction project, its NPV will be negative and the economic aim in considering alternatives is to reduce the negative NPV (more accurately NPC — net present cost) to as small a level as possible.

Discounted Cash Flow Return (DCFR)

DCFR is known by other names such as the *interest rate of return* and *internal rate of return*. It is defined as the discount rate, I, which makes the NPV of a project equal to zero:

$$\text{NPV} = 0 = \text{PV} = \sum_{n=0}^{n=t} \frac{C_t}{(1+I)^t}$$

From Figure 4-18 (b) it can be seen that, when the discount rate is 0 per cent, the project NPV is 320,000 mu (curve 1). As the discount rate is increased, the NPV falls until, at a discount rate of about 30 per cent, the NPV is zero (Curve 2). Therefore the value of I is 29.9 per cent per annum and this rate is the DCFR for this project. Increasing the discount rate beyond 29.9 per cent will produce a negative NPV.

The higher the value of the DCFR for a project, the more attractive it is. The minimum acceptable value of the DCFR is the cost of capital or market rate for the project. For a value of the DCFR greater than this, the project will show a profit; for a lesser value it will show a loss.

There is another way of interpreting DCFR. Suppose the funds to invest in a project are borrowed and interest is paid on the loan at a rate equal to the project's DCFR. Then, if the interest payments are now included as cash outflows in calculating the project cumulative net cash flow, the project will just break even at the end of its life. This is demonstrated in the "mortgage" cash flow of Curve 2 in Figure 4-18 (b).

The vertical scale here is cumulative cash flow and Curve 1 is the original project cash flow. Curve 2 is the project cash flow, assuming that funds for the project are charged interest at the DCFR rate and the interest payments are included as project cash flows. In the early years, the total debt increases rapidly as interest charges accumulate. When cash inflows begin, these are used to reduce the total debt and so reduce further interest charges. This continues until at the end of the project, the total investment and interest debt has been paid off by project income and the break-even point is reached. This interpretation of DCFR is analogous to paying off a mortgage.

Finding the DCFR for a project is a trial-and-error calculation, since the formula cannot be solved explicitly. If the calculation is done manually, a value of I is selected and the corresponding project net present value NPV is calculated. If NPV is positive, the value of I is too small; if NPV is negative, the value of I is too large. Graphical interpolation between two or three values gives I for NPV = 0 with sufficient accuracy. A demonstration of such trial-and-error calculations plotted on a graph of NPV versus discount rate is shown in Figure 4-19.

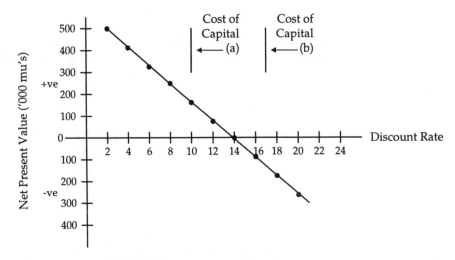

Figure 4-19: Project DCFR Diagram

Comparison of NPV and DCFR in Economic Evaluation

In calculating a project NPV, the cost of capital has to be explicitly included as I in the discounting calculations. In calculating the DCFR the cost of capital is not included. Instead, the value calculated for I is compared afterwards with the cost of capital to see whether the project is viable. There is, however, more than this superficial difference between the two methods in the way they are interpreted.

When a project's cash flows are discounted at the cost of capital the resulting NPV is a measure of the cash profit (in present value terms) that the project will produce after recovering the initial investment and meeting all costs, including the cost of capital. It is, therefore an absolute measure of the total project profit. Looked at another way, the initial investment could be higher by an amount corresponding to the project NPV and the project would still break-even.

On the other hand the DCFR for a project is a rate of return on investment. It is a measure of the efficiency with which the capital is employed and indicates the earning power of the project investment.

For the example shown in Figure 4-19, the DCFR of a project has been calculated to have a discount rate of 14 per cent. If the cost of capital was 10 per cent (see line (a)), then the project would be viable. If the cost of capital was 17 per cent (see line (b)), then the project would not be viable.

For a single project proposal considered in isolation, NPV and DCFR both lead to the same conclusion as to whether the project is economically acceptable. This is because, if a project has a positive NPV, it is also bound to have a DCFR above the discount rate used in the NPV calculation. The more common situations, however, involve selecting a portfolio of projects or selecting between mutually exclusive alternatives for the same project, and these involve optimisation.

Where a project sponsor's economic objective is to maximise the profits from the projects it undertakes, this is in cash terms, and is equivalent to maximising the total NPV of the projects undertaken. This corresponds with accepting all independent project proposals which have positive NPVs. This assumes, of course, that the supply of capital and other resources is adequate to undertake all projects with positive NPVs. Under these conditions of adequate resources and independent projects, the same result would be achieved by accepting all projects with a DCFR greater than the NPV discount rate.

If there are more potentially acceptable projects than capital to finance them, projects should be selected from those proposed in a way which maximises the total NPV within the permitted budget. Ranking projects in the order of decreasing DCFRs and selecting them until all the available capital has been allocated will give the same result, since it is a question of how efficiently a given total amount of capital can be used. Where there are other resource constraints besides capital, the selection of projects from a portfolio is not so straightforward and a mathematical programming approach is required. Other complications can occur in evaluating the effect of a portfolio of postponable projects, or of projects of different lifetimes.

Where a choice is to be made between alternative proposals for a project, these will have different cash flow patterns and different investments. In order to maximise the magnitude of the project's profits, the alternative with the greatest NPV should be selected. However, this is not necessarily the same as selecting the alternative with the highest DCFR. The reason is that the investment upon which the return is measured is not constant. Thus, a lower return on a larger investment could yield a greater cash profit than a higher return on a smaller investment. In order to select the best alternative using DCFR instead of NPV, it is necessary to look at the DCFRs of the incremental cash flows between alternatives.

Although DCFR is widely used in project evaluation, it is more limiting than NPV in its applications. NPV gives a direct cash measure of a project's attractiveness and NPVs are additive when dealing with multiple project selection, an essential requirement in many cases. DCFRs are rates of return on varying levels of investment and are not additive. This restricts the applications of DCFR and can lead to its incorrect use, with misleading results.

Quantifying Economic Uncertainty and its Implications

Sensitivity analysis demonstrates the effect of variations in contributing estimates on the economics of a project, but gives no indication of the probability that any variation of a specified magnitude will occur. The next step in trying to deal systematically and rationally with uncertainty in economic evaluation is to attempt to quantify the uncertainty in terms of subjective probabilities of possible alternative situations which could arise.

The essentially subjective nature of any method of measuring uncertainty in a project should be emphasised. No two projects are exactly alike. Even apparently similar projects differ in time or in location and are, therefore, influenced to different extents by economic, social or environmental factors. The experience gained with one project cannot be used directly to assess what is going to happen to another project, although, of course, such experience is still relevant and useful information.

Subjective probabilities are commonly used to quantify uncertainty. It is important to realise that they are merely a way of expressing personal feelings about uncertainty and that they have no objective reality. Objective probabilities can be demonstrated and tested. For example, the probability that a tossed coin will come down heads can be found by repeating the event a large number of times, or the probability that a person will live to a stated age can be found by analysis of population life records. There is no similar basis for probabilities about the future of a project, since there are not enough similar projects to reach a satisfactory conclusion and each project differs in some ways from previous ones. These subjective probabilities cannot be proved right or wrong; they depend on the estimator's knowledge of the situation and their relevant past experience. Note that once the situation occurs, past assessment of its probabilities is irrelevant. For example, if it is estimated that there is an 80 per cent chance of the capital investment for a project exceeding X mu, when the time arrives it either does or does not exceed X mu and the probability is then meaningless.

The advantage of using subjective probabilities as a means of expressing opinions about uncertain situations is not that the numbers have any objective reality (which they do not), but that they enable the consequences of these opinions to be explored logically and rationally. Thus, given that there is an 80 per cent chance of capital investment exceeding X mu, the effect on project NPV or DCFR can be evaluated and an appropriate decision taken. However, putting numbers on uncertainties in the form of probabilities in no way alters the fact that their subjective origin is based on experience, intuition, or mere hunch.

Decision-Making under Conditions of Uncertainty and Risk

Investment decisions under conditions of uncertainty and risk require the use of judgement in some form, but this does not mean taking decisions arbitrarily. Good judgement involves the systematic identification, consideration and weighing of all the relevant factors, and this is assisted by quantifying the problem, including its associated uncertainties, as much as possible.

Decisions are concerned with selecting a course of action from possible alternatives, remembering that "no action" is usually one possibility. Although readers should refresh their memories by referring back to Section 1, the basic steps involved are:

* identify possible actions;

* predict consequences of alternative actions to establish possible outcomes;

* evaluate each action in terms of the desirability of the resulting outcome;

- apply a criterion of desirability to select the preferred action.

The information relating to a decision can be presented in the form of a payoff table.

Simplest Case — No Uncertainty

Here the action which has the most desirable outcome is simply chosen. Suppose the decision is whether or not to invest in a project for a new plant that will provide monetary benefit. The two possible actions are "invest" or "don't invest". Each action has only one possible outcome. Let's suppose that the action "invest" will result in sales that over the project life will give an NPV to the project of 500,000 mu. A further assumption is that the action "don't invest" will enable the capital involved to earn interest instead on the financial market, equivalent to an NPV of 150,000 mu over the same time as the life of the project. The criterion is to maximise NPV and so obviously the preferred action is to invest in the project.

Decision with Alternative Outcomes

Suppose we suspect that a competitor may build a similar plant for the same product. If that happens, it will adversely affect our project and reduce its NPV to − 100,000 mu, i.e., a loss. If it does not happen our project's NPV will still be 500,000 mu.

Possible decision policies are:

- *Responding to the most likely situation*

Only what is considered to be the most likely situation is taken into account in deciding the preferred action. For example, if "no competition" is thought to be more likely than "competition", the decision is based on the consequences of "no competition" and the effect of "competition" is ignored. This policy of taking account only of the most likely situation and ignoring other possible ones is in effect what is done when single-valued estimates are used. It takes no regard of any risk that what is supposed to be the most likely outcome may not, in fact, occur.

- *Minimising the maximum loss*

At the other extreme, risk may be the dominant factor in selecting a course of action. Suppose that a project would absorb a substantial part of a sponsor's financial and other resources and that economic failure of the project would have disastrous consequences. Then an appropriate policy might well be to avoid the potentially worst situation at all costs. This is equivalent to selecting the course of action which minimises the maximum loss which could be sustained, even though it may be only a remote possibility. Thus in the example, the application of this "minimax loss" policy leads to selection of the negative action since this avoids the possibility of, say, a 100,000 mu NPV loss.

This policy of playing safe is always at the expense of the alternative chance of higher profits — here it gives up the chance of achieving a possible NPV of 500,000 mu should competition not materialise, and settles for the "safe" alternative of 150,000 mu whatever happens.

Giving Weight to Alternative Outcomes

Further progress in establishing policies towards uncertainty requires its measurement in terms of subjective probabilities of the possible alternatives. Suppose we feel that the odds against competition are 3 to 1. This means that probability of competition is 0.25, and of no competition is 0.75 (since the combined probability of either occurring must be one).

The so-called expectation of each course of action is calculated as the weighted average of the possible outcomes, each weighted according to its subjective probability. The expectations of alternative actions are then compared to select the best — in this case, the positive action to go ahead. If the assessment of the probabilities is different — for example, the reverse for competition and no competition — this would affect the relative standing of the alternative actions:

| E (invest) | = | $(0.75 \times -100{,}000) + (0.25 \times 500{,}000)$ | = | 50,000 |
| E (don't invest) | = | $(0.75 \times 150{,}000) + (0.25 \times 150{,}000)$ | = | 150,000 |

E is the expected NPV in mu. The "don't invest" alternative is better in this situation. Thus the use of expectation systematically allows for uncertainty in evaluating a project and selecting a course of action.

In practice, instead of deciding on values for probabilities and then evaluating the corresponding action, it is sometimes easier to start at the other end and find the critical values of the probabilities which change the action selected. It is then only necessary to judge whether the probabilities are greater or less than these critical values instead of fixing their values exactly. In the example, let P be the critical probability of there being competition. Then:

$$P \times (-100) + (1 - P)500 = 150$$

hence $-100P + 500 - 500P = 150$

from which $P = 0.583$

If the probability of competition is thought to be greater than 0.583 the "don't invest" alternative is the better course of action; if it is less than 0.583 then "invest" should be chosen.

In a repetitive situation, expectation measures the average effect of decisions. On any single occasion it will never be achieved, but in the long run the different effects will tend to average out at the expectation value. If a company has many projects in its programme and is primarily concerned with their average performance as a group rather than with the fate of any particular one, expectation is the measure to use. In project evaluation we are more concerned with the consequences of individual projects, and for a single project the expected value cannot actually be achieved — the actual value will either be more or less depending on the actual income. Nevertheless, it is a useful way of allowing for the effect of uncertainty in evaluating a project since it "discounts" the more attractive outcomes with the consequences of the less attractive possibilities. Note that DCFR cannot be directly included in expectation calculations since it is not an additive function which can be averaged.

Use of expectation with maximum permissible loss as a constraint on potential disaster generally works fairly well. In some situations, however, it may not adequately take account of the fact that in practice the subjective value of money appears to vary with the amount in question compared with the total available. For example, an additional 100 mu for someone who already has 100 mu is subjectively of more value to him (his incremental satisfaction is greater) than an additional 100 mu for someone who already has 1000 mu.

SECTION 4: A SELECTION OF OTHER DECISION-MAKING TECHNIQUES

Contents

- Aims and Objectives
- Criteria Weighting
- Correlation — Looking for Connections
- Line Fitting
- Time Series
- Linear Programming
- Summary of Key Points
- References

Aims and Objectives

The aims and objectives of Section 4 are to:

- Present the fundamentals of qualitative analysis;

- Provide the skills to evaluate data correlation;

- Explain how to carry out linear regression analysis;

- Describe time series and determine trends;

- Show how to use a graphical method to analyse linear programming problems.

Criteria Weighting

Section 1 dealt with the analysis of decisions in the light of a single objective (criterion), that of maximising a monetary payoff. But most situations are characterised by multiple criteria, many of which cannot be directly related to a form of quantitative measurement.

The decision-making process in cases incorporating multiple criteria can be facilitated considerably by arranging the relevant alternatives and decision criteria in a simple organised fashion (Goodwin and Wright, 1991). An initial step is to identify both the alternatives to be considered and the criteria relevant to the decision to be made. This is followed by scoring each alternative against each criteria in decreasing order of importance. A scoring system can range from 4 (high preference) to 1 (low preference). In some instances, this may be all that is necessary, for one of the alternatives could clearly dominate the others.

This procedure can be illustrated by the following decision matrix in which the numbers represent score grades rather than absolute values:

Criteria	Foreign Exchange Savings	Employment Creation	Increase in Output	Impact on External Partners
Alternative A	4	3	3	3
Alternative B	3	2	4	4
Alternative C	2	1	1	2
Alternative D	1	4	2	1

Each of the four alternatives produces different results with respect to the four criteria. Alternative A outranks all other alternatives in terms of foreign exchange savings, but Alternative D creates the greatest number of jobs. Alternative C, and perhaps Alternative D, could be eliminated because they are dominated by the other two, which have relatively higher overall scores. This can be shown by adding all the criteria scores for each alternative:

Alternative	Total Ranking Points
A	13
B	13
C	6
D	8

Let us, however, retain Alternative D for further analysis since it ranks highest in employment creation, and as yet we have to discover the importance of this criterion within the overall project.

To make a choice among Alternatives A, B and D, we need additional information concerning the relative importance of each criterion, which can be expressed in terms of ratios (or percentages) from 0.0 to 1.0 (or from 0 to 100 per cent). Ratios or percentages of this kind are called objective (criteria) weights. Let us assume that an analysis determines that the following weights are appropriate:

Criteria	Weight
Employment creation	0.3 or 30%
Increase in output	0.4 or 40%
Foreign exchange savings	0.2 or 20%
Impact on external partners	0.1 or 10%
Total	1.0 100%

The process of incorporating the criterion's weights in the decision is begun by normalising each column of the decision matrix. This is done by calculating the percentage distribution of each column so that it adds up to 100. Failure to normalise the columns would distort the comparison of the products of rank times weight. The resulting version of the matrix is:

Criteria	Foreign Exchange Savings	Employment Creation	Increase in Output	Impact on External Partners
Weight	(0.3)	(0.4)	(0.2)	(0.1)
Alternative A	50.0	33.3	33.3	37.5
Alternative B	37.5	22.2	44.4	50.0
Alternative D	12.5	44.4	22.2	12.5

Next the normalised column entries are multiplied by the relevant weights:

Alternative A = 0.3 (50.0) + 0.4 (33.3) + 0.2 (33.3) + 0.1 (37.5) = 38.7

Alternative B = 0.3 (37.5) + 0.4 (22.2) + 0.2 (44.4) + 0.1 (50.0) = 34.0

Alternative D = 0.3 (12.5) + 0.4 (44.4) + 0.2 (22.2) + 0.1 (12.5) = 27.2

The results clearly show that the relative position of Alternative D has improved owing to its output effect and that the previous tie (13 total ranking points) between Alternatives A and B has been broken. Under the conditions of this assessment, Alternative A produces the highest overall score. However, a different system of criteria weighting may produce different results.

Correlation: Looking for Connections

Project teams often have to deal with data where the need is to look at two variables simultaneously. For instance, a team developing a new computer system may wish to examine the performance of the lines of code being produced against the cost of the service being provided by a specialist. To carry out such an analysis requires the data to be collected in pairs. Such paired data is referred to as *bivarate* data.

Sometimes it is possible to look at paired data and observe some sort of causal relationship, but a more detailed analysis is normally required to determine if there is an association between the variables, the strength of this association, and the nature of the relationship between the variables. Before it is analysed the data needs to be presented graphically. Such graphical plotting of bivarate data is presented on what is called a scatter diagram.

A scatter diagram shows plots of one variable on the x-axis (horizontal) and the other variable on the y-axis (vertical). Normally the x variable is the one which is controllable (the independent variable), and in the new computer system project this would be the "production of lines of code". The y variable (the dependent variable) is the one of interest; in the system's project this would be the "cost of the service". The data pairs for the system's project for the variables described are shown plotted in Figure 4-20 (a).

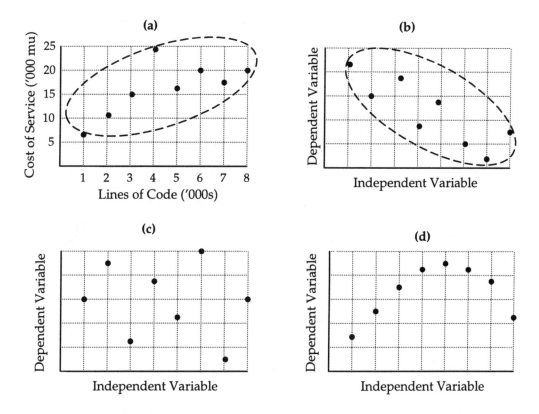

Figure 4-20: Scatter Diagrams

The diagram Figure 4-20 (a) shows a scatter of points indicating what is called a positive correlation; positive because as the number of lines of computer code increases so does the cost of this specialist service. Figure 4-20 (b) indicates a negative correlation which shows a decrease in the dependent variable as the independent variable increases. Figure 4-20 (c) indicates that no correlation exists between the plotted variables. A correlation does exist between the variables in Figure 4-20 (d), but it is not linear.

By drawing an imaginary ellipse around all the points on the scatter diagram, a means of categorising the scatter diagram is possible. An ellipse that points bottom left to top right indicates a positive correlation; if it were to lie top left to bottom right a negative correlation would be indicated; the closer the ellipse is to a circle suggests that there is little, if any, correlation.

An ellipse has been sketched on Figure 4-20 (a); this shows there is a positive correlation between lines of code and cost. The ellipse loop is relatively narrow, suggesting a reasonably strong correlation; the point representing 4,000 lines of code is a rogue pair, otherwise known as an "outlier".

The *correlation coefficient* measures the strength of the association between the variables. The correlation coefficient is measured on a scale between –1 and +1, so that –1 indicates a perfect negative correlation, +1 measures a perfect positive correlation, and 0 indicates no correlation.

The correlation coefficient is normally written as r and is given by:

$$r = \frac{n\Sigma xy - \Sigma x \Sigma y}{\sqrt{\left(n\Sigma x^2 - (\Sigma x)^2\right)\left(n\Sigma y^2 - (\Sigma y)^2\right)}}$$

Where n is the number of data pairs, x is the independent variable, and y is the dependent variable. Application of the formula is shown using the data in Figure 4-20 (a) and is tabulated as follows:

'000s of lines of code "x"	'000s cost of service "y"	xy	x^2	y^2
1.00	6.00	6.00	1	36.00
2.00	11.00	22.00	4	121.00
3.00	15.00	45.00	9	225.00
4.00	25.00	100.00	16	625.00
5.00	16.00	80.00	25	256.00
6.00	20.00	120.00	36	400.00
7.00	17.00	119.00	49	289.00
8.00	20.00	160.00	64	400.00
$\Sigma = 36$	$\Sigma = 130$	$\Sigma = 652$	$\Sigma = 204$	$\Sigma = 2352$

Substituting these Σ values into the formula for r gives:

$$r = \frac{(8 \times 652) - (36 \times 130)}{(8 \times 204 - (36)^2)(8 \times 2352 - (130)^2)} = \frac{5216 - 4680}{(1632 - 1296)(18816 - 16900)}$$

$r = 0.668$

This shows that for the variables and data pairs considered there is a fairly pronounced positive correlation. However, the correlation is on the basis of eight data pairs; more reliability could be placed on the correlation if there were twenty or more data pairs.

Line Fitting

The scatter diagram that was used in Figure 4-20 (a) has been reproduced as Figure 4-21 with a straight line drawn through the data pairs; this line represents the linear relationship between the two variables. The technique of linear regression attempts to define the relationship between the independent variable and the dependent variable by means of a linear equation of the type $y = a + bx$. This is the simplest formula between two variables; fortunately many relationships can at least be approximated by this type of relationship.

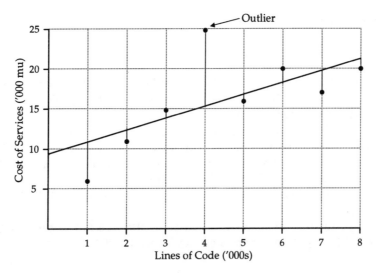

Figure 4-21: Line of Best Fit

It is possible to draw any number of straight lines by eye through the data as an attempt to define the relationship between the variables. To determine how "good a fit" a particular line is, it is necessary to measure what is called the "y errors". These are the measured distances between the actual value of where the drawn best fit line crosses a vertical representing the x value of all independent variables.

The y errors are shown on Figure 4-21 as vertical lines above and below the "best fit" line. The errors above the line are positive and the errors below the line are negative. By adding these errors it is possible to have a total error of zero for a number of different line positions. But by adding the sum of the square of the errors, the line of best fit is found when this sum is minimised. Therefore linear regression is finding the line that minimises the sum of the square of errors.

So from y = a + bx, the value of a and b that minimise the squared errors is given by:

$$b = \frac{n\Sigma xy - \Sigma x \Sigma y}{n\Sigma x^2 - (\Sigma x)^2}$$

$$a = \frac{\Sigma y}{n} - b\frac{\Sigma x}{n}$$

From the previous example — producing lines of code and their production cost — and using the Σx, Σx^2, Σy, and $\Sigma x \Sigma y$, the values of b and a give:

$$b = \frac{8 \times 652 - 36 \times 130}{8 \times 204 - (36)^2} = 1.5952$$

$$a = \frac{130}{8} - \frac{1.5952 \times 36}{8} = 9.0716$$

Therefore the regression equation is:

$$y = 9.07 + 1.60x$$

This indicates that for every 1000 lines of code being produced the cost of the service will be 1.60 times that, i.e. 1,600 mu, and with nothing being produced the cost of the service will be 9,070 mu.

To determine how well the regression equation fits the data and can be used as a good predictor for determining the dependent variable, it is worth determining the *coefficient of determination*. This is given by r^2. In the foregoing example the coefficient of determination will be 0.668^2 which is equal to 0.446. Hence it can be assumed that about 45 per cent of the service cost can be explained by the selected regression equation.

For an investigation of regression equations that are not linear the reader is recommended to refer to other specialist texts (Black, 1994).

Time Series

A time series can be likened to a set of bivarate data (data pairs) where the dependent variable of interest, such as production, is related to an independent variable, measured in units of time. The changing value of the dependent variable over a period of time is called a time series. Correlation and regression analysis which require the relationship between variables to be linear has little applicability because this rarely occurs in time series.

Analysis of a time series can provide details of behaviour of the dependent variable over a past time period — that is, for the period for which there is data. By making the assumption that the future will be exactly as the past, then the results of analysis will allow predictions to be made of the future value of the dependent variable. However, this method of forecasting is only suitable for the immediate future (up to five time periods ahead); other methods should be used for long-range forecasting. For time series analysis, two techniques are considered to be the easiest to understand, namely:

- the decomposition model;

- exponential smoothing.

An explanation will be provided here of the first form of modelling; the reader is advised to consult one of the more specialised texts listed at the end of Part 4 to read about exponential smoothing. Some of these texts will also provide guidance on long-term forecasting methods.

There are four components to the decomposition model: trend, seasonality, cyclic behaviour, and randomness. Trend refers to the past behaviour of the data, which can be increasing, decreasing, constant or nearly constant. Seasonality refers to fluctuations that have repeated themselves at periods of time in the past. Cyclic behaviour refers to the ups and downs that are often the pattern of data sets. Randomness refers to the variation that is always present in a time series. Figure 4-22 shows an example of a time series, based on the figures in the accompanying table.

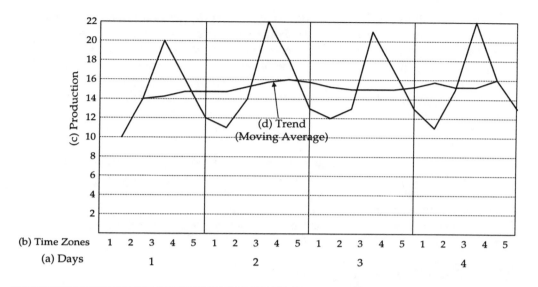

(a) Day	(b) Zone	(c) Production	(d) Moving Average	(e) SD	(f) S	(g) Predicted Sales	(h) Error
1	1	10					
	2	14					
	3	20	(10+14+20+16+12)/5 = 14.4	5.6	6.12	20.52	−0.52
	4	16	(14+20+16+12+11)/5 = 14.6	1.4	1.89	16.49	−0.49
	5	12	(20+16+12+11+14)/5 = 14.6	−2.6	−2.51	12.09	−0.09
2	1	11	(16+12+11+14+22)/5 = 14.6	−3.6	−3.85	10.75	0.25
	2	14	(12+11+14+22+18)/5 = 15.4	−1.4	−1.65	13.75	0.25
	3	22	(11+14+22+18+13)/5 = 15.6	6.4	6.12	21.72	0.28
	4	18	(14+22+18+13+12)/5 = 15.8	2.2	1.89	17.69	0.31
	5	13	(22+18+13+12+13)/5 = 15.6	−2.6	−2.51	13.09	−0.09
3	1	12	(18+13+12+13+21)/5 = 15.4	−3.4	−3.85	11.55	0.45
	2	13	(13+12+13+21+17)/5 = 15.2	−3.2	−1.65	13.55	−0.55
	3	21	(12+13+21+17+13)/5 = 15.2	5.8	6.12	21.32	−0.32
	4	17	(13+21+17+13+11)/5 = 15.0	2.0	1.89	16.89	0.11
	5	13	(21+17+13+11+15)/5 = 15.4	−2.4	−2.51	12.89	0.11
4	1	11	(17+13+11+15+22)/5 = 15.6	−4.6	−3.85	11.75	−0.75
	2	15	(13+11+15+22+16)/5 = 15.4	−0.4	−1.65	13.75	1.25
	3	22	(11+15+22+16+13)/5 = 15.4	6.6	6.12	21.52	0.48
	4	16				.	
	5	13					

Figure 4-22: Example of Time Series

The example shows a plot of production (c) against the periods of a day (b) which has been divided into 5 zones of 1½ hours each; this is referred to as the "series period". To isolate the trends, it is necessary to use the concept of moving averages. By taking the production average of five zones and starting with zone 1 in day 1, the moving average can be calculated as shown in the Table. The average of each group of five time zones is placed alongside the mid-point of each group; this is calculated in column (d). The reader is directed to specialist texts (Anderson et al., 1995) on how to isolate the trend when dealing with an even number of zones.

The complete moving average has been superimposed on the original time series diagram and is shown in Figure 4-22. The moving average concept has smoothed the data and therefore this second "time series", column (d), represents the trend. The trend appears to be fairly constant.

Seasonal swings can be normalised by either one or other of the following formulae:

$$Y = T + S + C + R \quad \text{(additive model)}$$

$$Y = T \times S \times C \times R \quad \text{(multiplicative model)}$$

where Y is the variable of interest, T is the trend, S is the seasonal component, C is the cyclic component, and R is the random element. The additive model is used when the seasonal swings are a constant difference from the trend. The multiplicative model is used when the seasonal swings are a percentage of the trend.

In the illustrated example, to obtain the seasonal differences, column (e), the additive model has been used and rearranged to $Y - T = S + C + R$. Column (e) results are obtained by subtracting column (d) results from column (c) results. This indicates that the value of the variable minus the trend value at any zone will give the seasonal difference plus the cyclic and random components. The cyclic component can be isolated only when the values of the variable Y are available over an extended period. As such information is quite rare it is normal to ignore the cyclic effects and accept that its effects, if any, will form part of the random element.

A way of examining seasonal differences is to construct a matrix of cells as below and place the differences in the correct cell. The average row gives the result of the average of the seasonal difference relative to each time zone:

Zone	1	2	3	4	5	
Day 1			5.6	1.4	–2.6	
Day 2	–3.6	–1.4	6.4	2.2	–2.6	
Day 3	–3.4	–3.2	5.8	2.0	–2.4	
Day 4	–4.6	–0.4	6.6			
Average	–3.87	–1.67	6.1	1.87	–2.53	$\Sigma = -0.10$
Adjusted Average	–3.85	–1.65	6.12	1.89	–2.51	$\Sigma = 0.00$

The adjusted average is obtained by taking the sum of the averages of all time zones, which is one-fifth of –0.10, i.e. –0.02 and subtracting this from the averages to obtain the figures in the bottom row. These are then placed in column (f) of the foregoing Table of results. Column (f) is added to column (d) to obtain column (g), the predicted sales.

Once the trend and seasonal components have been isolated it is a good idea to analyse the errors. Column (h) is the result of the error calculation and is obtained by subtracting column (g) from column (c).

One purpose for time series analysis is to forecast future values, say the next five time periods, of the series. Remember that, as stated at the beginning of this sub-Section, time series is not a method to be used for long-range forecasting. The procedure requires extrapolation of the trend and seasonally adjusted series, as shown by column (g) in the illustrated example. There are various methods of extrapolating. One method is linear regression, but this requires the past trend line to be approximately linear.

An essential aspect of any project management is planning for the future. As part of the decision-making process time series is an important technique which assists in both structuring the problem and analysing the problem. Good judgement, intuition and awareness are all useful attributes which give an individual a feel for what is likely to happen. Converting such feelings into numbers helps common sense.

Linear Programming

Linear programming is a problem-solving approach that has been developed to help managers make decisions. It is used when there is a need to maximise or minimise some variable. Another property of all linear programming problems is that there are constraints, or restrictions, which limit the degree to which objectives can be achieved. There is a special class of linear programming problem that is generally referred to as "network flow problems". The reader will find such problems also referred to as transportation and assignment algorithms (see Anderson et al., 1995).

Linear programming is concerned with the management of scarce resources. Its application is when there are two or more activities competing for these limited resources. Let's look at an illustration of a computer company where the objective is to maximise profits from the manufacture and sales of notebooks (N) and desktops (D) to a particular client. Within every ten computers to be sold, 15 mu of profit must come from notebooks and 45 mu of profit must come from desk-tops. The total number of labour hours needed to make notebooks is denoted by 2N and that required to make desktops is denoted by D. The sum of these two components must be less than or equal to 160 hours in any one day.

Because of a computer industry-wide restriction in the availability of "transducers", part of the electronic circuitry used in computers, the company has been restricted to a supply of 120 transducers per day. One transducer is required in each notebook and 2 in each desktop. Writing this information in mathematical form gives:

1) $P_{max} = 15N + 45D$ (profit)
2) $2N + D \leq 160$ (labour)
3) $N + 2D \leq 120$ (materials)
4) N and $D \geq 0$ (only positive values are sought)

If the inequality signs in equations 2 and 3 are replaced with equalities and a matrix prepared that compares the two variables N and D we have:

Constraint		N	D
Labour	(a)	0	160
	(b)	80	0
Transducers	(c)	0	60
	(d)	120	0

These two sets of data can then be plotted on a diagram as shown by Figure 4-23.

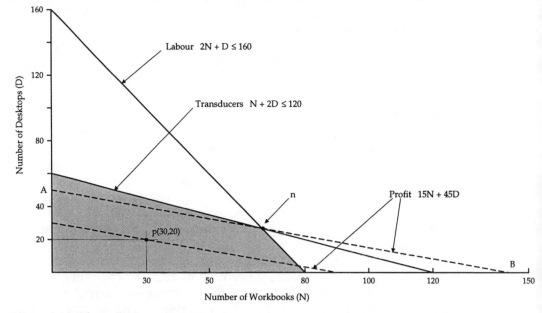

Figure 4-23: Linear Programming Diagram

The region that satisfies equations 2, 3 and 4 has been shaded; this is also referred to as the *feasible region*. This region can be found by drawing straight lines using the data in line (a), i.e. D is equal to 160 when N equals 0, and (b) i.e. N is equal to 80 when D is equal to 0. The resulting line satisfies the labour formula of $2N + D \leq 160$. The same procedure is used to plot the data in the matrix for transducers.

Point p is any point (30,20) which will satisfy equations 2, 3 and 4. By substituting the co-ordinates into equation 1 we get:

$P = (15 \times 30) + (45 \times 20) = 1350$ mu

When N is zero then D will be 30, and when D is zero N will be 90. This "profit" line is drawn on the graph and, as expected, passes through point p.

Is it possible to increase the P = 1350 value? As any profit line will always be parallel to the one drawn it can be observed that it will be necessary to increase the 1350 value because the profit line will be maximised when, remaining parallel to the profit line on the graph, will be furthest located from the origin (0,0). It is obvious that the profit line must coincide with a corner point of the feasible region; in this case point n. The co-ordinates of point n can be obtained by using simultaneous equations to solve equations 2 and 3, namely:

$$2N + D = 160$$
$$N + 2D = 120$$

x 2, change the sign, and add

$$2N + D = 160$$
$$\underline{-2N - 4D = -240}$$
$$0 - 3D = -80$$

Therefore D = 26.7 and N = 66.65 gives the position of point n. Substituting these values into equation 1 gives:

$$P_{max} = 15N + 45D = (15 \times 66.65) + (45 \times 66.65) = 3999 \text{ mu.}$$

The maximised profit line has been drawn on the diagram and is shown as A to B.

This has been a very fundamental introduction to graphical linear programming. Once again the reader is referred to the specialist texts at the end of Part 4 for recommended further reading.

Table 1: Discount Tables — What 1 mu Due in the Future is Worth Today (Present Worth)

Years	6% Present Worth	7% Present Worth	8% Present Worth	9% Present Worth	10% Present Worth	12% Present Worth	14% Present Worth	16% Present Worth	18% Present Worth	20% Present Worth	Years
1	0.943396	0.934579	0.926926	0.917431	0.909091	0.892857	0.877193	0.862069	0.847458	0.833333	1
2	0.889996	0.873439	0.857339	0.841680	0.826446	0.797194	0.769468	0.743163	0.718184	0.694444	2
3	0.839169	0.816298	0.793832	0.772183	0.751315	0.711780	0.674972	0.640658	0.608631	0.578704	3
4	0.792094	0.762895	0.735030	0.708425	0.683013	0.635518	0.592080	0.552291	0.515789	0.482253	4
5	0.747258	0.712986	0.680583	0.649931	0.620921	0.567427	0.519369	0.476113	0.437109	0.401878	5
6	0.704961	0.666342	0.630170	0.596267	0.564474	0.506631	0.455587	0.410443	0.370132	0.334898	6
7	0.665057	0.622750	0.583490	0.547034	0.513158	0.452349	0.399637	0.353830	0.313925	0.279082	7
8	0.627412	0.582009	0.540269	0.501866	0.466507	0.403883	0.350559	0.305025	0.266038	0.232568	8
9	0.591898	0.543934	0.500249	0.460428	0.424098	0.360610	0.307508	0.262953	0.225456	0.193807	9
10	0.558395	0.508349	0.463193	0.422411	0.385543	0.321973	0.269744	0.226684	0.191064	0.161506	10
11	0.526788	0.475093	0.428883	0.387533	0.350494	0.287476	0.236617	0.195417	0.161919	0.134588	11
12	0.496969	0.444012	0.397114	0.355535	0.318631	0.256675	0.207559	0.168463	0.137220	0.112157	12
13	0.468839	0.414964	0.367698	0.326170	0.289664	0.229174	0.182069	0.145227	0.116288	0.093464	13
14	0.442301	0.387817	0.340461	0.299246	0.263331	0.204620	0.159710	0.125195	0.098549	0.077887	14
15	0.417265	0.362446	0.315242	0.274538	0.239392	0.182696	0.140096	0.107927	0.083516	0.064905	15
16	0.393646	0.338735	0.291890	0.251870	0.217629	0.163122	0.122897				16
17	0.371364	0.316574	0.270269	0.231073	0.197845	0.145644	0.107800				17
18	0.350344	0.295864	0.250249	0.211994	0.179859	0.130040	0.094561				18
19	0.330513	0.276508	0.231712	0.194490	0.163508	0.116107	0.082948				19
20	0.311805	0.258419	0.214548	0.178431	0.148644	0.103667	0.072762	0.051385	0.036506	0.026084	20
25	0.232999	0.184249	0.146018	0.115968	0.092296	0.058823	0.037790	0.024465	0.015957	0.010482	25
30	0.174110	0.131367	0.099377	0.075371	0.057309	0.033378	0.019627	0.011648	0.006975	0.004212	30
35	0.130105	0.093663	0.067635	0.048986	0.035584	0.018940	0.010194	0.005546	0.003048	0.001693	35
40	0.097222	0.066780	0.046031	0.031838	0.022095	0.010747	0.005294	0.002640	0.001333	0.000680	40

Formula: $P = F\left(\dfrac{1}{(1+i)^n}\right)$

Table 2: Discount Tables — What 1 mu Payable Periodically is Worth Today (Present Worth of Annuity)

Years	6% Present Worth	7% Present Worth	8% Present Worth	9% Present Worth	10% Present Worth	12% Present Worth	14% Present Worth	16% Present Worth	18% Present Worth	20% Present Worth	Years
1	0.943396	0.934570	0.925926	0.917431	0.909001	0.89286	0.877193	0.862089	0.847458	0.833333	1
2	1.833393	1.808018	1.783265	1.759111	1.735537	1.69005	1.646661	1.605232	1.565642	1.527778	2
3	2.673012	2.624316	2.577097	2.531295	2.486852	2.40182	2.321632	2.245890	2.174273	2.106481	3
4	3.465106	3.387211	3.312127	3.229720	3.169865	3.03735	2.913712	2.798181	2.690062	2.588735	4
5	4.212364	4.100197	3.992710	3.889651	3.790787	3.60477	3.433081	3.274294	3.127171	2.990612	5
6	4.917324	4.766540	4.622880	4.485919	4.355261	4.11140	3.888668	3.684736	3.497603	3.325510	6
7	5.582381	5.389289	5.206370	5.032953	4.868419	4.56375	4.288305	4.038565	3.811528	3.604592	7
8	6.209794	5.971299	5.746639	5.534819	5.334926	4.96764	4.638864	4.343591	4.077566	3.837160	8
9	6.801602	6.515232	6.246888	5.995247	5.759024	5.32825	4.946372	4.606544	4.303022	4.030967	9
10	7.360087	7.023582	6.710081	6.417658	6.144567	5.65023	5.216116	4.833227	4.494086	4.197472	10
11	7.886875	7.498674	7.138964	6.805191	6.495061	5.93771	5.452733	5.028644	4.656005	4.327060	11
12	8.383844	7.942686	7.536078	7.160725	6.813692	6.19437	5.660292	5.197107	4.793225	4.439217	12
13	8.852683	8.357651	7.903770	7.486904	7.103356	6.42356	5.842362	5.342334	4.909513	4.532681	13
14	9.294984	8.746468	8.244237	7.786150	7.366687	6.62818	6.002072	5.467529	5.008062	4.610567	14
15	9.712249	9.107914	8.559479	8.060688	7.606080	6.81088	6.142168	5.575456	5.091578	4.675473	15
16	10.105895	9.446649	8.851369	8.312558	7.823709	6.97399	6.265060				16
17	10.477260	9.763223	9.121638	8.543631	8.021553	7.11962	6.372859				17
18	10.827603	10.059087	9.371887	8.755625	8.201412	7.24969	6.467420				18
19	11.158116	10.335595	9.603599	8.950115	8.364920	7.36578	6.550369				19
20	11.409921	10.594014	9.818147	9.128546	8.513564	7.46943	6.623131	5.928844	5.352744	4.869580	20
25	12.783356	11.653583	10.674776	9.822580	9.077040	7.84314	6.872927	6.097094	5.466905	4.947590	25
30	13.764831	12.409041	11.257783	10.273654	9.426914	8.05516	7.002664	6.177200	5.516805	4.978940	30
35	14.498246	12.947672	11.654568	10.566821	9.644159	8.17548	7.070045	6.215337	5.538618	4.991535	35
40	15.046297	13.331700	11.824613	10.757380	9.779051	8.24375	7.105041	6.233500	5.548150	4.996600	40

Formula: $P = A \left(\dfrac{(1+i)^n - 1}{i(1+i)^n} \right)$

Summary of Key Points

- Defined as a process rather than a single act, decision-making is characterised as a skill that can be learned and developed through practice. Good managers, it is said, are those who make good decisions. Everything that a manager does towards goal accomplishment should be based on a conscious, identified strategy that has the highest probability for success.

- Although qualitative skills are, to a greater or lesser extent, inherent in the decision maker, the skills of the quantitative approach can be learned only by studying the techniques available. A decision-maker can increase their effectiveness by learning more about quantitative methodology and by understanding better its contribution to the decision-making process.

- The four key elements contained within a decision are: the decision body, the decision options, the uncontrollable factors, and the consequences. Decisions may be classified as being: structured or unstructured, dependent or independent, and strategic or operational.

- The process of formal model building requires us to develop an accurate reflection of our perceptions of the decision area to aid the decision process. This can be done in one of three ways: descriptive models, analogue models, and relationship models.

- Cause-and-effect diagrams are a useful step in the process of understanding decision factors and the decision itself, however they are incapable of describing the nature of the relationships. To do that it is necessary at times to use symbolic models — in other words, mathematical models.

- Payoff tables are frequently the best method for representing non-complex decisions; complex decisions can be represented more lucidly in what is referred to as a "decision tree".

- Decision tree analysis is designed primarily to present a decision problem, with the alternatives and their relative merits, in a systematic manner that helps identify and evaluate the whole problem, and helps in the selection of the "best" decision or strategy.

- There are three methods of making assessments of chances, or more popularly called probabilities. These methods are: subjective approach, empirical approach, and *a priori* approach.

- Often we are confronted with probability problems where there is considerable data and we need to establish if there is a pattern to the data and if it belongs to one of the well-established patterns of data. These standard patterns are called *probability distributions*.

- Perhaps the most important distribution used to describe a continuous random variable is the normal probability distribution. In order to distinguish one normal curve from another we need to know the mean (where the peak occurs) and the standard deviation which demonstrates how spread out the distribution is.

- An economic evaluation of a project is based on estimates of the costs of the effort and resource usage, and of the monetary benefits expected. These are analysed with respect to time to find the rate of cash flow (in mu per year) and the cumulative cash flow (in mu) throughout the anticipated effective life of the project.

- The purpose of an evaluation is to assess the economic attractiveness or desirability of a project. The general shape of the cumulative cash flow curve itself is a qualitative guide to this. Many quantitative measures or indices are in use. Four types of such indices are: payback time, return on investment, net present value, and discounted cash flow return.

- "Payback time" and "return on investment" select particular features of the project cumulative cash flow and ignore others. For instance, they take no account of the pattern of cash flow during a project. The other indices, net present value and discounted cash flow return, are more comprehensive because they take account of the changing pattern of project net cash flow. They also take account of the "time value" of money.

- The greater the positive NPV for a project, the more economically attractive it is. A project with a negative NPV is not a profitable proposition. If, however, a project is not concerned with making a profit, but with meeting a necessary objective at the minimum overall cost, its NPV will be negative and the economic aim in considering alternatives is to reduce the negative NPC to as small a level as possible.

- The higher the value of the DCFR for a project, the more attractive it is. The minimum acceptable value of the DCFR is the cost of capital or market rate for the project. For a value of the DCFR greater than this, the project will show a profit; for a lesser value it will show a loss.

- Many situations are characterised by multiple criteria, many of which cannot be directly related to a form of quantitative measurement. The decision-making process in cases incorporating multiple criteria can be facilitated considerably by arranging the relevant alternatives and decision criteria in a simple organised fashion. An initial step is to identify both the alternatives to be considered and the criteria relevant to the decision to be made. This is followed by scoring each alternative against each criteria in decreasing order of importance.

- Project teams often have to deal with data where the need is to look at two variables simultaneously. Correlation coefficient measures the strength of the association between the variables. The correlation coefficient is measured on a scale between -1 and $+1$, so that -1 indicates a perfect negative correlation, $+1$ measures a perfect positive correlation, and 0 indicates no correlation.

- The technique of linear regression attempts to define the relationship between the independent variable and the dependent variable by means of a linear equation of the type $y = a + bx$. This is the simplest formula between two variables; fortunately many relationships can at least be approximated by this type of relationship.

- analysis of a time series can provide details of behaviour of the dependent variable over a past time period, that is, for the period for which there is data. By making the assumption that the future will be exactly as the past then the results of analysis will allow predictions to be made of the future value of the dependent variable.

- linear programming is a problem-solving approach that has been developed to help managers make decisions. It is used when there is a need to maximise or minimise some variable. Another property of all linear programming problems is that there are constraints, or restrictions, which limit the degree to which objectives can be achieved.

References

References used in the development of Part 4:

Allen, Derek H. (1991), *Economic Evaluation of Projects — A Guide*, 3rd edition, Institution of Chemical Engineers.

Anderson, David R., Sweeney, Dennis J. and Williams, Thomas A. (1995), *Quantitative Methods for Business*, 6th edition; West Publishing Company.

Black, Ken (1994), *Business Statistics: Contemporary Decision-Making*, West Publishing Company.

Churchman, C.W., Ackoff, R.L. and Arnoff, E.L. (1957), *Introduction to Operations Research*, John Wiley and Sons.

Cooke Steve, and Slack, Nigel (1991), *Making Management Decisions*, 2nd edition, Prentice Hall International (UK) Ltd.

Goodwin, Paul and Wright, George (1991), *Decision Analysis for Management Judgement*, John Wiley and Sons Ltd.

Humphreys, Kenneth K. (1991), *Jelen's Cost and Optimization Engineering*, 3rd edition, McGraw-Hill International Editions.

La Monica, Elaine (1994), *Management in Health Care*, Macmillan.

Morris, Clare (1996), *Quantitative Approaches in Business Studies*, 4th edition, Pitman Publishing.

Oakshott, L.A. (1993), *Quantitative Approaches to Decision-Making*; DP Publications.

Peck, M. Scott (1990), *The Road Less Travelled*, Arrow Books Limited.

ORGANISATIONAL THEORIES, ORGANISATIONS AND PEOPLE

Part 5 commences with a brief history of the development of organisational theories in the developed world. This is followed by an overview of a range of organisational structures currently available in the projects' environment.

Part 5 also deals with the management of project human resources, principally the skills and abilities consistent with achieving success in projects. Major people-related problems encountered in projects and the linkage between problems and skills are covered.

From a range of project organisational structures available to a performing organisation, the advantages and disadvantages of five different types are examined. Also discussed are the results of significant related research which indicates how the performing organisation should organise its project teams.

The role of the project manager (the responsible person leading the team/ project) is discussed; their competencies, skills, and training are presented. These aspects are linked to research findings and the known personal characteristics consistent with achieving project targets and delivering requirements.

The use of profiling to identify the natural team role that an individual performs within a project will be demonstrated through the use of self-perception profiling, linked to Belbin's team role characteristics.

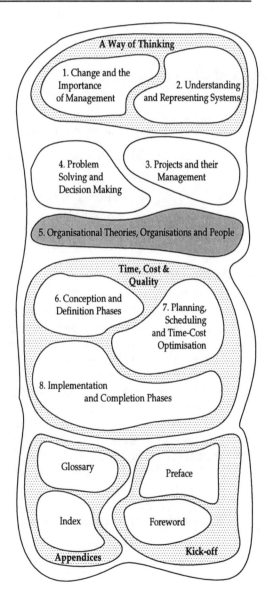

SECTION 1: ORGANISATIONAL THEORIES

Contents

- Aims and Objectives
- Scientific Management
- "Human Relations" Management
- Industrial Psychology
- Maslow's Theory of Motivation
- Theory X and Theory Y

Aims and Objectives

The aims and objectives of Section 1 are to:

- Outline the impacts of F.W. Taylor's work on management techniques;

- Describe the differences in concept between "scientific" and "human relations" management;

- Show the contributions of people such as Argyris and Maslow;

- Define theory X (classical organisational theory) and theory Y (nonclassical organisational theory) and explain the differences between the theories.

Scientific Management

From the unsophisticated 1930s to the relatively sophisticated current time there has been a fairly significant momentum in the discipline of management. There are no less than six schools of thought; it is hardly surprising that the on-looking individual is confused and the student of management frustrated in trying to understand the development of the subject.

The name of F.W. Taylor was introduced under the sub-Section "Randomness and Chance", in Section 2 of Part 1. Taylor's early publications were on piece-rate systems, shop management and similar topics; these were expanded into his book, *The Principles of Scientific Management*, in 1911. His work subsequent to 1911 and certain aspects of earlier work were collected in 1947 and published under the title *Scientific Management*.

Taylor (1856–1915) was obsessed with the idea of maximising efficiency in an organisation in order to maximise profits. He was one of the founders of the now well-established management techniques we know as organisation and methods (O and M) study. He assumed that:

- people could be related to their work, rather like machines, and made as efficient as it was theoretically possible to make them;

- properly used (monetary) incentives would get people to work harder to earn more;

- people would see the need to co-operate with management — the financial rewards from doing so would benefit the firm (more money) and the workers (increased wages).

Taylor could be described as the "father" of scientific management.He used his experience of the steel industry in the US to come to the view that all was not well in modern industry. Managers approached their jobs in arbitrary rule-of-thumb ways. Workers were casual and lackadaisical in meeting their work commitments.

He considered that the main obstacle to efficiency was a failure by managers to find ways to co-ordinate and control workers' output, and a failure to devise fair and satisfactory ways of paying the workers to ensure full co-operation and the desired output. Taylor recommended making management a science, resting on fixed principles instead of more or less hazy ideas. Taylor preached the doctrine of "cost effectiveness". Cost effectiveness implied control, which is really the central pivot of Taylor's message.

The main significance of Taylor's work was that it demonstrated the possibility and importance of a systematic analysis of business operations, and of the scope for using "scientific" methods in a new field.

"Human Relations" Management

Elton Mayo (1880–1949) was an industrial psychologist who, early in his career, used scientific management principles in his applied research work. He became well known for the work which he and his team did at the Western Electric Company's Hawthorne works in Chicago. There are many publications on management theory or management history that fully describe the Hawthorne tests.

The basic conclusions from the Hawthorne experiments are:

- work is a group activity;

- workers do not normally act or react as individuals but as members of groups. The need for security and belonging is more important than the work environment;

- these groups need not be the formal groups set up by management; informal groups throughout the factory exercise control over the way individual workers think and act;

- therefore, levels of work are not set by physical abilities, but by group attitudes.

Those who supported these ideas became known as the "human relations school".The human relations approach stressed the importance of the informal group leader in setting the group standards. Also, if the formal leader (supervisor) could become the informal one, he could get his standards accepted. This leads to a need for communication between all levels of employees for participation and decision-making and for a democratic style of leadership. The human relations approach is very much about "being nice to workers".

Once management developed social groups on the job and provided them with democratic, participating and communicative managers, then organisational life would be happy. Thus, paternalism was fostered; human relations experts appeared (and are still with us); the firm's directors began to talk about "teams" and "team work".

The teachings of the scientific management and human relations schools are in opposition to one another. The Taylor view was *what was best for the firm would also be best for the worker*; the human relations view was *what was best for the worker would be best for the firm*.

The two viewpoints gave rise to two related concepts. Scientific management pointed to the importance of the formal organisation — the hierarchy, the rules and regulations, the bureaucracy. Human resources management stressed the informal group — the attitudes, opinions and ideas of its members.

Industrial Psychology

From about 1900, industrial psychology was applied, initially concerning itself with such matters as fatigue and accident proneness. Later came the introduction of IQ and various aptitude tests for the selection and training of personnel. Later still, the interest shifted to the role of managers and management in the organisation. The interaction between managers and the managed and the amount of conflict that existed between them became the subjects of study by what we call "organisational psychologists". There are a large number of writers in the field of organisational psychology but the views of Argyris, Maslow, and McGregor are perhaps worth commenting on because of what they represented.

Argyris claimed that everyone has potential or undeveloped powers which, given the right environment, can be developed and fully realised. He approved of the development of people's potential, as it benefits not only the individual (in terms of maturity) but all those around, including the organisation to which the individual belongs. Regrettably, as we know, the majority of industrial and commercial organisations are organised to inhibit such personal development.

To explain the ways in which people behave at work, it is necessary to examine how far they have progressed from the childish ways of their earlier years. Argyris sets out seven different ways people, in a western environment, can be thought to develop.

from childhood	*to maturity*
• infant passivity	• increasing adult activity
• state of dependence on others	• relative independence as adult
• limited range of behaviour	• different, varied behaviour patterns
• erratic, casual, quickly forgotten interests	• deeper interests: doing things for their own sake
• short time perspective (the "now" dictates behaviour)	• longer time perspective (past, present and future all dictate behaviour)
• have an inferior/subordinate position in the family	• aspiring to equal/superior position in respect of fellows
• lack self-awareness, control over feelings/behaviour	• has self-awareness, can control behaviour, develops sense of integrity

Argyris's hypothesis was that, should anything interfere with or stop the development process in the growth from childhood to maturity, this would be harmful.

Argyris also considered the organisation: who chooses the goals, who sets the strategies it follows. We know that the impact made by any organisation upon any individual depends upon the organisation and the individual. For the sake of argument, if we take a relatively "Argyris mature" person in a formal organisation run on scientific management principles, then the impact between this person and the organisation means the individual:

- has little control over their working world;

- is expected to be passive, dependent and subordinate;

- uses only a few trivial abilities or skills repeatedly;

- is expected to produce.

The mature person is expected to behave in a less than mature way. This describes with reasonable accuracy the work lot of a great many people in western society. To cope with this it is not the individual but the organisation that must change. Management must:

- aim at the full development of individual potential;

- allow a more widespread involvement of subordinates, and let them express their ideas and feelings;

- see that jobs are "enlarged", not only to de-specialise them as much as possible, but to use people's abilities much more fully. Let people have more control over what is done in their own sphere of activities.

Maslow's Theory of Motivation

A.H. Maslow's theories (1908–1970) dealt with human need. His theories are simple, wide in scope, easy to understand, and have a convincing ring about them. They have been widely copied, or included in elaborate theories more or less unaltered.

Why do people go to work? To go further, why do people work at all and of those who work, why do some people work more enthusiastically or reliably than others? By observing any group of workers doing the same job, you will see that some do it well, others badly, some do it grudgingly and others gladly. This is true irrespective of the job role or the person's position within the organisation. Levels of ability can be put forward as the reason. Skill, expertise, training can all be put forward as the reason for work quality; a poorly trained operator could turn out bad work. However, explanations of this kind cannot cover every case. The reason given is that different work performances often reflect different levels of motivation, ambition, energy, drive and commitment to work.

Maslow attempts to solve the problem of what motivates people to work or do anything with his theory of the "hierarchy of human needs". He starts with the assumption that every human being has needs, the forces that drive them to act, and these needs can be arranged in a kind of hierarchy.

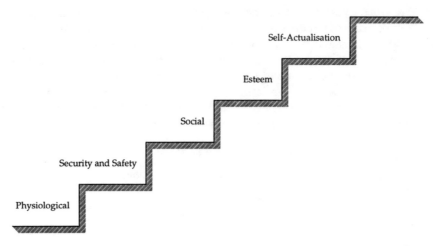

Figure 5-1: Maslow's Hierarchy of Needs

In Figure 5-1, as the steps are ascended, so the needs are of increasingly higher order.

The first needs, the *physiological* needs, are the basic needs necessary for the support of human life. Food, water, oxygen, sex, exercise, etc. are all characterised by the fact that they can be identified and linked to separate systems within the body. For example food and water are linked to the digestive system, oxygen is linked to the respiratory system, sex is linked to the reproductive system, and exercise is linked to the muscular and skeletal systems.

As Maslow puts it, the physiological needs are the most important of all. Survival of the individual and the human race are paramount. After the basic needs are satisfied, higher needs emerge and these are the next immediate matters to dominate human behaviour. Once these are satisfied, then newer and still higher needs emerge and so on. Satisfaction of a need means it is no longer important to us for the time being; only unsatisfied needs motivate people to do things.

The next level of need above the physiological need is the *security and safety* need. People in western society prefer a safe, orderly, and predictable world, and even if they may not show it on the surface, have a greater liking for the familiar than the unfamiliar. Safety needs are great motivators; whole societies can be brought together by danger. So the security of the steady job, constant income, home, life and property insurance policies, and the like are all important needs.

"Man" is a herd animal who prefers to live in groups which are often larger than the immediate family. Even in quite primitive societies a person may belong to different groups simultaneously. The average person may be a member of a family, a work group, a leisure group, a political group, an informal group, etc. The need to belong is very strong. Not to belong is to be divorced from your family partner, sacked from your job, dropped from the sports team, voted off the local council, ignored in the bar. In general, humans need "to receive and give love". This is what Maslow meant by "*social need*".

Most people want to belong and be respected as a person. Most people like praise and the approval and *esteem* of others. Group respect is sought through reputation, recognition, attention, importance and appreciation, and is satisfied through gaining self-confidence, adequacy, a feeling of being wanted and being useful in the world. Thwarting of these needs leads to inadequacy, feelings of inferiority, weakness and helplessness.

Self-respect is the other ego/esteem need and this relates to confidence, independence and the need to "hold your head high". Even if well-fed, with a secure income and with fellow human beings to relate to and be respected by, a person will become dissatisfied if they are not doing all that they are both capable of and like doing. *Self-actualisation* is not in itself a creative activity, but much creative work stems from the desire to satisfy this need. The whole emphasis is on the need for people to develop their whole personality, to grow and make the best use of their abilities, and respond to challenges.

There are exceptions to this general theory; Maslow makes the following comments:

- there are creative people who are motivated by the self-realisation need, despite or in spite of the fact that other needs are not satisfied.

- people may have very low levels of aspiration if their life experience has been narrow.

- satisfied needs lead to new wants, as we have seen. The new wants continue even when the lower needs suddenly become unsatisfied.

- some people have high ideals, religious views or values, which they will maintain against public opinion, the state and armed force. The need to maintain their values outweighs any other need.

Maslow's theory is worthy of consideration. Maslow's ideas are widely known in Europe, as well as America, and greatly influenced the work of others including Douglas McGregor (1901–1964) who drew heavily upon the need hierarchy.

Theory X and Theory Y

McGregor is best known for his analysis of behaviour of people at work. In what is known as "theory X", he sets down what he believes managers have felt about the workers in their charge and the traditional views of workers' attitudes to work. In his other theory, "theory Y", McGregor provided what he considered to be a much more realistic explanation of workers' motives and general behaviour.

Theory X behaviour can be summarised as follows:

- the average human being has an inherent dislike of work, and will avoid it if possible.

- because of the dislike for work, most people must be coerced, controlled, directed, threatened with punishment to get them to put adequate effort toward the achievement of organisational objectives.

- the average human being prefers to be directed, wishes to avoid responsibility, has relatively little ambition and wants security above all.

Theory X behaviour which is "management by control" relies upon external control of human behaviour and believes that the average person is indolent, irresponsible, resistant to change, gullible and not very bright. The implication of theory X is that about 95 per cent of the people are, at best, average and the brilliant 5 per cent have to do the world's thinking. If people are treated as if they are dumb, rebellious, easily led, then they may come to believe they are inferior and. furthermore, they will almost certainly rebel against such treatment.

If they rebel, the manager's beliefs about people are reinforced. The more they rebel, the more these notions are confirmed. The manager reacts by enforcing more control and applying more discipline. Managers who tend to hold views similar to those expressed in theory X, are called "theory X managers". Theory X is also synonymous with the term "classical organisational theory" and was primarily practised by organisations prior to 1950.

When setting out his alternative explanation of general human behaviour, McGregor called it theory Y, which can be summarised as follows:

- the expenditure of physical and mental effort in work is as natural as play or rest.

- external control and the threat of punishment are not the only means for bringing about organisational objectives. People will work and discipline themselves in the service of objectives to which they are committed.

- people are committed to objectives in proportion to the rewards associated with achieving the objectives.

- the average human being learns under proper conditions not only to accept but to seek responsibility.

- the capacity to exercise a relatively high degree of imagination, ingenuity, and creativity in the solution of organisational problems is distributed widely, not narrowly, in the population.

- under the conditions of modern industrial life, the intellectual potential of the average human being is only partially utilised.

Theory Y behaviour which is "management by objectives" is based on more adequate knowledge of human nature and motivation. McGregor's belief was that people are not passive by nature.

Theory Y advocates what we now call "participative management", the situation where workers join in decision-making under the chairmanship or leadership of their immediate boss. Theory Y, which is synonymous with the term "non-classical organisational theory", has evolved from the criticisms of classical organisational theory.

Theory Y implies that poor performance lies with management's methods of organisation and control. The essential task of management is to arrange organisational conditions where opportunities are created for workers, through the removal of obstacles, the encouragement of growth and the provision of guidance.

It is important to realise that most, if not all, contemporary management practices are based on non-classical organisation theory. Non-classical organisation theory uses a situational approach to leadership and a leadership style that is based upon understanding the general systems theory (see "Systems Theory" in Part 2) which provides a means for studying people within their environment and as shapers of their environment (La Monica, 1994).

SECTION 2: PROJECT ORGANISATION STRUCTURES

Contents

- Aims and Objectives
- Performing Organisation Project Structures
- Functional Structure
- Functional Matrix Structure
- Balanced Matrix Structure
- Project Matrix Structure
- Project Team Structure
- A "Best Form" of Project Structure
- Organisational Influences

Aims and Objectives

The aims and objectives of Section 2 are to:

- Outline the range of project organisational options available to the performing organisation;

- Define the structure, strengths, and weaknesses of:
  ◊ Functional organisation
  ◊ Functional matrix
  ◊ Balanced matrix
  ◊ Project matrix
  ◊ Project team

- Describe the effectiveness of the different project organisational structures.

Performing Organisation Project Structures

A project is an organisation unit that has been dedicated to the attainment of a goal(s); in general the goals are the successful completion of a development product on time, within budget, and in conformance with predetermined performance specifications.

As we read in Part 3, project management involves the planning, organising, directing and controlling of resources which have been established to achieve the predetermined objectives and goals of something that is unique. As discussed in Section 1 of Part 3, traditional management, which is related to project management, is applied to *processes*. Processes are continuations of something; in other words doing the same task today, and the day after, and the days after that, etc. Traditional management has characteristics that are, to a large extent, the exact opposite of the characteristics of projects.

However, it is worth noting that within *one* organisation it is possible to have some people engaged in *projects* while others are involved with *processes*. A typical example of this would be a company which manufactures road kerbing; the kerbing, in precast concrete, is made in hundreds and thousands of units each day and each week respectively. Casting shop management and the activities of the shop-floor personnel are very likely to fall under the traditional management approach. Conversely, upper management within this company could be organised in teams because what they do is not repetitive, but will vary each day and will reflect the characteristics of projects (unique, uncertain and temporary). Whether they are organised in teams will very much depend upon the culture of the senior personnel.

Project management is characterised by methods of restructuring management and adopting special management techniques. The purpose of project management is to obtain better planning, execution and control of the use of existing resources. Also, project management is often used because traditional management structures cannot respond to the rapidly changing environments found in the pre-investment activities, the design, procurement and execution of a wide range of projects.

Projects are typically part of a performing organisation which is larger than the project: corporations, government agencies, health care institutions, international bodies, professional associations and others. Even when the project is the organisation (joint venture, partnering), the project will still be influenced by the performing organisation or the organisation that set it up.

The management function of organising is concerned with developing a structure or framework which relates all personnel, work assignments, and physical resources to each other and to the enterprise objective. Usually this framework is termed organisation structure.

All organisations require both division and integration of personnel, functions, and physical factors. Organisation structure provides the blueprint that denotes the manner of dividing and combining components so that co-ordination toward intended system objectives can be effected. Major factors affecting this design are:

- the stability and complexity of the outer environment;

- the degree of development of the inner technology;

- the aspirations and capabilities of the organisation's personnel.

Project organisational structures can be characterised as spanning a spectrum from functional to projectised with a variety of matrix structures in between (Project Management Institute, 1996). The *classical functional organisation* is a hierarchy (each employee has one clear superior) with staff grouped by speciality (e.g. production, marketing, engineering, accounting, etc.). At the opposite end of the spectrum is the *projectised organisation*. Staff are grouped by project and often dedicated to the project. *Matrix organisations* are a blend of functional and projectised characteristics.

An organisation has several options available when choosing a project structure. Each option has its own strengths and weaknesses; the type of structure chosen can significantly affect the success of the project. Although there are many variants, there are basically five alternative organisational structures that can be found in the projects' environment (Gobeli and Larson, 1987). These alternatives are functional, functional matrix, balanced matrix, project matrix and project team. A brief explanation of each type follows.

Functional Structure

The functional option is the classical command structure and is considered to be the most prevalent structure used in organising projects. Separate work groups, usually divided by discipline, each has a functional manager(s) (FM) responsible for all aspects of a discipline. The functional managers and the management hierarchy co-ordinate the various activities. Under this arrangement, the project manager does not exist. If they do, it is in name only with little responsibility and no authority.

The project work is segmented from the organisation's standard operations and assigned to relevant functional areas and/or groups. The staff members within each function are denoted by S as shown in the Figure which follows; this applies to each of the Figures from 5-2 to 5-6.

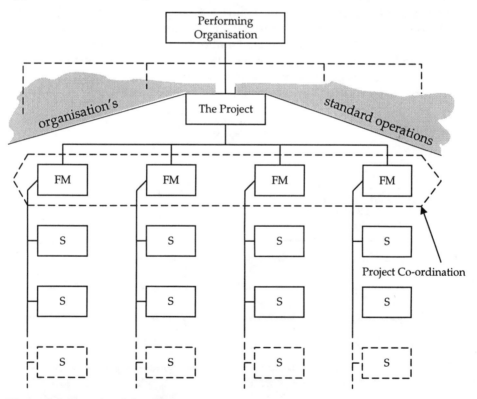

Figure 5-2: Functional Structure

Within the functional structure (see Figure 5-2), work is carried out within strict disciplines or departments. The functional managers liaise and co-ordinate the work at their level. Within this option there is therefore a large element of vertical work movement inside departments, with little horizontal integration except at the upper levels of organisational control.

This structure is therefore hierarchical, with functional units based on work or activity specialisation. A strength of the functional structure is its centralisation of similar resources. It is also considered easier to manage specialists if they are grouped together, with a functional head with training and experience within that particular discipline.

The weaknesses of this type of project organisational structure are:

- where there are multiple projects there is competition for resources;

- more emphasis is placed on function speciality (rather than on the goals of the project);

- there can be a lack of motivation and inertia.

Many companies use the function organisation structure for their project work as well as their standard operations.

Functional Matrix Structure

In the functional matrix option (Figure 5-3), the project work is segmented from the organisation's standard operations with, usually, a formally designated project "manager" who has very limited authority. The manager can be defined more accurately as a *project co-ordinator* with limited responsibility and no authority for achieving the project objectives or the completion of the project. This role is also referred to by some as "project management without risk".

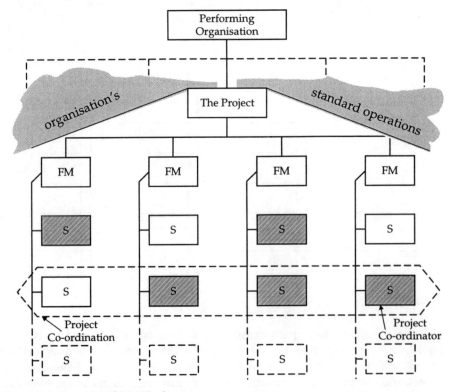

Figure 5-3: Functional Matrix Structure

The project co-ordinator co-ordinates the work across the functions; staff (S) will be assigned to work on the project but with direction on all matters coming from the FMs. The shaded boxes represent the staff that have been assigned to work on the project.

As an example, in the European construction industry, this role is predominantly played by a person or department, but more typically — on the large complex projects of an organisation — selected from one of the functional groups. For instance, either the building services consultant, the civil and structural consultant, the architectural practice, or other principal party will be appointed as the co-ordinator of the project. The primary point of this is that, although a manager formally exists, the role is normally restricted to planning and scheduling with no responsibility for the overall completion of the project.

Balanced Matrix Structure

In the balanced matrix structure, the project work is again segmented from the organisation's standard operations. The balanced matrix is the pure matrix form with a balance in power between the function resource managers and the project manager. The functional managers are usually responsible for *what* is undertaken, *how long* it takes and *how much* it costs. Under this option, the project manager formally exists, but power, or project responsibility, is shared almost equally with the functional managers. The balanced matrix structure is shown in Figure 5-4.

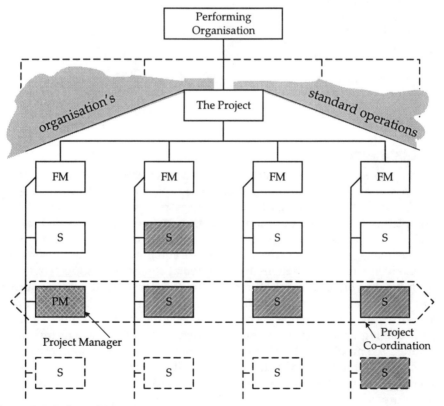

Figure 5-4: Balanced Matrix Structure

The essence of the balanced matrix structure is that the project manager formally exists but must share authority with the resource managers. The balanced matrix structure is one where there are two chains of command (two bosses), the functions are technical, and there is usually a project office responsible for budgetary and schedule control.

The advantages of the balanced matrix structure include:

- a balance between the project office and the functional departments in achieving the project objectives;

- integration of the project across functional departments;

- efficient use of the company's resources;

- effective dissemination of project information;

- technology and know-how not lost;

- higher morale;

- good training ground for project managers;

- no large lay-offs with project shut-down.

The perceived disadvantages of the matrix project structure are:

- there are two bosses;

- the organisational structure is more complex;

- problems with project priorities and resource allocation;

- top management must balance goals of functional departments and project teams;

- effects of conflict on management.

Project Matrix Structure

In the project management structure, the project work is again segmented from the organisation's standard operations. The project matrix structure (see Figure 5-5) provides the project manager with primary responsibility and authority for completing the project. Functional managers assign staff as needed and provide technical expertise. The key element of the project matrix is the strong role of the project manager (PM) who needs to exercise equally strong interpersonal skills.

Conventional organisations are not good at coping with added complexity and with the enormous amount of information to be processed on a modern project. Such organisations also find it difficult to fragment the problem. The project matrix structure was developed because of a need for an organisational form capable of managing very large, complex programmes. It was also a structure that would address the problem of functional departments' tendency to sub-optimise or solve problems within their particular discipline. It was also considered a way of overcoming functions and skills that are fragmented throughout the organisational structure.

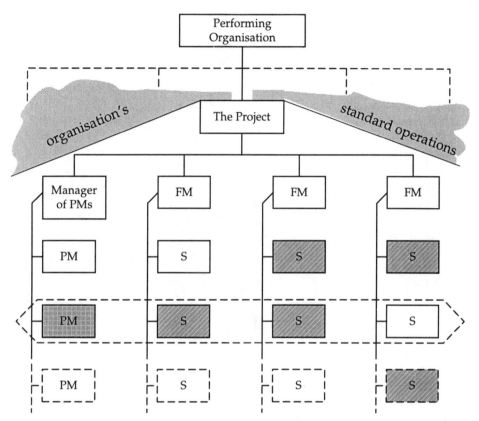

Figure 5-5: Project Matrix Structure

Project Team Structure

In the fifth project structure option (see Figure 5-6), a PM is put in charge of a project team composed of personnel drawn from several functional groups who are assigned on a full-time or an "as-required" basis. Functional managers have no formal involvement, but project team members may refer to functional managers for advice or even sharing of resources. The core group, the project team, will normally have the personnel resources to get the work done on its own.

This type of organisational structure is also referred to as a "projectised" organisation. The projectised structure is the opposite of hierarchical functional structure. The resources are usually set up as a self-contained unit headed by a PM. In large organisations the tendency is to set up a smaller temporary specific purpose structure for each project. The PM is given considerable authority and may acquire resources from either inside or outside the overall organisation. The PM has direct authority over all personnel.

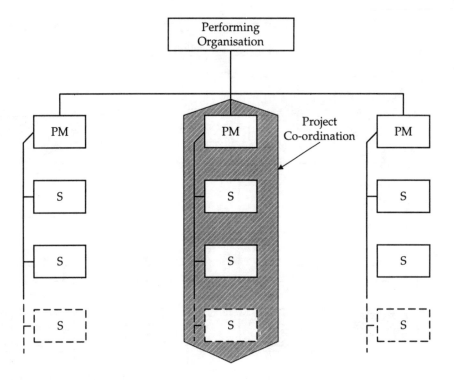

Figure 5-6: Project Team Structure

The advantages of the projectised structure are:

• it has singleness of purpose;

• there is unity of command;

• it generates an *esprit de corps*;

• it can operate with informal communications.

The disadvantages are:

• certain facilities may be duplicated;

• resources may not be used effectively;

• there can be a loss of job security.

A "Best Form" of Project Structure

Of the five organisational options that have been described, the functional and functional matrix structures could be seen as ineffective in relation to success in meeting the usual project objectives of performance (scope and quality), completion time and overall cost. The principal reason for their ineffectiveness is the slowness of these organisational structures to respond to the required dynamics found in the projects' environment.

The project matrix and project team organisational structures have been found to be the most effective in handling projects. The main reason for this is the strong influence of the PM. What really happens in both these structures is that the influence of the PM creates a horizontal line of communication and workflow, cutting across the bureaucratic vertical structure, with its strong, superior/subordinate linkage.

All the project organisational forms have advantages and disadvantages, but the project matrix and project team options offer real solutions for the running of complex engineering and construction projects. As can be seen from the results of recent research in Figure 5-7, this is generally the case whether the project is a new product, services, or construction.

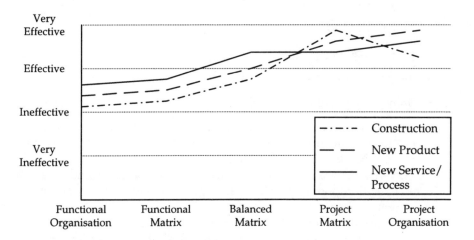

Figure 5-7: Organisation Structure Effectiveness
Source: Tobeli and Larson (1987)

Probably the most significant aspect of the project matrix or project team forms is that the individual's first loyalty is to the project. For this reason it is axiomatic that the project management position must be separated from any controlling interest of the functional managers and the functional department management's hierarchy. In other words, the project's managers cannot also be the project's designers.

In a projectised organisation structure, the PM requires the skills of a general manager. The planning and reporting system in a project organisation can be fairly simple (because the team is in close proximity). The opposite is true in the management of projects through a functional organisation. Information in the form of plans, schedules, budgets and reports is the key medium for integrating a functional organisation structure.

Organisations typically turn to using projectised structure or the matrix structure. But before giving up on the functional organisation, analyse the real problems and see if steps can be taken short of reorganisation such as:

- developing procedures (plans, budgets, schedules, review meetings) across functional department boundaries;

- ensuring direct contact between managers;

- having an informal liaison role;

- working in teams.

The basic factors that influence the selection of the best form of project management organisational structure include:

- project size and value;

- project complexity;

- project timescale;

- experience with project management organisational structures;

- philosophy and visibility of the owner/client;

- project location;

- available resources;

- unique aspects of the project.

By examining conditions on a specific project it is possible to choose the right organisational structure for a particular environment. An organisation developing many new but small projects with standard technology would most likely find a functional structure best. On the other hand, a company with a lengthy, large, complex and important project should probably favour the projectised structure. A company engaged in the pharmaceutical business with many complicated technologies would probably use a matrix structure.

It is possible for the same company to use all three structures on different projects. All three structures might also be used on the same project at different levels — for example, an overall matrix structure for the project with a functional sub-structure in engineering and a project organisation in another functional sub-area.

Before making a final choice, the following additional factors should be considered:

- what is the relationship between organisational design (type), the skills of the PM and the project planning/reporting system?

- are there ways to improve co-ordination and commitment in the functional structure without moving to a project or matrix structure?

- what variations exist in the matrix structure and what are the advantages of each variation?

Successful project management, regardless of organisation structure, is only as good as the individual who is in the key position of PM. These individuals need to have very good people-management skills and need to score highly in communications, organisation, leadership, team building, coping (stress), and technology.

In conclusion, proper project planning, organising, directing and control can only be performed by key individuals, with the correct skills, preferably working within the project team or project matrix form of organisational structure under the management of a skilled and experienced PM, ably supported by other project management specialists.

Organisational Influences

Functional organisations can undertake projects, but the perceived scope of the project is limited to the boundaries of the function (e.g., the engineering department in a functional organisation will do the project work independent of the other departments). In functional organisations most "projects" are sub-projects of the traditional work of the departments. Project issues are resolved by the functional heads.

In the projectised organisation most of the organisation's resources are involved in project work; PMs have a great deal of independence and authority.

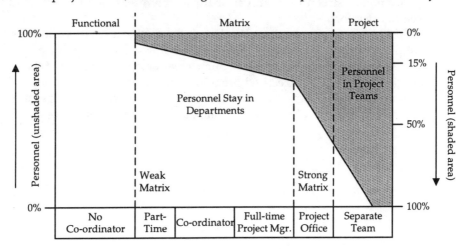

Figure 5-8: Team Member Location versus Organisation Option

From Figure 5-8, it can be seen that the three organisational forms (functional, matrix, and projectised) can be presented as a continuum as shown at the base of the chart. In the process from functional structure to matrix structure, there is no co-ordinator or part-time co-ordinator. The difference between project co-ordinator and PM can be seen as the difference between integrator and actual decision-maker respectively. The dividing line between strong matrix and project team demonstrates the difference between work that is still being performed in functional departments versus the team personnel being transferred to work together at the project team's location. It is rare to have all personnel transferred from their home department and assigned to work on the team.

The matrix type of organisation can range from being *weak* (basically equivalent to the functional matrix) to *strong* (basically equivalent to the project matrix); this does not infer bad or good. Weak matrices maintain many of the characteristics of a functional organisation and the PM's role is more of a co-ordinator or ex-

pediter than that of a manager. Similarly, strong matrices have many of the characteristics of the projectised organisation — full-time PMs with considerable
authority and full time project management administrative staff.

The matrix organisation structure maximises the strengths and minimises the
weaknesses of both the projectised and the functional types respectively; it combines the well-understood vertical hierarchy containing the various technical or
scientific functions with horizontal co-ordination.

One key problem with matrix organisations is that they can tend to overload
the functional departments with work. If a functional department is over-
committed (i.e. is required to do more man-hours than it has available), then
conflicts over priorities between projects are inevitable.

No specific organisational form can be guaranteed to work at all times, or to
improve productive output. However, it can be said that some organisational
forms have a better chance of working than others, particularly if they are designed to meet the needs of project work. The principal need in projects is for an
organisational structure that can handle the great complexity of a multi-
disciplinary effort.

Most modern organisations involve all these structures at various levels. For
example, even a fundamentally functional organisation may create a special project team to handle a critical project. Such a team may have many of the characteristics of a project in a projectised organisation. It may include full-time staff from
different functional departments, may develop its own set of operating procedures and it may operate outside the standard formalised reporting structure.

SECTION 3: PROJECT TEAMS — THE HARMONY AND THE CONFLICTS

Contents

- Aims and Objectives
- Building Effective Project Teams
- Characteristics of an Effective Project Team
- Barriers to Effective Project Team Building
- Managing Conflict within the Project Team

Aims and Objectives

The aims and objectives of Section 3 are to:

- Describe the basis for effective project teams;
- Discuss the barriers to effective project team building;
- Examine how conflict within project teams can be managed effectively.

Building Effective Project Teams

The issues in the building of an effective team are largely behavioural ones. Indeed it is fair to say that the behavioural dimension is often the forgotten element — this despite the fact that often what distinguishes an effective project team from an ineffective one is its concern for behavioural dynamics. There are a number of important sub-issues, namely:

- the nature of a team and characteristics of an effective project team;
- barriers to effective project team development;
- balance within the project team in terms of behavioural roles;
- team building as an on-going process;
- leadership within the project team;
- recommendations on effective project team building.

Characteristics of an Effective Project Team

The word "team" has a particular meaning within the behavioural context. The words "team" and "groups" are often used interchangeably, but they have distinct meanings in organisation behaviour.

- A *group* is an informal coming together of people for a particular purpose. Each member of the group still retains their individuality and sense of purpose independently of the group.

- A *team* consists of members who are willing to subordinate their own ambitions to the overall needs of team success. The team reflects credit on all the members.

This distinction is important. Effective project teams have particular characteristics. Little research has been done on this issue in Ireland; however research by Kerzner (1992) in the United States is very helpful and gives us some idea of the issues to be examined. He identifies the following characteristics of effective project teams:

- high performance and task efficiency;

- innovative/creative behaviour on the part of members;

- high levels of commitment on the part of team members to the project team goals;

- the professional objectives of team members are concerned with project requirements;

- team members are highly interdependent and interface effectively;

- there is a capacity for conflict resolution; however, conflict is encouraged when it can lead to beneficial results;

- there are effective communication systems within the project team;

- there are high levels of trust and a co-operative spirit;

- the project team has a results orientation — that is, effectiveness is a priority;

- team members have high energy levels and enthusiasm and there are high levels of morale;

- there is a change orientation within the project team.

These are characteristics which take a considerable amount of time and energy to develop and sustain but are essential to effective performance.

Barriers to Effective Project Team Building

The process of project team building is a difficult one. Many barriers may exist arising from many sources. An understanding of these barriers can help in developing an environment suitable to effective project team building. Thamhain and Wilemon (1979) have identified a number of these barriers. Their research was on large project management teams in the USA and has been reinforced by other studies. The barriers discussed here are typical of many project environments:

Divergent Outlooks, Priorities and Interests

Team members may have professional objectives and interests that differ significantly from the project objectives. Furthermore, certain supports to the project team may also have different interests and priorities.

Lack of Clarity on Project Objectives/Outcomes

Project teams with unclear objectives/outcomes produce a number of dysfunctional consequences such as power struggles, conflict between members, role ambiguity, role conflicts such as who does what within the team, etc. These problems must be avoided.

Team Leadership Definition and Structure

The research indicates that leadership problems are most likely to emerge at the early stages of the project life-cycle. There may be competition between formal and informal leaders. Team building is considerably hampered when the project leader suffers from poor credibility within the team or from other managers. This has implications for the commitment of team members. The credibility problems usually arise from poor management skills, limited technical expertise or a lack of relevant project experience. This may manifest itself in challenges to the project leader's ability and competence. The team may also lack an effective reporting structure and a clear definition of task responsibilities.

Poor Team Member Selection

Individuals may feel threatened during the staffing of a project. The project leader may have very little input in the selection process, with team members assigned to the team by functional managers. The project team leader may not have the human resources required. This can present several difficulties in building the project team. Furthermore, where team members are assigned to the team, they may have motivation problems, be unprepared for the project and may introduce conflict situations.

Team Member Commitment

This is essential to effective project team functioning. Poor commitment can arise for a number of reasons:

- feelings of insecurity associated with the project;
- professional interests which lie elsewhere;
- lack of clarity about the nature of the rewards forthcoming from project completion;
- interpersonal conflicts within the team;
- certain individuals on the project team get too much attention from the team leader. These "stars" can kill the motivation of the other team members.

Communication Problems

Poor communication significantly influences effective team development. It can exist at four different levels in the project team: communications among team members, between the project leader and team members, between the project team and top management and between the project leaders and the client. Communication problems often result from low motivation levels, poor team morale and lack of attention to detail. Poor communications within the project team can have severe consequences, including unclear objectives, poor project control and work flow problems.

Lack of Senior Management Support

Poor support from top management makes project team development difficult. Furthermore this commitment can vary over the project life-cycle. A perceived lack of support from top management can result in team member apathy, low levels of enthusiasm and poor commitment to the project. Also, top management may fail to give timely feedback on project team performance and there may be insufficient attention to creating the right environment for the project team as it starts its work.

Managing Conflict within the Project Team

Traditionally, the view held was that conflict within organisations was negative and must be eliminated. The more contemporary view is that conflict is a natural process within organisations and project management teams. Indeed it can be seen as healthy and can lead to positive outcomes. However, this very much depends on how effectively it is managed. The following aspects will be examined:

- the nature of conflict and the conflict process;

- the conflict environment of a project;

- conflict and the project life cycle;

- preparing for conflict resolution;

- the traits of an effective PM as conflict handler.

Nature of Conflict and the Conflict Process

Conflict is a widely defined term in the organisation behaviour literature. Conflict is defined as a process that begins when one party perceives that another party has negatively affected or is about to negatively affect something that the first party cares about.

There are a number of themes underlying this definition.

- conflict must be perceived by the parties (whether or not conflict exists is a perception issue);

- there must be an opposition or an incompatibility;

- there must be an interaction if it is to become an inter-party conflict.

A distinction can be made between functional and dysfunctional conflict. Functional conflict supports the goals of the project team and improves its performance. Dysfunctional conflict hinders project team performance. The line between the two is not precise, but the criterion that differentiates the two is project team performance.

Conflict within teams comes in many forms. We can identify four categories:

- *goal conflict*: in which desired end states or preferred outcomes appear to be incompatible;

- *cognitive conflict*: in which ideas or thoughts are perceived as incompatible;

- *affective conflict*: in which feelings or emotions are incompatible, i.e. people literally become angry with one another;

- *procedural conflict*: in which the parties differ on the process to use for resolving a conflict.

According to Robbins (1992) conflict can be seen as a process. Figure 5-9 represents the process which is comprised of five stages.

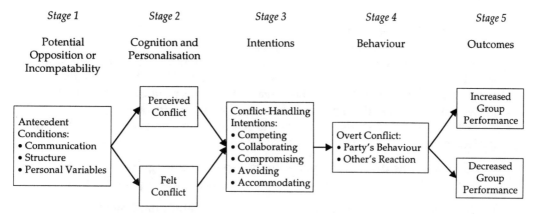

Figure 5-9: The Five Stages Of Conflict
  Source: Robbins (1992)

- **Stage 1 — Potential Opposition or Incompatibility:** The first step is the presence of conditions that create opportunities for conflict to arise. These conditions fall into three categories: (1) *communication*: This relates to noise in the communication channels, misunderstandings, etc. between people; (2) *structure*: This relates to variables such as size, degree of specialisation, team member goal compatibility, leadership style, reward systems, etc.; and (3) *personal variables*: These include the individual value systems that each person has and the personality characteristics that individuals have.

- **Stage 2 — Cognition and Personalisation:** The conditions outlined in stage one can only lead to conflict when one or more of the parties are affected by and aware of the conflict. Perception is required. However, just because a conflict is perceived does not mean that it is personalised. When individuals become emotionally involved, then frustration, hostility, etc. arise.

- **Stage 3 — Intentions:** Intentions intervene between people's perceptions and emotions and their behaviour. People make decisions and these decisions are intentions to act in a certain way. A lot of conflicts escalate merely because one party attributes the wrong intentions to the other party. There is also a great deal of slippage between intentions and behaviour, so that behaviour does not always accurately reflect a person's intention.

- **Stage 4 — Behaviour:** This is the stage where conflicts become visible. The behaviour stage includes the statements, actions and reactions made by the conflicting parties. They are usually overt attempts to implement each individual's intention. Sometimes these real behaviours deviate from original intentions. It is here that conflict management techniques are required to de-escalate the conflict.

- **Stage 5 — Outcomes:** The interactions between the conflicting parties result in consequences. These outcomes may be functional or dysfunctional.

This conflict process is important because it helps us to identify and apply appropriate conflict management methods.

The Conflict Environment of a Project
Conflicts are an inevitable feature of projects. These conflicts may involve issues relating to manpower resources, costs, responsibilities, personality clashes, scheduling problems, technical options and trade-offs. The extent of conflicts can vary in intensity depending on the stage of the project life cycle, the number of project constraints, and the person whom the conflict is with, etc.

Wilemon (1973) has identified several reasons why conflicts occur within the project team:

- the greater the diversity of disciplinary expertise among the participants of a project team, the greater the potential for conflict to develop among members;

- the lower the PM's degree of authority, reward and punishment power over those individuals and organisational units supporting the project, the greater the potential for conflict to develop;

- the less the specific objectives of a project are understood by team members, the more likely it is that conflict will develop;

- the greater the role ambiguity among the participants of a project team, the more likely it is that conflict will develop;

- the greater the agreement on subordinate goals by project team participants, the lower the potential for negative conflict;

- the more the members of functional areas perceive that the implementation of a project management system will undermine their traditional roles, the greater the potential for conflict;

- the lower the need for interdependence among organisational units supporting the project, the greater the potential for dysfunctional conflict;

- the higher the managerial level within a project or functional area, the more likely it is that conflicts will be based upon political considerations.

The extent to which conflict will emerge in the project is largely determined by its life cycle.

Conflicts and the Project Life Cycle
The life cycle concept is a much used one when studying organisations and projects. Figure 5-10 presents the life cycle of a project and the intensity of conflict

over the cycle. Conflict intensity is simply measured by calculating the product of frequency and magnitude of each conflict type.

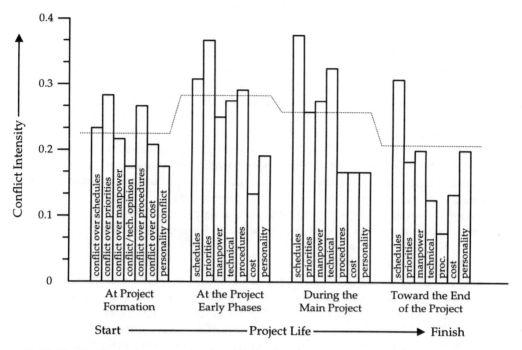

Figure 5-10: Conflict Intensity versus Project Life Cycle
Source: Thamhain and Wilemon (1975)

Thamhain & Wilemon (1975) point out that all phases of the project life cycle are characterised by conflict. These conflicts fall into three distinct categories:

- groups working on the project may have different goals and expectations;

- there may be uncertainty about who has the authority to make decisions;

- there are interpersonal conflicts between people who are parties with an interest in the project.

The conflict issues within each phase of the project life cycle follow.

At the project *conception phase* most of the conflict centres around the inherent confusion of setting up a project. The project's technical objectives may not be very well understood, and there may be a lack of clarity about the relative power/influence/authority of the PM and functional managers. The latter will be a major component of all conflict.

During the project build-up or *definition phase*, the period during which the project moves from a general concept to a highly detailed set of plans, there may be conflicts over technical issues and between the PM and functional areas. Functional departments will usually claim more technical expertise than the PM. However, the PM may also be a specialist. Such differences in perceptions will usually require some frank discussion in order to avoid dysfunctional conflict situations arising.

Time schedules are still a major source of conflict in the *implementation phase* of the project life cycle. Project plans have been developed and work is now under-way. There may be delays. Maintaining the project schedule is an exercise in managing trade-offs. Such trade-off decisions are extremely difficult and are prone to conflict.

Technical conflicts may be considerable during this stage. These technical conflicts may be concerned with interfaces. As the project gets larger, the number of interfaces increases. The motivation and skill to manage these interfaces and to correct incompatibilities is the key to dealing with conflict in this area.

The time schedule is a major source of conflict during the project *close-out phase*, the final phase. If schedule slippage has occurred in the implementation phase the consequences will be felt in the final phase. Technical problems are few during phase-out because most have been solved or by-passed earlier. Personality conflicts may emerge during close-out. This is mainly due to interpersonal stress caused by the pressure to complete the project and to an individual's natural anxiety about leaving the project and being assigned to another one. Conflict also arises between projects that are coming to an end and those just starting.

Preparing for Conflict Resolution

Analysis of conflict at different stages of the life cycle shows that the issues most likely to cause problems for the PM over the life of the project are disagreements over schedules, project priorities and human resources (Thamhain and Wilemon, 1975). The PM may have limited control over other issues that have an important impact. Conflict may be reduced if intensive planning is undertaken prior to the actual launch of the project. Planning can help the PM anticipate many potential sources of conflict before they occur. There will, however, be situations that defy forecasting.

Figure 5-11 provides an illustration of one of many methodologies that can be used by the PM for anticipating conflict and planning ahead.

Source of Conflict	Life-cycle Phases				Score	Overall Rank
	Conception	Definition	Implementation	Close-out		
Schedules	3	2	1	1	37	1
Priorities	1	1	4	4	34	2
Manpower	4	5	3	3	29	3
Tech. Issues	6	4	2	6	26	4
Admin.	2	3	5	7	27	5
Personality	7	6	7	2	22	6
Cost	5	7	6	5	21	7

Rank:	1	2	3	4	5	6	7
Score	10	9	8	7	6	5	4

Figure 5-11: Ranking Conflict Sources

As conflict varies between phases of a project it is necessary to rank the possible conflicts for each phase. The generic titles are used for the four phases: conception (pre-investment); definition (design); implementation (build); close-out (finish).

The seven sources of conflict are listed vertically to the left of the table. When assessing risk for the conception phase put a 1 by the most intense source of risk. Put a 2 for the second most intense source, a 3 at the third most intense source, and so on. Carry out this procedure for each of the phases. Weight the conflict scores using some sort of weighting, for example a 1 could be equal to 10 points and so on until a 7 would be worth 4 points. By adding the points horizontally the overall ranking of conflicts can be established for the total project. By rearranging the conflicts in decreasing magnitude the ranking can be obtained for each phase of the project. For instance during the implementation phase the ranked order would be: schedules (1), technical issues (2), manpower (3), etc.

The Project Manager as a Conflict Handler

Effective PMs should realise that conflicts are inevitable and that certain behavioural traits may be used to help solve them. We can examine this issue by looking at three areas: knowledge requirements, behavioural characteristics, and style.

The effective PM in a conflict situation has *knowledge* or understands:

- the organisation;

- the procedures for resolving conflicts;

- the conflict resolution process;

- the conflict motives;

- the feelings of others;

- the nature of the conflict.

The effective PM in a conflict situation should display the following *behavioural characteristics*:

- listens and understands rather than evaluates;

- maintains relationships with disputing parties;

- facilitates the communication process;

- pauses and thinks before acting and reacting;

- builds trust;

- maintains a give-and-take attitude;

- educates others tactfully of his views;

- is willing to say when he is wrong;

- keeps the conflict situation under control.

There are a range of *styles* open to the PM. Effectiveness means being aware of when to use these. They are as follows:

- *Accommodating*: When one party seeks to appease an opponent, that party may be willing to place the opponent's interests above their own. In order for the relationship to be maintained, one party must be willing to be self-sacrificing.

- *Compromising*: When each party to the conflict seeks to give up something, sharing occurs resulting in a compromised outcome. In compromising there is no clear winner or loser. Rather there is a willingness to ration the object of the conflict and accept a solution that provides incomplete satisfaction for both parties concerned.

- *Competing*: When one person seeks to satisfy their own interests regardless of the impact on the other parties to the conflict, they are competing.

- *Avoiding*: A person may recognise that a conflict exists and want to withdraw from it or suppress it. Examples of avoidance are trying to ignore a conflict and avoiding others with whom you disagree. This is not a satisfactory style for a PM to adopt.

- *Collaborating*: When the parties to a conflict each desire to fully satisfy the concern of all parties, we have co-operation and the search for a mutually beneficial outcome. In collaborating, the intention of the parties is to solve the problems by clarifying differences rather than accommodating various points of view. This is the ideal "win-win scenario".

SECTION 4: PEOPLE IN PROJECTS AND THEIR ROLES

Contents

- Aims and Objectives
- The Project Manager
- Project Manager Competencies
- Project Manager Personal Skills
- The Training of Project Managers
- Project Team Members
- Balance within the Project Team
- Summary of Key Points
- References

Aims and Objectives

The aims and objectives of Section 4 are to:

- Outline the role of the project manager;

- Define the competencies of the project manager;

- Describe the personal skills of the project manager;

- Provide a view on the training of project managers;

- Explain the "team role" or behavioural role of individuals and its importance relative to team effectiveness;

- Show a means of relating self-perception testing to "team roles" for the selection of team members.

The Project Manager

Generally speaking, the project manager's role is to create a *product*. In doing so, they have to manage two processes:

- the process to produce the product,

- the process to manage the production of the product.

The primary tool available to the project manager is the brainpower of those individuals who are professional specialists in diverse fields. They use this tool in all the phases of the creation of the product from conception through to close-out.

The functions of the project manager which must be understood are:

- what does a project manager do?

- what kind of person must they be?

- what training is prerequisite for success?

In considering these functions, the more or less autonomous project will be used, in which "real" management and personnel responsibility resides with the project manager. This autonomy is in contrast to the organisation in which the project function is maintained by a "project co-ordinator", who is often relegated to a staff position with responsibilities far outweighing their authority, and who must pursue tenuous relationships with a great deal of skill and persistence to achieve even modest performance goals.

Project Manager Competencies

Years ago, an individual in charge of a project only needed to be technically competent in a single discipline. A few centuries ago, in building and construction it was the master mason who was in charge (the project manager); he did everything. In more recent years the competent architect, working with several master craftsmen, was the "project manager".

These were times when the time schedule for the project might have been decades, labour was relatively inexpensive, and projects were not complicated. As projects have become complex and technically sophisticated, they have become multi-disciplinary in nature. Invariably, modern projects are subject to tight time schedules and constrained cost budgets.

The demand by society for sophisticated products and effective infrastructure, together with the advent of the computer has led to modern project management being seen as having three important ingredients. These ingredients are:

- organisational structure;

- people roles;

- procedures and techniques.

Today's project managers know that having a strong discipline background and a knowledge of the procedures and techniques are not the complete answer to running a successful project. The astute project manager knows that their personal attributes and the ability to lead, motivate and integrate the project team are equally important factors.

A project manager's success or failure on a project can be based on three factors (La Monica, 1994):

- *technical*: a solid foundation in a discipline appropriate to the type of project in which the manager is involved;

- *conceptual*: the ability to see the "big picture";

- *human*: competency as a manager of people in a project environment.

These three factors are shown in Figure 5-12, diagrammatically plotted against project position and competency level. The diagram should be interpreted relatively and not in absolute terms.

Successful project managers combine these three competencies. The distribution of each competency depends upon, amongst other determinants, the positional authority of the project manager, and the size and nature of the project. It is important that the project manager provides a balanced mix of these competencies throughout the project life cycle.

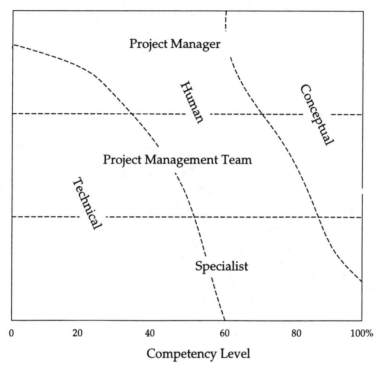

Figure 5-12: Management Factors versus Competency and Position

Typically, project managers would be well trained in a specific *technical* discipline. The technical competencies mostly relate to working with processes, tools, or physical objects.

They may have been very successful in their chosen discipline, and this fact probably contributed to their ultimate selection as a project manager. Because most of today's projects are staffed by well-educated individuals, many with a specialist knowledge, the project manager needs a different attitude regarding the classic management functions of plan, organise, direct and control. These competencies are needed to communicate effectively with the project team on matters such as, value, risk, time/cost/quality trade-offs, etc.

Project managers with good *conceptual* abilities are aware of how the performing organisation and parts of the performing organisation work and complement each other. They should also be "systems approach" converts who are capable of perceiving the environments beyond the project and can understand the relationships between the sub-systems and elements of other "systems" and the project they are responsible for.

Human competencies build co-operation between team members and between other teams, project stakeholders, and the project manager. The major skills required from the project manager include communication, team building, leaderships, etc. These skills are dealt with in the next sub-Section, "Project Manager Personal Skills".

The project manager's knowledge and experience in project management should include the management processes of planning and organising the work, tendering and contract procedures, supervising other peoples work, financial budgeting, status reporting and forecasting, human resource factors, etc. Figure 5-13 shows the project manager (and their team) as the central focus of all the normal management functions to be found within projects.

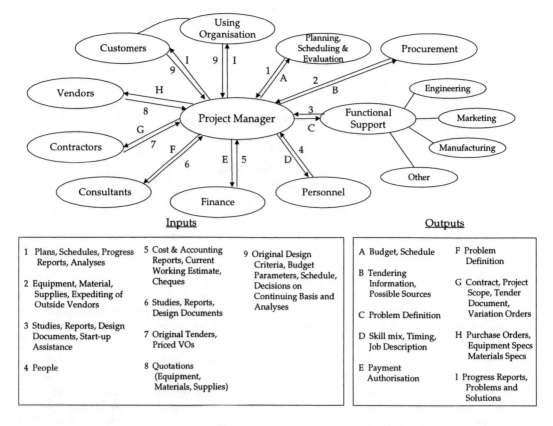

Figure 5-13: The Central Focus of the Project Manager

Ideally the project manager's competency would contain all or most of the following:

- concern for performance;

- leadership qualities;

- consistently high values;

- hard worker;

- ability to get and keep quality people;

- communicating skills;

- good discipline;

- effective work systems;

- enthusiasm;

- sensitivity to interpersonal relationships.

The project manager's training is likely to have been more haphazard than their formal education; however, much of the management knowledge will have been through self-initiative — in other words, self-taught.

Project Manager Personal Skills

Project managers need to have strong skills in the following areas:

- communication;

- organising;

- team building;

- leadership;

- coping (dealing with stress);

- technology of the project.

These project manager skills and some of the associated problems that can develop in a project if the skills are inadequate are shown in Figure 5-14. Of course, the relationship between skills and problems can be interpreted another way. The surfacing of certain project problems can be directly related to associated skills deficiencies in the project's manager. In other words, inadequate managerial skills can often precipitate a range of related project problems, and problems in the performance of a project can most often be traced to deficiencies in the manager's skills.

To be effective, project management requires good *communication*. Communication in a projects' environment may take any of several forms or combinations, depending upon the requirements and the situation. Generally, three types of communication used in projects are: oral, written and visual. In communicating, project managers need to be just as good at listening as they are at persuading others to do certain things. There is a range of communication environments that surround the projects' environment.

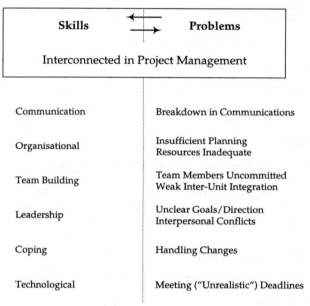

Skills	Problems
Skills ⇄ **Problems**	
Interconnected in Project Management	
Communication	Breakdown in Communications
Organisational	Insufficient Planning Resources Inadequate
Team Building	Team Members Uncommitted Weak Inter-Unit Integration
Leadership	Unclear Goals/Direction Interpersonal Conflicts
Coping	Handling Changes
Technological	Meeting ("Unrealistic") Deadlines

Figure 5-14: Project Manager — Skills versus Problems

Vannevar Bush (1949) noted the distinction in communication reaction between the military and academicians when he wrote many years ago:

> In the military there is vigorous and open debate on proposed actions before the decision. But when an officer with clearly constituted authority makes the decision, the antagonists, acting under a basic doctrine of their profession swing round to support actively a solution that they may have opposed earlier.
>
> In contrast, under the customs which prevail in academic circles, the duly established decision signals the start of the fight. In this environment, it is very difficult to learn the nature of the opposition to administrative planning, since academicians are not inclined to communicate freely in such matters. Consequently, after decisions are taken there tends to be considerable passive and sometimes active resistance in the execution of ideas.

From this tale, the lessons for the project manager are that considerable active effort must be expended in learning to communicate adequately and in helping others to develop the right communications attitude.

They need to be highly proficient in planning, goal-setting and analysing — the elements that are seen as prime project *organising* skills. The process of goal setting begins with the project manager establishing clear goals in their mind and then ensuring that they are understood in the minds of the team members. As it is time that drives projects, the project manager and the rest of the team will be focusing on future work. Future work is what is important; what has already happened is only important with respect to how it affects the future.

A major responsibility of the project manager is making decisions. During the planning phase of a project there are always key decisions which have not been made. The project manager should identify these decisions, schedule a date when each decision must be made, and assign the responsibility for making it. Everyone, including the project manager, must learn to distinguish the important tasks (self-imposed, large number of people, dealing with the future) from the urgent tasks (e.g. an individual action from the past that should have been done previously). It is important that the project manager responds to these urgent tasks, sometimes moving them up on the priority list and trying to find a way to minimise their number and their impact on the workday.

In setting project goals, it is worth noting what the four characteristics are:

1) the goals must be defined and measurable;

2) completion time has to be set;

3) resources to be used have to be allocated;

4) desired level of quality has to be determined.

Reference should also be made to the sub-Section "What is Project Management?", in Part 3, Section 1, where the matter of project objectives is discussed.

A prerequisite for *team building* is the visible commitment of top management to the team concept. Any company that is engaged in the management of projects would have to see team building skills as a necessity because of the technical complexity and multidisciplinary nature of projects. A closely knit group of people working together is usually more productive and will have higher morale than equivalent people with the same level of knowledge working separately. It follows from this that performance can be enhanced through building a team or teams to undertake projects.

The project manager needs to be the sort of person who can develop motivation in a project group and who has the ability to create a "spirit of belonging" or of being part of something exciting. Everyone in a project team will want to do a good job. In general, if a person understands what is wanted, the person will come much closer to fulfilling that expectation. If the person has an understanding as to why it is wanted and what it will be used for, the chances of satisfying the goals will be increased.

Ideally the project manager will be someone who has *leadership* skills. They will therefore have vision and can see the "big picture", in other words, can see beyond the detail of today's situation. Leadership skills will include setting good examples, being very energetic, being able to delegate and being positive.

Project management is concerned with accomplishing things through others by performing the functions of planning, organising, directing and control. Leadership adds another dimension by introducing extraordinary motivation for the followers. However, it should be noted that managers can manage without having to be leaders and leaders can lead without being good managers. The preferred combination of having a project manager that is a good manager as well as a good leader is not common. The principles of good management can be taught but leadership cannot be taught as it is instinctive. It is also found that good leaders generally become better leaders with added experience.

There is a considerable body of evidence to suggest that project managers are often selected without adequate consideration of their leadership style. The key issue is to achieve a balance between the technical and managerial requirements of the project. Wilemon and Cicero (1970) identify four possible scenarios:

- the greater the project manager's technical expertise, the greater their propensity to over-involve themselves in the technical details of the project;

- the greater the project manager's difficulty in delegating technical task responsibilities, the more likely it is that they will over-involve themselves in the technical details of the project;

- the greater the project manager's interest in the technical details of the project, the more likely it is that they will define the project manager's role as one of a technical specialist;

- the lower the project manager's technical expertise, the more likely it is that they will over-stress the non-technical project functions.

Having the ability to cope with the traumatic happenings that can be an everyday occurrence in projects is also a required attribute. Being flexible, creative, patient and persistent are all *coping* skills that need to be used from time to time in different project situations. Instead of the word "coping" we could substitute the word "negotiating".

All of us negotiate every day of our lives. With so much practice we should be very good at it. The problem is that we don't realise what we are doing. We do not go about it in an organised way. Most of the time we come away from negotiations having done a poor job, ending up with much less than we could have obtained. Most people do not really know what they want as a result of negotiation. They have not established the limits they will settle for. For them, negotiation is merely arguing to get the better of an opponent.

One important rule of negotiation that must be learnt is to concentrate on the issues and not on the people. We must learn to avoid being overly emotional in our negotiations. There is a real need to make negotiations "win–win". In other words, one party must not feel that it has come away from a negotiation having lost something at the expense of the other party having gained something. Unless both parties come out of a negotiation feeling that they can live with the final resolution, there has not been a successful negotiation.

Last, but not least, the project manager needs to be skilled in *technical knowledge* and be experienced in the type of work that the team will be required to handle as part of their functional responsibilities. In other words, if the project is the design and construction of an under-river tunnel as part of a transportation system, then it is advisable, if not essential, that the project manager has had experience on a project of this type.

The Training of Project Managers

Some of the qualifications that a successful project manager must possess are:

- their career must have been moulded in a technology environment;

- they must have a working knowledge of many technological fields;

- they must have a good understanding of general management functions;

- they must have thorough experience of the project management process;

- they must have a strong, continuous, active interest in teaching, training, and developing the skills of all team members.

An important aspect of these qualifications is that, in an operational sense they must be integrative. There is the ever-present requirement for the joining of these parts into a systemic whole.

For the project managers who have to lead high-tech, large, complex projects it is likely, but not conditional, that they will have commenced their professional career through undertaking study that will lead to a technical, or scientific, undergraduate degree. After some years of work experience, which is initially likely to be technical or scientific, the individual having been recognised as possessing managerial/leadership qualities will more than likely move towards the managerial function. When it is suitable, the individual should be considered for undertaking an advanced degree; this will usually be a Master's level course in project management or general management. A possible career path is shown diagrammatically in Figure 5-15.

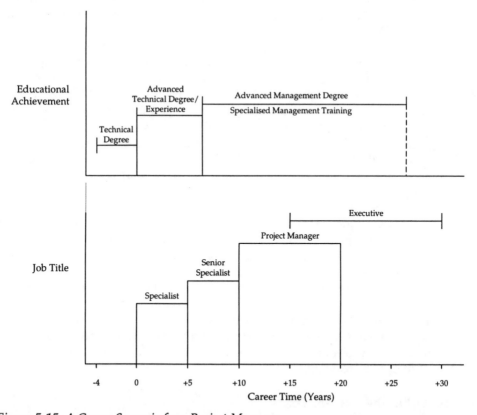

Figure 5-15: A Career Scenario for a Project Manager

The Figure shows a scenario of academic progress plotted against time in the upper chart within the Figure. The bottom chart shows typical job titles that an individual may hold as they progress in the organisation(s) from the time that they commence their professional career.

The career scenario that has been described is obviously only one of many, but for the type of project that has been assumed, the progress of the typical project manager working within a reasonably large organisation would be similar to that described.

What of the project manager working in smaller organisations, where the type of work would not be considered complex or of a high scientific content? The progress of the individual within the organisation is likely to be similar to that described. The academic progress may not extend beyond a primary degree but the individual will be best served by following some form of advanced training in the project management process as well as in specialist subjects of general management.

The Project Team Members

Many management texts suggest that a manager within an operations-type organisation should have no more than ten people reporting directly to them. In a project organisation, the span of management depends upon the range of technologies or trades involved and this can be as high as twenty-five, sometimes higher (House, 1988).

The project staff are likely to provide a mix of brainpower which will vary with the project's mission. For example, a project involving a high degree of "information systems" development, such as one devoted to a multimedia application, will have a high proportion of engineers and analysts to technicians, which means a high proportion of theoretically inclined individuals. In contrast, a project dedicated to linking two land masses with an under-water tunnel will have more labourers, artisans, and technicians than scientists and engineers.

In Section 2 of Part 3, within the sub-Section, "Human Resource Management", the processes of organisational planning, staff acquisition, and team development were described. The first and second processes are instrumental in transforming people requirements into people assignments.

Organisational planning is the process which identifies and assigns project roles, responsibilities and reporting relationships. As a result of this process, the roles are identified and an organisational chart prepared showing the reporting relationships and responsibilities of each individual.

The next process step is to acquire the people who will fill each of the roles. This may result in internal negotiations with functional or line managers for specific individuals, or procuring such personnel from outside, either from other organisations or through open recruiting. Outputs from this process are the assignment of the project staff and a directory, which will include the roles and responsibilities of all team personnel.

Balance within the Project Team

Research undertaken by Belbin (1981, 1993) illustrates that one of the essentials for effective team functioning is the requirement of balance in terms of team roles. A distinction is made between functional roles and "team roles", also referred to as "behavioural roles".

Behavioural roles are distinct from functional roles and concern processes within the team. Belbin points out the need to select the right mix of people. Team typing is useful in selecting the right people. This involves the identification of the skills and qualities that are possessed by individuals. These are then compared to the skills and qualities required in specific situations in which the project team is likely to become involved. In designing an effective project team, project managers should bear in mind the different qualities required and ensure that the right type of team member is selected. Balance in terms of team roles is essential. The team roles are shown in Figure 5-16.

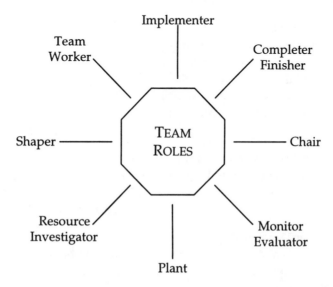

Figure 5-16: Belbin's Team Roles

In examining the behavioural roles necessary for effective teams, Belbin's nine characteristics are:

- **Chair (CH):**
  ◊ makes the best use of team resources
  ◊ recognises the team's strengths and weaknesses
  ◊ controls the team to achieve team objectives
  ◊ is calm, controlled and confident, but not necessarily creative.

- **Plant (PL):**
  ◊ puts forward ideas and looks for an innovative approach
  ◊ is individualistic, unorthodox and inclined to disregard practical details.

- **Resource Investigator (RI):**
  ◊ maintains external contacts which may be useful to the team
  ◊ reports on ideas, developments and resources outside the group
  ◊ is extroverted, enthusiastic and liable to lose interest once the initial fascination has passed.

- **Team Worker (TW):**
  ◊ fosters team spirit, helps communications and supports members
  ◊ understands team members' limitations and builds on team member suggestions
  ◊ tends to be mild, sensitive and indecisive in moments of crisis.

- **Monitor Evaluator (ME):**
  ◊ ensures that everything is evaluated
  ◊ wants the project team to make a balanced decision
  ◊ tends to be sober, prudent and lacking ability to motivate others.

- **Implementer (IMP):**
  ◊ this individual is good at implementation
  ◊ turns ideas and plans into practice and will carry out an agreed plan in a systematic and effective pattern
  ◊ tends to be conservative and predictable
  ◊ is unresponsive to unproved ideas.

- **Shaper (SH):**
  ◊ shapes the way that the team effort is applied
  ◊ imposes some pattern to group discussions
  ◊ ensures that attention is directed to the setting of objectives and priorities
  ◊ tends to be highly strung, dynamic, impatient and prone to provocation.

- **Completer Finisher (CF):**
  ◊ maintains a sense of urgency and progress within a team
  ◊ checks every detail to ensure that nothing is omitted or done that should not be done
  ◊ is conscientious, painstaking and worries over little things.

- **Specialist (SP):**
  ◊ single minded, self-starting, dedicated
  ◊ provides knowledge and skills in rare supply
  ◊ tends to contribute only on a narrow front and overlooks the broader picture

A team which has at least one person possessing one or more of these characteristics has the potential to be very effective. Each role identified has negative characteristics associated with it. Belbin takes the view that we should not try to eliminate these negative characteristics, rather we should manage them. Eliminating the negative characteristics may also eliminate the positive characteristics. This requirement for balance within the team has major implications for the project manager in terms of selection and training of team members.

Let's look at a way in which a first indication of the "team role" of individuals within a project team can be assessed. Figure 5-17 shows an analysis sheet for a self perception test based on Belbin's team roles. By answering certain questions using multiple choice answers it is possible to score your behaviour and hence determine your "strong" behavioural type(s) and your "weak" behavioural type(s).

Section		IMP		CH		SH		PL		RI		ME		TW		CF
Q1	g	3	d	2	f	2	c		a	3	h		b		e		
Q2	a		b		e		g		c		d		f		h		
Q3	h		a		c		d		f		g		e		b		
Q4	d		h		b		e		g		c		a		f		
Q5	b		f		d		h		e		a		c		g		
Q6	f		c		g		a		h		e		b		d		
Q7	e		g		a		f		d		b		h		c		
Total:																	

Figure 5-17: Self-Perception Inventory Analysis Sheet

Respond to each of the next seven questions (indicated 1 to 7 inclusive) by using the sentences which are listed below each question and using a total of ten points. Within each question distribute the 10 points across the sentences which you feel would be most appropriate and best describes your behaviour.

For example you may feel after reading Q1 and its statements a) to h) that a), d), f) and g) best describes "what you believe you would contribute to a team". Assuming your distribution of 10 points is 3, 2, 2, and 3 respectively, the scores would be placed against Q1 as shown in Figure 5-17. After all the questions have been scored, by adding the scores within each column IMP to CF, the individual will find those team roles in which they score highly (these are the team role strengths) and those in which they score lowly (these are the team role allowable weaknesses).

Q1.   What I believe I can contribute to a team:

a)   I think I can quickly see and take advantage of new opportunities.
b)   I can work well with a wide range of people.
c)   Producing ideas is one of my natural assets.
d)   My ability rests in being able to draw people out whenever I detect they have something of value to contribute to group objectives.
e)   My capacity to follow through has much to do with personal effectiveness.
f)   I am ready to face temporary unpopularity if it leads to worthwhile results in the end.
g)   I can usually sense what is realistic and likely to work.
h)   I can offer a reasoned case for alternative courses of action without introducing bias or prejudice.

Q2.   **If I have a possible shortcoming in teamwork it could be that:**

a)   I am not at ease unless meetings are well structured and controlled and generally well conducted.

b)   I am inclined to be too generous towards others who have a valid viewpoint that has not been given a proper airing.

c)   I have tendency to talk too much once the group gets on to new ideas.

d)   My objective outlook makes it difficult for me to join in readily and enthusiastically with colleagues.

e)   I am sometimes seen as forceful and authoritarian if there is a need to get something done.

f)   I find it difficult to lead from the front, perhaps because I am over-responsive to group atmosphere.

g)   I am apt to get too caught up in ideas that occur to me and so lose track of what is happening.

h)   My colleagues tend to see me as worrying unnecessarily over detail and the possibility that things may go wrong.

Q3.   **When involved in a project with other people:**

a)   I have an aptitude for influencing people without pressurising them.

b)   My general vigilance prevents careless mistakes and omissions being made.

c)   I am ready to press for action to make sure that the meeting does not waste time or lose sight of the main objective.

d)   I can be counted on to contribute something original.

e)   I am always ready to back a good suggestion in the common interest.

f)   I am keen to look for the latest in new ideas and developments.

g)   I believe my capacity for judgement can help to bring about the right decisions.

h)   I can be relied upon to see that all essential work is organised.

Q4.   **My characteristic approach to group work is that:**

a)   I have a quiet interest in getting to know colleagues better.

b)   I am not reluctant to challenge the views of others or to hold a minority view myself.

c)   I can usually find a line of argument to refute unsound propositions.

d)   I think I have a talent for making things work once a plan has to be put into operation.

e)   I have a tendency to avoid the obvious and to come out with the unexpected.

f)   I bring a touch of perfectionism to any job I undertake.

g)   I am ready to make use of contacts outside the group itself.

h)   While I am interested in all views I have no hesitation in making up my mind once a decision has to be made.

Q5.   **I gain satisfaction in a job because:**

a)   I enjoy analysing situations and weighing up all the possible choices.

b)   I am interested in finding practical solutions to problems.

c)   I like to feel I am fostering good working relationships.

d)   I can have a strong influence on decisions.

e)   I can meet people who may have something new to offer.

f)   I can get people to agree on a necessary course of action.

g) I feel in my element where I can give a task my full attention.
h) I like to find a field that stretches my imagination.

Q6. If I am suddenly given a difficult task with limited time and unfamiliar people:

a) I would feel like retiring to a corner to devise a way out of the impasse before developing a line.
b) I would be ready to work with the person who showed the most positive approach.
c) I would find some way of reducing the size of the task by establishing what different individuals might best contribute.
d) My natural sense of urgency would help to ensure that we did not fall behind schedule.
e) I believe I would keep cool and maintain my capacity to think straight.
f) I would retain a steadiness of purpose in spite of the pressures.
g) I would be prepared to take a positive lead if I felt the group was making no progress.
h) I would open up discussions with a view to stimulating new thoughts and getting something moving.

Q7. With reference to the problems to which I am subject in working in groups:

a) I am apt to show my impatience with those who are obstructing progress.
b) Others may criticise me for being too analytical and insufficiently intuitive.
c) My desire to ensure that work is properly done can hold up proceedings.
d) I tend to get bored rather easily and rely on one or two stimulating members to spark me off.
e) I find it difficult to get started unless the goals are clear.
f) I am sometimes poor at explaining and clarifying complex points that occur to me.
g) I am conscious of demanding from others the things I cannot do myself.
h) I hesitate to get my points across when I run up against real opposition.

A balanced team will be one in which all the team roles are found to be either a primary or a secondary strength of individual members. A team which is out of balance will under-perform. With under-performing teams it is necessary to identify the gaps in the team role composition, improve the self-insight of the team members, heighten the understanding between members of their respective team roles, and provide a reference point to allow members to agree how to divide the responsibilities between them.

Summary of Key Points

- The teachings of the scientific management and the human relations schools are in opposition to one another. The scientific view is "what is best for the firm will also be best for the worker". The human relations view is "what is best for the worker will also be best for the firm".

- Most, if not all, contemporary management practices are based on non-classical organisation theory (i.e. theory Y). Non-classical organisation theory uses a situational approach to leadership and a leadership style that is based upon understanding the general systems theory which provides a means for studying people within their environment and as shapers of their environment.

- All organisations require both division and integration of personnel, functions, and physical factors. Organisation structure provides the blueprint that denotes the manner of dividing and combining components so that co-ordination toward intended system objectives can be effected.

- The functional organisation structure is the classical command structure and is considered to be the most prevalent structure used in organising projects. Separate work groups, usually divided by discipline, each has a functional manager(s) responsible for all aspects of a discipline. The project work is segmented and assigned to relevant functional areas and/or groups.

- The balanced matrix organisation structure is the pure matrix form with a balance in power between the function resource managers and the project manager. Under this option, the project manager formally exists, but power, or project responsibility, is shared almost equally with the functional managers.

- The "projectised" or project team organisation structure is the opposite of the hierarchical functional structure. Usually the resources are set up as a self-contained unit headed by a project manager. The project manager is given considerable authority and may acquire resources from either inside or outside the overall organisation.

- By examining conditions on a specific project it is possible to choose the right organisational structure for a particular environment.

- No specific organisational form can be guaranteed to work at all times, or to improve productive output. The principal need in projects is for an organisational structure that can handle the great complexity of a multi-disciplinary effort.

- The issues in building an effective team are largely behavioural ones. Indeed, it is fair to say that the behavioural dimension is often the forgotten element despite the fact that what often distinguishes an effective project team from an ineffective one is its concern for the behavioural dynamics.

- The process of project team building is a difficult one. Many barriers may exist which arise from many sources. An understanding of these barriers can help in developing an environment suitable to effective project team building.

- The current view is that conflict is a natural process within organisations and project management teams. Indeed, there is the view that it is healthy and can lead to positive outcomes. However, this very much depends on how effectively it is managed.

- Analysis of conflict at different stages of the life cycle shows that the areas most likely to cause problems for the project manager over the life of the project are disagreements over schedules, project priorities and human resources.

- The project manager's role is to create a *product*. In doing so they have to manage two processes: the process to produce the product, and the process to manage the production of the product.

- Project managers know that having a strong discipline background and a knowledge of the procedures and techniques are not the complete answer to running a successful project. The astute project manager knows that their personal attributes and the ability to lead, motivate and integrate the project team are equally important factors.

- Project managers need to have strong skills in the following areas: communication, organising, team building, leadership, coping (dealing with stress), and technology of the project.

- Behavioural roles are distinct from functional roles and have to do with processes within the team. This involves the identification of the skills and qualities that are possessed by individuals. These are then compared to the skills and qualities required in specific situations in which the project team is likely to become involved. In designing an effective project team, project managers should bear in mind the different qualities required and ensure that the right type of team member is selected. Balance in terms of team roles is essential.

- A balanced team will be one in which all the team roles are found to be either a primary or a secondary strength of individual members. A team which is out of balance will under-perform.

References

References used in the development of Part 5:

Belbin, R. Meredith (1993), *Team Roles at Work*, Butterworth-Heinemann.

Belbin, R. Meredith (1981), *Management Teams — Why they Succeed or Fail*, Butterworth-Heinemann.

Bush, Vannevar (1949), *Modern Arms and Free Men*, New York: Simon and Schuster.

Fisher, R. & Ury, W. (1983), *Getting to Yes*, Penguin Books.

Geddes, M., Hastings, C. and Briner, W. (1990), *Project Leadership*, Gower.

Gobeli, David H., and Larson, Erik W. (1987), "Relative Effectiveness of Different Project Structures", *Project Management Journal*, Vol. XVIII, No. 2, June.

House, Ruth Sizemore (1988), *The Human Side of Project Management*, Addison-Wesley Publishing Co. Ltd.

Kerzner, H. (1992), *Project Management: A Systems Approach to Planning, Scheduling and Controlling*, Van Nostrand Reinhold.

Kliem, R.L. and Ludin I.S. (1992), *The People Side of Project Management*, Gower.

La Monica, Elaine (1994), *Management in Health Care*, The Macmillan Press.

Project Management Institute (1996), *A Guide to the Project Management Body of Knowledge (PMBOK)*, PMI Publications.

Robbins, S.P. (1992), *Organisational Behaviour*, Sixth Edition, Prentice Hall.

Taylor, Frederick Winslow (1911), *The Principles of Scientific Management*, Harper.

Thamhain, H.J. and Wilemon, D.L. (1975), "Conflict Management in Project Life Cycles", *Sloan Management Review*, Summer.

Thamhain, H.J. and Wilemon, D.L. (1979), *Team Building in Project Management*, Proceedings of the Annual Symposium of the Project Management Institute, October.

Thomsett, Rob (1980), *People and Project Management*, Yourdon Press.

Wilemon, D.L. (1973), "Managing Conflict in Temporary Management Situations", *The Journal of Management Studies*, pp. 282–296.

Wilemon, D L & Cicero, J P; "The Project Manager: Anomalies and Ambiguities", *Academy of Management Journal*, Vol 12 pp. 269–282; 1970.

PART 6

CONCEPTION AND DEFINITION PHASES

This Part deals with the very important pre-investment period in a project's life — normally referred to as the conception phase — when the decision "to proceed" or "not to proceed" is taken.

Assuming that it is worth proceeding with a project, the next step in the development process is termed the post-investment period.

After conception, many projects are transformed during the first stage (design) of the definition phase into paper or electronic drawings, specifications, or whatever is needed to convey the concept to whoever will be engaged in the implementation phase. Assuming that external goods and/or services are needed, the work involved in identifying and contracting with such interested entities is carried out within the procurement stage.

All knowledgeable project management teams should, as a matter of normal procedure during the conception and definition phases, be using such processes as estimating, value, risk and activity-based costing.

Section 2 deals with estimating and budgeting — the key to successfully conceived, managed and completed projects. An overview of the value process is given in Section 3. Some of the more popular techniques used in dealing with risk in projects are dealt with in Section 4. The reader interested in activity-based costing is directed to Part 7, in particular Section 3.

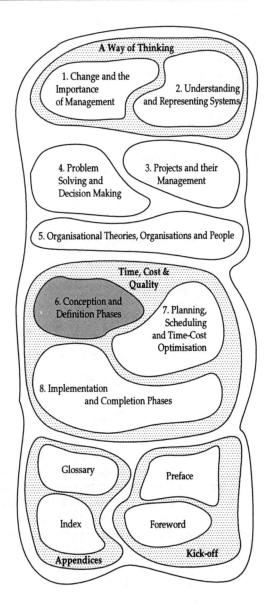

Section 1: The Phases of Greatest Impact

Contents

- Aims and Objectives
- Overview of the Initial Phases
- Project Owner's Requirements
- Conceiving the Project
- Preinvestment Analysis
- Preliminary Master Plan
- Definition Phase
- Concurrent Engineering

Aims and Objectives

The aims and objectives of Section 1 are to:

- Describe the deliverables from the conception and definition phases;
- Distinguish what is meant by the project requirements document;
- Explain the pre-investment (viability) process;
- Describe the work involved in producing the PMP, the preliminary master plan;
- Outline the management of the design process;
- Define the procurement process;
- Provide an overview of what is known as "concurrent engineering".

Overview of the Initial Phases

In Part 3, projects and their management were discussed, with a focus on the Project Management Institute's Body of Knowledge (PMBOK). This Part deals with what the present author considers to be the principal processes and sub-processes of the earlier project phases. New terms will be introduced, particularly when there is a need to show the integration of a sub-process across many of the knowledge areas. Many of these terms may not be found within the PMBOK. For instance, change control applies to many of the knowledge areas; this will be dealt with under what is referred to as configuration management. This is a term that has not been used previously.

Figure 6-1 illustrates the two distinct stages of the conception phase: preinvestment and post-investment. The definition phase also consists of two stages, as shown: the design stage and the procurement stage.

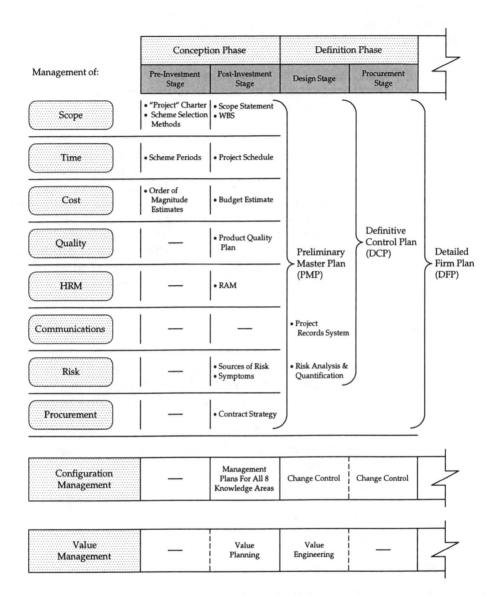

Figure 6-1: Model of PM Techniques for Conception/Definition Phases

Within each of the conception stages are the principal tools and techniques from the eight knowledge areas that are normally used in effective management of projects. The integration process (the ninth knowledge area) to a large extent comes under *configuration management* and, to some extent, *value management*. At the end of the conception phase a document referred to as the Preliminary Master Plan (PMP) provides the means for commencing the definition phase; this document, or its equivalent, is that phase's deliverable.

Configuration management, which relates to the development and control of management plans for all the knowledge areas, starts in the conception phase, normally after the viability of the project has been determined, and the owner has committed to the project. Configuration management is shown at the bottom of Figure 6-1.

Value management and its application is another process that should have its commencement as early in the project's life-cycle as possible. The value process, which is dealt with in Section 3, is shown as value management in Figure 6-1.

The first stage of the definition phase uses the PMP to advance the design(s) of the selected project to a very detailed level. Further development of all the constituents of the PMP including aspects of communications management and risk management, application of a change control system (which is part of configuration management), and further application of the value process, eventually the design stage deliverable, Definitive Control Plan (DCP) is produced. The DCP is used as part of the input to the procurement stage which, along with the application of the processes of procurement management (see Section 2 of Part 3), will produce what will be referred to here as the Detailed Firm Plan (DFP).

The DCP is normally the baseline against which the owner will decide on such matters as project budget. The DFP will be the baseline against which all project decisions will be based during the subsequent implementation and completion phases.

Project Owner's Requirements

The logical first step in starting a project is for the owner (or the project management team appointed for the purpose) to outline the work to be undertaken to complete the project and satisfy the need(s). The work to be carried out on any project is a function of the owner's objectives. The objectives must be known and clear to those who do the subsequent work. In defining the objectives, the owner is required to state them in some order of priority. This is done by means of a written document which is referred to here as the *requirements document*.

A summary of what the requirements document might consist of includes:

- official identification of the project;

- brief description of the envisaged project;

- relevant contract data affecting the work to be done;

- constraints and other conditions;

- stakeholder outline responsibilities;

- decisions that have already been made.

Having fully defined the project requirements, the next step is to define the "project strategy"; the *"how-we-are-going-to-get-there"* step. This strategy is the link between the objectives and the detailed planning. If we use the analogy of a journey, the project objectives should be seen as the ultimate destination, times of arrival and overall cost. The strategy is selecting the general direction to follow and the mode of travel to be used.

Project strategy depends to a large extent on what might happen in the future. Change, as we know, is likely to shift the objectives target. It is likely that alternatives will have to be considered and "what ifs" looked at. A well-thought-out strategy will offer and devise ways to do things differently, and better, for the specific project under consideration.

The tools and techniques shown in Figure 6-1 for the pre-investment stage of the conception phase are the main means for converting the owner's requirements and the strategy into tactics that will confirm, or otherwise, the need for a project and the viability of various options that could satisfy the need.

Recommendations for the proper introduction and execution of the conception phase are as follows:

- appoint a team leader (study or schemes' manager) who will have the single focus of "the project" and its effective management;

- through the manager confirm the requirements and outline the concept plan;

- appoint the best team to undertake conception of the project;

- carry out complete project conceptualisation to a depth that will ensure controllable later-stage variations within constraints such as quality, cost and time.

If these recommendations are followed the potential for project success will be enhanced significantly.

Conceiving the Project

The conception phase of any project is the important period between the time when an owner (also referred to as sponsor, developer, entrepreneur, or similar title) has an idea that is likely to be transformed into a project, and the start of the definition phase of the selected project. The conception phase consists of the pre-investment stage and the post-investment stage which are the periods before and after the owner's decision to financially invest in the project's implementation. This period is the time within the life-cycle of a project when a scheme(s) or idea(s) becomes a definable project, albeit in outline. It is also the time when the greatest effort is expected from the project's management (see Section 1 of Part 3).

Initially, the definition phase consists of the design stage which is followed by the procurement stage; this is usually not executed until the completion or significant completion of the design stage. Similarly, the design stage normally is not commenced until the concept work has been completed. Fundamental prerequisites for any project authorisation include:

- a feasible scheme;

- an "owner" commitment to the project;

- experienced technical (or other appropriate) resources;

- an appropriate level of funding to support the anticipated project costs.

A *feasible scheme* is one which if implemented can be demonstrated to be both technically and economically viable. In evaluating schemes it is necessary to gather data and market research relative to the type, size and location of what is needed to satisfy the owner's requirements. Alternative options (schemes) should be studied and compared during the feasibility study stage of a project's life-cycle. Feasibility analyses confirm, or otherwise, the viability of the schemes and whether or not there is an investment opportunity.

Figure 6-2 shows the sub-stages that may exist prior to the decision "to proceed". In other words, these stages are the pre-investment period of the conception phase. The terms that are used for the pre-investment stage vary considerably but *opportunity, pre-feasibility, feasibility,* and *funding* shall be used here to describe the sequence of events for the normal project. Opportunity studies are carried out when there might be a need or an idea but there is also the question: "Is it possible to conceive and implement?". These studies seldom incorporate economic evaluations but concentrate mainly on the technical viability of the various scheme options.

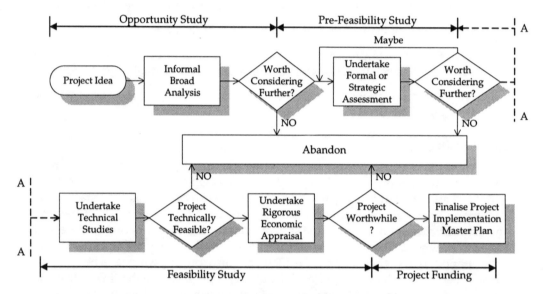

Figure 6-2: Model Flow Diagram of the Pre-Investment Process

Usually a prefeasibility study is instigated when the opportunity study has indicated that it may be worth considering the idea further or, having by-passed an opportunity study, there is sufficient technical knowledge on the viability of the idea or a need to proceed to a prefeasibility level of analysis. There are a number of best choice options under consideration at this time that could be the response to the idea or need.

If the more formal assessment of the idea shows itself to be supportable at a pre-feasibility level of analysis then the next step, to undertake a feasibility study, will demand a technical analysis of the surviving options and any new options that materialise during the feasibility period. The technical viability should be determined for all options before carrying out rigorous economic appraisals.

At feasibility study stage the cost comparisons are based on what is termed "order-of-magnitude". Such costs of alternative schemes will be relative and not absolute. In fact the cost comparisons are preliminary and are likely to be no better than + 50 per cent to – 30 per cent adrift of the absolute cost of each scheme. However, providing each scheme has been evaluated on the same basis, this level of accuracy (or inaccuracy) is quite acceptable for the purposes of scheme comparison.

It is generally found that the "best" option becomes more or less apparent, but the relative cost comparisons are influential in the selection of the "best" scheme. The best scheme is the one that is likely to provide the owner with the best benefit/cost ratio and will meet all of the project requirements. It must be remembered that the "do nothing" option is always a choice. *Authorisation*, which is the term used in the PMBOK (see Section 2, Part 3), is the process of recognising formally the existence of a new project (or that an existing project should continue into its next phase). Authorisation is the initial confirmation of the *owner's commitment* to the project.

Normally, projects are given the go-ahead in order to realise some particular advantage, or gain, for the project owner. The project can be a new IT system, the overhaul of a major piece of equipment, the installation of a new production line, a new water supply scheme, etc. The advantage of the project may be additional profit or an improved facility. It is one or other, or both, of these advantages that lead to the owner's commitment

In an ideal world, the owner's organisation would be expected to manage all its own projects. However, in reality this seldom happens and this is probably just as well. It is highly likely that owner personnel with corporate roles and responsibilities would not necessarily provide the impartial and unbiased single focus that is needed for good project management.

Assuming that "surrogate owners", in the form of independent project managers, are engaged, then it is imperative that the owner designates an in-house representative who will have continuous involvement with the project. Continuous involvement means day-to-day involvement with the detail of the project. Such an executive will be the owner's decision-maker on the designated project. This person needs to have the authority and commensurate project responsibility to act as the owner's representative within the conception team.

In general, the project manager should be *identified and assigned* as early in the project as is feasible. Where possible the project manager should be assigned at the start of execution of the conception phase. A *project charter* is the document that formally recognises the existence of a project. The project charter provides the project manager with the authority to apply organisational resources to project activities.

From the viewpoint of the unsophisticated owner, or the owner without adequate resources, the best contractual option is likely to be the one that requires the services of a project manager to take full responsibility for managing the project. The project manager must be independent of technical and commercial bias, and have the necessary skills and experience on a project of the type to be developed and executed (see Section 4 in Part 5).

Within a project management type organisational structure the project manager can directly appoint the *technical resources* needed to conceptualise the project. Technical resources should be obtained by using in-house resources or external resources, or a combination of both types of resource. External resources, in whole or in-part, should be procured through a limited competition based on the suppliers' background, the ability to work to tight time targets, the expertise and experience of the personnel; professional fees, although important, should not be used to determine the selection of any of the team members.

Funding for a project can be obtained from the owner's own equity, it can be borrowed, or it can be obtained through some other mechanism, such as build-operate-transfer for large infrastructure projects, or any combination of methods. Without a sound funding plan the "best" scheme is likely to remain no more than just that; funding availability is a sacrosanct determinant for the commencement of all projects.

Preinvestment Analysis

During conceptualisation and prior to taking the decision to invest in a project, there are likely to be a number of alternatives that need to be studied, analysed and evaluated. Project selection methods generally fall into two broad categories: benefit measuring methods and constrained optimisation methods (Project Management Institute, 1996). These methods are often referred to as *decision models*.

The *constrained optimisation models* are mathematical models, such as decision trees, linear programming and other similar techniques, some of which were dealt with in Part 4. *Benefit measuring models* are those which use comparative techniques such as cost benefit analysis, economic evaluations, etc., some aspects of which are also discussed in Part 4.

Pre-feasibility and feasibility study stages should include financial as well as technical analyses of alternative schemes — the difference between the two analyses being the greater refinement and detail in the feasibility study. By the completion of the feasibility study stage, the study team should be able to clearly identify the project to be invested in, providing of course that the "do not invest" option is not the recommended conclusion of the analysis.

As part of the viability analysis of the various schemes under consideration, the technical and economic evaluations will form the key elements of the viability process. The various schemes' technical feasibility should be investigated to a sufficient level of detail commensurate with good practice and within the budget constraint available for the preinvestment stages.

The economic evaluation process should use *payback period, return on investment, net present value and internal rate of return* as some of the methods available for comparing the economic attractiveness of various schemes. These methods were described earlier (Part 4, Section 3).

It is necessary, for meaningful scheme selection, that the time periods for the definition, implementation, and completion phases are assessed, and not guessed, for each option. As mentioned in the previous sub-Section, it is also necessary to ensure that each option have its costs estimated in accordance with a standard order-of-magnitude approach, and that this approach is held constant for all cost estimates.

Other aspects that may need action during this stage are to produce the quality definition for the project's product and process, and, if possible, introduce the first steps of the value process. The value process is described in Section 3.

Preliminary Master Plan

The project manager and the project team (or the owner's organisation, if it is more applicable) should, by the end of the conception period, have:

- established the project's scope of work and quality definition;
- managed the conception team to produce the conceptual design;
- produced a master time schedule;
- developed the project's overall estimate of costs;
- selected the most appropriate contract strategy.

These five elements are sometimes referred to as the "preliminary master plan" or PMP. The PMP is the deliverable from the conception phase. The PMP is the basis for the future unfolding of the design and implementation of any project. Projects that prove to have measurable failure elements inevitably have their problems traced to the inadequacies of the conception phase; in other words, the PMP has not been adequately undertaken.

Time spent on the conception of a project will always be time well spent. Extended periods in feasibility study and conception will ensure a higher level of project definition and therefore considerably reduce the risk of missing some aspect of the owner's requirements and the project objectives. Arguments regarding the expense of up-front owner costs should not be used to dilute the case for spending more time earlier in the project's cycle but they should be acknowledged in the sensible, balanced decision-making that should epitomise all projects at this phase in their life.

On the whole the project manager will execute and manage all the main elements with the exception of the technical design. The appointed concept team is responsible for executing the concept design. It is worth noting that the concept design team need only be appointed for the concept stage. A decision can be made by the owner and/or the project manager either to continue or to abort the concept team at the end of this stage.

The project manager is responsible for determining the work plan for the conception phase. This plan will be carried out as all plans should be: by establishing the phase objectives, producing the WBS, the OBS, the RAM, the logic diagram and then the scheduled plan.

The project manager and their management associates are the only entity within the team with the single focus of management; they are required to hold a "big-picture vision" of the project. The project manager directs and controls the concept team, ensuring that time targets are met, that quality of outline design and performance are consistently achieved and that the budgeted cost of the team's services is under control and is at, or below, predictions.

In parallel with managing the activities of the concept team, the project time schedule and the overall cost estimate to completion will be developed. From the ongoing concept designs, the project manager and other members of the project management team plan and schedule the detailed design, procurement, implementation, and completion phases. The work associated with this exercise of planning, scheduling and balancing the project's future activities will provide the master time plan, the estimated budget cost of the project (related to the scheduled activities), and the packaging of the project's physical works.

The PMP is concluded by deciding on the most appropriate contract strategy. The number of contract packages, the right form of contract, how the contracts are to administered, bonds, insurances, etc., are all matters that need to be included within the contract strategy.

The following brief summary is offered as practical advice on achieving success in the conception phase:

- create a study team of skilled individuals with complementary capabilities working under a study manager;

- select supplier organisations and/or implementation contractors to join the study team to provide a dimension of practical expertise;

- investigate a range of technical options and select the "best" options for financial sensitivity analysis;

- undertake a risk analysis exercise of the best options, identifying risks and analysing their effects, and determining the potential for allocation;

- compare a short-list of schemes using Net Present Value (Cost) analysis and select the "most likely project";

- produce a feasibility study report which is a "bankable" document dealing with all aspects of the recommended project and, if required, its impact on the environment, the benefits of the project, the financial aspects, and the economic effects;

- ensure that the PMP is complete and to an appropriate level of detail.

Definition Phase

The two stages of the definition phase are the design stage, and the procurement stage. These stages are identified in Figure 6-1.

Design

The project team during design has two organisational components, that, although related, are separate in what they do. The parts are:

- technical design;

- design management.

Technical design is by its very nature a creative, expansive process with each successive step of the continuum being both cyclic and iterative. For the optimum solution to emerge requires not just visionary and inspirational ideas but much hard work, research, skill, knowledge, and determination. Inspirational ideas and vision unfortunately cannot be predicted and programmed, and yet time and cost must be derived, and work progress must somehow be monitored and evaluated. As the design work progresses through its later steps the processes of: specifications, materials, documents, and other documentation become more real and manageable.

The technical specifications constitute an important element that will be used to control the performance of suppliers and contractors through contract documentation. Specifications need to be prepared so that the intent of the designer is clear and unambiguous. In determining the requirements of specifications, the author should appreciate the supplier's right to choose the method of execution. Specifications should portray clearly the required finished product of the project. The supplier/contractor will be held responsible for any aspects of the product that do not comply with the specification.

When an owner has to procure design services it is recommended that the design team should be secured on a similar basis to that used for the appointment of suppliers and contractors. The design stage should not be dealt with any differently to any other stage or sub-stage — the rationale being that within any system (project) the sub-systems should support a common strategy, the same overall objectives, and use methods and procedures that are consistent. In accordance with this approach, it is normal for the design stage to be planned, monitored and controlled in the same way as any other phase or stage. This aspect of design management is dealt with in this sub-Section.

The cost of design can usually be related to a percentage of the total cost of a project. A figure that is often quoted is 10 per cent but the cost of design can be significantly less or more than this; the figure used is dependent upon the business or development sector of the project. Since design costs normally represent only a small proportion of total costs, it becomes worthwhile, particularly on large projects, to increase the design effort significantly in order to achieve comparatively small percentage reductions in implementation cost, which in monetary terms can be many times the extra design cost.

Let's examine the following figures in order to understand the point that is being made:

| | Cost (mu) | | |
Item	Original Design	Revised Design	Change
Design	50,000	75,000	+50%
Implementation	950,000	855,000	−10%
Total Cost	1,000,000	930,000	
Overall Saving		70,000	+7%

The above Table shows a project that has an estimated total cost of 1 million mu, which includes a design cost of 50,000 mu; this equates to 5 per cent of the overall cost. The assumption is that if there was to be a 50 per cent increase in design effort, hence increasing the cost of design (50,000 to 75,000 mu), this would yield a savings in implementation cost of 10 per cent (950,000 to 855,000 mu). The net result is a 7 per cent reduction in total cost or an overall saving of almost three times the cost of extra design work, i.e. 70,000/25,000. Therefore the above indicates an ROI (return on investment) of about 3:1.

Does this ROI understate or overstate the issue? In reality, it probably understates rather than overstates. For example, when using the value process, project savings typically yield an ROI of between 10:1 to 20:1 of the extra design costs. The results of value process workshop exercises (see Section 2, "The Value Process") would indicate that even this ROI range understates the savings potential when operating, maintenance, and other on-going costs are taken into account. This would indicate that there is a strong argument for supporting an increased design effort; yet, with a few exceptions, pressure from owners or project sponsors normally mitigates against such action. Project managers need to balance increased design effort and cost against the potential for obtaining project total cost reduction.

Partnering arrangements between owner and design team are popular in certain industries. This is where the design team continues to provide a design service to an owner on a range of projects that are part of a "total program" of projects.

Throughout the definition phase the design team's performance will be measured by the management team against the original plan, the pertinent contract and the effect of all change orders to the project.

Good management methods can contribute to the achievement of good design. In addition to design skills it is now a requirement of successful project management that the designers have proven management abilities in addition to design skill and flair. It seems that future work for designers will centre more and more on the design service and less and less on other fringe services. In the future, competition and economic trends will determine that designers have, and use, demonstrable resource planning and control expertise.

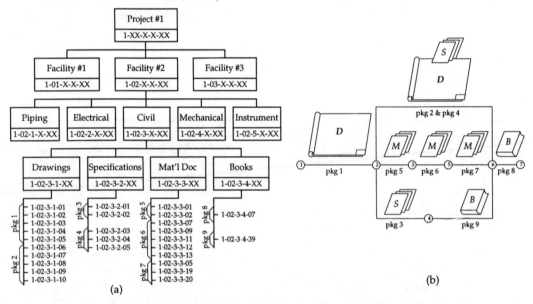

Figure 6-3: Model Planning and Control System for Design Documents

Figure 6-3 (a) shows a simple part-WBS of a project and (b) shows a representative network diagram for a 9 work-package project that will produce drawings (D), specification (S), materials documents (M), and technical reports (B) for one of the technical disciplines of one section of what is referred to as "project #1". The estimation of duration for each activity and how to analyse this type of activity network would be undertaken using the techniques explained in Part 7.

Often design expenditures are used to determine the state of progress of design work; this practice is not recommended. The principal assumption in using design expenditures as a progress measurement tool is that the ratio of cost-to-date to its total estimated cost is indicative of a project's design progress. This rationale is often extended to a broad range of project activities, in addition to design activities. In other words, a common procedure is to consider the per cent completion of something (in this case the design) to be 50 per cent complete when half of the associated budget has been spent. Obviously a substantial amount of a project's funds can be expended without any significant progress having been realised.

Assessment of work packages needs to be based on actual quantities rather than on actual expenditures. It is therefore necessary to establish "control points" and how to earn value when assessing progress. One recommended way in which a progress measurement system can be designed is shown in the following part-table layout which is shown for one item within one of the packages indicated in Figure 6-3.

col#1 Doc. no.	col#2 Reference		col#3 Items Budget	col#4 To-date Actual	col#5 Assigned % to CP					
	pkg	schd			#1	#2	#3	#4	#5	#6
1-02-3-S-07	4	2-6	25	15	20	15	40	5	10	10

col#6 A (actual) % compl. on CP						col#7 Percent Complete	col#8 Earned Value	col#9 Perform. Indicator	col#10 Current Forecast	col#11 Current Variance
#1	#2	#3	#4	#5	#6					
100	100	100	100	0	0	80	20	1.30	19	6

Columns #1 to #11 represent the columns within a spreadsheet presentation used for design (and other suitable activities) planning and control. Column #1 indicates the document identification number. Column #2 shows the package reference number and the schedule start and finish event numbers. The items budget and the to-date actual budget are shown in column #3 and #4 respectively.

The control points that have been selected for a specification document show that there are six control points; these could be assigned as follows:

CP	Earned Value	Description
#1	20%	Conditions of Contract
#2	15%	General Specifications
#3	40%	Detailed Specifications
#4	5%	Form of Contract
#5	10%	Owner's Comments Incorporated
#6	10%	Signed off, Printed and Bound

Column #7, percentage complete, is obtained by using the following formula:

$$\Sigma\, CP_i \times A_i \text{ (with i between the limits of i = 1 to i = 6)}$$

In the example shown this will give 80 per cent. What is referred to as "earned value" — column #8 — is given by column #3 x column #7/100. Column #9, the performance indicator, is obtained by dividing column #8 by column #4. The current forecast, column #10, is found by dividing column #3 by column #9. Column #11, the current variance, is obtained by subtracting column #10 from column #3.

This approach provides an integrated and quantitative management control approach for tracking the conception and definition phases of a project. The computed percentage complete for the various packages forms a more objective basis for updating and controlling particular parts of a project's schedule. There are other benefits, including:

- budget forecasts are also determined in an objective manner based on *actual performance*;

- performance indices are computed based on cumulative data that reduce the tendency of the forecast to be affected by a single bad period. The indices can be used to evaluate *personnel performance* and in creating a self-driven motivation for the highest possible performance;

- quantitative impact of the computed man-hours can be examined not only on project cost but also on *project milestones* and *completion dates*.

Delays and disruptions are the biggest destroyers of the productivity of design office output. Failure of a system usually manifests itself in shortage of key resources which includes, materials, people, equipment, or information (especially concerning decisions on critical issues). By far the most important of these resources is information. The engine which drives the design system is the brainpower of its members and the fuel which powers the engine is information. The design office is the quintessential information processing system: information drawn from a host of sources — the marketplace, design codes and standards, technical literature, the owner's terms of reference, the knowledge and experience of the designers — is processed into something which is (hopefully) elegant, useful, and economical.

Numerous reviews will be a fundamental function in the monitoring and control process of the project design. The project manager may need to decide on recovery options if the actual design performance should slip relative to the original (or last) scheduled plan and/or cost plan.

Procurement

One of the five parts of the Preliminary Master Plan (PMP) consists of determining the most appropriate contract strategy. This strategy includes such matters as:

- the basis for selecting contractors;

- number of work packages and hence contracts;

- the start, finish, and intermediate milestone dates for each contract;

- estimated budget cost, contingency sum, and the spend versus time profile of each contract.

Procurement management was explained in Section 2 of Part 3. It consists of the process of: *procurement planning, solicitation planning, solicitation, source selection, contract administration, and contract close-out.* The first of these items, procurement planning, is what would form the basis of the contract strategy as part of the PMP. Procurement planning is determining "what-to-procure-and-when". The contract strategy will include procurement planning but will also incorporate the procurement systems (contract types) to be used. From the various *procurement planning* decisions that need to be made, the scope of work, the extent of procurement, how the procurement activities are to be managed, etc. will have been refined and included as part of the DCP which is the deliverable from the design stage.

The procurement process normally follows a sequence of enquiry, comparison of bids, ordering, expediting, inspection and delivery. Figure 6-4 shows a schedule with the procurement activities in sequence (Bent and Humphreys, 1996). The Figure demonstrates the sequence of procurement steps and, based upon past experience, the approximate time periods in weeks that may be needed to complete each of the steps.

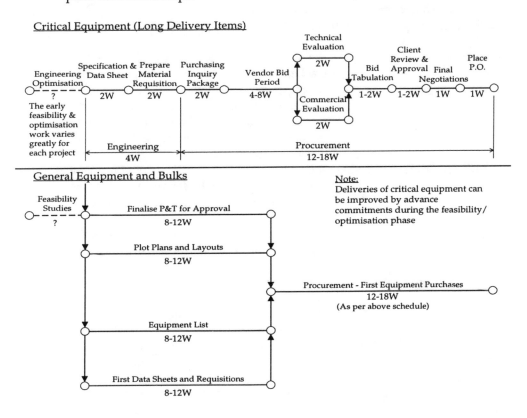

Figure 6-4: Typical Procurement Schedule

Enquiries should be issued only to potential suppliers with adequate and proven capability. Identifying potential suppliers should be part of a prequalifying exercise. Such companies should be included within the project's "bidders listing". Information contained within enquiries should be stated in a concise and unambiguous manner to obtain quality bids from suppliers.

Comparison of bids includes the bidding and evaluation strategy. The strategy, referred to earlier, will have identified options such as, open bidding, negotiated bidding, single source, multiple source, etc. Bids should be evaluated on a technical, delivery, financial, commercial, and economic basis and such information should be tabulated and included as part of a bid report that includes award recommendation.

Any negotiations between receipt of bids and placing of orders should be carried out with appropriate project stakeholders. Following approval of the bid the order should be placed with the recommended bidder.

The first step in the selection process is to choose an appropriate organisation to conduct the project. The process starts by eliminating types of organisations that obviously do not meet the needs of the project and the owner. To eliminate inappropriate organisations, three types of characteristics must be assessed by the owner. These will be referred to as project characteristics, owner characteristics and market characteristics.

The main project characteristics are:

- *time constraints:* the owner must decide if the project is to be fast-tracked — i.e., the design and implementation overlapped — or whether a more normal sequential arrangement of activities is needed.
- *flexibility needs:* the owner must decide how much flexibility is needed for design changes to be introduced during the implementation process.
- *pre-implementation services:* the owner must decide if the project needs services from a specialist to derive cost estimates, provide advice and contribute to the value process.
- *designer interaction:* the owner must decide how much interaction to have with the designer during the design stage of the project.
- *financial constraints:* the owner must decide if the project can be more effectively financed, either short or long term, by the owner or by the contractor.

The owner characteristics can be used to narrow further the choice of appropriate organisations. The owner characteristics are:

- *implementation knowledge:* the owner must conclude whether or not to have advisers.
- *current capabilities:* the owner must decide what staff can be committed to the project to administer, monitor and manage it.
- *risk aversion:* the owner must decide the amount of financial risk to bear.
- *restrictions on methods:* the owner must determine if there are any restrictions on the methods to be used in bidding for the project.

The market characteristics are used to help the owner to understand the business environment in which the project is to be awarded; this helps to determine the award method. The market characteristics are:

- *availability of contractors:*   the owner must determine that appropriate suppliers are available to work on the project.
- *current state of the market:*   the owner must determine the competitive state of the implementation market at the time of tendering.
- *project package size:*   the owner must decide how to package the project to maximise efficiency and to gain the most from market competition.

After analysing all these characteristics, the owner should have determined at least one desirable organisation and an associated contract type.

In selecting a contract type, the owner's decision is related to risk allocation. There are many risks inherent in implementation. However it is financial risk — what the final cost of the project will be — with which an owner is most concerned. Optimising the cost of the project depends on the proper identification and assessment of risk, its allocation, and ensuring that each party manages the risks allocated to them.

The identification of the project risks will be found in the main project characteristics and to some extent in the owner and market characteristics. Lack of final and/or complete information at the time of award creates the financial risk in a project's total cost. The balancing of risk between the owner, the designer and the contractor(s) should be sought in order to utilise the incentive value of bearing risk while minimising a contingency charged for accepting risk.

In determining the contract type(s) to be used for a project, numerous issues arise that will determine the choice. Such issues include:

- shortening the duration of the project by overlapping design and implementation and/or eliminating solicitation time;

- providing flexibility for introducing changes during implementation and completion;

- creating greater team-work between designer/"goods and services suppliers" (contractor) and accordingly reducing adversarial relationships;

- allowing a contractor to participate in the design process, thus augmenting the designer's implementation experience on such tasks as value, operability, etc.;

- providing incentives for the contractor to save the owner money;

- providing alternative financing methods.

The owner has the choice of using two main types of contract: fixed price and reimbursable. Fixed price contracts are also referred to as lump sum, unit prices or cap (fixed price set by the owner against which the contractor proposes a level of quality for a project). Reimbursable contracts are also referred to as cost plus or fixed fee. A hybrid of the two is called a guaranteed maximum price (GMP) which reimburses the contractor only to a certain point, the GMP, and beyond this price the contractor is liable for the costs.

The award method is the method used to select the supplier and/or the price to undertake the implementation. The award method is very important because of the unique "one-off" nature of most projects. The two extremes of award methods are lump sum competitive bidding which is open to anyone and single source negotiation which is carried out with only one contractor.

An outline explanation of each type of award method follows:

- *competitive bid:*   a contractor is selected by the lowest price proposal in competition with other bidders;

- *cap:*   a fixed price is set by the owner against which contractors propose a level of quality and options for a project;

- *negotiation:*   the price and/or the contractor are selected by negotiation between the owner and either several contractors or one contractor;

- *qualification and price proposal:*   the contractor is selected competitively based on qualification and price and is then usually ranked in decreasing order;

- *time and price proposal:*   the contractor is selected competitively based on the proposed schedule and price, and then ranked in accordance with a time-price formula;

- *qualification, time and price proposal:*   the contractor is selected competitively based on qualifications, proposed schedule, and price;

- *design and price proposal:*   the contractor is selected competitively based on proposed design and price and then ranked in accordance with a ranking formula.

The following brief summary is offered as practical advice on achieving success in the definition stage:

- from the concept design, master time schedule, and contract strategy, procure the services of a design team after competition and in accordance with a strategy that will evaluate a supplier's experience, capability of resources, planned methodology, and other factors that will be judged as important, if not more important, than the offered price of services;

- owners should be prepared to welcome increased design effort in order to achieve overall project cost optimisation;

- specifications prepared should be clear and unambiguous, and fair to both parties to a contract;

- the design team's contractual time schedule and contracted cost, along with declared productivity rates, are used to monitor and control the team's activities;

- the procurement team, using a pre-qualification/qualification process, select the organisation type, the contractor, and award method which best suits the project;

- ensure that the Definitive Control Plan and the Detailed Firm Plan at the end of the design stage and procurement stage respectively are complete and to an appropriate level of detail.

Concurrent Engineering

Recent studies have shown that in certain high-technology areas, such as semi-conductor manufacturing and telecommunications, where performance is increasing and price is dropping almost daily, survival of these types of production company depends upon the rapid introduction of new technologies. Being a few months late with a new product is worse than having up to, and more than, a 30 per cent development cost over-spend; this concept is described later within this sub-Section.

In the global market, successful companies will be those that learn to make and deliver goods faster than their competitors. To reduce cycle times three principles can be applied:

- reorganise the work;

- organise and reward performance;

- aggressively pursue cycle-time reduction.

A relatively recent trend in technology management is to perform all major components of design concurrently: this concept is known as *concurrent engineering*.

Concurrent engineering is based on time savings which can be obtained through undertaking parallel design of product components. Such an approach will shorten project life cycles and thus reduce the time-to-market for new products. Let's assume that a three-phase model reflects a product's commercial life. The assumption is that these three phases called growth, maturity, and decline refer to:

- *growth*: where sales increase at a fixed rate regardless of the entry time;

- *maturity*: the time period when sales start to level off to the time when sales start to decline;

- *decline*: where sales decrease to zero.

If the time periods for each of these phases are taken to be 6 months, 12 months, and 8 months, respectively, then being late in introducing a product to the market can mean the revenue generated could be reduced by 36 per cent. This point is shown demonstrated in Figure 6-5.

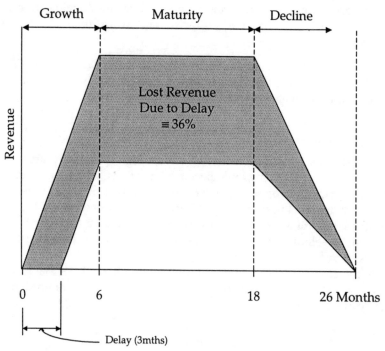

Figure 6-5: Lost Revenue from Delay in Reaching Market

From Figure 6-5 it can be seen that a delay of 3 months in 26 months, i.e. between one-eighth and one-ninth of the product life-cycle reduces the potential product income by over one-third.

Introducing and applying a concurrent engineering process is not an easy matter; the risks are greatly increased and many issues need to be addressed. Issues such as errors and change control, if not properly managed, can raise the risk of schedule and cost over-runs, and the performance of the design process. Time has become a critical element in the design process; today's successful companies need to have the ability to reduce the time required to develop new products and bring them to market quicker than their competitors. The two most prominent risks when using concurrent engineering are:

- organisational risk;

- technological risk.

Organisational risk can be rampant when there is no deliberate attempt to form project teams of people from the various functions needed to design and produce what the customer requires. Cross-functional project teams with the right attitude can help to reduce the potential for organisational risk.

Because it is not possible to "freeze" any of the design activities before commencing with succeeding activities, the *technological risks* are much higher than in sequential engineering. It is essential that the information used by all designers is current and correct. It is for this reason that configuration management (see Part 8, Section 5) should be used on most projects.

The basic idea of concurrent engineering is to use project scheduling and resource management techniques (see Part 7) for the design process. Although such techniques have always been common to the implementation phase it is now recognised that such techniques are vital to all life-cycle phases.

The conventional engineering approach is one of sequence compliance by which new product development starts with one organisational unit creating specifications based on customer requirements. These specifications are used to come up with a product design, which in turn serves as the basis for manufacturing engineering to develop the production processes and flows. This is then followed by support design during the manufacturing process. Sequential engineering takes longer because all the design activities are strictly ordered and in series.

Concurrent engineering depends upon designing, developing, testing, and building prototype parts and subsystems concurrently, not serially, while at the same time designing and developing the equipment to fabricate the new product. This means the team members from the various departments are required at times to make their contribution(s) in parallel. The basis of concurrent engineering is parallel activities, information sharing, teamwork, and constant communication among the team of people involved.

Concurrent engineering should be used if a project demonstrates some or all of the following characteristics:

- the project is of a developmental (novel) type or of an applications (routine) type;

- the project team has experience with the technology;

- the team has received training in total quality management and has had the opportunity to apply the concepts in its work;

- the scale of the project falls somewhere in the range of 5 to 35 full-time staff members for a period of 3 to 30 months;

- the goal is a product or family of products with clearly defined features and functions;

- success is not dependent on invention or significant innovation.

SECTION 2: ESTIMATING AND BUDGETING PROCESSES

Contents

- Aims and Objectives
- Cost Estimating
- Types of Estimate
- Direct and Indirect Cost Items
- Estimating Techniques
- Cost Budgeting
- Range Estimating

Aims and Objectives

The aims and objectives of Section 2 are to:

- Explain the process of capital cost estimating;
- Describe the five classifications of estimate types;
- Define the differences between direct and indirect costs;
- Explain various estimating techniques;
- Describe the elements of a project cost budget;
- Present the basics of range estimating.

Cost Estimating

Cost estimates, budget, work breakdown structure, and time schedule are interrelated concepts. The WBS and time schedule concepts are described in Parts 3 and 7, respectively. In projects, it is necessary to put practical constraints on costs so that realistic budgets can be established; cost estimating is the basis for developing budgets which in turn become the baseline for measuring project performance. The rate of actual cost expenditure compared to the estimated rate of expenditure, interpreted from the budget, is an important basis for project performance. Without good estimates it is impossible to evaluate work status or to determine how much the finished project will cost (Nicholas, 1990). The concepts of project status monitoring and performance are explained in Part 8.

As the term implies, "estimating" is a procedure which provides answers with significantly less than 100 per cent chance of being correct or even close (Humphreys, 1991). Estimating is imprecise and cannot be reduced to a sequence of mathematical expressions. Thus, understanding the accuracy limitations of the estimate and its potential variation is extremely important to the user.

A cost estimate may be defined as a compilation of all costs of the elements of a project or the cost of effort included within an agreed-upon project scope. To a contractor (supplier) this includes the cost that will most likely be incurred to complete the project as defined in the contract documents, and turn it over to the owner. The contractor's costs are made up of the contractor's internal costs as well as the cost of the work of any subcontractors, suppliers and other third parties.

The owner's costs are made up of: the owner's own costs for administering the project; the *price* (see comment in last paragraph at the end of this sub-Section) which the contractor(s) have charged for work performed; and the costs of consultants, engineers, and, other suppliers. Also included within the owner's costs, and where applicable, will be the cost of land, provisions for interim and permanent financing, plus numerous elements of the life cycle cost associated with the project, and hence the facility, ownership and operation, etc.

Capital investment is composed of two parts:

- the fixed capital investment to provide the physical facilities.

- the working capital investment (revolving fund to keep the facilities operating).

Cost estimates for capital projects consist of two parts:

- *direct costs*: all permanent equipment, materials, labour and other resources;

- *indirect costs*: all costs, other than direct costs, which do not become a permanent part of the facilities.

Further explanation of these costs are presented later in this sub-Section.

The process of capital-cost estimating is accomplished in three steps:

- *takeoffs*: this refers to measurement of the quantities of work and the cataloguing of cost items identified from the scope documents;

- *costing*: from takeoffs and information from the scope documents, the assignment of cost values to the elements of work and related items;

- *pricing*: determining the amount the owner is charged by the supplier of goods and/or services.

It is important to note the difference between *costing* and *pricing*. Costing is the basis of determining what the goods or services will cost if undertaken. Pricing is the basis of what someone will pay if they have to buy the goods or services.

Types of Estimate

Project cost estimating is essentially an intuitive process which attempts to predict the final outcome of a future capital expenditure programme, even though not all parameters and conditions are known, or are not fully defined, when the cost estimate is prepared. Accurate cost estimating is sometimes a difficult task; the range of difficulty being dependent on when in a project's life cycle the estimate is being carried out. In general, the earlier in the life cycle, the greater the difficulty.

Five classifications of estimating type named according to their common-usage term (along with an alternately used term) are (Goodwin and Wright, 1991):

- order of magnitude (ratio estimate)

- study (factored estimate)

- preliminary (budget authorisation estimate)

- definitive (project control estimate)

- detailed (firm estimate)

Let's look at three of these classifications to obtain some idea of what they mean.

Order-of-magnitude estimates are normally within an accuracy range of –30 to +50 per cent. This type of estimate is usually made without any detailed technical data. The estimate is often developed using cost-capacity curves, scale-up or scale down factors, or ratio estimating techniques. These estimates are used during the formative stages of a capital expenditure program when there is a lack of firm or verifiable information for the initial evaluation of the project. The accuracy of a preliminary estimate is usually very low.

Preliminary estimates are normally within an accuracy range of –15 to +30 per cent. This type of estimate refers to the owner's budget, not to the budget as a project control document. Where applicable, information such as flow sheets, lay-outs, and equipment details are necessary to perform this type of estimate. These estimates are used for the development of the PMP. These cost estimates are used for many purposes, including bid proposals, establishment of budgets, fair-price estimates for bid evaluations, contract change orders, extra work orders, etc.

Detailed estimates are normally within an accuracy range of –5 to +15 per cent. This type of estimate is developed from very defined technical data through specifications and drawings, etc. The accuracy of an estimate depends on the quality and quantity of available project information.

A guide for judging estimate accuracy and the type of estimate to be used, based on available information, is shown in the Figure 6-6.

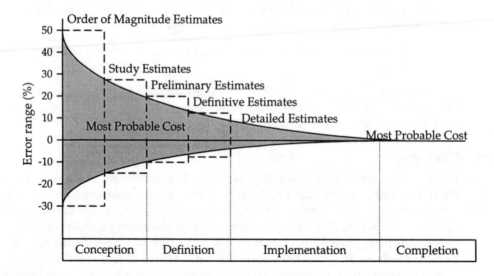

Figure 6-6: Accuracy Range of Cost Estimates

This shows a proposed range envelope, between minimum and maximum values, for five types of cost estimate within which the total capital cost estimate of projects would be expected to fall. The envelope is superimposed on the phases of a typical project life cycle. The most striking aspect of the relationship is the significant convergence in percentage error that takes place primarily within the earliest project phases. Ironically, this takes place at a time when cost information is scant and project costs are in the process of being developed.

Direct and Indirect Cost Items

Direct and indirect cost items must be kept separately. The reason for this is that indirect costs are usually specific to a particular contractor's or supplier's infrastructure. In order to compare elements of work or work activities more accurately between historical and future situations, then the less encumbered direct costs are, the more reliable will be the cost data for a new project.

A hierarchical structure (WBS) can be used for a cost estimate; such a structure might look something like:

- direct cost
  - ◊ labour
  - ◊ materials
  - ◊ equipment
  - ◊ subcontracts
- indirect cost
  - ◊ taxes
  - ◊ general conditions
  - ◊ risk
    - * profit
    - * contingency
  - ◊ overheads

These cost estimate elements can be briefly explained as follows:

Direct Costs

Labour can be broken into two components: basic wage (wage x hours worked), and labour burden (taxes, insurances, etc.). Burden is not always treated as a direct cost element since it is seldom directly proportional to the hours worked (use whatever is company practice).

Materials include the costs of materials or parts incorporated into a project. They are obtained from suppliers, etc. and are usually priced specific to a particular project. Most contractors include delivery charges as part of the direct costs and taxes as part of indirect costs.

Equipment refers to the cost of the equipment that a contractor uses to perform a contract. Operators' costs are usually included in the direct labour costs even though they are part of the operating costs.

Subcontracts are the cost of services provided by subcontractors performing a specific portion of a given project that the general contractor does not perform with its own forces.

Indirect Costs

Indirect costs vary significantly from location to location and by the tax-exempt status of the contractor. They are usually catalogued separately.

General conditions include the cost of items needed to perform a given contract as a whole. Usually these items cannot be charged to a specific element of the work and include such items as supervision, temporary facilities, utilities, small tools, etc.

Profit may be regarded as the amount of money included by a contractor as compensation for the risk, effort, and endeavour to undertake a project. The amount of profit added is usually subjective. It depends upon such factors as competition, how badly the contractor needs the project, the job market, local conditions and the economy.

In cost estimating, there is always an element of uncertainty, since estimates are based on assumed values of cost and productivity, which actually are subject to considerable variability. *Contingency* is added by management using subjective reasoning or structured risk analysis.

Overheads are in two categories:

- *Home office overheads*: this includes the fixed costs and expenses incurred in the course of doing business by a company, regardless of the amount of work completed or contracts received. This overhead includes office rent or lease, utilities, communications, advertising, salaries, donations, legal costs, accounting expenses, etc.

- *Job overheads*: this is another name for general conditions or job indirects and includes costs that are incurred at the job level in performing a specific contract but not chargeable to any specific item or element of that contract.

Estimating Techniques

Cost estimates are prepared using a number of techniques (Humphreys, 1991) based on:

- the cost of similar projects;

- the cost of project components.

A commonly used method for developing quick preliminary estimates draws on the "collective judgement" of a group of individuals (group consensus) with experience in cost estimating for similar projects in the past. The "comparison estimating technique" is a common method for estimating new capital projects and determining appraisals for existing facilities. Estimating by comparing, weighing, and relating the costs of similar past projects requires adjusting for the new location and time period, which usually requires judgement or well-defined adjustment factors.

When using published cost data, it is not always clear what is included in the cost. Published cost data should be used only for order-of-magnitude estimates since the assumptions made and the estimates' accuracy are seldom known.

Cost estimating techniques can be classified under the following types:

- graphic and tabular relationships;

- unit rate;

- resources allocation method;

- factor estimating;

- cost indices.

"Graphic and tabular relationships" are two estimating techniques. These methods are more quantitative and accurate than either "collective judgement" or "comparison estimating technique"; they are used in estimating during the conception phase. Examples of these techniques are:

- tabulations of data

- exclusion charts

- band charts

- upper and lower-limit charts.

Figure 6-7 (a) shows *tabulated* data (Humphreys, 1991) which, in this case, relates to the work-hours for the fabrication and erection of pipelines, including branches, valves, etc. that would be needed, for example, to transmit fluids. The tabulated data has been assembled into "operations" and "sources"; this information forms the columns of the Table. By using, say, the information from source C (could be a particular artisan) it would be possible to estimate the number of work-hours to fabricate and erect, say, 1,000 metres of 20mm pipe having 20 XH ells, 45 XH tees and fifteen 300 lb (135 kg) handled valves.

An *exclusion chart* is shown in Figure 6-7 (b), where the "early start" and the "late start" of a significant project activity is shown plotted on a chart where activity duration is the independent variable and activity cost is the dependent variable. The region of cost-time estimates is shown within the shaded area; all relationships outside that area are referred to as the exclusion zone(s).

An example of a *band chart* is shown in Figure 6-7 (c). This shows a relationship between the size of a unit and person hours. For instance the unit size could be lines of computer code to be written by a software analyst; the person hours would be the time taken to write lines of code. The shaded area shows the spread of the relationship; the plotted positive line (broken line) is "the line of best fit" obtained through carrying out a regression analysis (see Part 4, Section 4). Estimates are taken from the best-fit line or something close to that relationship.

An *upper and lower limit chart* is shown in Figure 6-7 (d). This shows performance versus base cost as a positive straight-line relationship (solid line) and upper and lower parallel lines (broken lines) that are the upper and lower limits set for the relationship. Estimates of "base cost" or "performance" are taken from within the set limits.

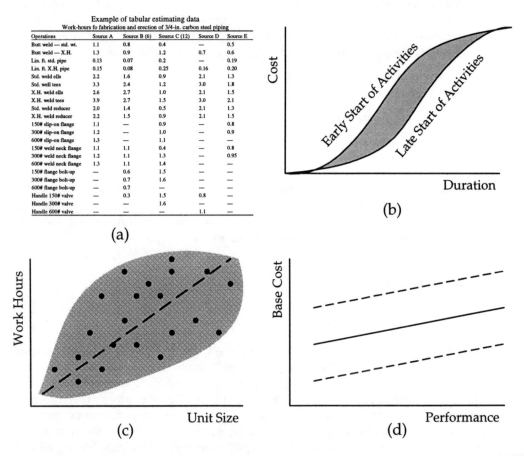

Example of tabular estimating data
Work-hours fo fabrication and erection of 3/4-in. carbon steel piping

Operations	Source A	Source B (6)	Source C (12)	Source D	Source E
Butt weld — std. wt.	1.1	0.8	0.4	—	0.5
Butt weld — X.H.	1.3	0.9	1.2	0.7	0.6
Lin. ft. std. pipe	0.13	0.07	0.2	—	0.19
Lin. ft. X.H. pipe	0.15	0.08	0.25	0.16	0.20
Std. weld ells	2.2	1.6	0.9	2.1	1.3
Std. weld tees	3.3	2.4	1.2	3.0	1.8
X.H. weld ells	2.6	2.7	1.0	2.1	1.5
X.H. weld tees	3.9	2.7	1.5	3.0	2.1
Std. weld reducer	2.0	1.4	0.5	2.1	1.3
X.H. weld reducer	2.2	1.5	0.9	2.1	1.5
150# slip-on flange	1.1	—	0.9	—	0.8
300# slip-on flange	1.2	—	1.0	—	0.9
600# slip-on flange	1.3	—	1.1	—	—
150# weld neck flange	1.1	1.1	0.4	—	0.8
300# weld neck flange	1.2	1.1	1.3	—	0.95
600# weld neck flange	1.3	1.1	1.4	—	—
150# flange bolt-up	—	0.6	1.5	—	—
300# flange bolt-up	—	0.7	1.6	—	—
600# flange bolt-up	—	0.7	—	—	—
Handle 150# valve	—	0.3	1.5	0.8	—
Handle 300# valve	—	—	1.6	—	—
Handle 600# valve	—	—	—	1.1	—

(a)

(b)

(c)

(d)

Figure 6-7: Examples of Graphical and Tabular Relationships
Source: Humphreys (1991)

The "unit rate" technique is one of the most widely used approaches in preliminary and detailed estimating during the definition phase. This method takes the form of either the so-called bare unit cost or the complete unit cost (see the example mentioned earlier regarding the use of Figure 6-7 (a), which is an example of bare unit rate).

The "resource allocation method" is popular in developing cost estimates for less tangible or non-repetitive items, such as applications of new technology, research and development projects, technical services, management services, consulting or advisory services. This method uses scheduled time periods of either weeks or months against project activities. Time spent by resources within each time period is costed using, say, unit rates; the matrix provides the basis for developing cost estimates.

"Factor estimating" is a technique generally used to arrive at an order of magnitude cost estimate during the conception phase. In this method a cost is estimated by multiplying one cost by a factor to get another cost. For example, if the average installed cost of equipment is about 1.5 times the purchase cost (the factor can vary considerably), the factor would be 1.5.

Another form of "factor estimating" called exponent estimating technique is sometimes used to prepare estimates during the conception phase. The costs of similar plants or pieces of equipment of different sizes vary with the size raised to some power. The relationship can be expressed as:

$$\frac{C_2}{C_1} = \frac{Q_2^x}{Q_1}$$

C_2 is the desired cost of capacity Q_2 and C_1 is the known cost of capacity Q_1. A frequent value for x is 0.6 so this relationship is often referred to as the six-tenths factor rule. The variable x can be determined by plotting actual historical costs for the equipment or plant as the ordinate on log-log paper and the equipment or plant size as the abscissa; the slope of the resulting line through the data will be the cost-capacity factor.

"Cost indices" are dimensionless numbers used to adjust the cost of an item from one time period to another. The adjustment is necessary because of the changing value of money with time. To convert costs from one time period to another:

$$C_2 = C_1 \times \frac{index_2}{index_1}$$

One of the major pitfalls of indices is the tendency to use them over too long a period. A rule of thumb is to use indices only to adjust costs for a 4–5 year time span. Using them over longer time spans greatly reduces the accuracy of the results.

Cost Budgeting

In the first sub-Section of this Section, the necessity of putting practical constraints on costs to establish realistic project budgets was presented. It was also stated that cost estimating is the basis for developing project budgets which then become the baseline for measuring performance. A budget is a plan for allocating resources. A budget is not simply one facet of a plan, nor is it merely an expression of organisational policy; it is also a control mechanism (Meredith and Mantel, 1995).

Within the sub-Section "Cost Management" (see Part 3, Section 2), project cost budgeting is defined as the allocation of the overall cost estimate to the individual work packages. The individual work packages are derived from the WBS activities. By costing the WBS activities, aggregating these activities into work packages, and then aggregating the work packages to arrive at a total project budget, the project budget can be interpreted as the scheduled plan in another form.

In most projects, work schedules and cost expenditures are difficult to control simultaneously. Two primary techniques for controlling the project are the scheduled plan and the cost budget; these techniques together provide what is referred to as *activity-based budgeting*.

Figure 3-17 (see Part 3) shows a time-based budget for a single work package. It can be envisaged that, by aggregating all work packages, a total project time – budget cost relationship can be developed. The total cost of each work package is distributed over the time period planned for each package. By adding the planned cost expenditure for the work packages for each time period — in this case 1 to 12 — the planned relationship between project time and cost can be obtained.

Another such relationship is shown in the following Figure.

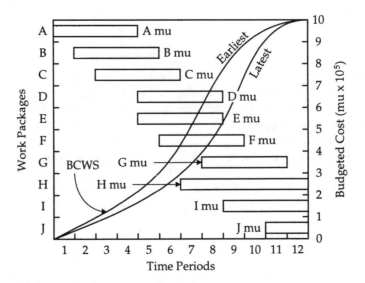

Figure 6-8: Budgeted Cost of Work Scheduled

Figure 6-8 shows what is typically referred to as an "S" curve relationship between project time and project budget. A generic term that is used is "budgeted cost of work scheduled" or BCWS for short. The Figure shows two BCWS curves, one representing the earliest start of activities, the other representing the latest start. It is normal to implement and hence control a project using only the earliest start relationship.

An important requirement when preparing a cost budget is a good cost code system. A modern cost code system must satisfy the owner as well as the project and it must be adaptable to computers and machine accounting. It must provide the cost feedback necessary for researching cost patterns, grouping like sub-components together, and it must also provide the detailed data required by the stakeholders in the project in a way that each stakeholder understands.

It is usual to adopt an eight-digit coding system in which the first four digits refer to major components and their functions, with the last four digits referring to cost elements. Such a coding would look something like this:

column	(1) (2) (3) (4)
digits	00-00-000-0

The first digit of column 1 refers to the major components that comprise the project. The first digit, having priority over all digits to its right, separates a project into major components, each one having some distinct difference from the others. This breakdown provides the desired summary sheet breakdown for the total budget.

Thus for the planning of a distance-learning (correspondence) educational project we could have as column 1 an abbreviated list of major components:

00	general
10	writing manuscript
20	editing manuscript
30	video production
31	*video #1*
32	*video #2*
40	outreach infrastructure
41	*centre A*
42	*centre B*
43	*centre C*
50	print course materials
60	(etc.)

It will be noted that the second digit can be used for a breakdown of the major components into "identifiable" major components, e.g. 31, 32 and 41, 42 and 43.

The second digit, having priority over all digits to its right, provides 10 subcodes for each major component. These two digits enable the components in the first column (1) to be divided into 10 main functions by using the first digit in column (2) followed by 10 sub-functions (2nd digit in the 2nd column). In all cases the digit on the left has priority over the digits to its right.

The third column (3) is for the project elements and is the main classification commonly used. The fourth column (4) is used when a detailed breakdown of the element into tasks is required.

Range Estimating

The basic problem with normal estimating and cost budgeting is that the bottom line estimate or "target total cost" is a single figure and, unless contingency has been thought about, the figure will likely exclude any contingencies. The problem with this approach is the effect of the uncertainties found in all projects. These uncertainties can lead to a situation where management makes an incorrect decision regarding the funding and hence the very viability of a project.

Michael Curran in his paper in James Bent's book (Bent and Humphreys, 1996), describes *range estimating* as a synergistic combination of Monte Carlo simulation, sensitivity analysis, and heuristics which enable the decision-maker to:

- identify the mathematical probability of overrunning the bottom line (target);

- estimate of the cost of a project;

- determine the maximum potential deviation above and below the target estimate;

- isolate and rank the reasons why that probability of overrun is as high (or as low) as it is.

A requirement in range estimating is to identify the "critical items" in a project. In the conception phase an element of cost estimate is deemed critical if it can vary, either favourably or unfavourably, by such a degree that the targeted total cost of the project would be underrun or overrun more than 0.5 per cent e.g. in a project with a targeted total cost of 6,172,630 mu the foregoing yields a value of 30,863 mu. Thus, if any cost element in the project can vary in either direction, by an amount such that the targeted total cost of the project would vary by more than 30,863 mu, then that element is critical.

As is expected from Pareto's law (refer to the next section, Section 3) relatively few elements in a project are critical. Typically there are less than 20 critical items in most projects. Once the critical items are identified, the range of values for determining the highest and lowest estimates need to be predicted. In range estimating it is usual to accept that there should be one chance in one hundred that the actual value could materialise above or below the highest and lowest estimate respectively. In other words, the lowest and highest estimates should form the boundaries of a range within which there is a 98 per cent probability of the actual value falling.

In determining the probability of an actual value not being greater than the target estimate, a simple procedure can convert qualitative values into a numerical context. One such procedure is to use the following guidelines:

- relatively little possibility of being greater than the   10%   (*unlikely*)
  target value

- some possibility of being greater than the target   25%   (*could happen*)
  value

- as much chance of being greater as being less   50%   (*as likely as not*)

- very likely to be greater than the target value   75%   (*very likely*)

- almost certain to be greater than the target value   90%   (*almost certain*)

The non-critical elements in a project can be aggregated and frozen. Aggregating items involves categorising them under labour, materials or equipment items. The non-critical elements are then frozen at their target estimates. Freezing non-critical elements presumes that the non-critical elements, as a group, will not overrun or underrun their target estimates by a significant amount.

The maximum possible deviations from the target total cost of the project, the so-called "theoretical limits" are 5,631,530 mu and 7,704,630 mu. These limits are shown on Figure 6-9. As these estimates are in the extreme, having been predicted on the basis of a 1 in 100 situation, they are interesting but somewhat beyond what would be considered to be "practical limits".

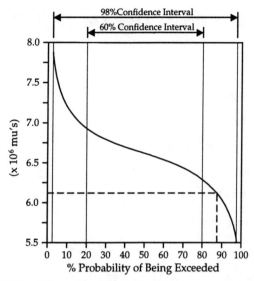

Figure 6-9: Probability of Exceeding the Project Cost

A range estimating model is generally little more than a series of simple relationships which show how the elements combine to produce the bottom line cost of the project. The estimates are then simulated using Monte Carlo techniques. The graphical overrun profile is shown in Figure 6-9. As can be seen, there is an 87 per cent probability that the actual cost will overrun the target total cost estimate of 6,172,630 mu. There is also a 60 per cent confidence that the project cost will be between approximately 6.275 million mu and 6.90 million mu.

SECTION 3: THE VALUE PROCESS

Contents

- Aims and Objectives
- The Effects of the Systems Approach
- Value and the Design Process
- Levels of Design
- The Issues for Producing Better Design
- The Key Elements of the Value Process

Aims and Objectives

The aims and objectives of Section 3 are to:

- Indicate some of the objections to fragmenting the elements of an enterprise;
- Outline the issues for producing better design;
- Introduce the value process through cultural acceptance or workshop intervention;
- Describe some of the more important value techniques available.

The Effects of the Systems Approach

Many professional designers have failed to adapt to the use of an integrated approach to design. There is still a tendency for project teams of technical specialists to work in isolated boxes. Often complex designs are developed without consideration of the discipline interfaces. Those concerned with design must be aware of the tendency for this to occur and take appropriate action to ensure full and proper co-ordination of these teams.

Some of the specific consequences for design arise from the rapidly growing importance of the "systems" approach. Not only the technical elements, but all elements of an enterprise must be integrated at the design stage. It is easy to understand why the mechanical, electrical, instrumentation and hydraulic systems of a concrete manufacturing plant must be harmonised and integrated in order to achieve the best and most reliable performance. It is not so easy to understand why the control of the implementation works and the complete management and administration of materials resources have to be planned in detail at the design stage of a project. This growing necessity of integrating every activity in an enterprise with the associated hardware at such an early stage causes great difficulties to those traditionalists accustomed to a rather fragmented and sequential approach.

Because of this shift in intellectual emphasis from the implementation phase to the conception and definition phases, it is essential that the project personnel have the ability to integrate, to pre-plan a multiplicity of options and be able to select that which offers the best solution. The onus is on the team to think through the totality of implementation performance requirements in the knowledge that failure cannot be compensated or overcome by the ingenuity of those who will use the facility (the term used for a project after the completion phase) during its operational life.

The design team (and the project team) must ensure that functionally the future facility will satisfy the owner's requirements and that the facility will be provided at least cost.

Value and the Design Process

It is very important that the relationship between value (Institution of Civil Engineers, 1996) and the traditional design process should be fully understood. There would be little benefit in applying the value process if everyone involved in design had perfect information and had used it effectively. However the complexity of today's projects, together with the increase in new technologies and techniques, render the concept of "perfect information" virtually impossible.

The design of relatively straightforward projects requires the interdependent working of a number of specialist designers, consultants and contractors. Such a team will often be working together for the first time. Its work does not form a simple sequence of activities, but will depend upon a complex pattern of multi-dependencies. Any one design decision is likely to have an important impact upon the work of other designers. In complex projects the implications of early design decisions are often difficult, or even impossible, to foresee.

The value process can be applied in two ways:

- as part of the design culture;

- using intensive workshop exercises.

In the "design culture" option, the key elements of the value process are carried out by the designers as part of an integrated thinking approach to project design. In the second option, the workshop exercise, the value process is carried out by an external facilitator or team of specialists who take a systematic approach and offer a "second look" at key design decisions taken by the design team.

There is, of course, benefit to be derived from the workshop exercise approach, irrespective of whether or not the original design was carried out with the value process as part of the culture.

Figure 6-10 shows the decreasing impact of decisions on project costs as the project moves through its life cycle. It also shows the influential stakeholder within each of the four generic phases. An important aspect to observe is where the greatest impact is achieved. This occurs during the conception phase and is a direct result of the decisions and actions of the owner. It could be said that this is conveniently at a time when the project cost is at a minimum; hence the benefit of addressing such impacts is maximised.

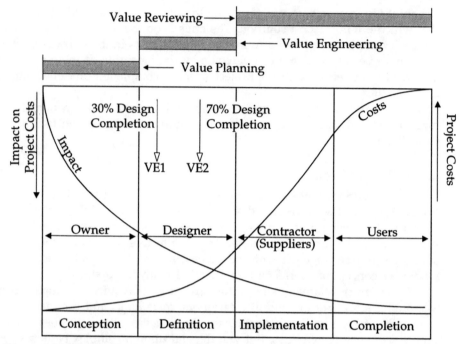

Figure 6-10: Stakeholder Impact on Project Cost

The timing for introducing the value process should be as early in the life of the project as possible. During the conception phase the process is referred to as "value planning" (VP), during the definition phase it is referred to as "value engineering" (VE), and during the remaining phases it is referred to as "value reviewing" (VR). Figure 6-10 shows when the workshop option (VE1 and VE2) should be used. In the cultural option, it is axiomatic that this should be part of the design team ethos from the commencement of design. In both of these approaches, the key elements of the value process are applied; these include:

- function analysis;

- creative thinking;

- cost models;

- cost and worth;

- life cycle costing;

- evaluation matrix;

- attitudes;

- contractual incentives.

These elements are dealt with subsequently in the sub-Section "The Key Elements of the Value Process".

Levels of Design

Design may be thought of in a hierarchical sense: at the top is the overall concept of the completed facility and at the bottom the detailed design of a myriad of tiny items and bits of systems, with a number of layers in between representing, from top to bottom, increasing levels of detail. The concepts and arrangements at the top level must be the responsibility of a small group, sometimes a single person. At the bottom they will be the creation of many people or groups located in different companies and possibly in different countries. At the top level, there is the general framework of relationships connecting all the elements or concepts which, taken together, make up the total project. Decisions made at this level will determine whether the project will be efficient or inefficient.

The design concept usually originates from an understanding of the process requirements and this is the basis from which the designer starts. Examples of the type of processes or systems to be understood could be:

- a business computer system requires detailed analysis of the business operation, the inputs, the elements to be integrated, the required outputs, and operator usage;

- a building design cannot really be attempted until the site location is selected, the use of the completed building is determined, site geotechnical information is available and local planning restrictions known;

- a manufacturing works cannot be designed until the manufacturing process is known and the manufacturing lines, flow rates and manning levels are defined.

Providing there is an adequate understanding of the process, or system, then it is possible to devise a project concept. This is a generalised idea of how to meet the requirements which have been given a systematic identity through the study of associated process(es) and will eventually be given form and substance by the design brief.

Designers are experts in their own fields and they conform to known and accepted practices, often favouring a particular "doctrine". They are creative by temperament and usually need the challenge posed by clear boundary conditions to bring out the best in them. In order to be good at their job they need to immerse themselves in an immense range of knowledge and understand how to apply it to best advantage. Indeed they bear a resemblance to outstanding performers in other fields e.g. athletes, academics, etc. It is obvious that all of these characteristics will be found in only a very few designers. Because of this, the use of workshop exercises is recommended for all projects, irrespective of whether or not the designers are cultured in the value process.

For every project, the design problems at the definition phase must be solved against a particular set of constraints. Whatever these are, and however numerous they may be, the designer must either know or be aware of them. Some of the most common constraints are: time, performance, safety, environment, space, and costs.

At the design stage, compromises must be reached between all the competing requirements within one or more of the limiting constraints. There is seldom a single correct solution, and a number of choices will usually be studied and compared.

At the design stage the project must have the benefit of high quality detailed design of the process or of the system's elements and components. This is necessary because:

- every component in every system must be able to make its proper contribution to the functional performance of that system;

- frequent and unpredictable component, and thus system, failure must be avoided;

- component wear-out rates and maintenance tasks should be harmonised so that repairs can be planned and controlled.

The Issues for Producing Better Design

Designs of most projects are complex. They require investment and experienced and talented people. Regardless of how capable or able a designer is, there will always be unnecessary costs hidden in their design.

Society is increasingly suspicious of professionalism and sees it not as upholding standards but rather as a restrictive practice designed to protect the self-interests of the professions. To change this view, it will be necessary to address certain key issues.

The first issue is the criterion that is often used for designer selection: the owner wants more for less. This is unsatisfactory because it stifles innovation. Innovation provides owners with projects that functionally satisfy their objectives. Innovation provides minimum cost projects. The current system of commercial interest works only because it over-rules the professional stance of design consultants.

The second issue is the theory of competitive bidding and the idea that the designer with the lowest bid will produce the most efficient and innovative design. In practice, the lowest bid frequently comes from the highest risk-taker; the result being that claims are often made as compensation for the problems caused by misconceptions.

The third issue is the need to communicate with a contractor at an early stage in the design process to ensure that BOD (buildability, operability, designability) are adequately addressed. The fourth issue is the general lack of formal techniques and procedures for managing the design process; this is found to be a hindrance in producing better quality designs.

The fifth issue is the skills, experience and drive of the people who have real influence through their position as buyers of goods and/or services. It is they, through synthesis and harmonisation, who have the power to produce the required big-picture thinking. Extreme specialisation and fragmentation is not what is wanted.

The Key Elements of the Value Process

As stated earlier, the key elements of the value process are: function analysis; creative thinking; cost models; cost and worth; life cycle costing; evaluation matrix; attitudes; and contractual incentives.

Function Analysis

Function is the keystone of the value process. The functional approach is what separates the value process from other cost reduction techniques. The concept of function is used to obtain a precise description of purpose. But what is *function*? Function is the basic purpose of an item or an expenditure. It may also be a characteristic that makes the item work.

The cost of a project, or an element of a project, and alternative approaches that can reduce cost, cannot be intelligently analysed without first determining the function that the project, or element, is to perform. We first investigate the function of the total system (the project) and then break the system down into quantifiable parts. Thinking about what a system or element does and assigning a value to that action forces us to think in greater depth and to make more comparisons than we would have without the function approach.

The application of function is function analysis. The project and its elements are evaluated by identifying the function in two words. A verb (action word) and a noun (measurable noun) are used to identify what the item does. For example, a water pipe has the function of transmitting water — transmit (verb) water (noun).

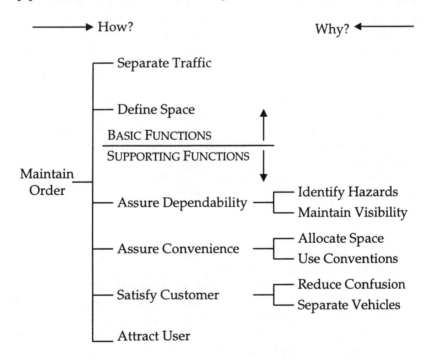

Figure 6-11: Function Analysis System Technique (FAST) Diagram

Figure 6-11 shows a FAST diagram for the ground marking of a multi-vehicle carpark to show the allocation of individual vehicle parking spaces. Most people are familiar with the painted "yellow lines" that mark off car spaces in public carparks. The main requirement is to "maintain order". The *needs*, that which will satisfy the requirement, are provided by the basic functions; see comments on basic function which follow. The *wants*, that which will sell the requirement are provided by the supporting function; see comments on secondary function which follow.

When analysing function, the following list of questions is useful:

- what is the purpose of the project (or element)?

- what does it do?

- what does it cost?

- what is it worth?

- what alternative would do the same job?

- what would that alternative cost?

The functional approach also helps us to think deeper about the project by classifying the functions as primary or secondary functions.

Primary functions are the specific work or purpose the project or an element must achieve. *Secondary functions* are support functions that may be a necessary part of the project but do not themselves perform the intention of the project or element. For example, in considering the functional analysis of a bridge deck, the primary function is to "allow passage". The elements of the bridge may be bridge deck, structural steel beams, piles, pile caps, excavation and guard rails. The bridge deck is the only element that "allows passage" to traffic; other elements of the bridge are support elements. In analysing the primary function of the bridge deck, let's assume that the load-bearing embankment fill used for the approach roads can be extended to eliminate several of the pile-supported deck sections. Thus, a part of the bridge deck is now replaced with the road surface, which provides the same function as "allow passage".

In the value process it is usual to perform a functional analysis on the total project first and thereafter provide separate functional analyses on each of the elements.

Creative Thinking

In simple terms, quality means doing what is now being done, only better. Doing old things with more quality may not, however, be part of the solution. There may be a need for change in what is being done or a need to do things differently. Creativity is the skill of bringing into being something that was not there before. Creativity has much to do with the way we think.

The brain can only see what it is prepared to see and it usually sees these as existing patterns. When we analyse data we can only pick out ideas we already have. If you can rid yourself of these inhibitions, you will be creative. But to be creative you have to use your right brain.

Intelligence has traditionally been seen as an inherited potential. People have been, and still are, IQ tested and judged in accordance with their IQ scores. For years, intelligence was considered to be something which we all have in some measure but which cannot be increased to any great extent. On the other hand, creativity was perceived as something which could be developed through the application of various techniques for creating ideas, within a stimulating environment. Creativity was seen as being much more related to the environment, even though some considered that certain creatively gifted people were born with such abilities.

Today the functions of the brain are better understood. The debate is now less centred on intelligence and creativity; it has more to do with the left and right hemispheres of the brain. The left hemisphere can generally be related to the concept of intelligence, the right hemisphere to the concept of creativity. Logical, evaluating, criticising and analysing activities are dealt with by the left-brain, and intuitive and creative activities are dealt with by the right-brain. Some characteristics of the two hemispheres can be summarised as follows:

left brain	*right brain*
• deals with information in logical order	• connects things in new ways
• analyses, evaluates, criticises	• thinks in pictures, deals with wholes and not detail
• controls verbal aspects	• controls artistic endeavours
• recognition of words and numbers	• recognition of people, objects, and experiences
• common sense	• intuition, spontaneity, and feelings

Within each of us, one of the brain hemispheres is normally dominant over the other. The ideal situation is to try to develop a balance between them. When the two hemispheres are working together the brain is being optimised. How can this be done? If we do develop the side which has been neglected, how will this help us? By using the left *and* right brains we:

- become more creative

- solve problems faster

- learn things quicker

- improve our memory

- decipher "body language" better

- improve communications.

We are now beginning to appreciate how important it is to develop both sides together. In general our schooling tends to encourage a preponderant use of the left-brain; this has led to a neglect by many of the right-brain. In other words, at this crucial time in our lives, most of us learn reading, writing and arithmetic, but learn much less, or nothing, on systemic thinking (thinking in wholes), mapping our thoughts, how to daydream, etc.

The dominant feature of all projects are the people which make them happen. Each person who is a "stakeholder" in a project is a sub-system or an element of that project but they are also a system in their own right. Within each stakeholder's system there are sub-systems, one of which is the brain. The probability is that all these brains are operating well below their whole collective potential and considerably less than their optimum. Within a projects' environment there is a finite time available, and certainly little time for individuals to develop the other brain hemisphere. The creativity which is needed from the stakeholders during the relatively short project duration is best created through the technique known as brainstorming. The technique is basically to:

- create as many ideas as possible (right-brain)

- evaluate them one by one (left-brain)

Brainstorming is synonymous with deliberate creative effort through a group process. Edward De Bono (1992) is of the view that an individual can be even more creative in their own right given the proper skills. Most project stakeholders are unlikely to have the individual skills needed, so brainstorming and group sessions could be expected to be two of the classical techniques used in a projects' environment. The problem is that this is not the case in most of today's projects.

It would seem that creative thinking can be applied in at least three ways:

- through improvement,

- within problem-solving,

- as part of the value process.

Improvement is perhaps achieved by either creating "a better way" of doing something or by "removal of faults". Creative thinking is not always necessary. When there are faults, logical problem-solving or using some of the available quality techniques can be used. When there are no faults, there is a greater need for creative thinking in seeking a better way. Better ways can include such issues as: lower cost, less time, fewer errors, or more humane, simpler approaches.

Cost Models

The cost model is the tool used to organise and distribute estimated costs that can be easily defined and quantified into functional areas. The purpose is to use past historical costs and the experience of team members in considering the present design and to ascertain those areas, or elements, with abnormally high costs.

Figure 6-12 shows a cost model for an institutional-type building (Institute of Civil Engineers, 1996). The cost differentials represent areas of potential cost savings. The elements of the cost model should relate to a cost estimating system that can be organised easily into functional areas and trade breakdowns. The model identifies all costs within functional areas of the project.

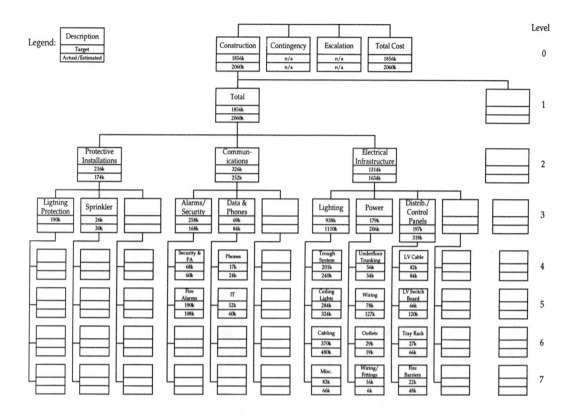

Figure 6-12: Example of a Cost Model

A further method for representing the total project cost is to use Pareto's principle (Michaels, 1996). Vilfredo Pareto (1848–1923), an Italian economist, postulated that if all the wealth, influence, and power in the world, which resides mainly in the hands of a few people, were distributed evenly among all people of the world, the wealth, influence, and power would inevitably return to the hands of the few. The expressions "the vital few", usually taken at about 20 per cent of the items of interest, and "the trivial many", usually taken at about 80 per cent, can be used to help identify the vital few cost elements in a project.

Figure 6-13 shows a histogram of principal cost elements (A to P) of a project, plotted in decreasing order of magnitude against the top scale. Superimposed on the histogram is a cumulative curve of project cost in which an element cost has been added to the previous sum of all elemental costs and the result plotted, as shown by the smooth curve, against the bottom scale. At the 80 per cent point of the total project cost, point "a" on the bottom scale, when projected vertically to the smooth curve shows that elements A to G represent the ($\cong$ 20 per cent) vital few.

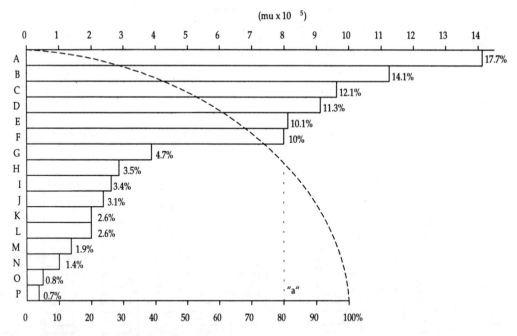

Figure 6-13: Application of Pareto's Principle

Cost and Worth

The basic means of measuring function is through its cost. Cost is what is paid for an item; it can be seen as the designer's estimate. The worth of a function is the least cost for performing the function.

Project: Building		**Item:** External Doors		**Basic Function:** Provide Access				**Date:** Dec '95	
Quantity	Unit	Component or Element	Function			Explanation	Original Cost	Worth (% of Cost)
			Verb	Noun	Kind			
10	No	Warehouse Door	Provide	Access	B		2,500	400
			Exclude	Elements	B			800
			Provide	Security	RS			600
			Enhance	Appearance	S			
		Ironmongery	Control	Door	B		1,000	450
			Enhance	Appearance	S			
		Painting	Protect	Material	B		500	350
			Enhance	Appearance	S	cost/worth = 4,000/2,600 = 1.54	4,000	2,600

Key: B=Basic, RS=Required Secondary, S=Secondary

Figure 6-14: Example of Cost/Worth Ratio Calculation
Source: Institute of Civil Engineers, 1996.

Figure 6-14 shows an example of the completed analysis of function. Having identified the basic, secondary and required secondary functions, the next step is to assign a worth to the function elements. In assigning worth, it is necessary to speculate on the least cost for performing the function. Many of the ideas generated may seem fairly crude. However, this is an effective way of developing a list of alternative solutions to the original design.

The relationship between total cost of an element and the worth of the primary functions is then found. This is called the cost-to-worth ratio. Experience shows that cost to worth greater than at least 1.50: i.e. cost/worth > 1.50, will usually indicate that there is unnecessary cost within the element being considered.

Life Cycle Costing

Life cycle costing (LCC) is the total economic cost of owning and operating a facility or a part of a project. The life cycle costing analysis reflects present and future costs of the project, or an element of it, over its useful life. It allows an assessment of a given solution and it is a tool for making comparisons.

Criteria for making life-cycle analyses include values for maintenance costs, long-term cost of money, salvage values and the expected life of the facility or the element being analysed. Costs given with reference to a particular time help us to get a clearer picture of the differences between expenditures at the present time and the equivalent value of that money at some future date.

Item: Conventional vs. High Frequency Lighting		HF Lighting		Switch Start	
Life Cycle: 60 years　　　　　Date: '97		Est. Cost	Present Cost	Est. Cost	Present Cost
Initial Cost	Based on 144 sq. m. room @ 500 Lux: 36 Fittings (16 Twin)	4140	4140	3600	3600
Salvage/ Replacement Cost	HF Tubing　　　　　　　　　　　PW Factor Every 4 yrs　4/56　　　　　　　4.456143	135	602		
	Conventional Tubing Every 3 yrs　3/57　　　　　　　5.045697			135	682
	Fittings Every 15 yrs　15/30/45　　　　　0.664025	4140	2750	3600	2390
Annual Cost	Maintenance:　　　　　　　　　PWA Factor Cleaned every 2 yrs　　　　　　7.806036	81	632	81	632
	Operations: High Freq.　£274/yr/144 sq. m　16.1614	274	4429		
	Conventional　£348/yr/144 sq. m			348	5624
	Meger Test　Every 5yrs　　　　2.836664	81	230	—	—
Total Net Present Cost			12,783		12,928

Figure 6-15: Life-Cycle Cost Comparison of Alternatives

The example used in Figure 6-15 is a comparison of high frequency versus traditional lighting and associated fittings over an economic life period of 60 years. You can see that the economic evaluation of the traditional lighting is contained within the last two columns and the HF lighting is contained within the first two columns. PW factor refers to the present worth discount factor and is obtained from discount tables for a specific discount rate and particular years of application. PWA factor relates to present worth annuity, and is obtained from discount tables for continuous payments.

Evaluation Matrix

The evaluation matrix is a decision-making tool. Along with the application of the "criteria weighting" technique (see Part 4, Section 4), the techniques combine under what is called SMART (simple multi-attribute rating technique) which was put forward by Edwards (1971) and is explained by Goodwin and Wright (1991). Although the SMART technique has wide application, it is of considerable benefit to a project when applied to a decision problem that is considering a range of qualitative attributes.

The evaluation matrix technique is designed to take criteria that affect an element of a project and develop a weighting system that will permit an evaluation of the response of various alternatives (properties and/or costs) against the criteria. Total weighted evaluation scores aid the decision-maker in the selection of the best alternative. The input data consist of the criteria and their weighting and the alternatives developed.

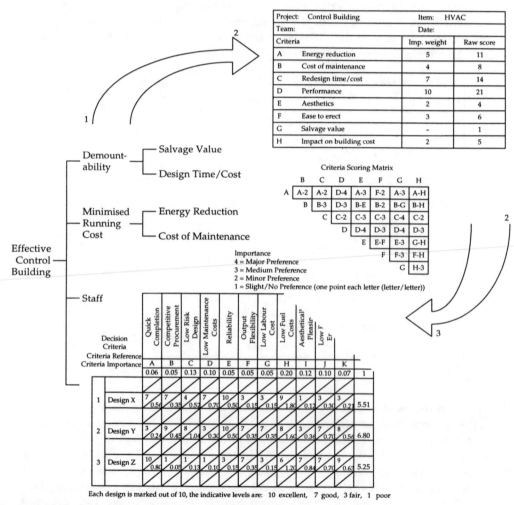

Figure 6-16: From Decision Problem to Evaluation Matrix

After listing the input data on the standard form (as shown in Figure 6-16), each alternative is evaluated against each of the criteria and ranked using the following marking system: excellent 10; good 7; fair 3; poor 1.

The ranking is selected to take into consideration how each alternative compares with the criteria. The next step consists of multiplying the rank of each half block with the weight of each criteria and entering the total in the upper half block. The alternatives can then be ranked for selection, the one having the highest total score being the "best alternative". But of course the capital cost or initial cost of each alternative must also be taken into account before deciding on which alternative to finally select.

Attitudes

Attitudes support the continuation of existing habits and may cause mind-blocks in the individual. Attitudes play a large part in our decision-making ability. Mind-blocks are quite often expressions of our attitudes and cloud the true facts. They colour reality. They kill off many good ideas before the ideas have a chance to develop.

Your attitudes are probably no different to this. Ask yourself and reflect on the following three questions:

1) Have I thrown out a good idea because I was guided by opinion rather than by facts?

2) Have I thrown out a good idea because I had a preconceived notion as to the solution?

3) Have I thrown out a good idea because I could not break my habits?

Like most people you have probably killed new ideas unfairly. Designers kill off ideas unfairly. Prejudice — and everyone is prejudiced in some manner — influences our opinions and our attitudes.

A primary concern of designers and contractors is with their past failures. When faced with something similar to a past failure, the tendency is to refuse to proceed. However a similar situation may have been handled successfully by someone else, whose experience would therefore be valuable. The tendency is not to want to investigate new occurrences, new developments of the product or different applications. We may not feel we have the time, the money or the inclination to do it. It is especially difficult when living in a time of explosive technical change. New products, new materials, new methods of implementation all add to the somewhat overwhelming choice of combinations that can be used to put projects together.

Contractual Incentives

The inclusion of incentives within contracts allows successful suppliers to share in any savings that can be developed in their contracts. The objectives of such incentive provisions are:

- supplier know-how;

- criteria improvement;

- reduction of operation and maintenance costs;

- a contractual means of providing a win-win situation.

Incentive clauses in contracts enlist the support of suppliers by paying extra fees or by rewarding them with extra profit for worthwhile proposals. Such proposals usually tend to inspire better, more economical decision-making by the design team.

Under these arrangements, bidders bid on contract documents which include value sharing provisions. These provisions do not affect the basis of the bid. After award, the successful supplier may submit value proposals that, if accepted, would create a change to the contract and effect a saving to the owner.

SECTION 4: THE RISK PROCESS

Contents

- Aims and Objectives

- Project Risk Management

- Risk Identification

- Risk Quantification

- Risk Response

- Summary of Key Points

- References

Aims and Objectives

The aims and objectives of Section 4 are to:

- Explain what is meant by project risk management and how to classify risks;

- Describe how to identify project risks;

- Enable the quantification of risks using a number of techniques;

- Outline briefly the process for the allocation of risk.

Project Risk Management

Corporate management has the responsibility to make formal judgements and appropriate decisions that will lead the organisation to a successful destiny. Organisational survival in today's world is achieved by pursuing opportunity within the spectrum of uncertainty. In taking advantage of these opportunities, a projects environment is typically created.

Uncertainty is the likelihood of an event occurring. Risk is the probability of an event occurring and the significance of the consequence of the event if it occurs. The word risk derives from an early Italian word (*risicare*) which means to dare (Bernstein, 1996). Risk would appear to be a choice rather than a fate. How free we are to make choices determines how much we dare to take actions. These actions can otherwise be referred to as opportunities; opportunity and risk go together. Future outcomes that are favourable can be viewed as opportunities, while those where the outcome has the probability of being unfavourable represent risk.

Project risk is the cumulative effect of the chances of uncertain occurrences adversely affecting project objectives. Project risk management is the art and science of identifying, assessing and responding to project risk throughout the life of a project and in the best interests of its objectives (Wideman, 1992). The constant goal of project risk management should be to move uncertainty away from risk and towards opportunity. The goals of risk management, therefore, are to identify project risks and develop strategies which either significantly reduce them or take steps to avoid them altogether. This process has to commence early in the life of a project; that is, in the conception and definition phases.

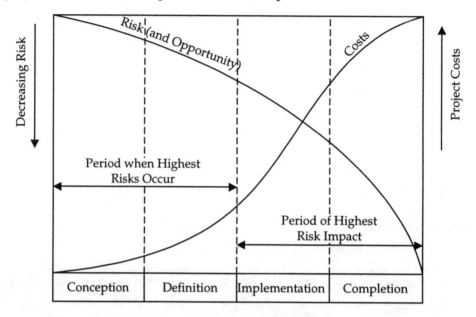

Figure 6-17: Opportunity and Risk versus Project Life Cycle

Figure 6-17, which has a close connection with Figure 6-10, shows the typical relationship between risk and the monetary investment for each of the four generic phases of a project. Risk (and opportunity) are highest during the conception and definition phases, but because of the relatively low level of capital investment during these phases the related cost of risk is low. During the implementation and completion phases, and as the level of monetary investment increases, the remaining unknowns progressively transform into knowns; the result being a decrease in risk to the project. During this same period the capital investment increases rapidly and the financial impact of risks can be substantial. The Figure shows this as the period of greatest risk impact; this should be compared with the period when risks are typically incurred.

Risks may be classified in a number of ways. One way is to describe the uncertainties in terms of *knowns, known-unknowns* (UNK), and *unknown-unknowns* (UNK-UNK). A *known* is an item or situation which contains no uncertainty; in fact, there is total certainty — it *will* happen. An UNK is an item or situation which is an identifiable uncertainty. An UNK-UNK is simply an item or situation whose existence cannot be imagined.

Another way in which risks can be classified is according to their impact on the principal targets, namely: scope, time, cost, and quality. A difficulty with this type of classification is that risks can have impacts on more than one of these knowledge areas at the same time. Yet another way of classifying risk is to separate them according to their nature, or derivation, e.g. contractual, political, financial, managerial, technical, etc., but again such classification may impact on two or more areas of a project leading to significant confusion and the potential for double counting when planning how to provide for such risks.

The Project Management Institute's "Body of Knowledge" (PMBOK) classifies risk in accordance with five categories: external, but unpredictable; external predictable, but uncertain; internal, non-technical; technical; legal. This classification concentrates on source of risk rather than risk effect.

The most serious effects of project risk are: failure to keep within the cost estimate; failure to achieve the required completion date; and failure to achieve the required quality and operational performance. When serious overruns occur on project cost estimates and time schedules, the effect on the overall project can be very damaging. In extreme cases, time and cost overruns can invalidate the economic case for a project, turning a potentially profitable investment into a loss-making venture.

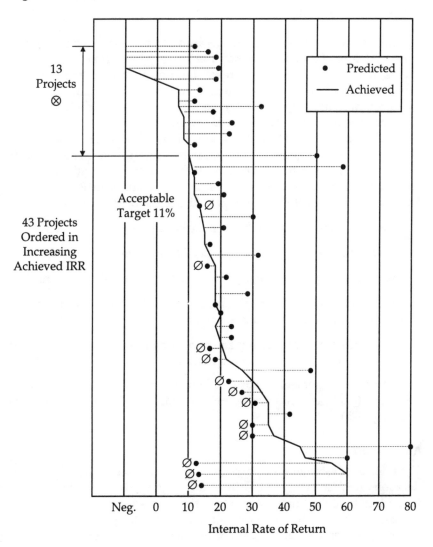

Figure 6-18: Graph of Projects Target and Achievable IRRs

Figure 6-18 reproduces (Thompson and Perry, 1992) a range of projects that were funded by the World Bank during the 1970s. The Figure shows that 13 projects out of 43 achieved an IRR that was less than the acceptable target set by the Bank; these are shown by ⊗. The acceptable World Bank target (at least in the 1970s) was a discount rate of 10 per cent. Out of 43 projects only 12, indicated by ∅, had IRRs that were the same or greater than the predicted IRR. What this implies is that 13 projects should never have been attempted, 28 were questionable in that they didn't reach their economic targets, and only 12 could be accepted as being economically attractive.

Time and cost overruns can invalidate the economic case for a project, turning a potentially profitable investment into a loss-maker. The evidence would indicate that too many projects overrun both cost and time targets. Better project management will produce significant improvement in meeting predetermined targets. Better project management includes identifying, measuring and responding to risks.

Targets are sometimes missed because of unforeseen events that even an experienced project manager cannot anticipate. More often it happens because of events that are predictable in general, but not in specific terms. This will not always lead simply to a list of potential calamities. Cost may be less than anticipated, the weather may be kind, revenues my exceed expectations (risks may be beneficial but they must always be taken into account), etc.

Another reason for the early identification of risk is that it focuses the attention of the project's management on the strategies for the control and allocation of risk, for example through the choice of contract strategy. It will also highlight those areas where further design, development work, and clarification may be needed. Risk management within projects provides major benefits. It can:

- enable decision-making to be more systematic and less subjective;

- allow robustness of projects and specific uncertainties to be compared;

- make the relative importance of each risk immediately apparent;

- give an improved understanding of the project through identifying the risks and thinking through response scenarios;

- have a powerful impact on management by forcing a realisation that there is a range of possible outcomes for a project.

Project risk management consists of four processes: risk identification, risk quantification (analysis), risk response development, and risk response control (Pilcher, 1992).

Risk Identification

The realism of estimates increases as the project proceeds but, of course, the major decisions are made early in the life of the project. So despite the difficulties, a realistic estimate of the final cost and duration of the total project is required as early as possible. It is at that time that all potential risks and uncertainties, which can affect these estimates, and act as constraints on the projects, should also be identified. This effect was demonstrated in Figure 6-17.

What are the major sources of risk? Here are some examples (Thompson and Perry, 1992):

source	example
owner/government/regulatory agencies	bureaucratic delays, changes in local regulations
funding/fiscal	changes in funding policy, co-financing relationships
project definition	changes in scope
project organisation	authority of project management, involvement
design	adequacy to meet need, realism of design programme
local conditions	local customs, weather
permanent equipment	degree of novelty, damage/loss during transportation
contractors	experience, financial stability
materials	excessive wastage, quality reliability, delivery
labour	industrial relations, availability of skills
temporary equipment	resale value, spares availability
logistics	remoteness/difficult access
estimating data	availability/relevance to specific project
inflation	management of national economy
exchange rates	unexpected changes in parity
force majeure	floods, earthquakes, etc.

Risk identification consists of determining what sources of risk and which risk events may reasonably be expected to affect the project. Risk identification is not a one-time event; it should be performed on a regular basis throughout the project. Risk identification may be accomplished by identifying causes-and-effects (what could happen and what will ensue) or effects-and-causes (what outcomes are to be avoided or encouraged and how each might occur).

To commence the identification process, the nature of the product of the project, its constraints and assumptions, are factors that will have a major effect on the risks identified. The scope statement, WBS, staffing plan, procurement management plan, etc. should all be used as inputs in identifying the risk items.

Checklists are used to organise sources of risk. What actually happened on previous projects can be helpful in identifying potential opportunities and threats. In addition to project files and project team knowledge, risk-oriented interviews with various stakeholders can be helpful in identifying risk items.

Outputs from risk identification include sources of risk, potential risk event, risk symptoms, and inputs to other processes. Sources of risk and potential risk events are the categories of possible risk events and discrete events respectively which may affect the project for better or worse. The list of sources and events should be comprehensive. Identifying risk events should generally include estimates of a) the probability that the risk event will occur, b) the alternative possible outcomes, c) expected timing of the event, and d) anticipated frequency.

All project risks may be characterised by (Wideman, 1992):

- *risk event*: precisely what might happen to the detriment of the project;

- *risk probability*: how likely the event is to occur;

- *amount at stake*: the severity of the consequence.

The ranking of risks (risk event status) is determined by:

$$risk\ event\ status = risk\ probability \times amount\ at\ stake$$

Some risks can be of low probability and low severity, while others, at the opposite end of a spectrum, can be of high severity and high probability — these are obviously the most serious of the range of risk events.

Risk Quantification

Risk quantification sets out to analyse the effects on the project of the major risks that have been identified. Only on very few projects is the matter of risk considered in a consistent and logical way. In analysing risk, the first step is to decide which technique to use. Analytical techniques have now been developed specifically for this task. The excuse usually given for not using these analytical techniques is commercial pressure from the owner, contractors, consultants, etc.

The analysis of the impact of risk extends to judging the probability of occurrence of each risk and its consequences. The collective effect of many risks is to delay implementation and commissioning, both of which can affect the total project cost. Risk quantification produces estimates expressed in terms of ranges — not as single figures. The accuracy of the range and the probability improves with elapsed time.

Quantifying risk can be fairly subjective but an estimate of the degree of uncertainty can be arrived at by using such techniques as:

a) influence diagrams;

b) probability distribution;

c) probability trees;

d) risk modelling;

e) sensitivity profiles.

Two of these techniques — b) and c) — are described in Part 4. Care needs to be taken in using the results of the above techniques; at best they provide estimates that are based on experience and opinion.

Influence diagrams (Goodwin and Wright, 1991), which are closely related to decision trees, are sometimes used to summarise the dependencies among events that act within a decision. They are often used to elicit decision tree representation from decision-makers. They are often used before constructing decision trees because they are more easily revised and altered as the decision-maker relates to the graphic representation of a decision problem.

As with decision trees, the basic symbols used are: event nodes are represented by circles and decision nodes by squares; arrowed lines between nodes represent influences of one node on another. An event node that precedes another event node indicates that the probability associated with the succeeding event (chance variable) depends on the outcome of the preceding event (chance variable). Likewise a decision node that precedes an event node indicates that the probability of the succeeding chance variable depends upon the preceding decision. An arrow pointing to a decision node indicates that either the decision is influenced by a prior decision, or, on the occurrence, or not, of prior events.

Statistical techniques can be used to sum probability distributions of cost estimates, quantity estimates and similar items. By convention, project cost estimates are either triangular or beta. Schedule simulation (based on some form of Monte Carlo analysis) uses a representation or model of a system to analyse the behaviour or performance of the system.

Expected monetary value, as a tool for risk quantification, is the product of two numbers: risk event probability (an estimate of the probability that a given event will occur) and risk event value (an estimate of the gain or loss that will be incurred if the risk event does occur). The result of this calculation is generally used as input to further analysis (e.g. in a decision tree) since risk events can occur individually or in groups, in parallel or in sequence.

Risk modelling (Michaels, 1996) means representing some attribute of a system or product for the prediction and control of the risk exposure contribution of that attribute; the attributes are normally time or money. There are three broad categories of risk modelling; network risk analysis (CPM, PERT, etc.), decision risk analysis (decision trees, expected monetary value, etc.), and cost risk analysis.

Sensitivity analysis is used to identify the impact on the total of a change in a single risky variable (Flanagan and Norman, 1993). The major advantage of sensitivity analysis is that it shows the robustness of the ranking of alternative schemes or projects. This method of analysis identifies the point at which a given variation in the expected value of a cost parameter changes a decision. A spider diagram is an effective way of presenting the outcome of sensitivity analysis. A spider diagram can be constructed using the following sequence:

- estimate the total life-cycle cost (LCC);

- identify the risky variables using a decision tree approach;

- select one variable and calculate new LCCs using variable values ± 1 per cent, 2 per cent, etc.;

- plot the results;

- repeat for other variables.

The result of this sequence is shown as a series of non-linear lines in Figure 6-19. The flatter the line the more sensitive the LCC will be to changes in that parameter. For instance parameter 1 and 4 will have much greater impact on the LCC than either parameter 2 or 3.

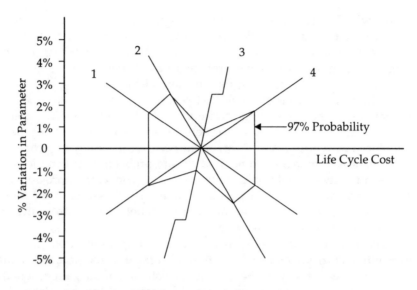

Figure 6-19: Spider Diagram Showing Sensitivity Profile

Although LCC has been chosen as the independent variable for this illustration, other parameters, such as IRR, the duration of a project, etc. could be used.

As part of the sensitivity analysis illustrated above it is useful to know how likely the cost parameter will vary within a particular range. Probability analysis, using, say, the central limit theorem, can be used to determine probability contours such as shown on the diagram for a 97 per cent probability. The 97 per cent probability, which is equivalent to all values within ± 2 standard deviations, would define the ± percentage effect on the LCC of that variable. This procedure would then be carried out for each variable. The procedure would then, if required, be extended to other probabilities to create a series of contours.

Sensitivity analysis gives guidance for further investigations; it provides the critical factors and it shows which parameters should be considered. Evidence shows that the eight largest risk parameters in a project will typically cover up to 90 per cent of the total risk impact (Flanagan and Norman, 1993).

Risk quantification is primarily concerned with determining which risk events warrant response. It is complicated by a number of factors including, but not limited to: opportunities and threats can interact in unanticipated ways; a single event can cause multiple effects; opportunities from one stakeholder may be threats to another; and mathematical techniques used can create a false impression of precision and reliability. Part 4 deals with some of these quantitative methods.

Risk Response

Once the decision has been made to respond to a potential opportunity or risk, response development is the process of deciding specifically what to do. The greater the uncertainty associated with a project, the more flexible the response must be. There are three ways to respond to risk:

- avoidance;

- mitigation;

- retention.

Avoidance refers to eliminating a specific threat, usually by eliminating the cause. All risk can never be completely eliminated, but specific risk events often can be.

Mitigation relates to reducing the expected monetary value of a risk event by reducing the probability of occurrence (e.g. using proven technology to lessen the probability that the product of the project will not work) reducing the risk event value (e.g. buying insurance), or both.

Retention means accepting the consequences. Retention can be active (e.g. by developing a contingency plan to execute should the risk event occur) or passive (e.g. by accepting a lower profit if some activities overrun).

In the extreme, risk may have such serious consequences as to demand a reappraisal of a project or even its complete abandonment. It is, however, more likely that risk identification and analysis will reveal a need for redesign, more detailed design, further investigatory work, a different packaging of the work content, use of alternative contract strategies, etc.

If risks can be transferred their consequences will be shared with, or totally carried by, someone other than the owner. The owner should expect to pay a premium for such transfer; the decision must, therefore, lie with the owner, who should ensure that it is in their interest to transfer the risk.

Risk response control involves executing the risk management plan in order to respond to risk events over the course of the project. When changes occur, the basic cycle of identify, quantify and respond is repeated. It is important to understand that even the most thorough and comprehensive analysis cannot identify all risks and probabilities correctly; control and iteration are required.

Inputs to risk control are: the risk management plan, actual risk events, and additional risk identification. Some of the identified risk events will occur; others will not. The ones that do occur are actual risk events and the project management team must recognise this so that the response developed can be implemented. As project performance is measured and reported, potential risk events not previously identified may surface.

If the risk event was not anticipated, or the effect is greater than expected, the planned response may not be adequate. It will be necessary to repeat the response development process (and perhaps the risk quantification process as well). As anticipated risk events occur or fail to occur, as risk event effects are evaluated, estimates of probabilities and value, as well as other aspects of the risk management plan, should be updated.

Project management has a vital role to play in managing risk. In the work leading to the approval of funds, project managers can contribute to sound economic appraisal by producing realistic estimates of cost and time based on a clearly defined standard of the quality of work and the operational requirements. The key elements for success are:

- an in-depth study of risk and uncertainty on all projects;

- estimates of cost and time that include specific contingency allowances;

- proposals of ways of at least reducing the effects of risk and uncertainty;

- the adoption of methods for allocating the remaining risks to the various parties in a way which will optimise project performance;

- recognition that risk and reward go hand-in-hand and that the allocation of a risk to a party should be accompanied by motivation for good management;

- an open-minded approach to innovative solutions to problems and a special awareness of the problems of overseas owners;

- regular and, preferably, independent review of project proposals and conceptual design to reduce misunderstandings and ensure that the full spectrum of uncertainties is exposed.

Summary of Key Points

- At the end of the conception phase a document referred to as the Preliminary Master Plan (PMP) provides the means for commencing the definition phase; this document, or its equivalent, is the deliverable from the conception phase.

- The recommendations for proper introduction and execution of the conception phase are: appoint a study team manager with the commensurate responsibility and authority; the manager confirms the project requirements; the right team is appointed to plan and undertake the conception work; and full and total project conceptualisation is carried out.

- A feasible scheme is one which can be demonstrated clearly to be both technically and economically viable if implemented. Feasibility analysis confirms, or otherwise, the viability of the schemes and whether or not there is an investment opportunity.

- The economic evaluation process should use payback period, return on investment, net present value and internal rate of return — some of the methods available for comparing the economic attractiveness of various schemes.

- When an owner has to procure design services it is recommended that the design team should be secured on a similar basis to that used for the appointment of suppliers and contractors. The design stage should not be dealt with any differently to any other stage or sub-stage.

- Since design costs normally represent only a small proportion of total costs, it becomes worthwhile, particularly on large projects, to increase the design effort significantly in order to achieve comparatively small percentage reductions in implementation cost, which in monetary terms can be many times the extra design cost.

- During the procurement process the first step in implementation planning is to decide on an appropriate organisation to undertake the project. The second step is selecting a contract type which best reflects the owner's degree of risk acceptance. The award method, the third step, is used to select the supplier and/or the price to undertake the implementation.

- Capital cost estimating is essentially an intuitive process which attempts to predict the final outcome of a future capital expenditure programme even though not all parameters and conditions concerning a project are known or are not fully defined when the cost estimate is prepared.

- Cost estimates for capital projects consist of two parts: direct costs, which are the costs of all permanent equipment, materials, labour and other resources, and indirect costs which relate to all costs, other than direct costs, which do not become a permanent part of the facilities.

- Work schedules and cost expenditures are, in most projects, difficult to control simultaneously. Two primary tools for controlling the project are the scheduled plan and the cost budget. These tools can be consolidated to provide a very powerful time-based budget.

- An important requirement for the gathering of costs is a good cost code system. A modern cost code system must satisfy both the owner as well as the project and it must be adaptable to computers and machine accounting.

- Range estimating is a method of analysis which will provide a means for identifying high risk items most likely to result in cost overruns, for identifying the probability of achieving a given cost estimate, and for helping owners maintain adequate contingency funds.

- In any project the onus is on the design team, during the definition phase, to think through the totality of implementation performance requirements in the knowledge that failure cannot be compensated for, or overcome by, the ingenuity of those who will use the facility (the term used for a project after the completion phase) during its operational life.

- Designs of most projects are complex. They require investment and experienced and talented people. Regardless of how capable or able a designer is, there will always be unnecessary cost hidden in their design. The design team must ensure that functionally the future facility will satisfy the owner's requirements and that the facility will be provided at least cost.

- The key elements of the value process are: function analysis, creative thinking, cost models, cost and worth, life cycle costing, evaluation matrix, attitudes, and contractual incentives. The objective of the value process is to increase functionality and reduce (life cycle) costs.

- Organisational survival in today's world is achieved by pursuing opportunity within the spectrum of uncertainty. In taking advantage of these opportunities, a projects environment is typically created. Project risk is the cumulative effect of the chances of uncertain occurrences adversely affecting project objectives.

- When serious overruns occur on project cost estimates and time schedules, the effect on the overall project can be very damaging. In extreme cases, time and cost overruns can invalidate the economic case for a project, turning a potentially profitable investment into a loss-making venture.

- Risk identification consists of determining what sources of risk and which risk events may reasonably be expected to affect the project. Risk identification is not a one-time event; it should be performed on a regular basis throughout the project.

- Risk quantification sets out to analyse the effects on the project of the major risks that have been identified. In analysing risk, the first step is to decide which technique to use. The analysis of the impact of risk extends to judging the probability of occurrence of each risk and the consequences. Risk quantification produces estimates expressed in terms of ranges — not as single figures.

- Once the decision has been made to respond to a potential opportunity or risk, response development is the process for deciding specifically what to do. The greater the uncertainty associated with a project the more flexible the response must be. There are three ways to respond to risk: avoidance, mitigation, and retention.

References

References used in the development of Part 6:

Bent, James A. and Humphreys, Kenneth R. (1996), *Effective Project Management through Applied Cost and Schedule Control*, Marcel Dekker, Inc.

Bernstein, Peter L. (1996), *Against the Gods: The Remarkable Story of Risk*, John Wiley and Sons Inc.

Cleland David I. and King William R. (1972), *Management: A Systems Approach*, McGraw-Hill Inc.

De Bono, Edward (1992), *Serious Creativity*, Harper Business.

Edwards W. (1971), "Social Utilities", *Engineering Economist*, Summer Symposium Series 6.

Flanagan, Roger and Norman, George (1993), *Risk Management and Construction*, Blackwell Science Publications.

Goodwin, Paul and Wright, George (1991), *Decision Analysis for Management Judgement*, John Wiley and Sons Ltd.

Humphreys, Kenneth K. (1991), *Jelen's Cost and Optimization Engineering*, 3rd edition, McGraw-Hill Inc.

Institution of Civil Engineers (1996), *Creating Value in Engineering*, ICE Design and Practice Guide, Thomas Telford Publishing.

Levy, H. and Sarnat, M. (1982), *Capital Investment and Financial Decisions*, 2nd ed., Prentice Hall.

Meredith, Jack R. and Mantel, Samuel J. (1995), *Project Management, A Managerial Approach*, 3rd ed., John Wiley and Sons.

Michaels, Jack V. (1996), *Technical Risk Management*, Prentice Hall.

Nicholas, John M. (1990), *Managing Business and Engineering Projects: Concepts and Implementation*, Prentice-Hall International Editions.

Pilcher, Roy (1992), *Principles of Construction Management*, 3rd edition, McGraw-Hill Book Company Europe.

Project Management Institute (1996), *A Guide to the Project Management Body of Knowledge (PMBOK)*, PMI Publications.

Raftery, John (1994), *Risk Analysis in Project Management*, E&FN Spon.

Thompson, P.A. and Perry, J.G. (1992), *Engineering Construction Risks: A Guide to Project Risk Analysis and Risk Management*, Thomas Telford.

Wideman, R. Max (1992), *Project and Program Risk Management: A Guide to Managing Project Risks and Opportunities*, Project Management Institute.

PART 7

PLANNING, SCHEDULING AND TIME–COST OPTIMISATION

Part 7 deals with the integration of time and cost, and shows why traditional forms of accountancy are no longer valid when considering the management of complex project work.

The connection between setting objectives, planning and scheduling will be explained. The establishment of objectives, outline specifications, and a schedule of milestone constraints are part of the initiating process. The work and organisation breakdown structures, the responsibility and accountablitity matrix, and the development of flow diagrams — all steps in the planning function — will be fully described.

Developing a project's cost breakdown structure (CBS), including the estimating process, and how the CBS is linked to the WBS will be described.

The fundamental concepts of activity-on-arrow and activity-on-node networks are compared; this leads to the application of the critical path method (CPM) of analysis. CPM is a decision-making method used by managers to determine when, how, and with whom project activities can be undertaken. It also provides a means for managers to determine resourcing levels, "least cost" scheduling, and other project decision issues. The application of the more comprehensive precedence diagramming method (PDM) is also fully demonstrated using worked examples.

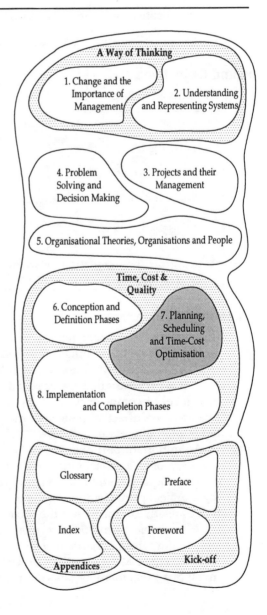

SECTION 1: CREATING THE PROJECT PLAN

Contents

- Aims and Objectives
- The Meaning of Planning
- Work Breakdown Structure
- Sequencing the Activities
- Organisation Breakdown Structure
- Responsibility and Accountability Matrix

Aims and Objectives

The aims and objectives of Section 1 are to:

- Define what is meant by planning;
- Describe the difference between planning and scheduling;
- Present a relational breakdown of the work required to carry out a project;
- Show how to draw logic diagrams;
- Identify a project's stakeholders through an "organisation breakdown structure";
- Contrast the interaction between the WBS and OBS to create a responsibility and accountability matrix (RAM).

The Meaning Of Planning

Effective project management, as with other management functions, is essentially the ability to do three things well: leading the people doing the work, making decisions, and communications. To make effective decisions and take related actions, it is necessary that the project manager and the members of the team have a high level of competency in planning, scheduling, and control. Although these functions are directly connected, they are mutually exclusive. The first of these terms, planning, is defined here.

An important part of a project manager's responsibility is the co-ordination of a variety of related activities that constitute the project scope. Determining the content, sequence, and inter-relationships of such activities assist greatly in creating a project plan. Comparing the unfolding actual performance of a project's activities relative to the plan is the project manager's chance of applying control.

When project activities are relatively limited and repetitive in nature, fairly simple diagrams or charts may be used to present the information needed for effective control. More usually a project is unique, large, complex and diverse and involves a great many organisations or subgroups. Accordingly, the project manager requires a clear view of this complicated network of inter-dependencies. The project manager needs to think of the project in its entirety, viewing it as a "total system".

A project's activities that have had the benefit of earlier planning and are being, or will be, carried out according to that plan stand a better chance of achieving success than those that have not been planned. Even though we are likely to grasp this, most often we feel we are being rushed into showing progress on work achievement. Under these or similar circumstances pre-planning is ignored, and a half-hearted attempt is made create do some sort of plan as the work proceeds.

It can be said that *we cannot control what needs to be done if we don't plan*. Planning and control are two closely connected elements in the project management process. Planning precedes control — planning usually consists of 80 per cent memory of historic procedures and 20 per cent synthesis or creative thought. A proactive, structured approach to planning will yield very significant benefits as compared to a reactive or random approach.

Studies that were carried out recently on the performance of projects show that an exceptional planning effort can yield as much as 40 per cent cost savings over reasonable planning. A poor planning effort can cause time overruns of as much as 400 per cent and as much as 50 per cent over-budget costs on a project when compared to projects that have had a reasonable planning effort. These figures, obtained from studies undertaken in the 1980s, do not overstate the issue; rather, they probably understate the real situation. Whatever the true figures, they support a general recommendation for an exceptional planning effort at all times.

Planning can be defined as making decisions now with the objective of influencing the future. Planning can also be seen as the desk study rehearsal of what is anticipated will happen in the future. To try to ensure that we are not presented with future surprises that have not been anticipated, planning needs to be an important part of both our personal and business lives.

One of the most important responsibilities in a project is the planning of project activities, analysing and integrating their effects, and executing the resulting project plans. Because of the relatively short duration and prioritised control that exist in many projects, there is a non-negotiable requirement for formalised detailed planning. This is done through the development of a project scheduled plan; the first version of this plan is developed during the conception phase.

For successful project management, there is a strong need for planning and control to ensure that one — or as few as necessary — forgotten or delayed activities do not hold up the entire project, or a vital part of it. A view of the network of inter-relationships may reveal where resources can be shifted or rescheduled to enable a significant reduction in the overall time for project completion.

A network portrayal of sequences and interrelationships will aid greatly in coordinating inputs and activities and reducing confusion and delays. Network models have special significance because they have certain mathematical characteristics that enhance their value in finding optimal solutions for complex problems.

Weiss and Wysocki (1992) put forward 25 action steps that expand the project management process into a detailed set of procedures. Within the 25 steps are ten steps that together constitute planning. The ten steps consist of five steps for each of the two sub-processes of initiating and planning; these and the other sub-processes were described in Part 3, Section 1, within the sub-Section, "The Project Management Process".

Initiating, although technically not part of planning, is a necessary input to planning and therefore needs explanation. Initiating a project, or each phase of a project, requires the following procedures:

- stating the problem;

- identifying the goals;

- listing the objectives;

- preliminary determination of constraints;

- identification of assumptions and risks.

The output from the initiating process should be a document that clearly establishes the requirements for the project, or project phase. This document can be referred to using many terms; the author recommends the use of the term "requirements document".

The five steps — the detailed procedures of the planning process — are:

- identifying the activities;

- determining the sequence of activities;

- estimating the time duration of each activity;

- identifying the critical activities;

- modelling the allocation of resources.

Technically, the last three steps are really part of what is called scheduling; this is dealt with in Section 2.

Scheduling is the conversion of the planned activities into a calendar-related plan. Having identified the difference between planning and scheduling, from here on the words planning and scheduling shall refer to the sequenced work required to reflect the scope of the project, and the sequenced work set against a calendar timeframe, respectively.

Planning and scheduling are an art needing personal skills acquired only after years of study, observation and experience.

There are a number of outputs from planning and scheduling, namely: the work breakdown structure (WBS), a project network diagram, and a selected project time plan that will provide "part of the means" for controlling the subsequent processes of executing and closing. Scope, cost, and quality will be the other "part of the means".

As was observed in Part 3, Section 1, sub-Section "The Project Management Process", initiating and planning will happen at least once in every phase of a project. Initiating, as can be seen from Figure 3-8 in Part 3, Section 1, happens at the beginning of a phase and extends for a relatively short time within the phase period. The planning process happens at the same time. It extends for the full period of the phase, and its intensity is greater during the early part of the phase than in the later stages.

Work Breakdown Structure

The identified project activities are grouped into a system which is broken down into subsystems and elements. The work breakdown structure (WBS) is the breakdown of the project into all the activities and tasks needed to design, procure, implement and complete the project. The WBS is a means of displaying the physical subsystems to be developed or produced; it relates the elements of work to be accomplished to each other and to the end product. Typically, when creating a WBS (refer to the sub-Section "Scope Management", in Part 3, Section 2) it is necessary to divide the work of the project into greater and greater levels of detail.

The WBS shows successive subdivisions of the work on a chart analogous to that used for conventional organisational charts. The number of levels depends upon the size and complexity of the project; there could be 5, 6 or more levels. The purpose of the WBS is to divide the project into what are referred to as work packages which will allow the assignment of time and cost estimates, management, and activity and task responsibility (Kesbom et al., 1989).

Activity No.	Activity Description	Responsibility
00/1.0	Start PSL Package	
1.1	Specification for PSL	Owner
1.2	Finalise Order with Contractor	Owner
1.3	Install Equipment	Contractor A
1.4	Commission	Contractor A
1.5	Validate Equipment	Owner
1.6	Document - As Built Drawings	Owner/Contractor A
01/1.0	Effluent Package	
1.1	Define Requirements	Owner
1.2	Allocate Contract	Owner
08/1.0	Mezzanine Package	
1.1	Define Requirements	Owner
1.2	Identify Pipe Runs, Wiring an d Ducts	Owner
1.3	Prepare Quotation Invitation	Owner
1.4	Obtain Quotes	Owner
1.5	Appoint Contractor/Supplier	Owner
1.6	Install Mezzanine	Contractor N
1.7	Install Computer Panels	Contractor C
1.8	Install CIP	Contractor H

Figure 7-1: Work Breakdown Structure

The WBS layout shown in Figure 7-1 is similar to Figure 3-11 in Part 3 except that it has been presented in the form of divisions, sub-divisions, etc. in the same way as the contents of a document are set out. This "listing" arrangement is more convenient than a hierarchical type of diagram, particularly if the project is large and consists of many levels or activities. The WBS activities should all have an activity (code) number, a description, and an assigned responsibility. At this stage it is only necessary to state the performing organisations under the heading "responsibility". Only work items that are definable and assignable should be included.

The first step in creating a WBS is to divide the total project into major work sub-projects (or objectives or categories). These sub-projects are then subdivided into units (or sub-objectives or sub-categories) which, in turn, are sub-divided and so on. This level-by-level breakdown continues so that the scope and complexity of work elements is reduced with each level of breakdown. This analysis will reduce the project into elements that can be thoroughly and accurately defined, budgeted, scheduled, and controlled. The WBS approach helps ensure that all elements, down to the smallest, are accounted for.

A typical WBS will consist of a series of levels, each level having a number indicator. Figure 3-11 (Part 3, Section 2) illustrated the following breakdown:

0 — total project
1 — sub-project
2 — unit
3 — area
4 — account
5 — work package
6 — activity.

In reality the number of levels varies and the description at each level is arbitrary.

A work package may be defined as an identifiable grouping of related work from one or more disciplines. It represents a manageable segment of the work to be performed. Continued subdivision of the work packages into related activities and tasks, or sub-activities, is part of the process of deriving the WBS. As a general rule, work packages should consist of similar or related activities, and should be of about similar size; one source suggests 200 hours as a minimum.

Individual tasks below this level should be subdivided to as small a number of hours as is necessary. As a general guideline:

- if the project duration is < 6 months, tasks of 1 day (10 hours) or less can be ignored.

- if the project duration is < 1 year, tasks of 2 days (20 hours) or less can be ignored.

- if the project duration is > 3 years, tasks of 6 days (60 hours) or less can be ignored.

Of course any task that would be less than these guidelines but is of crucial importance in executing and controlling the project should not be excluded. There is therefore a need for great discretion. The main objective of this "analysis" is to reduce the project into work tasks that are so clearly defined they can be thoroughly and accurately scheduled, budgeted, and, during the execution of the project, controlled. If carried out with great care, the WBS ensures that all tasks are accounted for.

Concurrent with the development of the WBS is the process of work definition. As each activity and task are identified, so the work associated with each element is further elaborated and more clearly specified. During this process, the questions that the team needs to ask include "What else is needed?" and "What has been missed?". By the time the WBS is completed, all work on the project has been completely defined.

In association with this listing is a unique number code that is assigned to each activity; this assumes that the project is large and complex and computerised scheduling will be needed to handle the volume of information. Further discussion on this matter is contained within the sub-Section "Cost Breakdown Structure" in Section 3 of this Part.

Sequencing of Activities

The next step in the planning process is to develop what is called a logic diagram, which can also be called a "sequential activity diagram" or "flow diagram". The logic diagram is often used in process engineering. It presents the project activities in the form of boxes (the activities) connected by arrowed lines that point from left to right (all flow diagrams used in the planning of projects should "flow" from left to right). The logic diagram is what it says it is. It presents a procedure, a sequence, for undertaking the project activities.

A sequence of adjacent points connected by lines is called a chain. When the chain is oriented so that it is possible to move along it from point to point, it is called a directed chain or a path. A chain that begins and ends at the same point is a cycle or circuit network. Logic diagrams can contain a number of paths or chains.

The development of a logic diagram can be undertaken by the traditional method using large paper areas on a desk or wall or electronically using a PC and one of the numerous planning software packages available. There is much to be said for not using the computer too soon, but using it later in the process as an aid to examining numerous alternatives.

Each activity listed in the WBS is written into a box on the logic diagram sheet. The activities are then connected together to form a logical sequence. In labelling the activities and event boxes it is recommended, where possible, to abbreviate the activities and tasks by using one noun and one verb. Sometimes this is not possible, so more words are used, but where possible the abbreviated form should be the norm. Activity descriptions should generally be reviewed for accuracy; descriptions often affect activity sequencing.

When connecting an activity to the others in the diagram, it is necessary for the planner (the person undertaking the planning) to keep asking the same three questions:

- What activities must be done before the activity I am considering?

- What activities can be commenced after the activity I am considering?

- What activities can be carried out at the same time as the activity I am considering?

This can be referred to as the planner's "thought spiral".

There are three designations given to activities:

- *predecessor* — these are all activities that come before the activity being considered;

- *successor* — these are all activities that come after the activity being considered;

- *concurrent* — these are all activities that can happen at the same time as the activity being considered.

These designators and their relationships can be demonstrated by referring to Figure 7-2.

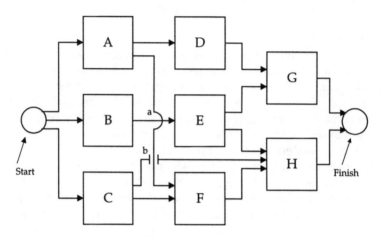

Figure 7-2: Activity Sequencing

If "activity E" is considered then:

- activity B is a predecessor to E;

- activities G and H are successor activities to E;

- activities D and F are likely to be concurrent to E.

The Figure show a flow diagram with a "start" node and a "finish" node; that is, they demonstrate the start and finish of the diagram. These nodes are optional but it is good practice when preparing logic diagrams not to have what is referred to as *dangles*. Dangles are activities which are missing either a connecting line coming into the left of their box or a connecting line leaving from the right of their box.

The lines which connect boxes demonstrate that there are relationships between those activities which are connected. These connection lines are known as dependencies, of which there are two types: mandatory and discretionary.

Mandatory dependencies — otherwise referred to as hard logic — are those which are inherent in the nature of the work being done. For example, it would be impossible to undertake an activity "test assembly" until all components of the assembly have been connected and checked as being complete.

Discretionary dependencies, otherwise referred to as soft logic, are those which are defined by the project team. They fall into two categories: those activities which are being sequenced due to knowledge of *"best practices"* — sequences that are desirable and customary so long as the project's overall duration is not affected. Those activities which are being sequenced due to knowledge of some unusual aspect of the activity are called *preferential logic*.

Most dependencies are internal to the project; in other words they are dependencies between two project activities. Some are *external dependencies* involving interfaces with other projects or with non-project activities of one or more stakeholders.

Any of the dependencies may require specification of a *lead or lag* in order to accurately define the relationship. For example, there may be a two-day delay between completing F and starting H. When drawing connecting lines that cross, then either create a bridge, see a, or cut one of the lines, see b.

It takes a little imagination to visualise the way in which logic diagrams can be useful in analysing projects that require the performance of a number of activities, some of which must be completed before others are begun. A logic diagram represents the essential tasks that must be performed to complete the project. Such a representation forces one to define carefully the tasks that must be performed and to specify any linkages that exist between tasks. An obvious result is a picture that shows which activities await the completion of others and which can be conducted simultaneously. Once the logic diagram has been completed, the project plan is complete. This is also referred to as the "model plan".

Of course project planning is not a once-off process. As additional information or changes to the project occur, then adjustments must be made to the model plan. Such adjustments are usually quite simple to achieve as the initial planning process is so comprehensive.

Documentation of the project plan provides a benefit to the project participants in providing a formalised, systematic, learning process. Remember: *a significant part of the planning process involves learning from history.*

Organisation Breakdown Structure

The organisational structure of a project should be designed as early as possible in the project's life cycle. The range of organisation structures was dealt with in Section 2 of Part 5. A clear definition of communication channels, responsibilities, and the authority of each participating entity are key elements affecting project success. The most appropriate structure depends on the nature of the project, on the environment in which the project is performed, and on the structure of the participating entities.

The organisational breakdown structure (OBS) is a graphical representation of the participating organisations. In the same way as the WBS can be arrayed in a hierarchical treelike form, so the OBS can be represented.

The OBS is the people organisation structure that will be needed to undertake the conception, definition, implementation and completion phases. It is necessary for the project management team to determine the disciplines and plan the numbers of skilled personnel that will be needed to execute the tasks identified in the WBS.

The OBS, as shown in Figure 7-3, is normally presented with the organisations shown horizontally and the hierarchy of skilled personnel listed in vertical format. It shows how each entity and each stakeholder fits into the "project organisation", the different levels of individual involvement, and the lines of communication. In the OBS, the lines of communication (dashed lines in Figure 7-3) between and within organisations are defined, and procedures for work authorisation, and report preparation and distribution are also established.

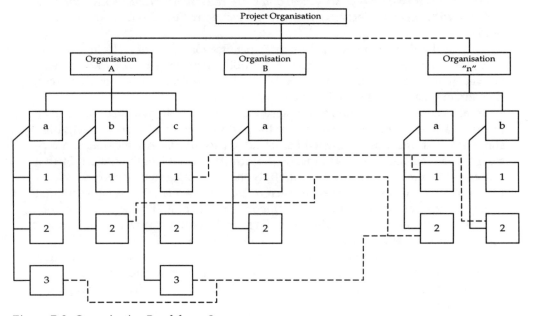

Figure 7-3: Organisation Breakdown Structure

Once the organisational structure is defined and each participating unit is assessed for which package(s) of work, or range of activities, it is likely to have responsibility for, it is then possible to further define and break the work content into additional activities and tasks, and then estimate each activity's duration. This breakdown is part of the planning process, but the estimating of the durations of activities, which is dealt with in Section 2, is part of the scheduling process.

The factors that need to be taken into consideration when selecting an organisation structure are (Shtub et al., 1994):

- number of projects and their relative importance;

- level of uncertainty in projects;

- type of technology used;

- project complexity;

- duration of projects;

- resources used by projects;

- overhead costs;

- data requirements.

If the performing organisation is only infrequently dealing with projects, then a functional structure may be the most appropriate one. When there are *many projects* to be dealt with and their *relative importance* — which is measured by comparing the total budget for projects relative to the total organisational budget — then the project's organisation structure should be either matrix or project team.

Structures which can react faster to change and can get all the information on actual performance directly from those who are actively involved are best for handling uncertainty. Uncertainty is countered by having a feedback control system that measures changes from the original plan and detects trends. A project team type structure is preferred when high levels of *uncertainty* are expected.

When a single *technology* predominates in a project, a functional structure is likely to be the best choice. When a number of different technologies are used, but not on a continuous basis, then the matrix structure could be preferred. When there are many technologies and a number of personnel are engaged on a full-time basis then the project team structure may be best.

High *complexity* is best handled by the project team structure and low complexity can be handled by either functional or matrix structures. In most circumstances short *project durations* are perhaps best handled by a matrix structure, whereas long duration projects will justify a project team structure. When there is much sharing of common *resources between projects*, the functional matrix is likely to be the best structure. If there is little sharing of common resources, then the project team structure is likely to be best.

A matrix organisational structure is likely to be the best for reducing *overhead costs*. If many projects have the same *data requirements* and such information is to be made available to other individuals not involved in the projects, then the functional structure is likely to be preferred.

Factor	Organisational Structures		
	Functional	Matrix	Project
• Uncertainty	Low	High	High
• Technology	Standard	Complicated	New
• Complexity	Low	Medium	High
• Duration	Short	Medium	Long
• Size	Small	Medium	Large
• Importance	Low	Medium	High
• Customer	Diverse	Medium	One
• Interdependency (within)	Low	Medium	High
• Interdependency (between)	High	Medium	Low
• Time Criticality	Low	Medium	High
• Resource Criticality	Depends	Depends	Depends
• Differentiation	Low	High	Medium

Figure 7-4: Some Factors Affecting the Choice of OBS

In addition to the foregoing factors there are others that need to be taken into account. Figure 7-4 looks at a number of factors compared for the functional, matrix and project team structures and presents a general assessment of how well they will be satisfied, or not satisfied, by each of these three types of organisation structure options.

Responsibility and Accountability Matrix

The responsibility and accountability matrix (RAM), also referred to as the linear responsibility chart or LRC, is a tool for combining the WBS and the OBS so that each work activity will have identified the members of the participating organisations who will make contributions to its completion. In other words it will show not only the activity as "the what" but it will specify who has which responsibility for that activity. For example, to produce a drawing for a particular component of the project will require someone to draw it, someone to check it, someone to approve it etc.

The RAM summarises the relationships between the project participants, the stakeholders, and their respective responsibility for each activity required to carry out the project. An activity as we have seen previously is any element of a project that needs to be performed. These are displayed as rows in the matrix, and by reading across for a particular activity, it can be discerned who has been allocated the responsibility for certain actions. A responsibility acronym often used is PARIS which relates to (Project Management Institute, 1996):

P performs
A approves
R reviews (or is notified)
I   inputs (contributes to)
S supports

A sample part-RAM is shown in Figure 7-5. As can be seen, each activity has been identified and coded. By reading across each activity the actions or responsibilities have been assigned using as many actions within PARIS as are needed for each activity. By reading down the columns of the RAM, each project participant can see their responsibilities and actions both as a total individual effort, and as a specific effort on certain activities. All individual effort should be reviewed with the particular participant. At the initial phase of a project, this may only be possible at organisation or department level; as the planning becomes more refined, the participating individuals can be identified. The RAM becomes an input and a very useful device for determining resource requirements.

Code	Activity Description	Owner				Contractors											
						a				b				c			
		1	2	3	4	1	2	3	4	1	2	3	4	1	2	3	4
1.1	SELECT TEAM	A												S			
1.3.1	General Arrangements	A			R	I				P				S			
1.3.1.1	Prepare Drawings - Pipe Run	A	I		R					P				S			
1.3.1.2	Prepare Drawings - Manifolds	A			R					P							
1.3.1.3	Prepare Drawings - Tank Conns.	A	I		R					P					S		
1.3.1.4	Prepare Drawings - HVAC Ducts	A			R	I				P					S		
1.3.2	Detailing	A								P							
1.3.2.1	Pipe Run	A	I		R					P		S					
1.3.2.2	Manifolds	A	I		R					P		S					
1.3.2.3	Tank Connections	A			R					P							
1.3.2.4	HVAC Ducts	A	I		R					P		S					
1.3.3	MTO	A	I		R					P		S					
1.3.4	Issue for Procurement	A								P							
1.4	PROCESS																
1.4.1	Tank Specification	A				I				P	R			S			
1.4.1.1	Specification	A								P	R			S			
1.4.1.2	Outline Drawings	A								P	R						
1.4.1.3	Release for Procurement	A				I				P	R			S			
1.4.2	Pump/Motor Specification	A				I				P	R				S		
1.4.2.1	Release for Procurement	A	I							P	R			S			
1.4.3	HVAC Specification	A								P	R						
1.4.3.1	Release for Procurement	A															

Figure 7-5: Responsibility and Accountability Matrix

The project team should use the RAM to review the completeness and adequacy of the WBS activities. The matrix may throw up duplicated activities, missed activities, critical interfaces between activities, or matters requiring special attention. Iterations between the RAM and the WBS should be carried out as many times as needed to ensure completeness and they accurately reflect what is seen to be the totality of the planned work.

Another major advantage of the RAM is that it provides an overview of "the what?", "the who?", and "what do I have to do on the what?". Project personnel, their department heads and their organisations can easily see what their involvement and responsibility is on the various work packages and activities, and the interfacing with other personnel, departments and organisations. Should project personnel feel it necessary to further break down short-duration (one or two days) assignments, then these assignments can be broken down as sub-RAMs and the respective tasks assigned to additional individuals.

Since the RAM prescribes how individuals within organisations need to perform, it is a very useful planning tool for monitoring and assessing how well responsibilities are being carried out.

SECTION 2: SCHEDULING THE PROJECT PLAN

Contents

- Aims and Objectives

- Definition of Scheduling

- Types of Scheduled Plan

- Activity Durations

- Creating Network-Based Scheduled Plans

- PERT and CPM — Two Types of Network Model

- Precedence Diagramming Method

Aims and Objectives

The aims and objectives of Section 2 are to:

- Define what is meant by scheduling;

- Contrast the different types of scheduled plan;

- Estimate activity durations;

- Demonstrate the preparation and analysis of network-based plans;

- Contrast the differences between CPM, PERT and PDM.

Definition of Scheduling

The logic diagram, which is the end of the planning stage, gives the sequence of project activities. The next step is to schedule the plan, that is, to relate the plan to calendar time. The sequence of activities can become a scheduled plan by estimating the duration of each activity and then setting these activities against a calendar timeframe. The primary advantage of a schedule is to produce the necessary time-related planning which all successful projects require.

Scheduling is the determination of the timing of activities and it follows logically from the planning process. The schedule is a reflection of the plan; the plan must come first. The process of scheduling may uncover flaws in the planning which will lead to revision of the plan. The scheduled plan is used to compare physical and other progress. Updating the scheduled plan and, where needed, changing it, is part of the scheduling process. The purposes of schedules include:

- predicting project completion (financial penalty/liquidated damages)

- predicting how long design and implementation will take (warranty of completion)

- predicting when specific activities will start and finish (subcontractors)

- exposing and adjusting conflicts (between trades, etc.)

- controlling a variety of resources (to plan cash flows etc.)

- evaluating the effect of changes on project completion and cost

- recording the project's progress

- giving notice of claims or extensions of time

The scheduled plan is a tool to determine the activities necessary to complete a project and the sequence and timeframe within which the activities must be completed. Scheduling systems achieve this by forcing members of the project team to think through the entire project in detail at the outset. This detailed thought process avoids inefficient and poor sequencing of the project. Understanding how the entire project will be completed permits recognition of the effects that unexpected events or alternative actions have on progress. Sequences can be changed to overcome or reduce the impact.

Which scheduling type should be used depends upon the characteristics of each project. If there are few activities or a large number of activities that have little interaction, then perhaps a *bar chart* or a *line of balance* would be quite appropriate. Where there are many activities or there is continuous interaction, then it is likely that a *network diagram* will be required. These and other terms are explained in the following sub-Section, "Types of Scheduled Plans".

Developing a schedule is not merely a mechanical exercise. Many judgements need to be made — the schedule's reliability depends largely on its quality. Scheduling is done by people, not computers; the scheduler must be equipped with:

- mechanistic and scheduling skills;

- ability to query and listen to discussions and to collect needed data;

- judgement and presence to probe bias and identify efficient linkages;

- persuasiveness to get the project team to "own" the schedule.

Delayed projects and disputes are closely related: a 1983 survey showed that half of owners who had projects behind schedule had been involved in litigation or arbitration. There is clear evidence to show that scheduled plans can reduce delays, cost over-runs and disputes. Without a scheduled plan, the probability of delays, cost overruns and disputes is higher.

Types of Scheduled Plans

The reasons for producing a scheduled plan for a project include:

- to incorporate all project activities needed to implement the project and inter-relate with the necessary resources and any imposed milestones;

- to establish the relative priorities of all project activities;

- to reflect both the base-line (current) plan and all subsequent plans;

- to produce a single time-related document that can be used by all project participants;

- the provision of a management tool for decision making and project control.

Regardless of the selected scheduling technique to be used, it must be structured to the specific project in order to facilitate its application and to attempt to maximise its resultant benefits as a control tool.

There are three basic scheduling methods that can be used:

- bar charts

- line of balance chart (linear scheduling method)

- network-based diagrams

Which technique(s) is used depends upon the type and complexity of the project. More than one of these methods may be used on any one project. Again, this would depend upon the complexity and type of work to be undertaken. If the project has activities of work that are repetitive, then "line of balance" would be the preferred choice. If the activities that constitute a project, or part of a project, are simple and straightforward then a "bar chart" would be the likely choice. In most other circumstances a "network" diagram would be the best option.

What are these techniques and what are the differences between each type? The following is a brief explanation of each type.

Bar Charts

Bar charts were first used by Henry Gantt in the early part of the twentieth century and accordingly are also referred to as Gantt charts. Bar charts are perhaps the most familiar method of scheduling. They show in graphical format when each activity to be undertaken starts and ends, and therefore how long each activity will take.

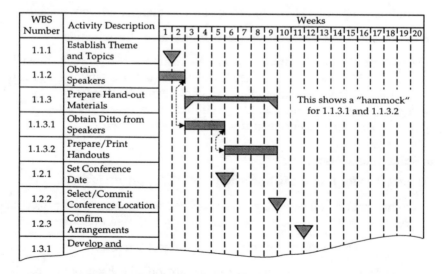

Figure 7-6: A Sample Bar Chart

Bar charts are very simple to prepare and easy to read. Their main disadvantage is that they can't show which activities are dependent on which, or whether or not various activities are dependent on each other. That is, as Figure 7-6 demonstrates, they cannot show:

- if some activities must be finished before others can start;

- if two or more activities can be performed at the same time.

Another limitation is how far the adaptation of bar charts can be taken. Revisions to these types of charts are difficult to make as they require a great deal of time to update, especially for large and complex projects.

There are many innovations that can be included within the bar chart format. Dependencies between activities can be shown by using dotted lines as shown between activity 1.1.2 and 1.1.3.1 or 1.1.3.1 and 1.1.3.2 in Figure 7-6. For simple projects with a relatively large number of activities, the drawing of dependencies linking bars would be quite demanding, but the ability to read and interpret the relationships might prove extremely difficult.

Although bar charts suffer from serious limitations as a scheduling technique, their main application is in the presentation of a scheduled plan. The most common method of presenting scheduled plans is through the use of bar charts. Bar charts, except for the very simple project, should therefore be seen *as an end presentation method of other scheduling methods.*

Line of Balance

The line of balance (LOB) method originated in the Goodyear Company in the 1940s and was developed by the US Navy during World War II. The method is used principally on large production jobs, but it can be applied to other types of production and to maintenance, research and development, etc.

Like the bar chart method, the LOB is an uncomplicated scheduling method that can be performed manually. The LOB is used when the activities or the work within a project consists of a number of units that are the same. LOB can be used for subset routines which may be a repetitive part of a network schedule. It is often used where the same activities are to be performed by the same team. LOB is also referred to as the linear scheduling method, and is also commonly called the "vertical production method".

LOBs fill a void between bar charts and network schedules:

- they are easier to prepare than a network schedule

- they provide more information than a bar chart

Network scheduling can be used to schedule repetitive activities, but only if there is a relatively small number of related activities to be scheduled. If there is a large number of related activities the scheduling exercise becomes boringly repetitive and that is not the primary attractiveness of network scheduling. On the other hand, bar charts can be used for such applications but, as stated earlier, they do not indicate activity inter-dependence, nor can they easily display variations in the rate of progress.

Each line on an LOB indicates the rate of progress of an activity; the intention is to keep all activity progress lines as close and as parallel as possible. Neither bar charts, nor, as you will see shortly, network schedules have the ability to show rates of progress. The LOB compares time and location or sequence number of repetitive elements (Callahan et al., 1992).

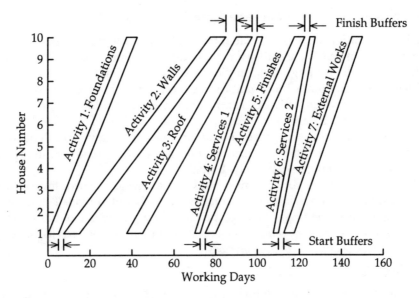

Figure 7-7: A Sample Line of Balance Chart

As can be seen from Figure 7-7 the horizontal axis plots time while the vertical axis plots location or distance along the length of a project. Individual activities are plotted separately, resulting in a series of diagonal lines. The slopes of the diagonal lines represent the planned rate of progress at any time of any activity. The completion time for each activity is a function of the rate of progress and the amount of work to be undertaken.

The rate of progress for an activity may vary due to location or time. When beginning an activity, the productivity rate is usually less than optimum. Individual production on an activity may vary as conditions change, e.g. increase or decrease of resources, a preceding or succeeding activity has a production rate change, etc.

Time spacers or buffers are sometimes required between adjacent activities in order to prevent one activity interfering with another and to accommodate differences in production rates between activities. Buffers can be at the start or finish or any intermediate location between the start and finish of two adjacent activities.

The LOB can also be used to show the start and finish of an activity at any location. The activity interval is the term used to refer to the period between the start and finish of an activity at a particular location.

As mentioned earlier, the LOB is easier to prepare than a network diagram and it presents more information than a bar chart. LOB shows rates of progress, which neither bar charts or networks are capable of indicating. A significant advantage of LOB diagrams is their simplicity in conveying a detailed work schedule. Another advantage of LOB is that it can be applied even when the activities are not repetitious sequential activities, but where there is a need to evaluate the best combination of individual progress rates. A major difficulty in LOB scheduling is determining the buffer interval. Sometimes buffer intervals can best be determined when the production rates of adjacent activities are known.

Network-based Diagrams

Modern planning and scheduling techniques have their origins in the late 1950s through two developments known as CPM (critical path method) and PERT (program evaluation and review technique). These developments produced what is referred to as network-based scheduled plans.

Such techniques were derived in part from bar charts (Gantt charts) of the 1910s. As seen earlier in this sub-Section, bar charts, although a useful technique, do have serious drawbacks when it comes to planning large, complex projects. The introduction of the CPM and PERT techniques were the modern response to these drawbacks.

Logic diagrams shows a sequence of work, including whether activities can be done at the same time or have to be done in a particular order. Network diagrams, in addition, include the start and finish dates for each activity. They can also show whether or not the timing of a particular activity is crucial to finishing the project by the given completion date or a part of it by a predetermined milestone date.

There are two types of basic diagrams used in network scheduling: activity-on-arrow (AOA) and activity-on-node (AON). AOA is the scheduling method applied when using PERT and AON is the scheduling method applied when using CPM.

AOA diagrams, like logic diagrams should always move from left to right, and as shown by Figure 7-8 the lines or arrows should always consist of a sloping section and a horizontal section. The reason for this is simply to provide a convenient platform for displaying the analysis of what will become a network-based schedule, as will be demonstrated in a later sub-Section within this Section, "PERT and CPM — Two Types of Network Model".

The AOA is also known as the "i–j" method; originally in 1961 it was referred to as the "circle and connecting line". In this type of diagram the nodes show events; these are activities which have no duration — that is they take no time, such as the start or finish of an activity. The arrows connecting the nodes represent the activities. The nodes are usually numbered as a means of identifying the activities in the network.

In activity on arrow (AOA) diagrams, "i" is the designation given to the start node of an activity and "j" is the designation given to the finish node of the same activity.

Each node should have its own unique number. The same number should not be used more than once. The best procedure is to work out the sequence of activities first without nodes, then number the nodes after a satisfactory network has been drawn. Usually "j" number node is greater than "i" number node, but this is not mandatory. Forward numbering helps prevent loops.

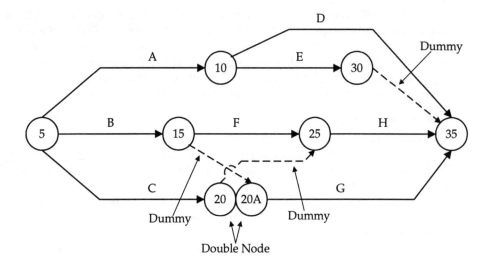

Figure 7-8: Activity-on-Arrow Diagram

The numbering of nodes is very important because the activities are normally referred to by their "i"th and "j"th designators. For instance, activity A in Figure 7-8
would be referred to as 5–10. Each activity should have unique i–j node numbers
and at no time should two activities have the same i–j numbers.

For example, if "H" is activity 25–35 then i=25, j=35. Both i and j represent
events and points in time. Unlike activities, events do not need time for their execution. To start (i) something, or finish (j) something does not require time; the
time taken for these events is finite. It should be noted that the i node of F is also
the j node of B.

In AOA the nodes are represented by circles big enough to contain an event
number. It is advisable not to use consecutive numbers but to use multiples of 2,
3, 5 or 10 to allow for adding node numbers later — that is, for accommodating
additional activities. There are times when it is necessary to include what is called
a "double node", such a node is shown as 20/20A.

There are six paths between nodes 5 and 35:

1) 5–10–35

2) 5–10–30–35

3) 5–15–25–35

4) 5–15–20A–35

5) 5–20–25–35

6) 5–20/20A–35

The Figure shows dotted lines as dependencies between events 15 and 20A, 20
and 25, and 30 and 35; these are called dummies. They are not activities but are
necessary to show that there are dependencies between certain activities. For example, activity H has two predecessor activities, namely C and F. Activities B and

C are predecessors to activity G. To show these dependencies, it is necessary to include dummies. AOA diagrams should always be drawn with a minimum number of dummies.

As can be seen, the AOA is a somewhat difficult concept because it requires the use of dummies. They do two things: indicate correct logic, and ensure that each activity has a unique set of node numbers. The dummy 30–35 is necessary to ensure that both D and E would not have the same start node number and finish node number. In other words, without the dummy both D and E would have the start node 10 and the finish node 35, and of course this is not permitted.

As with AON networks, the premise of the AOA network is that a given activity cannot start until all the activities that immediately precede it have been completed. In other words the dependency found in AOA networks is "finish-to-start" (FS). This and other dependencies are explained in the last sub-Section of this Section. This assumption makes the calculations of early dates and late dates fairly straight forward. Of course the reality is that perhaps up to 5 per cent of a succeeding activity can remain undone while the following activity(ies) can be started.

In i–j diagramming, the scheduler can minimise the chances of including logic loops by keeping the activity's j node number larger than its i node number. A logic loop exists whenever it is possible to trace a path from a point on the diagram back to the starting point. A first step of "good practice" is to avoid using any relationship arrow on the diagram that is not essential. With the exception of the start and finish nodes, all activities should have at least one preceding activity and at least one succeeding activity.

Frequently an activity will be related to two activities which at the same time are related to each other. This may result in unnecessary or redundant relationship lines and arrows. Redundancies result in needless computation and added diagramming effort; they should be avoided where possible.

When preparing an AOA network, it will be found that cross-over of lines in network diagrams are hard to avoid. Use breaks or bridges as explained in Section 1, sub-Section "Sequencing of Activities", and as shown in Figure 7-2.

The AON diagram is constructed using boxes containing activities; these boxes are called nodes. Arrowed lines, representing relationships with other activities, flow into the left of the node and leave on the right of the node. The arrowed lines, as in logic diagrams, show the "flow" or sequence of the activities. Lines in AON diagrams represent the logical relationships among the activities. It is normal to draw these lines (dependencies) in what is referred to as staff format, which means the lines are either vertical or horizontal and all connections being orthogonal. The same activities and their relationships that were used to develop the AOA diagram (Figure 7-8) are used to develop the AON diagram shown in Figure 7-9, view (a).

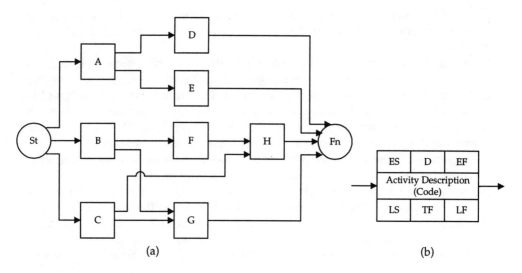

(a)   (b)

Figure 7-9: Activity-on-Node Diagram

The AON activity boxes need to contain space for:

- activity duration (D),
- activity description and code,
- early start date (ES),
- early finish date (EF),
- late start date (LS),
- late finish date (LF),
- total float (TF).

A proposed node layout that would suitably contain such information is shown as view (b) in Figure 7-9.

A single time value is assigned to each activity's duration. The code that is used for each activity is taken from the code that was used in deriving the WBS.

In AON scheduling, the convention is that only one kind of dependency or logical relationship between activities is allowed — that is, "finish-to-start" (FS). In other words, the preceding activity must be complete before the succeeding activity can commence. As FS dependencies are the most common relationship found in practice between activities, then the AON network can be accepted as a valuable method of analysing plans.

Activity Durations

In most scheduling procedures, each work activity has an associated time period that is needed to complete the activity. The time taken to carry out an activity is called its duration. Durations are usually estimated, based upon experience. These durations are necessary in preparing a schedule. All formal scheduling procedures rely upon estimates of the duration of the various project activities as well as the definitions of the predecessor relationships. Durations can be measured in hours, days, weeks, months, or whatever other units are most representative of project requirements.

Activity durations are a function of the quantity of work to be carried out, the average productivity per worker and the number of workers. An activity's duration D_{ij} can be estimated from:

$$D_{ij} = \frac{Q_{ij}}{P_{ij}N_{ij}}$$

where Q_{ij} is the required quantity of work specified, depending on the type of project, as lines of code (software design), number of pages (manual preparation), area of wall (building construction), and so on. P_{ij} is the average productivity of a standard unit resource having the required skills to do the assigned work, and N_{ij} is the number of unit resources to be used.

Such a formula can be used when the work to be undertaken and the production rate are quantifiable, and can be derived with a relatively high degree of accuracy.

The calculation of durations using this formula is only an approximation of the actual duration for a number of reasons:

- each project has its own peculiarities;

- there is a learning stage in each activity;

- the difference in resource skills;

- random factors (e.g. weather, use of averages, etc.).

The same activities in different projects are unlikely to be identical; therefore the use of an average production rate needs adjustment based upon the particular *peculiarities* of each project. The planner-scheduler needs to adjust the calculated D_{ij} based on their experience of whether the production rate should be lower or higher and by how much.

Productivity on an activity is often lower, sometimes much lower, at the initial stage of an activity's duration as the resource becomes familiar with the activity, and, when the number of resource units is >1, with the work habits of the rest of the resource team. This is referred to as the *learning stage* of the activity and it can have a major, or minor, effect on the average productivity.

If the project is undertaken outdoors, as is the case with most building and construction projects, the *weather effects* are often very important and can have significant influences on the productivity rates of activities. The use of *average production factors* will, in general, result in optimistic estimates of activity durations. This is due to the non-linearity of the relationship between durations and the reciprocal of productivity rates. For example, an increase in productivity rate of 25 per cent will, all other things remaining the same, result in a decrease in duration of 20 per cent.

The variability of an activity's duration may also be taken into account but the method used in its calculation uses the probability distribution of an activity's duration as well as the expected or most likely duration. A probability distribution indicates the chance that a particular activity duration will occur but there is no certainty regarding how long the activity will actually take. In other words, this approach is used when there is little historic information on activity durations — or put another way, there is a high degree of uncertainty regarding activity durations. This is often the case in certain projects, such as designing new computer software, and basic research projects, but can also be the case on an individual activity within a project that otherwise consists of activities with a high degree of certainty relating to their durations.

The probabilistic approach handles uncertainty by requiring three estimates of an activity's duration. The terms used for these estimates are:

- optimistic time (t_o)

- most likely time (t_m)

- pessimistic time (t_p)

Optimistic time represents the shortest (best) possible time within which the activity can be completed, i.e. there is little chance that the duration will be less than t_o. *Most likely time* represents the most realistic estimate of the activity's duration. It is the mode of the time distribution. The *pessimistic time* represents the longest (worst) possible period of time that can be required to form the activity. These time estimates and their relationship to a probability distribution curve can be seen in Figure 7-10.

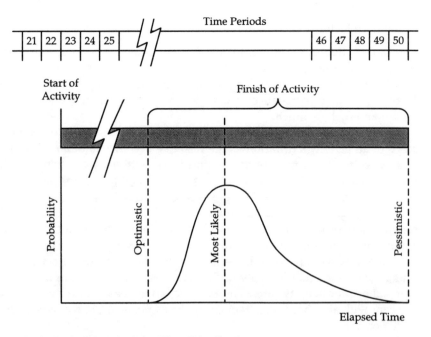

Figure 7-10: Estimating Activity Time Distribution

An expected time (t_e) of an activity can be arrived at by using these three estimates and the formula for expected time:

$$t_o = \frac{t_o + 4t_m + t_p}{6}$$

$$\sigma = \frac{t_p - t_o}{6}$$

$$\text{or } (\sigma^2) = \left(\frac{t_p - t_o}{6}\right)^2$$

Each activity's duration can be represented by a continuous probability distribution whose mean t_e, standard deviation σ, and σ^2 can be calculated. Hence the duration of any activity is assumed to be a random variable with beta distribution. An activity's continuous probability distribution can be described by its t_e, σ, and σ^2. The standard deviation (σ) is estimated as being one-sixth of the distance between the pessimistic and optimistic duration periods:

Creating Network-Based Scheduled Plans

Schematic models have significant value for a manager because they make it possible to visualise the major elements and interrelationships that describe a system. As a management device, the scheduled plan shows the activities necessary to complete a project, the sequence of activities, the timeframe within which the activities must be completed, and the overall timeframe of the project.

The project plan is scheduled by setting the activities in accordance with their logic against a calendar of time by:

- estimating the resources needed for each activity and the time duration to complete each activity;

- undertaking mathematical evaluation of the overall project duration;

- defining the working calendar for the project;

- if needed, balancing the schedule to better utilise resources.

So scheduling the plan is a four-step process. The first step requires the project team to determine an estimate of equipment, labour and materials that will be required to complete each activity. From this the durations of all activities can be established; this was dealt with in the previous sub-Section "Activity Durations".

Once the activities' durations have been established, the scheduling of the network can be carried out. This requires what is called a *forward pass* calculation, and thereafter a *backward pass* calculation. This procedure provides the early start (ES) date and early finish (EF) date and the late start (LS) date and late finish (LF) date for each activity respectively. The procedure also provides what is referred to as the critical path, activity total float, and, where it exists, free float between activities.

The next step is to determine the working calendar for the project. The choices available are wide: single shift, double shift, triple shift, 5-day working, 7-day working, statutory holidays, working holidays, vacation days, etc. The choice of calendar will be made to suit one or more of the following: the project completion date, the availability of resources, the location of the project, the complexity of the project, the contract strategy, etc.

Determining the work calendar permits the network to be converted into a *calendar schedule plan*. This expresses the plan in terms of actual calendar dates (day, month, year).

Once the first three steps in the scheduling process are completed, the scheduler has to analyse the results to determine whether there is a need to carry out further iterations of these three steps. In other words, it may be necessary to review the sequence of activities, the ascribed resources, the calendar, etc. in order to end up with a balanced scheduled plan that will work and reflect how the project management team perceive that the project will be implemented. Some resources may have to be shifted because they are limited or work loads need to be levelled out.

Scheduled plans are by their very nature evolutionary project documents and their application is often dictated by the amount of information they contain. The first scheduled plan will have been carried out during the conception phase of the project. During the conception phase, the scheduled plan will likely consist of few activities and the identification of only one or two target events (milestones). Typically, this first scheduled plan relates to broad functional categories of project work with little in the way of detail.

Network-based diagrams and their analysis reveal interdependencies and problem areas that are neither obvious or well defined by other scheduled planning methods. The network method determines where the greatest effort is needed for a project to remain on schedule. Another advantage of networking is its ability to evaluate the effects of changing activities, their sequence, their resources, etc.; this is referred to as "what if" scenarios. This is dealt with in Section 3 of this Part.

In essence, the fundamental information obtained from network-based diagrams is as follows:

- the impact of late starts;

- the impact of early starts;

- the effects of "crashing" the overall schedule;

- what activity or schedule slippages can be allowed.

Most large and complex projects require the production of multiple (usually four levels) scheduled plans: summary schedules for executive management, co-ordination schedules for project management, detailed schedules for contract package management and task schedules for product management. These are shown in Figure 7-11. As planning is carried out on a "top down" approach, the three or more levels of scheduled plan are automatically designed into the planning process.

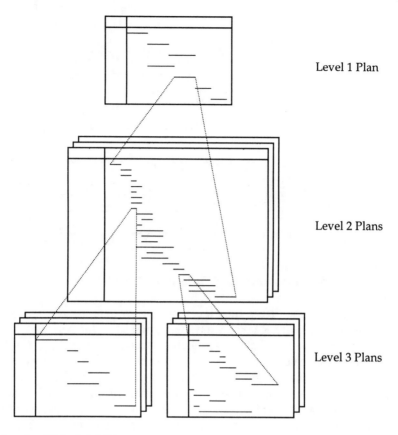

Level 1 Plan

Level 2 Plans

Level 3 Plans

Figure 7-11: Levels of Scheduled Plan

Forward Pass Calculation

A forward pass is always made in the direction from left to right — in other words in the same direction used in preparing the logic diagram and its normal flow.

After time durations have been assigned to each activity, the ES date and EF date can be determined. ES is the earliest date an activity can start after completion of the preceding activities. It is calculated by taking the project start date and adding each activity's time duration following the logic diagram. The EF is the earliest date an activity can finish if it was started at its earliest start date and is completed using the estimated time duration.

In analysing networks, there are a few other conventions that have to be stated and understood. It is convention to commence calculating the project at what is referred to as midnight on day 0. This is referred to as the project start date. This convention means that any activity's actual start date has to be interpreted as meaning a finite time after midnight, i.e. just into the start of the next day. For example if activity R takes 3 days and starts at day 12 its calculated activity start date is day 12 but its actual start date will be day 13. This is shown diagrammatically in Figure 7-12.

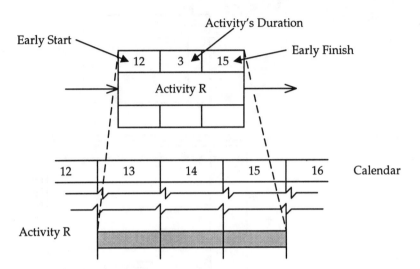

Figure 7-12: Interpretation of Calculated ES and EF

As can be seen from the Figure, the finish date, as you would expect, is day 15. Because activity R takes 3 days its actual calendar period will be days 13, 14 and 15. Any activity that immediately succeeds activity R will have its start date as day 15 for calculation purposes, but in real time this means day 16.

Where there is more than one preceding activity the largest value of earliest EF is always selected as being the early start of the succeeding activity. The reason for this can be explained by assuming the simple example of two preceding concurrent activities, S and T, and one succeeding activity, U. This is shown in Figure 7-13.

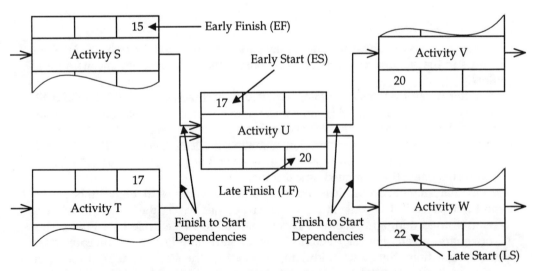

Figure 7-13: Determining ES of Successor and LS of Predecessor Activities

If S finishes on day 15 and T finishes on day 17, and both S and T have finish to start dependencies with U — i.e., S and T must be finished before U can start — then U cannot start until the latest finishing date (which is the same as the largest value of early finish date of S or T). In this example U could not commence until midnight day 17.

The forward pass calculations are carried out for all activities in a network. The calculations provide the ES date and EF date of these activities and, after analysis of the last activity, the overall time period and the finish date of the project can be determined.

Backward Pass Calculation

The backward pass calculations are made from right to left on the network-based diagram.

The LF is the latest date an activity can be completed without delaying the scheduled project completion date. The backward pass calculation is commenced by taking the project EF completion date, which is also the project's LF date, and subtracting each activity's duration, following the logic diagram, to derive an activity's LS date. This provides the latest start date of all predecessor activities to ensure that all succeeding activities will start on their latest start dates.

LS is the latest date an activity can be started if it is to be finished at its latest finish date. The LS date of an activity is calculated by subtracting the activity's time duration from the LF date.

Where there is more than one succeeding activity dependent upon an immediately preceding activity then the smallest value of LS date of the succeeding activities is always selected. The reason for this can be explained by again referring to Figure 7-13. V and W are succeeding activities to the predecessor U. If the LS dates for V and W are day 20 and day 22 respectively, then obviously U's LF will be dictated by V's LS of day 20.

Critical Path

When the ES and LS dates and the EF and LF dates are the same for an activity, this activity is said to be "critical". In other words critical activities must commence on their stated start date, must take no longer than the stated time duration, and must be complete no later than the stated finish date.

Critical activities form a continuous chain through the network called the "critical path". The critical path is the longest path through the network. In other words, it is the total time that the project will take assuming that the plan and the time durations are correct.

In small networks, it is likely that only one critical path will exist. In general, there can be numerous critical paths in a network.

Float

Activities with early and late dates which do not match are flexible. Such activities do not have to begin or end with the early start date or early finish date to permit completion within the scheduled completion date. In such activity's the flexibility is called *float* (or slack). Float measures the amount of time a particular activity's performance can be delayed while still permitting the activity to be completed within the scheduled time. The more float an activity has, the less critical the activity is.

Total float (TF) of an activity is the difference between the earliest and latest start dates or earliest and latest finish dates and can be written as:

TF = LS – ES or LF – EF

Free float (FF) is the difference between an activity's early finish date and the earliest start date of any dependent succeeding activity and can be written as:

$$FF = ES_s - EF_p$$

FF can occur when more than one succeeding activity is linked to a predecessor.

PERT and CPM — Two Types of Network Model

The Program Evaluation and Review Technique (PERT) and the Critical Path Method (CPM) were developed at about the same time (1957–1958) by separate groups, both of whom were attempting to develop more effective means for performing the planning and control functions in the management of major projects.

PERT was developed to facilitate management of the huge Polaris program. Personnel in the Special Projects Office of the Department of the Navy, together with a team of experts from Lockheed Corporation and Booz, Allen, and Hamilton developed the technique, which was credited with making it possible to save as much as two years in the research and development phases of the Polaris missile system program. Since its successful application in this project, which was of significant importance to US national defence, PERT has been used extensively for many civilian as well as other government projects.

During the same period, operations researchers from E.I. duPont de Nemours and Company, and computer specialists from what was then Remington Rand's Univac division, combined their talents to develop a method to schedule and control all the activities involved in constructing chemical plants. The result of their efforts was a network model termed CPM, which rapidly gained acceptance throughout the construction industry.

The original PERT and CPM models differed in the way they treated time and cost factors. In fact, as originally conceived, PERT considered only the time variable. The reasons for these principal differences between the two methods are understandable when one considers the orientations of the organisations whose needs gave rise to the development of the techniques.

In the midst of the cold-war period, the US Department of Defense was most anxious to match a potential adversary's capacity to deliver nuclear weapons. The Department of the Navy was correspondingly anxious to demonstrate its capacity to develop the Polaris delivery system and maintain itself as a viable part of the armed forces. Beyond the use of the technique to co-ordinate several thousand contractors, the Navy wanted to reduce the time required for the completion of the project. Therefore, one of their prime goals was to identify the longest time path of events and then work to reduce the time required for the completion of individual events that combined to define the longest path.

In the research and development activities associated with Polaris, or any other research-based project, uncertainty is obviously a major factor. Research implies the "breaking of new ground". The time required for a particular event (discovery) to result from scientific work (for example, the invention of new fuels or a guidance system) cannot be programmed. On the other hand, the orientation of the CPM team was not dependent on time alone, but rather on the relationship between time and cost of performing each major activity required in the design and implementation of a major production facility. In a project of this type, when a particular task is not performed on schedule, costly delays in the initiation of subsequent tasks can result.

Efforts initiated to overcome or break up bottlenecks can lead to overtime labour costs, special freight charges, higher materials costs, and other additional charges that add significantly to the total project cost. CPM was designed to facilitate identification of potential bottlenecks, to control the flow of activities, and to provide a means for evaluating the effects of trade-offs between the project completion time and project cost factors. Furthermore, although a large number of activities are involved in the projects for which CPM was devised, they are not research-type activities. They are activities that have been performed many times in other contexts; therefore, estimates of time and cost can be made with a reasonable degree of certainty.

Given this background, it is not difficult to understand the reasons for the principal differences between these two network models. These differences are summarised in Figure 7-14.

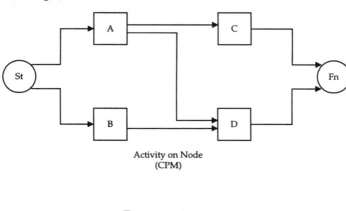

Activity on Node
(CPM)

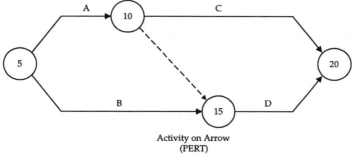

Activity on Arrow
(PERT)

Figure 7-14: Comparison of CPM and PERT Diagrams

Uncertainty with respect to the amount of time required for the completion of activities is recognised in PERT by using three duration estimates, namely: optimistic time, most likely time, and pessimistic time. This was dealt with under "Activity Durations" earlier in this Section of the book.

Duration times for CPM networks are assumed to be known. Furthermore, CPM views time as something that can be programmed; that is, the duration time, to a certain degree, can be controlled by the project manager.

Although cost was not an explicit feature of the original PERT models, CPM models treated cost as a major feature. They therefore served as tools of cost as well as time control.

Network analysis is common to both models. However, because of the difference in orientation, the points or nodes in the PERT network schematic represent events, and the lines indicate activities that must be performed for the events to occur. An event is the instant in time at which a specific part of the project is completed (or started).

Because the developers of CPM were dealing with projects for which the time and cost of activities required to complete the project were known, they naturally emphasised activities rather than events; hence, the points or nodes of the CPM network represent activities, and the connecting lines show the sequencing requirements of the project.

Comparison of the two Figures suggests that they could represent the same problem. Note that each is a directed network; activities flow from left to right. The distinction between using points to represent events and lines to indicate activities in PERT and points to represent activities in CPM has virtually disappeared in practice. Although of some conceptual importance, this distinction has little practical significance. Some practitioners follow the PERT convention, and others the CPM.

Precedence Diagramming Method

Precedence diagramming method (PDM) is a somewhat more complex version of the critical path method (Archibald, 1976). The complexity arises through the greater number of dependencies between activities and events. In addition to a greater range of dependencies, lags or leads between activities are also accommodated by PDM.

As with CPM, in PDM the left side of the node box represents the activity's start and the right side represents the activity's finish.

Dependencies and Lags

In PDM there are four logical relationships (compared with the one, finish to start, in CPM) and they are:

1) finish to start (FS).

2) start to start (SS).

3) finish to finish (FF).

4) start to finish (SF).

These four relationships are shown in Figure 7-15.

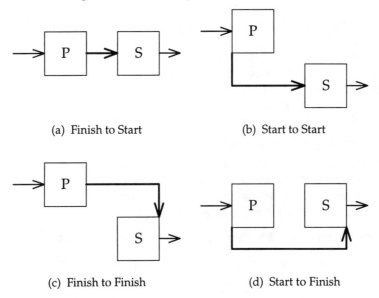

(a) Finish to Start   (b) Start to Start

(c) Finish to Finish   (d) Start to Finish

Figure 7-15: Four Dependencies Used within PDM

A *finish-to-start* dependency links the finish of the predecessor, activity P in (a) of Figure 7-15, with the start of the successor, activity S in the Figure. As in CPM, this means that the successor activity cannot commence until the predecessor activity has been completed.

In PDM, the assignment of relationships and lags can be shown quite simply. For example FS = 5 between two activities means that the successor activity must lag the predecessor activity by 5 time units. Or, in other words, the succeeding activity can start no sooner than 5 time units after its preceding activity has been completed.

A *start-to-start* dependency links the start of a predecessor with the start of a successor, (see Figure 7-15 (b)). An SS dependency should, if possible, be drawn with the relative activities drawn above one another (it makes it easier to read). Start to start relationships with zero lag between activities mean that the activities are started concurrently.

The term negative lag (lead) is used in situations which permit succeeding activities to begin before preceding activities have been completed. However this type of relationship can be shown by using a SS relationship with positive lag (simply reverse the arrow). SS relationships with negative lag are complicated and difficult to understand — they should be avoided.

A *finish-to-finish* dependency links the finish of the predecessor with the finish of the successor, as shown in Figure 7-15 (c). It indicates that the predecessor activity cannot finish until the successor activity has finished. FF relationships are used to show the relationship between the finishes (or completion) of two activities. Again, negative lag is difficult to understand and increases the complexity of the calculations to determine the critical path. Use of negative lag should be avoided.

A *start-to-finish* dependency links the start of the predecessor activity to the finish of the successor activity, as shown in Figure 7-15 (d). SF relationships should be avoided as there are generally less confusing methods for showing inter-dependencies.

Activity relationships can be better clarified by using two or more of the four possible relationships than by using only one relationship. PDM can express relationships between start and finish of activities. It is usual that if two activities have an SS relationship they will also have an FF relationship. Activities with both SS and FF relationships can be either partly or completely concurrent.

Calculation of early start and early finish (continuous work)

Continuous work assumes that an activity, when started, proceeds to the finish without a break. As with CPM the analysis of an activity's early start and finish is calculated by carrying out a forward pass. In carrying out a forward pass there a number of rules that have to be acknowledged:

- the smallest possible value for an early start time is zero.

- the activity's early finish time is the activity's early start time plus its duration.

- the value for early start "trial values" of the start of an FS or FF relationship is the activity's EF time. The arrow's trial-value ES/EF time is calculated by adding the arrow's lag to the arrow's trial value EF time respectively.

- the trial value for ES of the start of a SS or SF is the activity's ES time. The arrows trial value ES/EF is calculated by adding the arrow's lag to the arrow's ES time respectively. Note if an arrow has negative lag (lead), the lag value is added algebraically (subtracted).

- after the early times for all arrows terminating at the left side of an activity have been calculated, the activity's start time may be determined. The activity's ES time is the latest early finish of any relationship arrow entering the left side of the activity.

- after the trial-value ES for all activities terminating at the right side of an activity have been calculated, the activity's EF time may be determined. The activity's EF is the latest trial-value EF of any activity entering the right side of the activity *or* the activity's ES plus its duration, whichever is the largest.

- looked at symbolically and mathematically:

  i is for predecessor
  j is for activity being evaluated
  k is for successor
  t_j is the duration of activity j

predecessor type	calculation
F_iS_j	$ES_j = EF_i + F_iS_j$
S_iS_j	$ES_j = ES_i + S_iS_j$
F_iF_j	$ES_j = EF_i + F_iF_j - t_j$

EF for all activities: $EF_j = ES_j + t_j$

Early start (ES):
- For activities, the ES date of an activity is equal to the latest EF of preceding SS or FS constraints.

- For SF or SS constraints, the ES date is equal to the ES date of its preceding activity.

- For an FS or FF constraint the ES date is equal to the EF of its preceding activity.

Early finish (EF):
- For activities, the EF is equal to the latest of either the ES + duration or the latest EF of any SF or FF constraint ending on that activity.

- For all constraints, the EF = ES + duration.

- *Calculation of late start and late finish*
As with CPM, the late start and late finish is calculated by carrying out a backward pass. In carrying out a backward pass. there a number of rules that have to be acknowledged. The rules are:

- the largest possible value for any LS or LF is the project duration. Therefore the last activity is assigned a late finish time equal to the project duration.

- the value of the activity's LS time is the activity LF minus its duration.

- the value of an arrow's trial-value LF for the finish of an FF or SS arrow is the LS of the succeeding activity. The arrow's trial-value LS time is calculated by subtracting the arrow's lag.

- the value for LF for the finish of an FF or SF arrow is the LF of the succeeding activity. The LS for the arrow is calculated by subtracting the arrow's lag. Note that if an arrow's lag value is negative, the late start time must be calculated algebraically by adding its absolute value.

- after the trial-value late times have been calculated for all arrows starting at the left side of an activity, the LS time may be determined. The activity's LS time is the earliest LS of all relationships starting at the left side of the activity, or the activity's LF minus its duration, whichever is earlier

- looked at symbolically and mathematically as before:

successor type	calculation
F_jS_k	$LF_j = LS_k - F_jS_k$
S_jS_k	$LF_j = LS_k - S_jS_k + t_j$
F_jF_k	$LF_j = LF_k - F_jF_k$

LS for all activities: $LS_j = LF_j - t_j$

Late start (LS):

- For an activity the LS date is the earliest of either its LF – duration or the earliest LS of an SS or SF constraint leading from that activity.

- For all constraints the LS = LF – duration.

Late finish (LF):

- For an activity, the LF is the earliest LS of any succeeding FS or FF constraint leading from that activity.

- For an SF or FF constraint the LF is equal to the LF date of its succeeding activity.

- For an FS or SS constraint the LF is equal to the LS of its succeeding activity.

Calculation of float

In PDM there are three kinds of activity float, total float (TF), start float (SF) and finish float (FnF).

TF is calculated by subtracting the early start time and duration from the activity's late finish time, i.e.

$$TF = LF - ES - t;$$

Total float (TF):

- For both activities and constraints TF = LS – ES.

Free float (FF):

- For any activity the FF is the least FF of any constraint leading from the start or finish of the activity. All end activities have FF = 0.

- For FS or SS constraints FF = (ES of the succeeding activity) – (EF of the constraint).

- For SF or FF constraints FF = (EF of the succeeding activity) – (EF of the constraint).

$$SF = LS - ES;$$

$$FnF = LF - EF$$

An activity with zero total float is a critical activity. The completion of an activity may be critical even though the activity itself is not critical (remember FF relationships).

The critical path in PDMs is not as easy to follow as in i–j diagrams. The critical path may go through arrows and activities and parts of activities. If an activity's ES and LS are the same, the start of the activity is critical. If the EF and LF are the same the finish is critical. To be critical both the starts and finishes must be critical and the total float equal zero.

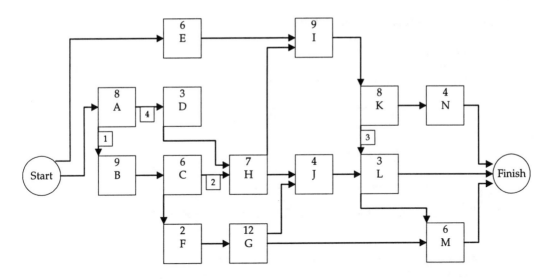

Figure 7-16: Precedence Diagram Example

Figure 7-16 shows a precedence diagram with its activities (letter-designated, A to N), their durations in days (above the activity letter), and the dependencies between activities. Lags between activities are shown as "flags"; for example, between A and D there is a four-day lag.

The application of a forward and backward pass reveals the analysis as shown on Figure 7-17.

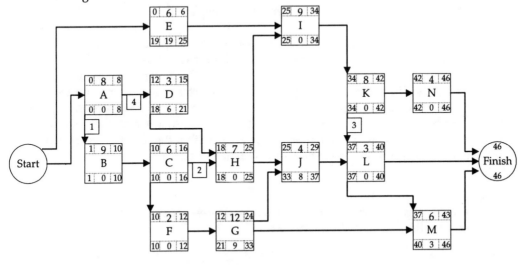

Figure 7-17: Analysis of Network Shown in Figure 7-16

The critical path is given by A-B-C-H-I-K-N. Activities F and L are critical but only by virtue of their start to start dependencies with C and K respectively. The total float in each activity is shown in the bottom centre box on each node.

Effect of Activity Splitting (Discontinuous Work)

- Forward pass

ES dates for all activities with no FS or SS predecessor relationships: set $ES_j = 0$. For all other activities calculate ES_j as follows:

predecessor type	calculation
F_iS_j	$ES_j = EF_i + F_iS_j$
$S_iS_j > a_i$	$ES_j = EF_i + S_iS_j - t_i$
$S_iS_j <$ or $= a_i$	$ES_j = ES_i + S_iS_j$

Finally set ES_j equal to the maximum ES_j's calculated above.

EF:

for all activities, calculate: $EF_j = ES_j + t_j$ (1)

for activities with
F_iF_j relationships: $EF_j = EF_i + F_iF_j$ for each F_iF_j (2)

Finally set EF_j equal to the maximum of the EF_j's in (1) and (2):

if (1) is a maximum, set $a_j = t_j$

if (2) is a maximum, set $a_j = t_j - F_iF_j$, using that F_iF_j which yielded the maximum EF_j in (2).

T (project duration) $T =$ maximum EF_j for all j's

The effect of the rules in a forward pass is to start each job as soon as allowed by its FS or SS predecessor relationships and to finish as soon as allowed by its duration or by its FF predecessor relationships. If the EF is determined by an FF relationship, say F_iF_j, and not by a duration, then the activity will be interrupted. The split will be such that the first portion is a_i days long and the last portion F_iF_j days long with the last segment commencing at EF_i (the point at which the predecessor activity i just finishes. a_i is the first work period within the duration of an activity before the discontinuity when no work is carried out).

- Backward pass

LF for all activities with no FS or FF successor relationships, set $LF_j = T$. For all other activities, calculate LF_j as follows:

successor type	calculation
F_jS_k	$LF_j = LS_k - F_jS_k$
$F_jF_k > b_k$	$LF_j = LS_k - F_jF_k + t_k$
$F_jF_k <$ or $= b_k$	$LF_j = LF_k - F_jF_k$

Finally set LF_j equal to the minimum of all LF_j's calculated above.

LS:

for all activities, calculate $LS_j = LF_j - t_j$ (1)

for activities with S_jS_k relationships $LS_j = LS_k - S_jS_k$ (2)

Finally set LS_j equal to the minimum LS_j's in (1) and (2):

if (1) is a minimum, set $b_j = t_j$

if (2) is a maximum, set $b_j = t_j - S_jS_k$, using that S_jS_k which yielded the minimum LS_j in (2).

In the backward pass, each activity finishes as late as allowed by the FS or FF successor relationships, and starts as late as allowed by its duration or by its SS successor relationships. If LS is determined by the later, say S_jS_i and not by the duration, then the job will be split. The first portion will be S_jS_i days long, ending just at the point successor job k begins (LS_k); the second portion will be b_j days long.

SECTION 3: RESOURCES, COSTS, AND OPTIMISING PROJECT DURATION

Contents

- Aims and Objectives
- Resource Aggregation and Balancing
- Cost Breakdown Structure
- Duration–Cost Relationship
- Least Cost Scheduling
- Central Limit Theorem
- Summary of Key Points
- References

Aims and Objectives

The aims and objectives of Section 3 are to:

- Show the development of resource histograms and how these are used to make decisions on resource utilisation;

- Demonstrate the relationship between a project's cost breakdown structure and the WBS and OBS;

- Define the relationship of activity and project duration to cost;

- Show how to derive the optimum duration for a project;

- Analyse project durations when activities do not have discrete durations.

Resource Aggregation and Balancing

Putting together a workable schedule that satisfies all constraints is not an easy task. After having evaluated the work to be performed and the most logical and cost-effective sequence of performing that work, there remains further analysis to produce a workable and efficient schedule.

Shortage of resources can significantly affect the initiation, performance and completion of activities. Limits imposed on resources can be dealt with in several ways. One way is to level the use of resources so that the project completion date can be met and the ES and LS dates and EF and LF dates can be respected. This process is known as "resource levelling".

In some cases it may be impossible to schedule activities so that the maximum numbers of resources does not exceed the available resources while maintaining ES, LS, EF and LF schedule dates, so it may be necessary to extend the overall project duration. This process is known as "resource-restrained levelling".

Using the logic diagram produced during the planning of the project and the time durations developed for scheduling the plan, it is possible to identify the resources that will be used in each activity. From this it is possible to develop an assessment of the total hourly, daily or weekly resources that will be required, based on the activities beginning on their ES dates and, similarly, based on activities beginning on the LS dates. This process is known as "resource loading".

Resource levelling attempts to arrive at the same number of personnel to be utilised during each day of the project. Resource levelling is the end result of a series of steps.

In estimating the duration of an activity, we have, until now, assumed that whatever resources might be needed to carry out the activity would be available. However, in many instances this is not the case.

The first step in resource aggregation is to derive a barchart from the network that was developed for the project. The completed barchart is used to unite the resources with the time schedule. This is simply carried out by determining the resources needed for each time unit — hour, day, month — for each activity. The resources are then aggregated for each time unit. Different types of resource can be aggregated separately. Resources can be equipment, labour or materials.

Through the use of network-type scheduled plans and float it is recommended that all resource levelling should be undertaken in the sequence:

Network — Barchart — Histogram

The total demand for each type of resource can be shown as a histogram drawn below the bar chart. Displaying it this way shows how the resource(s) vary with time. The development from the early-start/early-finish network to a histogram indicating the aggregated resources is shown in Figure 7-18.

The network is connected to a barchart and it is normal to plot the ES and EF of each activity; these are shown as bars on Figure 7-18 (b) (the shaded bars are the critical activities). Float, for those activities which are not critical, can best be shown as a dotted line, as in Figure 7-18 (b).

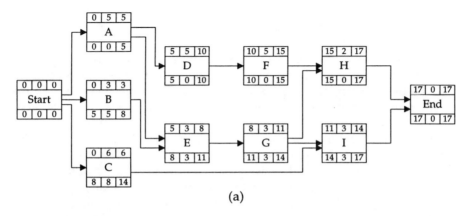

(a)

Figure 7-18: (a) Network Schedule

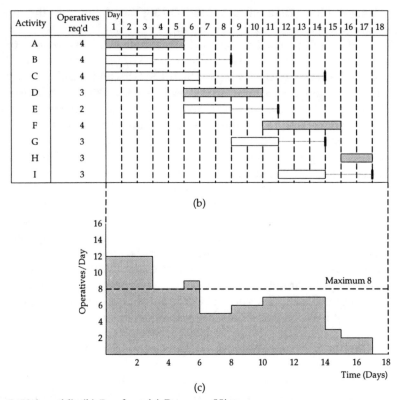

Figure 7-18 (cont'd): (b) Barchart (c) Resource Histogram

A histogram could also be developed for the late-start/late-finish but it is normal to analyse resources on the early network-based findings.

The Figure shows that there are a total of nine operatives required on day 6. Let's assume that there are only eight operatives available to the project; this is known as resource availability. By showing this availability as a horizontal line, it is clear where and when the over-demand exceeds resource availability. If the resource demand exceeds the resource availability during any one time period (day) then either the resources will need to be rescheduled or the schedule of activities will need to be amended.

Having more than one type of resource means that the histogram has to show the different types, or else a separate histogram will be necessary for each type.

From an organisation's point-of-view, to achieve maximum benefit from the individuals working on the project, the target should be to keep everyone fully occupied. It is desirable in achieving this target to avoid having an over-demand on some days and then later having these resources idle or nearly idle. The ideal is to try and keep the resources as nearly constant as possible.

To change the shape of the histogram, the position of some of the activities will have to change. This can be done by delaying the start of an activity. Whenever peaks and troughs exist on a resource histogram, it is normal to try to even out these variations. Such evening-out is known as resource levelling; the effect is shown on Figure 7-19.

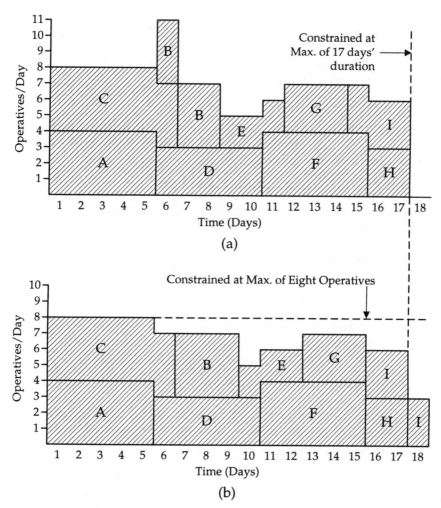

Figure 7-19: *The Effect of Resource Levelling*

Usually when levelling resources, one of two options can be used:

1) The project must be completed by a particular date to satisfy the owner's objectives. In this situation it is assumed that there is no upper limit on resources (but you must use them effectively). The requirement is to reschedule the activities without increasing the total project duration. This is known as *time-constrained levelling*.

Or

2) the number of resources available is limited and there is no possibility of bringing in additional resources. After the non-critical activities have been rescheduled, there may be no other alternative but to delay a few of the critical activities and consequently increase the total project duration. This is known as *resource-constrained levelling*.

The basic rules for each option is the same. Firstly, the resources are levelled. In the time-constrained case, so long as you haven't increased the total project duration, you are finished at this point. In the resource-constrained case, if the revised histogram is telling you that you still need more resources than are available, then you have to try one more time using another set of rules.

Time-constrained rules:
- use early dates and show the resource histogram for each activity as a block on the histogram (first plot the greatest float activity when two or more non-critical activities have the same ES date);

- all critical activity resource blocks will be fixed;

- reschedule the non-critical activities within their available float to obtain a resource histogram that is as level as possible.

Resource-constrained rules:
- schedule the project in, say, weeks

- at week 1 allow all activities to start if resources available;

- when more than one activity is to start but resources aren't available give priority to the activity with the earliest LS date. If there is more than one activity with the same LS, then select the one with the shortest duration.

- continue with this procedure until all activities have been rescheduled.

Figure 7-19 (a) shows the effect of time-constrained levelling of the example shown in Figure 7-18, and (b) shows the effect of resource constrained levelling. To complete the project in 12 days will require 8 operatives for the first 5 days and between 5 and 7 operatives for the remaining 12 days, except on Day 6 where 11 operatives will be required (see (a)). By allowing discontinuous working, which is the approach that should be adopted here, it will be possible to obtain a more level resource histogram without extending the duration of the project. To complete the project with a maximum of 8 operatives, while maintaining the project's logic, will require the project duration to be extended by 1 day (see (b)).

Cost Breakdown Structure

On small projects, planning and assigning budget costs can be undertaken using simple budgets for the project as a whole. Such budgets will be a matrix of time period (usually weeks or months) against expenditure item; an example of a typical simple budget layout was shown in Figure 3-17 in Part 3 for one element within a much larger project having a range of elements. Control of costs for such simple projects is carried out by including a constant comparison of actual expenditures versus planned expenditures.

On larger projects, a single project-wide budget is not sensitive enough to be used as a control device. Under such an arrangement, once a project is underway it would be difficult to locate the source of a cost increase or decrease simply because of the size of the project and the number (hundreds, even thousands) of cost elements that could be the contributor(s) to such change. To overcome this difficulty, the project budget is broken down into smaller segments called cost accounts (Nicholas, 1990). Larger projects may have tens or even hundreds of cost accounts.

The WBS technique used within the planning process describes the work activities of a project in a logical hierarchy which can be used for a number of related management control activities. Integrated with the WBS should be a cost breakdown structure (CBS).

The CBS enables the cost components to be aggregated based on some classification system. With due care in designing a system it should be possible to find and locate specific activities, specific subsystems, etc. within the CBS. The CBS is therefore a framework which links cost components to organisational units in the OBS, and to WBS elements (Shtub et al., 1994). For convenience, Figure 3-17 from Part 3 is reproduced as Figure 7-20 to demonstrate the inter-relatedness of WBS, OBS, and CBS.

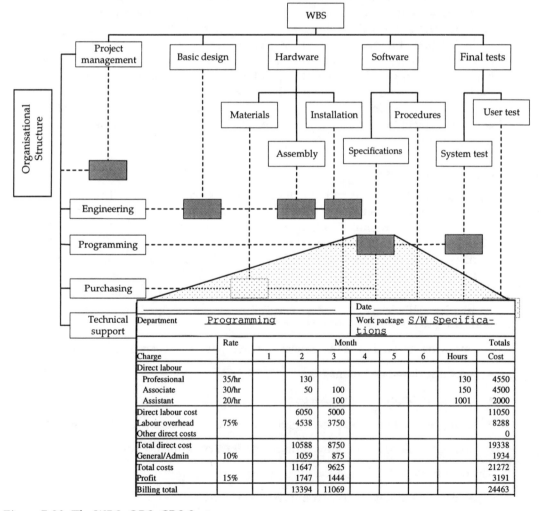

Figure 7-20: The WBS–OBS–CBS System

To help keep track of project activities, each category, task, etc. is coded with a unique number. The numbering code becomes the basic tracking and control unit for the project.

A system of cost accounts is set up in conjunction with the WBS. In practice, both the schedule and the time-phased budget are developed simultaneously. Cost accounts and work packages are analogous. Each cost account should include a description of the work, a time schedule, who is responsible, a time-phased budget, and material, labour and equipment required. With the exception of the time-phased budget, all this information is obtainable from the WBS.

A horizontal consolidation of cost accounts is used for monitoring the performance of individual departments or responsible parties to the project. A vertical consolidation of cost accounts is used to track and control individual work packages.

The WBS allows integration of the schedule and the budget in a single system, so that meaningful tracking can be carried out. The use of the WBS also allows better organisation of the work so that the accounting requirements of the project are more easily met and job charges are arranged through use of a coding system.

In the past, the percentage of physical progress on a job was tracked independently, using the time schedule as the baseline. The cost of the project was based on tracking and making "to complete" predictions against the baseline of the budget. As there was no relationship between the two, it was difficult to relate cost and progress. In Part 8, a highly recommended method of integrated time and cost control for the larger project, which is referred to as "earned value", is fully defined.

Duration–Cost Relationship

Up to now we have dealt with the development of schedules as a "first schedule", but for many reasons the first schedule may not be acceptable. It may be that, if time is "not at a premium", a longer period could be taken than that first scheduled. It may be that there is a need to shorten the first schedule period. To help in management decision-making a profile of the project's overall duration versus the cost of the project would be helpful. The first schedule provides management with nothing more than one point on the duration-cost profile (relationship).

In very many cases there is a need to shorten the completion period of all, or part, of a project. Reasons for this need include:

- satisfying the wishes of the project's owner, who wants it as soon as possible;

- avoiding liquidated damages;

- taking advantage of financial bonuses;

- taking advantage of seasonal weather variations (outside project);

- taking advantage of holiday periods/other calendar restrictions.

The easiest way of reducing the duration of a project are:

- eliminate unnecessary constraints between activities;

- re-sequence activities (divide them into smaller activities that can be carried out concurrently);

- adjust durations.

The process of expediting a project is often called "crashing". The term refers to the reduction of activity durations with the overall effect of reducing the project duration.

The crashing process uses an assessment of activity variable cost with time to determine which durations to reduce to economically minimise the overall project duration. Crashing can happen in one of the following ways:

- multiple shift-working;

- extended workdays;

- use larger/more productive equipment;

- increase the number of project personnel;

- use materials with faster installation methods;

- use alternate methods or sequences.

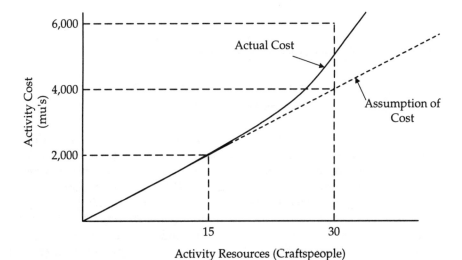

Figure 7-21: Resource–Cost Relationship

Let us briefly examine the option of increasing the project personnel. Figure 7-21 is a graph of the typically assumed relationship between resources and cost of a specific activity (Callahan et al., 1992). The typical assumption is that there is a linear relationship (straight line in Figure 7-21) between the activity resource and the activity cost, such that if resources are doubled the cost will be doubled. For instance, the example shows the situation for a particular type of work requiring skilled craftspeople where 15 people when increased to 30 people will increase the cost from 2,000 money units (mu) to 4,000 mu. In other words, double the independent variable (craftspeople) and the dependent variable (cost) doubles.

However, what is normally found is that when resources are doubled the costs are likely to be more than doubled. This is shown as the "actual cost" curve on the same Figure. This non-linearity is usually due to the fact the least expensive resources, or more accurately, the most productive resources are used first. Although this does not fully explain all the factors that can affect the linearity concept it does highlight the inadequacy of the "straight line" assumption.

Let us briefly examine the effect that increasing the project personnel would have on the activity's duration.

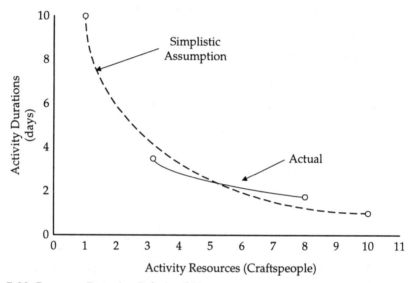

Figure 7-22: Resource-Duration Relationship

It is typically assumed that if "n" units of resource takes time "t" to do something, then "t" units of resource can do the same thing in "n" time. In other words if one person takes ten days to write 4,000 lines of text or code, then ten people could write the same number of lines in one day. This simplistic assumption is shown as a concave negative curve and labelled "assumption of duration".

Also imposed on Figure 7-22 is a more realistic "actual" curve which shows something different. It may be that the maximum number of people that could do this work would be eight and the minimum would be three. These upper and lower constraints can be due to available space, availability of equipment, etc. The reason why the actual curve is different to the assumed curve is again due to productivity which in this example is affected by "crowding".

Combining these foregoing concepts, it is possible to illustrate the basic duration-cost relationship for an activity (as well as for a total project) as shown by the curve in Figure 7-23.

At a particular position on the duration-cost curve there is a point at which the cost will be minimum; at this point the activity's duration could be referred to as "optimum". By applying more resources in the form of added personnel, or by extending the work day or by working shifts, the duration of the activity will be reduced but the cost of the activity will rise.

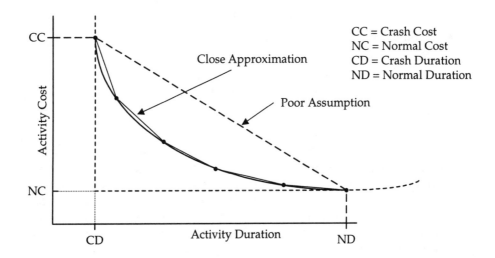

Figure 7-23: Duration-Cost Relationship

By continually applying resources, there comes a time when maximum effort has been applied and the duration cannot be decreased further; the activity is said to be crashed. The arc that is formed between the crash point and the minimum cost point can be poorly approximated by a straight line. It can be more closely approximated by a series of short straights, a–b, b–c, c–d, and so on. It is this concept which is used when analysing activity duration–cost relationships in selecting activity duration for "crashing" the overall project schedule.

Using the simplest case of the straight line approximation, it is possible to calculate the cost slope per unit time using the formula (Callahan et al., 1992):

$$\text{cost slope} \quad = \quad \frac{CC - NC}{ND - CD}$$

where CC is the crash cost, NC is the normal cost, ND is the normal duration, and CD is the crash duration. The cost slope is how much the cost of the job would change if it was sped up or slowed down. In general, the steepness of the cost slope increases with the cost of accelerating an activity.

The cost slope concept can be used to determine the most efficient way of shortening a project; this is dealt with in the next sub-Section.

Least Cost Scheduling

The network analysis described in Section 2 assumes that each activity is performed in the most economical way. Thus the combination of resources assigned to each activity is assumed to be selected to minimise the total cost of performing that activity. In the previous sub-Section it was demonstrated that it is often possible to reduce an activity's duration by spending more money. Thus it is possible to have a project duration and cost that lies between the limits of minimum cost/optimum duration and "maximum" cost/minimum duration.

Selecting the duration and cost of a project will require close collaboration with the owner of the project, who may wish to have the opportunity of deciding:

- a minimum duration project, hence accepting the additional cost of earlier completion, **or**

- the optimum duration project, i.e. minimum cost, that would result if the activities are carried out in the normal way, **or**

- some trade-off between the previous two options.

The technique of crashing activities uses network analysis to develop alternative schedules for a project. To reduce a project's duration, the critical path must be shortened. Thus, in reducing the length of the critical path, the first step is to identify the activity of which it is least expensive to reduce its duration. If there is more than one critical path, then the least expensive activity on each path have to be reduced. These activities are crashed and the process continues step-by-step with the next least expensive activity on each critical path being reduced by a unit of time, and so on.

If the duration of an activity is to be crashed then:

- the normal cost for the project is the sum of the normal costs for each activity.

- the first activity which should be crashed is the one on the critical path which will add the least amount to the overall project cost (activity with the flattest or least cost slope).

- the second and subsequent activities which should be crashed are again activities on the critical path with the next flattest cost slope.

- if there is more than one critical path then there should be a thorough inspection of crashing one activity on each path with the flattest cost slopes.

If the project duration time is to be reduced it will be necessary to obtain the following cost data for each activity:

- the cost required for undertaking the work on a normal time basis;

- the expenditure required for accomplishing the work on an expedited or crashed basis.

The two sets of data can then be used to develop alternative schedules and determine the best activity schedule in terms of minimum additional cost. The procedure is:

- list the activities (1), their normal duration (2) and direct cost.

- determine the crash time (3) and hence crash cost (5) of each activity.

- determine the crash cost per unit time (8).

- determine the minimum cost of reducing the project duration by one time interval (9).

- perform the same process to reduce the project duration a second time interval (10).

- repeat the process to a point where the project is fully crashed in terms of critical activities (12).

- determine the indirect cost for the project for the normal duration and the shortened durations (c).

- add the original direct cost (a) or the "crashed" direct cost and the indirect cost (b) to determine the total cost (c) at the various time intervals considered.

- identify the time interval, or project duration, at which the total cost will be at a minimum.

Normal activity durations are those that can be carried out at minimum cost. However, minimum cost rarely coincides with minimum duration.

The figures in parentheses above relate to the columns or rows in the Table below in which the relevant data is located; this Table shows a typical worksheet for an example project:

(1)	(2)	(3)	(4)	(5)	(6)	(7)	(8)	(9)	(10)	(11)	(12)	
Activity	Duration		Cost (£)		Δ£	Δd	Δ£/d	Weeks shortened by 1				
	N	C	N	C				1	2	3	4	5
A*	7	6	14,700	17,200	2,500	1	2,500					
B*	5	4	7,500	9,500	2,000	1	2,000					
C*	9	7	9,000	11,300	2,300	2	1,150			1	1	
D	19	16	9,500	11,900	2,400	3	800				1	
E	10	8	6,000	6,800	800	2	400					
F*	8	7	6,400	7,000	600	1	600		1			
G*	5	4	1,125	1,400	275	1	275	1				
H	11	8	3,520	4,510	990	3	330		1	1	1	
I*	6	5	9,000	10,000	1,000	1	1,000					
								275	930	1480	2280	**

Duration (weeks)				40	39	38	37	36

(a) Original direct cost			66,745	67,020	67,950	69,430	71,710

(b) Indirect cost						
	40 weeks@200	8,000				
	39 weeks@200		7,800			
	38 weeks@200			7,600		
	37 weeks@200				7,400	
	36 weeks@200					7,200

(c) Total cost						
	40 weeks	74,745				
	39 weeks		74,820			
	38 weeks			75,550		
	37 weeks				76,830	
	36 weeks					78,910

* activities that are on the original critical path
** it is not possible to crash the network by more than 4 weeks.

This information can be graphed to show the relationship of total cost against project duration. For the example shown in the foregoing Table the relationship between project duration and project cost is presented as Figure 7-24.

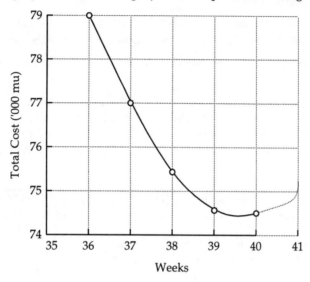

Figure 7-24: Project Duration Versus Project Cost

The Figure shows the minimum cost occurring at 40 weeks and the crash cost of £78,910 occurring at 36 weeks. With this information, a decision-maker can choose the planned duration against which the project will be undertaken. The choice of duration will determine the project's attendant cost.

Central Limit Theorem

In Section 2, under the sub-Section "Types of Scheduled Plans", under the sub-heading "Network-Based Diagrams", it was explained that activity-on-arrow is the scheduling method applied when using the PERT technique. A concept known as the "central limit theorem" (CLT) is used in PERT computations.

Before describing this theorem it is necessary to clarify the use of the PERT technique. PERT is a technique used to assist planning when no, or very little, historical duration or cost data is available. It is used when project duration is critical to the overall success of a project. PERT is used in both basic and applied research, new product development, software development, and other similar projects where there is a high degree of uncertainty associated with the overall duration.

PERT is a technique which focuses on events and not activities through using AOA network diagrams (see the sub-Section "PERT and CPM — Two Types of Network Model" in Section 2. This requires a probabilistic approach to the determination of activity durations which can then be used to determine the most probable project duration.

The variability of activity durations using the probabilistic approach was explained within the same Section, under the sub-Section "Activity Durations". Using this approach, the duration of an activity is assumed to be a random variable with a beta distribution. Three estimates of activity duration are made to compute the statistical limits that describe the activity duration and the distribution. As described in the earlier sub-Section, a formula is used to reduce the three estimates to one time estimate and a measure of dispersion for each activity.

CLT, central limit theorem, provides a means for combining activity duration distributions. The parameters needed to describe a distribution and to use the CLT are the expected duration, the standard deviation, and the variance. Calculation of these parameters were again illustrated in the earlier sub-Section. The theorem provides a means to combine activity duration distributions.

The CLT involves three concepts that apply to the adding of independent probability distributions:

- *the mean of the sum is the sum of the means:* The mean of the critical path T_E is the sum of the means t_e of the activities on the critical path.

- *the variance of the sum is the sum of the variances:* The variance of the critical path V is the sum of the variances of the same activities. Therefore the standard deviation of the critical path $\sigma_{TE} = V^{1/2}$.

- *the distribution of the sum is a normal distribution regardless of the shape of individual distributions.*

CLT is used to determine the probability of completing either the project or the individual activities at any specific time. It is also possible to determine the time duration for a given probability. The expected or mean time to reach an event is simply the sum of the mean times for each activity leading to that event.

The variance for the total time elapsed is equal to the sum of the variances for each of the activities in the chain of activities leading to the event. Therefore the standard deviation for the event time is equal to the square root of the total variance of the event time. It should be noted that it is not possible simply to add the standard deviations of the individual activities to arrive at the standard deviations of the event time. The CLT states that the variance of each activity is added to arrive at the total variance.

Having found the event standard deviation and the mean event time, the third concept in the CLT can be applied — the distribution of the chain of activities to an event is a cumulative normal distribution. It is possible to calculate the probability of various event times other than the mean event time. By reducing all the distributions to a common normal distribution, one can quickly identify the probabilities associated with these distributions from a standard table, such as the one shown in Figure 7-25.

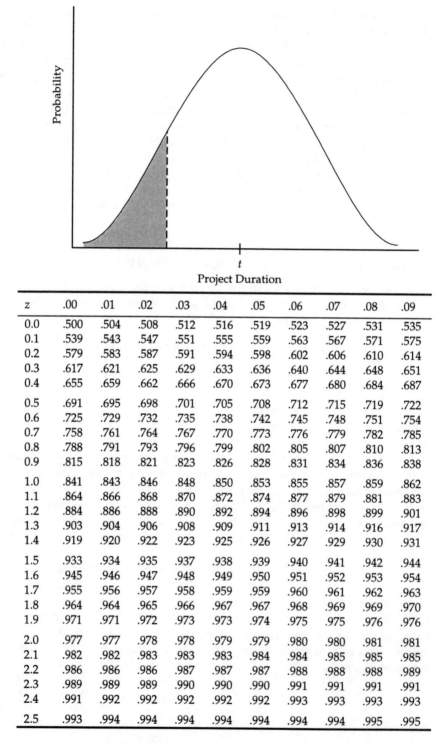

z	.00	.01	.02	.03	.04	.05	.06	.07	.08	.09
0.0	.500	.504	.508	.512	.516	.519	.523	.527	.531	.535
0.1	.539	.543	.547	.551	.555	.559	.563	.567	.571	.575
0.2	.579	.583	.587	.591	.594	.598	.602	.606	.610	.614
0.3	.617	.621	.625	.629	.633	.636	.640	.644	.648	.651
0.4	.655	.659	.662	.666	.670	.673	.677	.680	.684	.687
0.5	.691	.695	.698	.701	.705	.708	.712	.715	.719	.722
0.6	.725	.729	.732	.735	.738	.742	.745	.748	.751	.754
0.7	.758	.761	.764	.767	.770	.773	.776	.779	.782	.785
0.8	.788	.791	.793	.796	.799	.802	.805	.807	.810	.813
0.9	.815	.818	.821	.823	.826	.828	.831	.834	.836	.838
1.0	.841	.843	.846	.848	.850	.853	.855	.857	.859	.862
1.1	.864	.866	.868	.870	.872	.874	.877	.879	.881	.883
1.2	.884	.886	.888	.890	.892	.894	.896	.898	.899	.901
1.3	.903	.904	.906	.908	.909	.911	.913	.914	.916	.917
1.4	.919	.920	.922	.923	.925	.926	.927	.929	.930	.931
1.5	.933	.934	.935	.937	.938	.939	.940	.941	.942	.944
1.6	.945	.946	.947	.948	.949	.950	.951	.952	.953	.954
1.7	.955	.956	.957	.958	.959	.959	.960	.961	.962	.963
1.8	.964	.964	.965	.966	.967	.967	.968	.969	.969	.970
1.9	.971	.971	.972	.973	.973	.974	.975	.975	.976	.976
2.0	.977	.977	.978	.978	.979	.979	.980	.980	.981	.981
2.1	.982	.982	.983	.983	.983	.984	.984	.985	.985	.985
2.2	.986	.986	.986	.987	.987	.987	.988	.988	.988	.989
2.3	.989	.989	.989	.990	.990	.990	.991	.991	.991	.991
2.4	.991	.992	.992	.992	.992	.992	.993	.993	.993	.993
2.5	.993	.994	.994	.994	.994	.994	.994	.994	.995	.995

Figure 7-25: Cumulative Probabilities of the Standard Normal Distribution

Before the Table can be used it is first necessary to convert the expected time and standard deviation to normal standard deviation. This is accomplished by taking the event under study and subtracting from it the expected event time and dividing this difference by the event time standard deviation. This produces what is called the "z" value. The z value is provided in the cumulative normal tables. z is calculated from (Callahan et al., 1992):

$$z = \frac{T_s - T_E}{\sigma_{TE}}$$

where:

Z is the number of standard deviations from the mean.
T_E is the critical path mean of the project.
σ_{TE} is the critical path standard deviation of the project.
T_s is any date you choose.

A cumulative normal probability distribution for project duration illustrates how this information can be used to determine the likelihood of completing a project before a particular date. If the z-value is positive then the percentage is read directly from the Table. If the z-value is negative then the percentage is subtracted from 1 and the difference represents the probability of achieving the event in the specified time or less.

One drawback of assessing the probability of meeting the scheduled dates with this method is that only critical activities can be considered.

The best way to understand CLT is to review the following example:

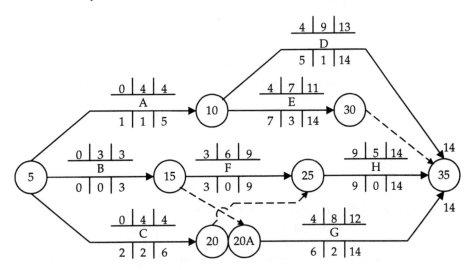

(Example taken from Figure 7-8)

Figure 7-26: Application of CLT

Events	t_o	Weeks t_m	t_p	t_e	σ	σ^2	σ^2 critical path
5 – 10	2	4	6	4	0.67	0.444	
5 – 15 *	1	3	5	3	0.67	0.444	0.444
5 – 20	3	4	5	4	0.33	0.109	
10 – 30	4	7	10	7	1.00	1.000	
10 – 35	8	9	10	9	0.33	0.109	
15 – 20A	-	-	-	-	-	-	
15 – 25 *	4	6	8	6	0.67	0.444	0.444
20 – 25	-	-	-	-	-	-	
20A – 35	5	8	11	8	1.00	1.000	
25 – 35 *	4	5	6	5	0.33	0.109	0.109
30 – 35	-	-	-	-	-	-	
					$\sigma^2 = v =$		0.997
					$\therefore \sigma =$		0.9985

This example was referred to in Section 2 of Part 4, so if you have read Part 4 these figures will be familiar to you.

The example shown in Figure 7-26 and the Table above show the activities, their relationships, the range of durations for each activity, the calculations for t_e, σ, and σ^2. The analysis shows that the project duration will be 14 weeks, and σ is 0.9985. Based on this, we are going to assess the probability associated with completing the project in 13 days; the z-value will be:

$$z = \frac{13 - 14}{0.9985} = -1.0015$$

from Figure 7-23, a z-value of –1.0015 gives a value of 0.844 for the cumulative normal distribution which, because the calculated value is negative, has to be interpreted as 1 – 0.844 = 0.156. In other words there is a 15.6 per cent chance that the project can be completed within 13 weeks.

Let's now see what the chances are of completing the project within 16 weeks. The z-value will be:

$$z = \frac{16 - 14}{0.9985} = 2.003$$

from Figure 7-23, a z-value of 2.003 gives a value of 0.977. In other words there is a 97.7 per cent chance that the project will be completed within 16 weeks.

Another calculation that could be performed would be to determine the duration equivalent to a probability of 75 per cent chance of being achieved. The z-value of a 75 per cent probability, obtained from the Table in Figure 7-23, is 0.68. The duration can be calculated from:

$$0.68 = \frac{T_s - 14}{0.9985}$$

from this, $T_s = 14.68$ weeks; in other words by completing the project in, say, 15 weeks there will be a greater than 75 per cent chance that it will be achieved.

Knowing the probability of completing a particular activity on a given date can be very helpful in making decisions about the sequencing of a project. A PERT approach with probabilistic analysis can be used to predict the amount of time necessary to complete a project with little risk of overrunning the duration. This type of information can be very valuable when making decisions about the viability of projects.

Summary of Key Points

- One of the most important responsibilities in a project is the planning of project activities, analysing and integrating their effects, and executing the resulting project plans. Because of the relatively short duration and prioritised control that are functions of many projects there is a non-negotiable requirement for formalised detailed planning. This is done through the development of a project scheduled plan.

- There are a number of outputs from planning and scheduling: the work breakdown structure (WBS), a project network diagram, and a selected project time plan that will provide "part of the means" for controlling the subsequent processes of executing and closing. Scope, cost, and quality will be the other "part of the means".

- The WBS shows successive subdivisions of the work on a chart analogous to that used for conventional organisational charts. The number of levels is dependant upon the size and complexity of the project; there could be 5, 6 or more levels. The purpose of the WBS is to divide the project into what is referred to as work packages which will allow the assignment of time and cost estimates, management, and activity and task responsibility.

- A logic, or sequenced flow, diagram represents the essential tasks that must be performed to complete the project. Such a representation forces one to define carefully the tasks that must be performed and to specify any linkages that exist between tasks. An obvious result is a picture that shows which activities await the completion of others and which can be conducted simultaneously. Once the logic diagram has been completed, the project plan is complete.

- The OBS is normally presented with the organisations shown horizontally and the hierarchy of skilled personnel listed in vertical format. It shows how each entity and each stakeholder fits into the "project organisation", the different levels of individual involvement, and the lines of communication.

- The responsibility and accountability matrix is a tool for combining the WBS and the OBS so that each work activity will have identified the members of the participating organisations who will make contributions to its completion. This tool summarises the relationships between the project participants, the stakeholders, and their respective responsibility for each activity required to carry out the project.

- The scheduled plan is a tool to determine the activities necessary to complete a project and the sequence and timeframe within which the activities must be completed. Scheduling systems achieve this by forcing members of the project team to think through the entire project in detail at the outset. This detailed thought process avoids inefficient and poor sequencing of the project.

- There are three basic scheduling methods that can be used: bar charts, line of balance chart (linear scheduling method), and network-based diagrams. Which technique(s) is used depends upon the type and complexity of the project. More than one of these methods may be used on any one project.

- Network-based diagrams and their analysis reveal interdependencies and problem areas that are neither obvious or well-defined by other scheduled planning methods. The network method determines where the greatest effort is needed for a project to remain on schedule. Another advantage of networking is its ability to evaluate the effects of changing activities, their sequence, their resources, etc.; this is referred to as "what if" scenarios.

- The Program Evaluation and Review Technique (PERT) and the Critical Path Method (CPM) were developed as a more effective means for performing the planning and control functions in the management of major projects. Network analysis is common to both models. Uncertainty with respect to the amount of time required for the completion of activities is recognised in PERT by using three duration estimates. Duration times for CPM networks are assumed to be known. Although cost was not an explicit feature of the original PERT models, CPM models treated cost as a major feature.

- Precedence diagramming method (PDM) is a somewhat more complex version of the critical path method. The complexity arises through the greater number of dependencies between activities and events. In addition to a greater range of dependencies, lags or leads between activities are also accommodated by PDM.

- To achieve maximum benefit from the individuals participating in a project, the target should be to keep everyone fully occupied. It is desirable in achieving this target to avoid having an over-demand on some days and then later having these resources idle or nearly idle. The ideal is to try and keep the resources as nearly constant as possible. This can be analysed by resource aggregation and balancing of resources.

- The process of expediting a project is often called "crashing". The term refers to the reduction of activity durations with the overall effect of reducing the project duration. The crashing process uses an assessment of activity variable cost with time to determine which durations to reduce to economically minimise the overall project duration.

- The cost breakdown structure enables the cost components of a project to be aggregated based on some classification system. With due care in designing a system, it should be possible to find and locate specific activities, specific subsystems, etc. within the cost breakdown structure. The CBS is therefore a framework which links cost components to organisational units in the OBS, and to WBS elements.

- The technique of crashing activities uses network analysis to develop alternative schedules for a project. To reduce a project's duration, the critical path must be shortened. Thus, in reducing the length of the critical path, the first step is to identify the activity of which it is least expensive to reduce its duration. If there is more than one critical path then the least expensive activity on each path has to be reduced.

- The central limit theorem is used to determine the probability of completing either the project or the individual activities at any specific time. It is also possible to determine the time duration for a given probability. The expected or mean time to reach an event is simply the sum of the mean times for each activity leading to that event.

References

References used in the development of Part 7:

Archibald, Russell D. (1976), *Managing High-Technology Programs and Projects*, John Wiley & Sons.

Callahan, Michael T., Quackenbush, Daniel G. and Rowings, James E. (1992), *Construction Project Scheduling*, McGraw-Hill Inc.

Humphreys, Kenneth K. (1991), *Jelen's Cost and Optimization Engineering*, 3rd edition, McGraw-Hill Inc.

Kesbom, D.S., Schilling, D.L. and Edward, K.A. (1989), *Dynamic Project Management: A Practical Guide for Managers and Engineers*, John Wiley & Sons.

Meredith, Jack R. and Mantel, Samuel J. (1989), *Project Management: A Managerial Approach*, John Wiley & Sons.

Nicholas, John M. (1990), *Managing Business and Engineering Projects: Concepts and Implementation*, Prentice-Hall Inc.

Pilcher, Roy (1992), *Principles of Construction Management*, 3rd edition, McGraw-Hill Book Company.

Project Management Institute (1996), *A Guide to the Project Management Body of Knowledge (PMBOK)*, PMI Publications.

Shtub, Avraham, Bard, Jonathan F. and Globerson, Shlomo (1994), *Project Management: Engineering, Technology and Implementation*, Prentice-Hall Inc.

Stevens, James D. (1990), *Techniques for Constructing Network Scheduling*, McGraw-Hill Publishing Company.

Weiss, Joseph W. and Wysocki, Robert K. (1992), *5-Phase Project Management*, Addison-Wesley Publishing Company.

Westney, Richard E. (1992), *Computerised Management of Multiple Small Projects*, Marcel Dekker Inc.

PART 8

IMPLEMENTATION AND COMPLETION PHASES

This Part contains some of the techniques and deliverables that are features of the implementation and completion phases of projects. It is during these phases in a project when the application of resources, including finances, is at a maximum; it is also the period of highest risk impact. Management of the implementation phase is dealt with in Section 1.

As the project progresses through its life cycle, so needs change from intense planning to intense control. Section 2 demonstrates how to measure work progress and monitor project performance through earned value and how such information can be presented as "reported status" in non-complex communications. This Section also describes other uses of time/cost planning and control.

Progress payments, trend and sensitivity analysis and claims for delay are considered in Section 3. Quality and its documentation is dealt with in Section 4, while Section 5 looks at communications and information, the life-blood of projects. Section 5 also deals with the configuration management process, status reporting, and structured meetings and their impact on project control.

The all-important completion phase of a project from the end of the implementation phase to final close-out is explained in Section 6. The close-back loop of "lessons learned" is also considered in the last Section.

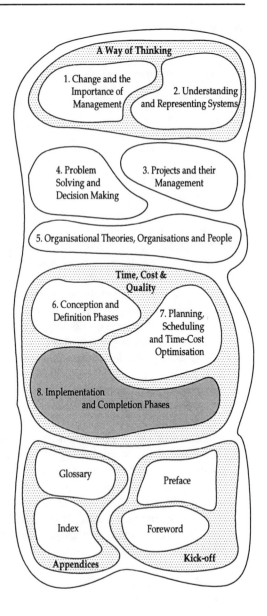

SECTION 1: MANAGING PROJECT IMPLEMENTATION

Contents

- Aims and Objectives
- Management of Implementation
- Contractor Performance
- Contract Administration

Aims and Objectives

The aims and objectives of Section 1 are to:

- Establish the primary elements in managing the implementation phase;
- Identify those characteristics used in determining contractor performance;
- Outline what management activities are included within contract administration.

Management of Implementation

Success in managing the implementation of a project depends on the efficiency and skill of the project management team, the effective control of the design team and the "implementation team", and the completeness and accuracy, primarily, of the preliminary master plan (PMP). Success also depends upon managing the subsequent refinements of the PMP, the definitive control plan (DCP) and the detailed firm plan (DFP).

How well the various parties, such as the owner, project management team, design team, implementation team (in the form of suppliers, such as contractors, vendors, subcontract specialists, etc.) work together will depend upon, *inter alia*, the efficacy of the PMP, the forms of contract selected and the behavioural personalities of the individuals involved. This "project" team is likely to consist of a range of companies, firms, partnerships and possibly individual specialists, usually referred to as experts.

The contract strategy, developed as part of the PMP during the conception phase, and refined during the detailed design and procurement stages as additional and more accurate information becomes available, will to a large extent determine the working environment for the implementation phase. This establishes who will contribute to the implementation work, how they will make their contribution, where they will be needed, and, in conjunction with the master time schedule, when they will be needed.

It is important during this period of "putting it all together" that each member of the project team recognises and appreciates the expertise of other team members and that the "big picture" requirements are continuously kept in mind by all.

Contract administration procedures need to be implemented for reviewing and evaluating such things as the properties of materials, dimensional accuracy, workmanship, etc. The project management team needs to check that material specifications are met, the results of any material or equipment tests are acceptable, that what is shown on the drawings is provided or built, that the goods are provided in accordance with the contract, and so on. This responsibility covers making sure that the configuration management procedures are adhered to; that all documentation is properly recorded, updated and filed for ongoing retrieval as reference materials. Configuration management is dealt with in Section 5.

Goods are usually procured with performance warranties and certification. Part of the project management team's duties is to verify all warranties and other certification. Minimum acceptable standards of workmanship have been developed for virtually every conceivable trade skill. Minimum levels of workmanship must be specified in the procurement process and verified by the administrator.

On most projects, substitution of specified items requires a formal change order signed by both parties to the contract (or by the project manager on behalf of the owner). The acceptance of substitution is usually a matter of judgement for the design professionals, contract administrator, the owner or contractor. Records must accurately reflect the item substituted, the original item, the reason for substitution, date of action, effect on project time period and price adjustment, if any.

The initial planning, adjusted when necessary to suit conditions, is the basis for monitoring and controlling the activities up to the commencement of implementation. The start date for implementation signals the beginning of this important period. The start date is set based on the detailed planning and scheduling which were undertaken during various preceding phases and stages of the project life cycle.

The scheduled plan developed during the conception phase and used to monitor and control the design and procurement stages needs to be updated and modified to accomodate the implementation plan. Major projects require a planned time schedule to be produced by the contractor (and subcontractors); this is usually a contractual requirement. The project's master time schedule is suitably adjusted with the information produced by the contractor at the commencement of the implementation phase. This upgraded scheduled plan then becomes the "implementation (completion) time schedule".

The planning and scheduling of the implementation and completion work is based on conformance with the overall scope of work and the contractor's proposed methods of carrying out the work. As part of the contract between the owner and the contractor, it is usual to obtain the contractor's proposed schedule for the works. At this time, the initial plan and schedule are enhanced with the contractor's detailed plans and schedules for the works to be executed. The broad assumptions made previously in addressing the implementation period and the implementation works are now replaced with detailed method statements, detailed plans, time schedules and other information that displace the broad assumptions.

In developing the time schedule for the implementation and completion phases, the contractor and his suppliers and subcontractors will have considered the time periods and the sequencing of the various work packages. This information provides the contractor with resource requirements and allocations and also provides the anticipated cashflow of earnings and expenditure and which items are critical and how much float is contained within all other items. This information is extremely useful to the owner in determining the cashflow of payments for the project, when they will be involved in approvals, staged handovers, etc., and when performance bonuses are due (if applicable), etc.

Detailed reports, usually daily, form a principal element of the project's management documentation. These reports, the implementation time schedule, the PMP and the change order forms are the most important reference materials for approving payment of invoices, resolving disputes and recreating job history. The preparation and review of the detailed progress reports are the project management team's most important tasks. Summary reports are usually prepared monthly; they relate the current status to project targets and objectives and to the planned situation at that time. Prompt and knowledgeable reviews of such data are vital to maintaining project progress.

Subjective reports, called exception reports, are normally made when unusual or significant events occur during implementation; all interested parties to the project need to be advised of every exception report.

The contractor is normally responsible for preparing the periodic payment certificates; these are reviewed and approved with or without amendment by the project management team. Periodic payments usually mean monthly payments to the contractor based on work done. All costs during implementation are divided into payments to the contractor and payments to others. Payments to contractors are further divided into regular or periodic payments of originally contemplated work, variations, extra work, etc. A complete record of all changes, indicating the percentage change to each contract and to the overall project cost, needs to be maintained.

The project management team needs to relate all project costs to a larger base; this requires the evaluation of individual element or package costs as a percentage of total/overall project cost. Periodic payments for individual contracts, assuming there are many, also need to be related to the overall project cost.

Usually an amount of money equal to a percentage of work completed is retained in case an estimating error, non-conformance to performance standards or implementation error is uncovered. This is normally set at 10 per cent of the value of work completed at the end of any time period. Releasing earned funds while withholding all unearned funds is a constant challenge to the project management team.

Most projects need contingency plans for unforeseen circumstances. This is covered by the risk management activities of the project management team; risk management is presented in Part 6, Section 4.

Ideally changes should be recognised in sufficient time for materials, design and fabrication/installation to be estimated, altered, actioned, received, and a fair price and effect on the project negotiated. Often this is not possible and work proceeds before all effects have been evaluated and/or agreed. Change frequently involves extra work on a project. The management of change is perhaps one of the most significant challenges faced by the management team during the implementation phase.

The project management team has a very important part to play during the implementation of the project, which of course is driven by the contractors and their support team. The project team's responsibilities are to maintain the "big picture" view of the project and to ensure that there is a balanced judgement in meeting the project targets of performance (scope and quality), time of completion and cost at completion.

Once the planning, design, bidding and award stages are completed, the continuing success of any project is dependent on completing the implementation and completion works to the required specification, within the predetermined time and the allotted financial budget.

The start of implementation is an event that signals a change in the "driver", from the professionals (design team) to the prime contractor. However, although the management of the implementation works is now in the hands of the contractor(s), the management of the project remains in the hands of either the owner, or the owner's appointed project management team.

Contractor Performance

The following are some of the main issues that arise in determining contractor performance:

Planning and scheduling

The contractor is concerned with the efficient utilisation of human resources, making sure that the skills of each individual are applied at all times on the most critical tasks. In most circumstances, planning during implementation is an exercise in fine-tuning and takes advantage of all opportunities to maximise the performance effort under changing conditions.

From the overall plan for the implementation works, the contractor needs to undertake monthly planning *and* weekly or daily planning as a way of keeping the project's implementation work on schedule. Implementation planning needs to be more comprehensive and detailed simply because of the "many people, many tasks" syndrome. These short range plans and schedules are needed to pinpoint exactly what will be done by whom, or by which squad, and when, i.e., which day, shift or, if appropriate, hour.

Identification of ongoing and anticipated problems becomes a significant factor in maintaining a schedule. Many things that happen during implementation could not have been anticipated by the planner/scheduler working months before the implementation actually started. All new factors need to be considered when preparing the detailed work plans.

Timely communication of all current plans will help to create a positive attitude throughout implementation. Performance indicators, similar to that discussed in Section 3 of this Part, are one of many methods of communicating performance between sub-contractors and others. Sub-contractor personnel, if motivated, will take more pride in their accomplishments.

Material control

All materials required for the project are defined, specifications written, quantities determined, and schedule requirements set. Control begins during the procurement stage and continues through manufacturing (or fabrication), transportation and delivery to the project location. On-site material control procedures track materials beyond that point — that is, from receipt at the project location to installation in the project works.

The material control objectives are to know at all times:

- what materials have been received at the project location;

- that the materials have been properly stored;

- when the materials are scheduled for installation;

- that the materials can easily be retrieved from storage;

- that commodity materials are pre-packaged for issue;

- that claims are filed promptly for items damaged in shipping;

- that shortages and surpluses are anticipated.

The project manager should ensure that the objectives of project material control are understood by those responsible as well as those individuals who actually carry out the work of materials receipt, storage, and issue.

Cost control

By the time the implementation works are under way, most of the project costs have been established, leaving three areas where the cost outcome of the project can still be affected: (1) on-site productivity; (2) schedule duration, and (3) fine-tuning of the implementation techniques.

Using the productivity information, the project manager can predict future performance and translate these projections into cost forecasts. Several techniques may be used for projections of future performance:

- future performance will be the same as past performance;

- future performance will be the same as budgeted;

- future performance will be a combination of the two;

- other techniques.

Refer to Section 3 for an illustration of a commonly used forecasting technique.

The following indicator, which has been referred to as Quadplot IV (Hamilton and Thomas, 1997), is an easily understood, easily produced device, and it can be a powerful motivator. A more detailed explanation is given in Section 2. This device is a simple way of showing project historical performance at each past time period (at the end of each week or each month), and a means of presenting time and cost performance for the current period, on a four quadrant chart. The quadrant within which the performance point falls each period shows the cost/schedule performance of the implementation to that date. A typical example is shown in Figure 8-1.

The horizontal axis is the "schedule performance index" and the vertical axis is the "cost performance index". The box in each quadrant indicates the state of the project at any reporting time. For instance, the lower left box indicates that a project's status in this quadrant would be "behind schedule and over budget". At the end of any time period, if a project's schedule and cost indices place the project within this quadrant, it is obvious that the project is not in a particularly healthy state; in fact, it is the worst state a project can be in. The healthiest state for the project is the top right quadrant "ahead of schedule and under budget".

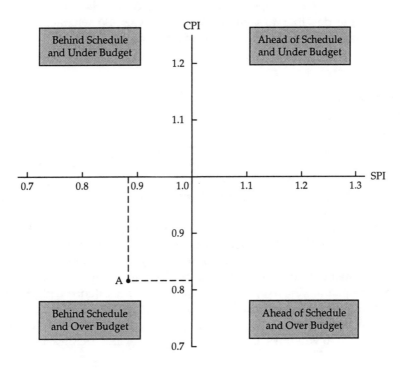

Figure 8-1: Model of a Project Control Chart

How the chart is constructed and used is dealt with in Section 2. Point A on the chart relates to an example described in Section 2. Point A is typical of a project's status where the project is both behind (time) schedule and above (cost) budget.

Changes to the Project

Project changes are a fact of life. The project can be expedited or delayed, depending on how these changes are handled. Two opposing factors are involved in changes during implementation. Proper control in many organisations dictates that the central head office or regional office must be involved in approving any change. Expediency, on the other hand, implies that implementation changes should be actioned by the implementation team and approved by the project management team.

The contract may have provisions which limit approval of changes during implementation. The project manager should understand just what the limitations are in delegating authority to the project team which represents the owner and/or the designer's interests. Changes regarding specifications or exceptions to drawings need to be referred to the proper engineering or technical authority. Any changes to the documentation should be fully recorded, giving reasons for the change.

If oral approval is given for a change because of time constraints, the approval should be documented as soon as possible.

Remember, the change control process requires the project manager and, if needed, the designer to sign-off their approvals. So whatever way approval is given, there is a need to ensure that it firstly has these sign-offs.

Contract Administration

Co-ordination

It is the project manager's responsibility to ensure that every possible effort is made to assist each contractor (and subcontractor) to establish mutual co-operation and respect among all the parties involved in the implementation works. If each contractor and subcontractor knows where their squad, or crews, are expected to be working, who is working adjacent to this squad, and when this squad and others are expected to start and finish their respective work, then the co-operation required will evolve.

Each contractor or subcontractor has the right to expect that they can perform the work that falls within their responsibility in an efficient manner. From time to time, there will of course be problems during the implementation work. For example, when one subcontractor's squad does not complete their work in time for another squad taking over to add something in accordance with the schedule. For instance, the plastering squad does not complete a particular room on time, and this affects the start of the carpentery squad who are scheduled to fit skirting boards, cills to windows, doors to door openings and architraves around the door openings.

The simple answers to getting over many of these types of problem are:

- excellent planning;

- good communications.

These actions, together with good relations between all contractors and subcontractors, make a difficult job easier.

Implementation and completion co-ordination is difficult, but fortunately it deals with the realities of what is happening, what should have happened and what needs to be done. In other words the project manager is dealing with things that can be seen and clearly perceived.

SECTION 2: PROJECT TIME AND COST CONTROL

Contents

- Aims and Objectives

- Making the Expected Happen

- Levels of Control

- Developing a Cost Schedule

- Work Progress

- Updating the Schedule

- Earned Value

- Forecasting

Aims and Objectives

The aims and objectives of Section 2 are to:

- Define project control;

- Analyse work progress of project activities;

- Show work progress on charts;

- Use earned value to determine the percent complete of activities and projects;

- Describe and calculate performance variables;

- Present performance variables in useful control chart formats;

- Produce forecasts of cost and time to project completion.

Making the Expected Happen

It is impossible at the start of any new project to foresee all problems or to anticipate all changes that the project may need. Every effort needs to be made throughout the project to regulate work, minimise changes to the plan and guide the project toward the predetermined performance, time and cost objectives. The process of keeping the project on target and as close to the predetermined plan as is feasibly possible, is the subject of this Section.

The control of project work can be expressed as "those measures that are necessary to make sure that the expected happens". Control with respect to time schedule, cost and performance (the triple constraints) is fundamental to achieving project success. The control activities in any project must be supported by the entire project team.

Let us be clear about what is meant by control! We can never actually control time but we can control what is done to achieve the time schedule. Neither do we actually control costs, but we do contain the costs to complete the work within the budget.

In the first instance, performance standards are defined and expressed in terms of technical specifications, budgeted costs, time schedules and resource requirements. Performance standards are derived from the owner's requirements, and are a part of the PMP. They are further refined as part of the DCP at the end of the design stage, and are refined again, if needed, as part of the DFP at the end of the procurement stage. These standards precisely define the cost, time schedule and technical factors to be regulated and the boundaries within which they must be maintained. One of the most powerful performance standards used in project management is *earned value*.

In the second instance, the standards are compared with the actual project performance to date. Schedules, budgets, and performance specifications are compared to current expenditures and work completed. The time and cost of work still remaining are estimated and used to forecast the anticipated date and cost of the completed project. Comparing actual performance with planned performance is explained in this Section.

Finally, when actual performance deviates significantly from the standards, corrective action needs to be taken. Such action is likely to include altering the scope of work or expediting the work, or altering the time schedule or revising the standards, etc. When the work performance is deficient, resources are either added, shifted or altered, or any combination of the three. When original estimates or expectations prove unrealistic, then project goals are likely to be changed and the performance standards revised.

The scheduled plan is a rehearsal on paper of what is going to happen; if it happens that way the management team know that it will be completed on time and to cost. Effective project management must continuously compare the project progress (time), project expenditures (cost) and technical performance (work scope and quality). The scheduled plan is the basis for project control.

Projects cannot be controlled unless they are properly planned, and projects cannot be planned unless there is a clear knowledge of the owner's requirements and the project objectives. It is obvious from the importance of the scheduled plan that it is time that drives projects, and it is for this reason that we use networked scheduled plans that are time-based.

It is not cost that drives projects; cost is an outcome of time expended. It should be remembered that budgets are only one of the constraints that affect what can be done and how it should be done.

If a project falls behind schedule, the implementation work should be accelerated or, if considered feasible by the project manager, the owner must allow more time by agreeing to an extension of the completion date; it may be necessary to take both measures. If the project becomes overspent or underspent, then the project management team need to analyse the reasons for this. They need to decide on corrective action and, with the implementation team undertaking the necessary adjustments, change management activities, work activities, resources, sequence, or any other elements needed to achieve recovery of the project schedule.

The conception phase of the project provides the planned time schedule and the scheduled cost of the works. With this information, suitably updated to the start of implementation and in cashflow format, a powerful method of control, called earned value, allows the management team to monitor both the time performance and the cost performance of the project.

Levels of Control

The levels of control on a project differ according to the project management organisation and its procedures, but classically there are four levels of control in a project:

- summary;
- co-ordination;
- detail;
- task.

These can be represented pictorially as shown by Figure 8-2.

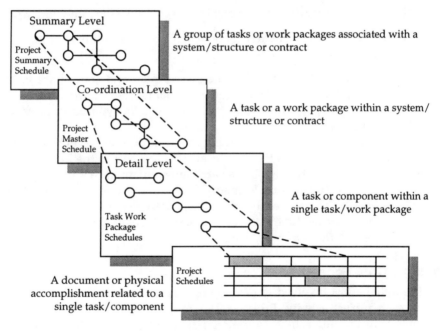

Figure 8-2: Four Levels of Project Control

At the *summary level*, the project plans and controls are generally viewed only by corporate or higher management. At this level there is no real management activity; this is principally an information level. As you can imagine, this upper level does not include or require much detail, in fact, the less detail the better. This level is therefore a summary of the detailed tasks or activities which make up the project's work breakdown structure.

At the *co-ordination level* of control, more time and cost data and details are required and used to plan and control the project. At this level, all the contract work packages have been identified in summary and correspond with the project time schedule developed within the PMP. It is at this level where the project manager (and, where appropriate, the project team) undertake the general management and control of the project. There are two more levels that form the detail of the co-ordination level. When a potential control problem is noticed at the co-ordination level it is necessary to further explore the problem by examining the package level and, if needed, the task level.

Projects are controlled at the second level of scheduled plan —co-ordination. The requirements of an effective tracking and control system include:

- clear communication of the scope of work required to complete the project;

- thorough planning of the work to be performed to complete the project;

- good estimating of activity time and its associated costs;

- a disciplined budget and authorisation for expenditure;

- timely accounting of physical progress and cost expenditures;

- periodic re-estimation of time and cost to complete the remaining work;

- frequent, periodic comparisons of actual progress and expenditures to schedules and budgets.

At the *detail level*, it is usual that the project plan and control are linked to the WBS. The WBS is used to determine work boundaries or work packages. It is at this level that the project is controlled. Control is likely, in most cases, to be on a day-to-day basis.

The most detailed level of planning and control is one level below the detailed level and is referred to as the task level. This *task level* is the lowest control point on the project and is typified by the assignment of an individual responsibility for the budget, schedule and performance of the task. Properly assigned task responsibilities can be aggregated to create WBS activities, which can then be further aggregated to create, firstly, the co-ordination level of control and, at the highest level of control, the summary level.

Developing a Cost Schedule

The initial effort involved in developing a cost schedule is determining the costs for each project activity. Project costs are developed for each work item in the same way that the activity durations are developed (see Part 6, Section 2). The activity costs and the project cost established from the planning and scheduling processes are those generally used for budget purposes; it is therefore important to use the best possible estimates at that time.

The eight-step procedure for developing a cost schedule is as follows:

i)   prepare the associated logic diagram and complete the network analysis;

ii)   derive an early start/finish bar chart from the network;

iii) prepare a tabulated format to determine the cost/unit time;

iv)   determine the time increments at which costs are to be considered;

v)   prepare a tabulation format to determine costs for the time increments;

vi) total the costs for each time increment;

vii) total the costs for all the time increments to obtain the total project cost;

viii) plot the total for each time increment on a cost distribution graph using the bar chart time schedule.

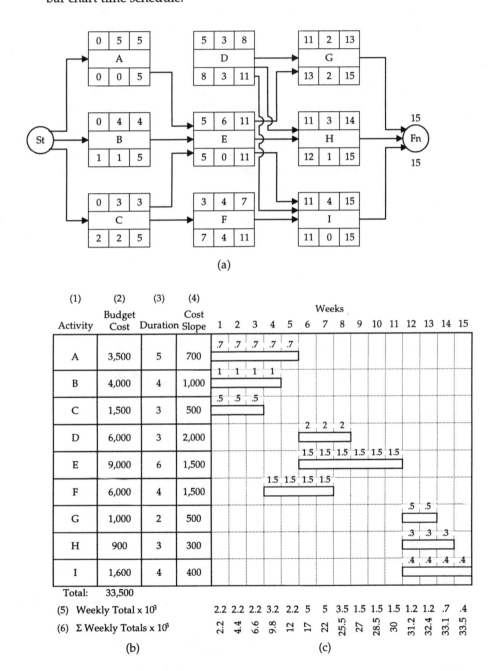

(a)

(b)

(c)

Figure 8-3: Network Example and Associated Barchart

The best way to understand this procedure is to see it in action. Let us assume that the network example shown in Figure 8-3 (a) is used to represent step (i). From this network, the bar chart shown in Figure 8-3 (b) represents the early-start/early-finish situation; this is step (ii). The next step, step (iii), requires the preparation of a Table with headings shown in Figure 8-3 (c).

As you can see from Figure 8-3 (c) one method of approach is to prepare the required Table as worksheet columns to the left-side of the bar chart — Figure 8-3 (b). This form of worksheet is a convenient way of understanding and presenting the resulting information.

Step (iii) requires the entry of each activity's cost into column 2 and each activity's duration into column 3. The cost slope, which is equal to the cost incurred in performing a job activity per unit length of activity time, is calculated by dividing each activity value (column 2) by the activity's duration (column 3). For further explanation of cost slope, reference should be made to the sub-Section "Duration–Cost Relationship" in Part 7, Section 3. In this case, the cost slope is given in mu per week, and the value is entered into column 4. The units selected are determined by the requirements of the project and are a natural development of the network schedule.

Step (iv) requires the determination of costs for each activity against a time period; in this case a time period of 1 week will be used. This is step (v). By way of explanation on how these values, on the bar chart and below the bar chart, have been derived, let's look at one or two activities. Take activity A. The slope cost of A is 700 mu/week. In week 1, there is 1 week of cost at 700 mu, which is placed on the activity A bar in week 1 (shown as .7 — all mu in Figure 8-3 (c) are in 1,000s).

To complete step (vi), total the costs for each time period — each week in this case. This is shown as row 5. For instance, the total for week 1 is relatively straightforward. It is 2,200 mu, i.e. 700 + 1,000 + 500, which are the weekly costs of A, B, and C respectively, totalled for week 1. Step (vii), the accumulated total, is given by row 6.

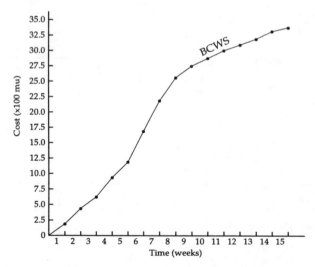

Figure 8-4: Time-Cost Graphical Relationship for Worked Example

Step (viii) is the plotting of the row 6 values, accumulated weekly total values, against the bar chart time-schedule. This is shown as Figure 8-4.

Work Progress

Only rarely is a scheduled plan followed precisely from the start of a project to completion. Marking progress on the schedule and making sequencing adjustments to the plan to match actual progress is called "updating". (This process also includes transferring project status/logic adjustments to the schedule and recalculating the schedule).

Sometimes due to lack of progress, changes or unanticipated problems, a project is delayed. This requires the schedule to be completely revised — this revision is called "rescheduling". Updating and rescheduling are needed so that the schedule can continue to be used to predict project completion and to manage the remaining work. Need arises because:

- it is important for the owner, designer and vendors to know the current status;

- it is important to know what is needed to recover delays;

- if the project is delayed, those involved will wish to know why;

- it provides an important record of the project;

- it provides a more accurate forecast of the future.

The frequency and detail of updating are dependent upon the size, overall duration, and complexity of the project. The frequency of updating can be daily, weekly, bi-monthly, or monthly. The degree of detail can deal with start/finish dates, work that is either completed or progressing, estimated percentage complete — used to determine value of progress payments — or all of these aspects.

The work activities and tasks required to complete a project include all those needed to provide the deliverables for the definition, implementation and completion phases. During these phases, the progress of the associated activities and tasks can be measured using different methods. The methods include:

- units completed

- incremental milestones

- start/finish

- opinion

- cost ratio

- weighted (equivalent) units

"Units completed" is the most appropriate method when the activities and tasks are repeatable. The units of measurement that can be used in this method include: number, linear measurement, square area, cubic volume, etc. Examples of activities using these measurements could be: testing pipeline valves (number); writing lines of software program code (linear); painting a wall (area); removing a materials stockpile (volume).

To find the percentage complete while the work is in progress, the completed measured work is divided by the total estimated work for that activity. For example, if 2,000 square metres of wall have to be painted, and 800 square metres have been completed to date, then the work is 40 per cent complete.

The "incremental milestones" method of assessing work progress is applied when what has to be controlled includes subtasks that must be handled in sequence. An example of this would include inward storage of goods where the sequential subtasks are considered to be milestones and when "completed" represents a percentage complete of the overall task.

The percentage milestones are normally evaluated based on the number of work-hours required to achieve that milestone as a proportion of the total work-hours. For example the subtasks and their percentage milestones might include: receive goods (15 per cent), check against order (25 per cent), inspect goods (50 per cent), store goods (80 per cent), update storage inventory (100 per cent). Should a particular batch of materials (task) received by stores have reached the stage of inspection of the batch having been completed, then that task would be 50 per cent complete.

The "start/finish" method of assessing work progress is applicable to those activities and tasks which are not readily definable as incremental milestones or where the effort-time is not easy to estimate. For such tasks, a percentage complete is assigned to the start and 100 per cent is recorded when the task is complete. In other words a percentage value is known at the start and the finish but no intermediate milestones are measurable. An example would be the delivery and moving of new equipment into a building. The arrival of the vehicle carrying the equipment to its installation location could have a 40 per cent equivalent "moving start" and when in approximate position within the building would be recorded as 100 per cent complete.

The "opinion" method of assessing progress is subjective and is usually made by someone who has knowledge of the activity and who simply makes a judgement of the percentage complete. If this method is used, it should be restricted to minor tasks.

The "cost ratio" method is applicable to long tasks which take as long as the project itself. Examples would be administrative support, quality assurance, and similar bulk allocations of either associated cost or time. The percentage complete at any time is simply obtained by evaluating the actual cost or work-hours expended to that time divided by the forecasted cost or time to completion. For example, if the activity is administration support to the project and the cost to date is 30,250 mu for what has been estimated will cost 55,000 mu, then administration is 55 per cent percent complete.

The "weighted or equivalent units" method is applicable where the task is a major effort involving a long period of time and is composed of two or more overlapping subtasks, each with a different unit of work measurement. For instance, if the work task is "design, supply, install something" the subtasks could be design (percentage measure), supply (unit), and install (square measure); the units of work measurement are shown in brackets. Each subtask is weighted according to the estimated level of effort (usually work-hours) that will be devoted to that subtask. As quantities of work are completed for each subtask, the quantities are converted into equivalent work-hours.

Using the example presented in the last sub-Section, let's assume that the following is the status of the project at the end of week 5:

- B, C complete

- A started, 60 per cent complete

- D, E to start in a week's time

- F started, 50 per cent complete

- G cancelled

Using the percentage complete milestones, it can be discerned by examining Figure 8-3 (b) that A can be completed in two weeks (i.e. 40 per cent left to complete) and F can be completed in two weeks (50 per cent left to complete).

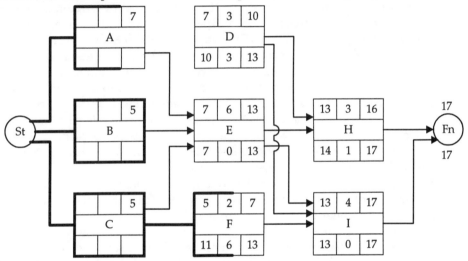

Figure 8-5: Network of Example Showing Progress and New Duration

Based on the information at the end of week 5, A will require 2 weeks to complete (weeks 6 and 7), B and C are shown complete at the end of week 5, F has two weeks to complete, and G has been removed (cancelled activity).

Figure 8-5 shows how you would show progress on an AON diagram and a re-analysis of the network to find the new duration of the project. With the status given at end of week 5, the project duration will be 17 weeks (against the original duration of 15 weeks).

Updating the Schedule

Why does the schedule need updating? Only in the rarest circumstances is the planned schedule followed precisely from the start of the project until its completion.

Effort is required during the project to check the actual progress against the planned schedule; sometimes the time and effort can be considerable. Marking progress on the schedule network and making sequencing adjustments to match the actual design activities, procurement activities and implementation activities are referred to as updating.

The various reasons that necessitate the updating of networks include:

- the inaccuracy of the initial project plan or schedule;

- the manner in which work is carried out in practice is often different to that originally envisaged;

- unforeseen problems that develop after project start, such as more knowledge required, change orders, adverse weather, etc.

Most of the stakeholders in a project need to understand how a project is progressing. Distribution of an updated schedule is a good way to keep the participants informed. The designer needs to be aware of the changes in priorities of design drawings and shop-drawings. The contracts administrator, or whoever is responsible for the purchasing and expediting of bought-in items, needs to be aware of the schedule changes. The supplier needs to know in order to take appropriate action to get the project back on schedule or to request appropriate time extensions. Trade contractors and sub-contractors of equipment and materials need to know how their work relates to the supplier and to the work and activities of other trade contractors, etc. The buyer needs to know if the project is behind schedule so that any changes that are necessary in plans related to the definition and execution of the project, or in the associated financing plans, can be taken. Priorities can be reviewed continuously and determined by studying the updated schedule's critical path or near-critical activities.

If a project's scheduled completion date is delayed, those involved in the project will want to know the cause. Those responsible for the delay may face significant financial penalty. The contractor may be responsible for liquidated or other delay damages to the owner if the contractor's actions have caused the delay. The owner may be responsible for the contractor's delay costs if the owner has caused the delay. The designer may be responsible for either the contractor's or the owner's delay costs if the designer caused the delay. All those potentially responsible for project activities need to know the cause of delay and be able to explain or defend the delay, and more importantly to investigate what needs to be done to bring the project back on schedule.

An updated schedule provides an important record of the project status at a specific time. A network regularly updated to show the effect of changes, errors or delays can be used to determine and allocate responsibility.

Frequency and Level of Detail of Updates

Updates may occur daily, weekly, bi-monthly, monthly, or less frequently, depending on the size, complexity and characteristics of the project. Monthly updates are the most common. The frequency of updates should be determined by the project team, in conjunction with the owner, and such updates should become part of the regulated project procedure.

The degree of detail in updating may include any, or all, of the following:

- identify actual start and finish dates for each activity;

- show the estimate of percentage completion for each activity;

- re-evaluate the remaining durations of activities;

- revise the logic to show the current plan for completion.

We are not going to deal with actions that a project team may take when presented with a project update. This Section is about the mechanism of updating and interpreting status using the various planning methods.

Bar Charts

To allow us to produce a bar chart from this project network we can work with only the earliest starts and earliest finishes. In other words, to turn networks into bar charts all that is needed is to carry out a forward pass; this is demonstrated with the logic diagram of Figure 8-3 (a) which is transposed into the bar chart (Figure 8-3 (c)). By examining the status of the project at the end of week 5, (see Figure 8-5), the information contained on the network can be transferred to the barchart in order to present the week 5 update. By using colour, shading or other suitable method, it is possible to show the updates for all weeks on one chart.

Line of Balance Charts

Updating LOB charts uses a similar method to that described for bar charts. The date of the update is marked with a vertical line. Progress can be marked on these charts in contrasting colours or shading which parallels the activities' performance line, or by symbols located on the line.

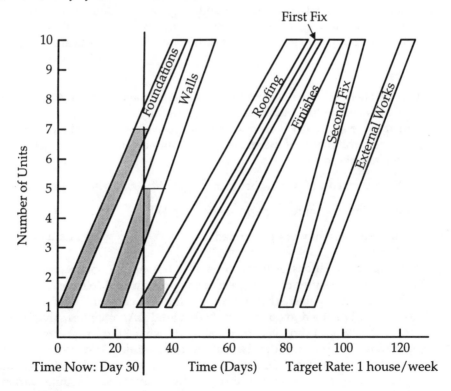

Figure 8-6: Update on Line of Balance Chart

Figure 8-6 represents a schedule for building 10 identical houses; reference should be made to Part 7, Section 2, which contains a description of this method of scheduling.

Network Diagrams

One advantage of network schedules is their ability to easily incorporate scheduling changes as the project progresses. Like updated bar charts, an updated network diagram is based on the initial network schedule or the latest update.

The first step in updating network diagrams is to mark project status on the logic diagram. This is shown in Figure 8-5. These are marked to show either no duration remaining for activities that have been completed or a revised duration for those activities which have not yet been completed. Actual dates for start or finish of activities should also be noted on the logic diagram.

Remaining durations can be determined in one of three ways:

- by subtracting the time actually expired on an activity from its scheduled duration;

- the remaining duration may be directly proportional to the scheduled duration;

- using percentage of work complete or actual rates of progress.

In addition to revising durations and start and finish dates, network diagrams should also show activity sequence updating. Once this information is at hand the project team can then reschedule by carrying out forward and backward passes and determining the revised project completion date and critical path(s).

Earned Value

It is often necessary to measure the actual performance of a project and compare it to what was scheduled at an earlier date, usually at project commencement. The earned value approach is used for this purpose. To measure the performance of a project, several pieces of information are required concerning the activities, or the project, and these are:

- the budget cost of work scheduled   (BCWS)   "what I plan to do"

- the budget cost of work performed   (BCWP)   "what I did"

- the actual cost of work performed   (ACWP)   "what I paid for"

By using combinations of these three, it is possible to obtain cost and schedule performance measures of the project at any point in time (Nicholas, 1990).

Performance against schedule is then simply a comparison of the singular actions "what I planned to do" against "what I did". Another term that is often used to describe "what I did" is earned value. If "what I did" is greater than "what I planned to do", it means that I am ahead of schedule. Conversely if "what I did" is less than "what I planned to do", then I am behind schedule. Schedule performance can be determined through two variables, schedule variance and schedule performance index. These variables can be explained symbolically as:

schedule variance $\qquad$ SV = BCWP – BCWS

schedule performance index $\qquad$ SPI = $\dfrac{\text{BCWP}}{\text{BCWS}}$

Both BCWS and BCWP can be measured in work hours or in monetary units. If measured in monetary units, SV requires conversion to time units for this variable to reflect schedule variance realistically.

To convert SV from monetary units to time units the assumption is that the earned value slope — the slope of the BCWP curve — for the more recent periods is constant. Although BCWP and BCWS are, as shown in Figure 8-7 by a and b respectively, the vertical difference in monetary units at any time in the project, this is converted graphically to time units. The schedule variance is given by the measurement between c and b.

Performance against budget is a comparison of the singular actions "what I did" against "what I paid for". If "what I did" is greater than "what I paid for", it means that I am under budget. Conversely if "what I did" is less than "what I paid for" then I am over budget. Budget performance can be determined through two variables — cost variance and cost performance index. These variables can be explained symbolically as:

cost variance $\qquad$ CV = BCWP – ACWP

cost performance index $\qquad$ CPI = $\dfrac{\text{BCWP}}{\text{ACWP}}$

Under favourable conditions of performance, both the cost and schedule performance indices should be greater than 1.0. If SV is negative, the project is behind schedule and if CV is negative the project is over budget. Assume that the following data refers to the example project examined earlier. We need now to find the project's performance at the end of week 5. To do this we are required to find:

a) the earned value

b) the percentage completion

c) the schedule variance and SPI

d) the cost variance and CPI.

Assume that it is the earliest starts and finishes to which the project performance must be related, and that the budget of each activity is evenly dispersed throughout each activity. The project is currently at the end of week 5 and the Table provides the associated information about the project at that time.

(1)	(2)	(3)	(4)	(5)	(6)	(7)
activity	original duration	original budget	expended cost	percent complete	earned value	notes
A	5	3,500	2,200	60	2,100	
B	4	4,000	4,600	100	4,000	
C	3	1,500	2,000	100	1,500	
D	3	6,000	-	-	-	
E	6	9,000	-	-	-	
F	4	6,000	4,200	50	3,000	
G	2	1,000	-	-	-	cancelled
H	3	900	-	-	-	
I	4	1,600	-	-	-	
earned value (BCWP)					10,600	
money spent (ACWP)			13,000			

Earned value compares the budgeted cost of work scheduled, BCWS, with the two other variables of interest, BCWP and ACWP. BCWS is the baseline cost of the project at any time during the duration of the project. The outcome is a "costs" curve — a BCWS curve. An example of this curve is shown in Figure 8-4; it is also known as an "S" curve.

By using the progress information from the Table above, of the physical work completed to date (say at the end of week 5), the budgeted cost of the work performed, BCWP, can be established. The BCWP takes the measurement of the work's physical progress achieved and evaluates the work at the budgeted costs. The difference between the BCWS and BCWP (the schedule variance) is calculated in monetary units. For the example shown the schedule variance is:

SV = 10,600 – 12,000 = –1,400

The BCWS of 12,000 is given from the Σ weekly total at the end of week 5, or it can be read from the BCWS curve (Figure 8-4). The SV of –1,400 mu can be converted graphically to related time using the diagram shown in Figure 8-6. The variance shows whether the project is ahead of or behind schedule. If the value is negative, the actual performance is behind what was planned; if positive, it is ahead of what was planned. In this case, the Figure shows that the project is about 5 days behind schedule out of a (5 x 7 day) 35 day period to the end of week 5.

The actual cost of work performed, ACWP, takes the measurement of the work's physical progress achieved and evaluates the work at actual cost (not budgeted cost). The difference between the ACWP and the BCWP (the cost variance) is calculated in monetary units. This variance shows the apparent budget overrun or underrun to date; it shows the difference between what the project was supposed to cost and what it has actually cost. If the value is negative, this represents an overspend; if the value is positive, this represents an underspend. For the example shown the cost variance is:

CV = 10,600 – 13,000 = –2,400

This is also shown on Figure 8-7. As can be discerned, the example project is both behind schedule and over budget at the end of week 5.

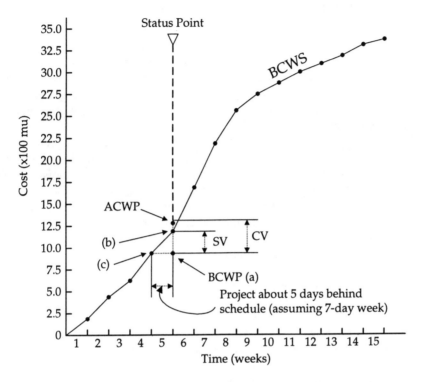

Figure 8-7: Graph showing Example Cost and Schedule Variances

Earned value is used to determine the progress on a project from the progress assessments of various activities. The earned value method can be used on projects where the budget changes and it will still provide meaningful information. With the earned value approach, a relationship exists between the current budget for an activity and the measurement of percentage complete.

Another way of calculating the performance of a project at any time is to use the concept of CPI and SPI. The three variables that are evaluated at the end of any period are used to determine both these indices. For the example project that is used in this sub-Section, these indices have the following values:

$$CPI = \frac{10,600}{13,000} = 0.815$$

$$SPI = \frac{10,600}{12,000} = 0.883$$

These values can then be plotted on a Quadplot IV chart similar to that shown in Figure 8-1 in Section 1. Point A in Figure 8-1 shows the above values of the example project. This type of chart shows immediately the status of the project. One other benefit of this form of analysis is the value of the variable CPI. This shows the benefit which is being obtained for every unit cost incurred up to that point in time. For instance, the example project shows that for every 1.0 mu spent on the project, only 0.815 mu is being earned.

Forecasting

Although BCWS and BCWP are usually measured in terms of money, they are really measurements of quantities of work expressed in terms of monetary units. Monetary units are the best all-encompassing way to measure, because other measures of achievement are expressed in a range of measurement units (Hamilton and Thomas, 1997).

New estimates derived from current information are the basis of trend analysis. Estimates tend to improve as actual progress is made. This is due to the completion of activities for which actual duration and cost become known, as well as improved information on workforce productivity and the availability and cost of resources. The indices for schedule and cost can be used to generate an estimate of the likely situation, in terms of time and cost, of the project at completion

EAC is the estimated cost at completion and is based on the current trend of SPI and CPI continuing to completion, and is given by:

$$EAC = ACWP + \frac{BAC - BCWP}{CPI}$$

where   EAC = the cost at completion
        BAC = the basic or budgeted cost at completion

ETC, the estimated time to completion, is given by:

$$ETC = ATE + \frac{OD - (ATE \times SPI)}{SPI}$$

where   ETC = estimated time to completion
        ATE = actual time expended
        OD = original duration

By the use of these two formulae, the time and cost to completion can be estimated at any status point or update point in a project.

SECTION 3: PROGRESS PAYMENTS, TRENDS, AND CLAIMS

Contents

- Aims and Objectives

- Progress Payments

- Trend Analysis

- Sensitivity Analysis

- Contractual Claims

Aims and Objectives

The aims and objectives of Section 3 are to:

- Demonstrate a method for determining progress payments cashflow;

- Show ways of determining trends from actual durations and hence forecast new durations for any project participant;

- Answer the "what if" in trends to forecast final out-turn;

- Show how network analysis can be used as a reactive tool to support or defend past delays.

Progress Payments

Progress payments, which are paid periodically to the contractor during the implementation of a project, are based on the amount of work accomplished to date.

If we assume that the information provided in Figure 8-3 is the direct cost assessment by the contractor for undertaking the implementation of some project, let's also assume the contractor's indirect costs are 200 mu/week and the contractor is working on a 3 per cent profit margin on both direct and indirect costs. Based on these assumptions, the cash-flow profile of the contractor's anticipated earnings can be calculated.

This information is also of importance to owners and other stakeholders. From the contractor's network schedule, the contractor's anticipated cash-flow of income can be generated. This information can be used as the basis for the owner when planning the project finances and the weekly/monthly outgoings; the implementation cost is one of those outgoings (Hamilton and Thomas, 1997).

The total predicted earnings or expenditure, which we will call "e", in one week is derived from:

total "e" = direct "e" + indirect "e" + profit

The values of total earnings or expenditure are presented in the following Table — column 5 for the earliest start option and column 9 for the latest start option.

For the owner to ensure that at any week's end there are sufficient funds to cover the contractor's earnings, it is necessary that the upper limit of the contractor's earnings is covered. This means that the earliest start earnings will need to be provided for.

Column 10 is the likely maximum contractor cumulative earning requirements, providing that the original activity's logic and duration schedule is adhered to. For instance, if you look at week 6, the anticipated cumulative progress payment to the end of week 6 is 18,800 mu; this amount will cover both the earliest start and the latest start options.

Tabulating the input data in columns 1 to 4 and 6 to 8 inclusive:

(1) time period	(2) early start direct Σ	(3) early start indirect Σ	(4) profit 3% of 2 + 3	(5) total "e"	(6) late start direct Σ	(7) late start indirect Σ	(8) profit 3% of 6 + 7	(9) total "e"	(10) progress payment Σ	(11) progress payment (monthly)
1	2200	200	72	2472	700	200	27	927	2500	2500
2	4400	400	144	4944	2400	400	84	2884	5000	2500
3	6600	600	216	7416	4600	600	156	5356	7500	2500
4	9800	800	318	10918	6800	800	228	7828	11000	3500
5	12000	1000	390	13390	9000	1000	300	10300	13400	2400
6	17000	1200	546	18746	10500	1200	351	12051	18800	5400
7	22000	1400	702	24102	12000	1400	402	13802	24200	5400
8	25500	1600	813	27913	15000	1600	498	17098	28000	3800
9	27000	1800	864	29664	20000	1800	654	22454	29700	1700
10	28500	2000	915	31415	25000	2000	810	27810	31500	1800
11	30000	2200	966	33166	30000	2200	966	33166	33200	1700
12	31200	2400	1008	34608	30400	2400	984	33784	34700	1500
13	32400	2600	1050	36050	31100	2600	1011	34711	36100	1400
14	33100	2800	1077	36977	32300	2800	1053	36153	37000	900
15	33500	3000	1095	37595	33500	3000	1095	37595	37600	600

Column 11 is derived by subtracting the current period's cumulative total from the subsequent period's total in order to find the current period contractor's anticipated earnings or the owner's anticipated expenditure. For instance, to find week 6 anticipated earnings or expenditure the following is used:

$$\text{period}_n \text{ "e"} = \text{cumulative}_{n+1} \text{ "e"} - \text{cumulative}_n \text{ "e"}$$

where n is the current period; therefore

"e" in week 6 = cumulative "e" in week 7 – cumulative "e" in week 6

$$= 24,200 - 18,800 = 5,400 \text{ mu}$$

Figure 8-10 shows the profile of anticipated potential earnings that the contractor would expect as financial inflow to his company; it is also the anticipated progress payment that the buyer would expect to make provision for as the anticipated outflow from the buyer's organisation. This is shown as a solid stepped line. The earliest start and latest start cash-flows have also been added as dashed lines to compare them with the anticipated progress payments.

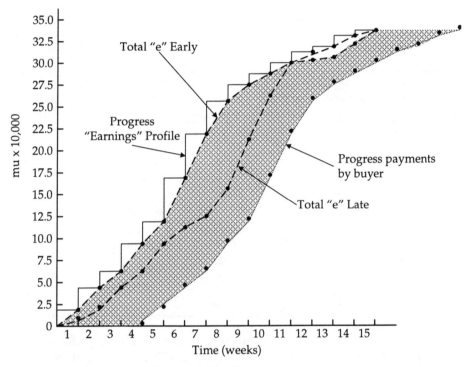

Figure 8-8: Progress Earnings/Payments Profile

As buyers are traditionally given 30 days, otherwise known as the credit period, to provide monthly payment to the contractor for work completed, it is more likely that the progress payments profile will be shifted to the right by one month as shown by the chain-dotted line. The shaded area between the cash-flow line and this actual payment line is therefore a potential overdraft situation that the contractor must allow for elsewhere or have the bank charges built-in to his indirect costs for this project.

Trend Analysis

In order to identify trends in activities we have to introduce a new input field which is called category (Hamilton and Thomas, 1997). Several categories can be added, but within this sub-Section we will deal with one only. Category is based on the attributes of the activity and identifies those activities that possess common features, such as:

- which stakeholder is responsible for the activity? — *responsibility components;*

- is the activity one of many within a regional or project area? — *major components;*

- is the activity one of many requiring the same disciplines? — *functional components;*

- is the activity one of many carried out by a project stakeholder? — *element components.*

The "responsibility component" concept will be used to show what is meant by trend analysis. Let's look at an example of trend analysis. The activity durations are given in days.

(1)	(2)	(3)	(4)	(5)	(6)	(7)	(8)	(9)
		preceded	original	remaining	comments	days		APF
activity	category	by	duration	duration		used	remaining	
A	PC	-	9	-	(complete)	10	-	1.11
B	SA	-	13	-	(complete)	12	-	0.92
C	PC	A	12	4	inprogress	9	4	1.08
D	SA	A	8	3	inprogress	10	3	1.63
E	SB	B,F	11	8	inprogress	9	8	1.55
F	SB	-	8	-	(complete)	6	-	0.75
G	PC	B	5	2	inprogress	4	2	1.20
H	PC	D	7	7	not started			
I	PC	E,G	17	15	"			
J	SA	I	4	4	"			
K	PC	H,L	10	10	"			
L	PC	C,D,E	13	12	"			

The project, it has been assumed, is to be executed by a prime contractor (PC), subcontractor A (SA) and subcontractor B (SB). Each one of these responsible parties has been assigned project activities that they must execute. The input data on category is given in column 2. The data provided is assumed to be the situation on an update, which is day 15 of the project. The status of each activity on that day is measured and noted (column 6). The number of days used is also noted (column 7) and an estimate made of the remaining duration for each activity (column 5).

The initial network schedule which meets the contractual time requirement is called the contract schedule. This contract schedule is used when updating by incorporating the actual performance to date. The difference between the planned durations and the actual durations for completed activities and in-progress activities is calculated and an activity performance factor (APF) is generated. The APF is the ratio of planned to actual performance and is calculated as follows:

APF =   actual duration
              planned duration

Within the Table, in column 9, the values for each activity are therefore calculated by adding the values in columns 7 and 8 together and dividing by the value in column 4. The addition of the values in columns 7 and 8 give the "actual" duration and column 4 gives the "planned" duration.

At this point, an analysis can be carried out on the completed and in-progress activities to determine an overall performance factor for the category. The category performance factor is calculated as follows:

$$CPF = \frac{\Sigma \text{ APF for the category}}{\text{number of activities for the category}}$$

A check can also be made on the variance of the APFs within the categories to determine which ones are consistent and which ones are random. Those categories whose APFs are fairly consistent may represent a trend. Using the updated data, the CPFs, the number of activities involved, the number of activities over or under the estimated time, and the high and low APFs are derived as shown in the following tabulation:

(1) Category	(2) CPF	(3) # activities	(4) # over	(5) # under	(6) high APF	(7) low APF
PC	1.13	3	1	2	1.20	1.08
SA	1.28	2	1	1	1.63	0.92
SB	1.15	2	1	1	1.55	0.75

The CPF factor in column 2 is calculated using the formula quoted earlier for CPF. For example, if we look at the category PC we see that there are three APF values at this update. Therefore the figure 3 is the denominator in this formula. The APF values are: 1.11, 1.08 and 1.20. Putting these values into the CPF formula presents the following:

$$CPF = \frac{1.11 + 1.08 + 1.20}{3} = 1.13$$

The figures in column 3 are simply a total of the number of activities in that category, either complete or in-progress. The figures in column 4 and 5 are a total of the number of activities within a category that have a value greater than column 4 or less than column 5, the CPF value. For instance, for the PC category, there is one value, 1.20, that is greater than the CPF (1.13) and two values, 1.11 and 1.08 that are less than the CPF value. Column 6 and 7 highlight the upper and lower APF values within the category range. When compared with the CPF value, this is useful in giving a first impression of the skewness or distribution of the values within a range.

At this stage it can be decided which of the activities appear to indicate a trend that can be taken into account for the remainder of the schedule. The information available at this stage should also help in indicating where there may have been poor estimating by one or more of the responsible parties. It should also show those categories that have the expected normal variation in performance.

For those categories that seem to indicate a trend, it is now possible to simulate the remaining schedule to observe what would happen if the apparent trend were to continue. This is accomplished by applying the CPFs to the remaining activities to get new durations and then recalculating the network schedule.

New durations are calculated as follows:

new duration = old duration x CPF

For example, in the exercise above, the durations of the remaining PC activities are multiplied by 1.13 to obtain a set of new durations. Undertaking this simulation is called a "what if". In other words the project team, or the scheduler, looks at "what happens to the project if . . .".

While this exposition only addresses one category, i.e. responsibility, the logic can be applied to a multi-category situation. For instance, activity A may have categories that represent disciplines, use of equipment, and so on, in addition to the responsibility category.

New durations are therefore calculated as follows:

new duration = old duration x CPF_a x CPF_b x CPF_c x ..... x CPF_n

where the subscripts a, b, c etc. are the different categories.

Sensitivity Analysis

In the previous sub-Section, the undertaking of simulations — performing "what ifs" by varying something — we saw what the effect on the project would be. Another term that is normally used to describe such a procedure is called sensitivity analysis. This type of analysis can be explained by example. Taking the same example as in the previous sub-Section, but this time taking account of the planned network for the project, the network is as shown in Figure 8-9.

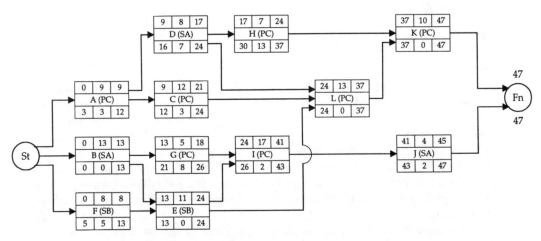

Figure 8-9: Example Network Showing Category "Responsibility"

The responsible entity for each activity is shown in brackets within the description box at each node. The durations are given in days. The original total project duration is 47 days. It may be of interest to do a sensitivity test on SA (subcontractor A) while assuming that PC and SB are held constant. Such an analysis will allow us to determine how crucial the performance of category SA will be on the completion of the project.

We can see from the previous Table that the CPF value for SA is within the range 0.9 to 1.7 (figures rounded off upwards and downwards respectively) and is probably around 1.28. To carry out a sensitivity analysis on SA we should take a CPF range between, say, 0.8 and 1.8. Taking CPF values of 0.8, 1.0, 1.2, 1.4, 1.6 and 1.8 for sensitivity analysis should be sufficient to give an indication of trends. The first step in the analysis is to prepare a Table of results for CPF = 0.8. The results are as shown in the following Table:

activity	original duration	CPF	new duration	ES	EF
A	9		9	0	9
B	13	0.8	10.4	0	10.4
C	12		12	9	21
D	8	0.8	6.4	9	15.4
E	11		11	10.4	21.4
F	8		8	0	8
G	5		5	10.4	15.4
H	7		7	15.4	22.4
I	17		17	21.4	38.4
J	4	0.8	3.2	38.4	41.6
K	10		10	34.4	44.4
L	13		13	21.4	34.4

With a CPF of 0.8 for SA the project duration is given by the earliest finish of the final activity, activity K ; the duration is 44.4 days. Let's just accept the fraction of a day for the present. If the same calculation is carried out for the range of CPFs decided upon the results are as follows:

CPF for SA	0.8	1.0	1.2	1.4	1.6	1.8
Project duration (days)	44.4	47	49.6	52.2	55.2	57.4

or rounding off the parts of a day upwards to the next full day:

45   47   50   53   56   58

So this type of sensitivity analysis tells us that SA's performance, which is indicating a CPF of 1.28, could mean an increase of about 5 days, i.e. somewhere between 50 and 53 days total duration, to the project's completion, unless some action is taken that will change this trend. Although the demonstration of sensitivity analysis is carried out on one category, the same exercise can be carried out for all categories that are involved in a phase of a project or the totality of a project.

Contractual Claims

In implementation claims, a delay is the time during which some part of the implementation work has been extended or not performed due to an unanticipated circumstance. Delays may be caused by any of the stakeholders.

Many things can cause delays. The following are just a few of the causes:

- late provision of project information;

- changes in owner's requirements or design requirements;

- project-site ground conditions;

- inclement weather;

- unavailability or lateness in provision of labour, equipment or materials.

Network schedules can play an important part in implementation-delay claims (Hamilton and Thomas, 1997). Delays can be identified, defined, and explained by schedules. By re-calculating (or re-running through a computer) the schedule with the delays, the effect of the delays on the project completion date can be shown and the effect of future delays can be previewed.

Types of Delays

Implementation delays fall into two major categories: excusable and nonexcusable (or inexcusable). Excusable delays are ones that can be justified. Nonexcusable delays are those delays that cannot be excused and therefore are not justifiable. Examples of each of these types depend upon which one of the stakeholders is being considered. Let's assume that we look at delays from the standpoint of the contractor because it is, after all, mainly from contractors that contractual claims emanate. Examples of each type are as follows:

excusable	*nonexcusable*
owner initiated changes	failure to perform work
unanticipated weather	unavailability of labour, etc.
labour disputes	subcontractor failures
acts of God	defective work that has to redone

Generally, whether a delay is excusable or nonexcusable is a matter of contract. Most contracts specify the types of delay that will entitle a contractor to some form of compensation. Compensation is normally in the form of:

- an extension of time to the original project duration;

and/or

- expense based on the cost of delaying the contractor.

Compensable and Noncompensable Delays

Excusable delays can be further classified as compensable and noncompensable delays.

If the delay is deemed compensable, the party will be entitled to additional compensation for the costs of the delay. A compensable delay does not always mean that an extension of time is also due. Generally speaking, a delay that could have been avoided by due care of one party is compensable to the other, innocent, party who has suffered because of the delay. An example of this is an owner who has taken too long to secure a permit. The contract completion date may not have been extended (the contractor finished on time) but the delay in furnishing the permit may have caused the contractor's costs to increase. In other words, if the delay in issuing the permit had taken place at the start of the project, hence delaying the start, the contractor would then have been engaged in accelerating the works in order to complete the same amount of work within a shorter project duration.

A noncompensable delay is what it implies: it is a delay for which there would be no compensation paid to the party that has been affected by the delay.

Critical and Noncritical Delays

Not all delays result in delay to the overall project completion. Delays that result in extended project completion are known as "critical delays". Delays that do not extend the project completion date are called noncritical delays. It is generally found that a contractor is not entitled to a time extension for an excusable delay unless the delay extends the overall project completion.

Analysis of Concurrent Delays

The term "concurrent delays" is used to describe two or more activity delays that occur at the same time, any of which, had it occurred alone, would have affected the completion date of the project. Concurrent delays can be classified to include the following combinations:

- excusable delay and non-excusable delay;

- excusable delay and compensable delay;

- excusable delay, non-excusable delay and compensable delay;

- non-excusable delay and compensable delay.

As an example of a concurrent delay, suppose the owner failed to supply certain materials on time and at the same time the workers who would have installed the materials were on strike. This is a concurrent delay of the compensable type (owners delay in supplying materials) and excusable type (workers on strike). The legality of concurrent delays can be regarded as follows:

concurrent delay	remedy
any delay concurrent with excusable	time extension
compensable with non-excusable	time extension or apportionment

In the case of concurrent excusable and compensable delays, the constructor should be entitled to a time extension but not to damages. The constructor does not get entitlement for both. When excusable and non-excusable delays are concurrent, the constructor should be entitled to an extension of time. Thus, for concurrent delays with an excusable delay, the available remedy will most probably be a time extension.

For concurrent delays in which the owner and the constructor are both responsible for delays in completing the work, there are two possible routes. In the first route liquidated damages are not allowed and each party suffers its own losses; a time extension is allowed to the constructor. In the second route, apportionment of liquidated damages is carried out. To undertake apportionment, it is imperative that the project records are used to establish some genuine formula for assigning culpability.

Before analysing construction delays it is necessary to make available the following three major scheduling documents:

- as-planned schedules;

- as-built schedules;

- adjusted schedules.

As-planned Schedule

The as-planned schedule illustrates the initial work plan to achieve the scope of work conforming to the contract requirements. It serves as a criterion for measuring actual fulfilment of the work.

As-built Schedule

The as-built schedule reflects the actual succession of the activities that happened during execution of the project. It is established from careful inspection of project reports and documents.

Adjusted Schedule

The adjusted schedule serves to quantify and identify the impact of schedule variances on the project. It is useful in determining the effects of different types of delays on the project completion date.

SECTION 4: QUALITY AND ITS DOCUMENTATION

Contents

- Aims and Objectives
- Basic Concepts
- Basic Elements of Quality
- Historical Relevance
- Economics of Quality
- Organisation for QA
- Some of the Tools of Quality

Aims and Objectives

The aims and objectives of Section 4 are to:

- Explain the basic concepts of quality and its management;
- Introduce some of the more important gurus of quality;
- Provide an explanation of the relationship between quality and value;
- Describe briefly the cost of (non)conformance;
- Provide an insight into some of the tools used for quality improvement.

Basic Concepts

The target of any project is to meet time, cost, and quality objectives. Quality objectives are met if the project delivers products conforming to established requirements. To do this requires development of a quality management plan (Project Management Institute, 1996). This plan is composed of the requirements themselves, the plan for communicating these requirements to those responsible for compliance, any training required to ensure that workers have the capability to meet these requirements, and techniques for measuring compliance.

Quality is defined as "the totality of characteristics of an entity that bear on its ability to satisfy stated or implied need" (Project Management Institute, 1996). A critical aspect of quality management in the project context is the necessity to turn implied needs into stated needs through project scope management.

Quality criteria affect all phases of a project. The key aspects of quality can be related to planning, assurance, and control.

Quality Planning

This term describes procedures used to ensure that the engineering and design for the various implementation elements are undertaken in accordance with mandatory criteria that have been set by the regulatory agencies. These procedures and the associated standards are revised frequently, and it is important that all those associated with the engineering of projects use up-to-date applicable standards.

Quality Assurance

Quality assurance is not a particularly well-defined term. In general, it is considered to be a broad, all-encompassing term for the application of standards and procedures to ensure that a product or a facility meets or exceeds the required performance criteria. Quality assurance also usually includes the documentation that is needed to verify that all steps in the procedures have been dealt with satisfactorily.

Quality assurance transcends both quality engineering and quality control. In other words, it includes both the design of "something" that has an end use and the development of procedures which will ensure that the "something" attains its designed quality.

Quality Control

This process includes:

- setting specific standards for the implementation works through the instructions emanating from the definition phase (drawings, specifications, etc.);

- measuring the differences, or what is referred to as the variances, between what the standards require and what is actually being provided;

- taking whatever action is necessary to correct or minimise adverse variances;

- continually planning for improvement in both the standards themselves and in the process which is trying to conform with the standards.

So you can see that quality control is all about setting standards and making sure that the physical work conforms to those standards.

Basic Elements of Quality

Now let's look at the basic elements of quality (Hamilton, 1997).

Quality Characteristics

Quality characteristics include such factors as shape, physical dimensions, strength, temperature, colour, etc. Quality characteristics are one or more properties that define the nature of a product for quality-control purposes.

Let's look at an example of this: let us consider the material concrete. The quality characteristics that specify and control concrete quality include compressive strength after a fixed curing time, the amount of slump of freshly mixed concrete, the size of aggregate, the ratio of water to cement, surface finish and, sometimes, colour.

Quality of Design

No human undertaking produces absolutely perfect results. In recognition of this fact, designers often specify not only the desired quality characteristics; but they also define the tolerances or acceptable range of variations from the standard.

For example, let's look again at the material concrete. By setting a concrete compressive strength of 200 kg/cm^2 and stating that no more than 20 per cent of the compressive-strength test cubes can fall below this value is a recognition of the statistical nature of work processes.

In design, if the standards are raised such that there are higher standards and tighter tolerances, then design costs are raised. Of course, if the standards are too low and the resulting quality introduces what is called rework then the costs of this type of quality are also high. In other words if the standards are too low or too high, the cost of design is also high. This phenomena is shown in Figure 8-10.

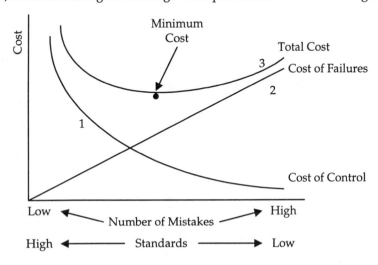

Figure 8-10: Cost of Quality

Curve 1 shows the trend if the standards are high in order to maintain a low level of mistakes (or defects). Curve 2 shows the situation when the standards are low and the cost increases with the number of mistakes. By adding curve 1 and curve 2 together, as shown in the Figure, curve 3 is obtained; this curve is referred to as the total cost. The lowest point on curve 3 is referred to as the minimum cost point. This point may, or may not, be the appropriate point to select as the starting point to design the "something" that is required.

It is highly likely that the more appropriate design standards will require a lowering of the number of mistakes and hence the true design cost will be somewhere to the left of the minimum point. In other words, you can see that the cost of achieving a lowering of mistakes increases the costs. Design standards must therefore be set to provide what is appropriate to satisfy the intended function.

Quality of Conformance

Once the quality of design has been specified, the quality of conformance is defined as the degree to which the physical work produced conforms to this standard. In the example, 3 concrete cubes per 100 that have strengths below 200 kg/cm^2 gives a much higher quality of conformance than 10 per 100.

As with quality of design, there is a close correlation between standards for conformance and the cost of achieving those standards. There are trade-offs to be considered between costs of the work methods and quality control procedures and the cost of mistakes.

The Quality System

The relationship between the elements that have been described so far is shown in Figure 8-11.

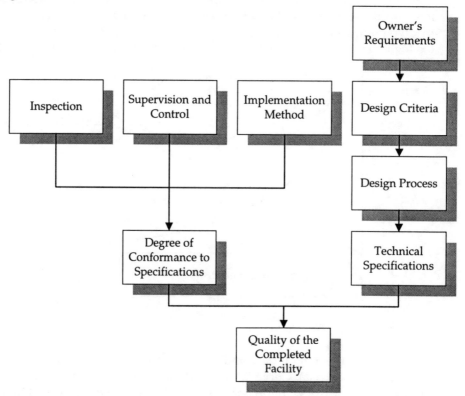

Figure 8-11: The Elements of Quality

The process starts with the owner's requirements. From these requirements, the design criteria are established and from these criteria the engineering and design processes can be planned and operated. Out of the process the technical specifications will be produced; it is these specifications that set the quality of design.

The quality of conformance is influenced by:

- the implementation methods;

- supervision and management controls;

- the inspection and quality control procedures.

Quality of design and conformance together determine the quality of the completed facility. It is worth knowing that, during implementation, very often the problem area within the quality system is inspection. Factors such as poor statistical analysis, miscalibration or inaccurate tools/equipment used for quality control are the reasons for poor inspection and inadequate quality.

Historical Relevance

The field of quality management has been strongly influenced by such people as Deming, Juran, Crosby, Feigenbaum, Ishikawa, Garvin, Shingo, and Taguchi.

Dr. W Edwards Deming originally concentrated on statistical process control (SPC) and later in his working life he was associated with quality management theories. Deming was always of the view that management must have an appreciation of statistical variation, because chance will account for a certain degree of natural variation. He was of the view that without management action or support, significant improvement seldom can be made. Deming's rule of thumb was that perhaps 80 per cent of improvement requires management effort, while only 20 per cent is actionable solely by front-line personnel.

Deming produced a 14-point plan which is seen now as a complete philosophy of management, not just quality management (Gitlow et al., 1987). In addition to the 14-point plan, he was also an advocate, if not the originator, of PDCA (plan, do, check, act), which is now a universal improvement methodology. The idea of PDCA is to improve constantly and to reduce the difference in the (project) requirements and the performance of the (projects) process.

Dr. Joseph Juran (Juran, 1979) emphasises the need for on-going quality improvement. He maintains that this is achieved only through "project-by-project" improvement — in other words, by a succession of small improvement projects carried out throughout an organisation. Project-by-project improvement is perhaps similar to the Deming PDCA cycle, and leads straight into the quality trilogy. The quality trilogy comprises quality planning, quality control, and quality improvement. These actions are seen as parallel to the financial processes of budgeting, cost control, and cost reduction.

He was also responsible for the introduction and use of Pareto analysis (see Part 6, Section 3) for the universal solving of problems. He used the principle within the quality process to identify the "vital few" as opposed to the "trivial many" or the "useful many". This refers to the fact that there will always be a relatively few processes or people or defects or problems that somehow take up most of the time or effort or cost.

Phil Crosby, like Deming, also produced a 14-step plan for quality improvement, but he is perhaps best known for the "four absolutes". These are:

- the definition of quality is conformance to requirements;

- the system of quality is prevention;

- the performance standard is zero defect;

- the measurement of quality is the price of non-conformance.

Crosby (1989) is of the view that once the *requirements are specified*, then quality is judged solely on the criteria of whether or not they are met; aesthetics and feelings don't play a part. It is the duty of management to specify the requirements. The concept of SPC deals with understanding the process, looking at what's wrong, and taking *preventive actions*. ZD, or *zero defects*, has to be the aim; nothing less than perfect quality is needed. Crosby classifies costs into the price of conformance and the price of *non-conformance*, and uses such information as a prime motivator for management.

Armand Feigenbaum (1991), an American engineer, was the originator of the concept of total quality. He recognised that quality begins and ends with the buyer, and in between, many people and functions must play a role; in fact everyone has a role and the responsibility must be shared.

Feigenbaum is also known for his concept of the "hidden plant". He was of the view that in every factory (organisation) a certain proportion of capacity is wasted through not getting it right first time. He quoted a figure of up to 40 per cent of the capacity of the plant being wasted. Even today, some investigative managers are witness to the accuracy of this figure.

Kaoru Ishikawa (1985), a leading contributor from Japan, was the inventor of quality circles; groups of personnel dealing with quality issues as an extension of their job. This was closely aligned to his approach, which maintained that management must conduct it all with a "belief in humanity". He believed that circle activities must be part of a wider total quality effort. Managers must understand both total quality and the functioning of circles before circle activities begin. Those supervisors in whose area circles are in operation require special training. Members of a circle must be volunteers. Circle members must be trained in appropriate tools, but must also learn to appreciate the wider aspects of quality throughout the organisation. Effective evaluation of circle efforts must be made.

David Garvin, a professor at Harvard Business School, has made his contribution to the concept of quality as a strategy and to the understanding of just what is meant by quality.

Shigeo Shingo is associated with the concept of just-in-time, but he will probably be best known for "*pokayoke*". *Pokayoke* is about adding devices to machines and processes in order that defects are simply not produced.

Genichi Taguchi is best known for his work during the 1980s regarding quality through design. His principal contribution was to add to our understanding of what product specification really means for quality and how such specifications can be translated into cost-effective production.

Economics of Quality

One of the outcomes, if quality procedures are not established and followed, is that mistakes will be made. It is very expensive to correct mistakes once implementation has begun. For instance, a simple mistake on an engineering drawing, such as a bolt-hole in a large girder, which is to link up with a similar hole in an adjacent girder so that they can be bolted together 40 metres above the ground, being placed in the wrong position, is an example of an expensive mistake.

You can imagine the loss of time and money, and the frustration of the people involved when the erector, lying out on the end of this girder with a large bolt in one hand and a much larger spanner in the other, finds that the girders cannot be bolted together! Down he has to come, down the girders have to come, the lifting cranes and operators have to be stood down, the riggers have to be stood down, the design team has to be called, drawings and specifications have to be studied, a discussion has to take place, a decision has to be made to either drill insitu, if that would be permissible, or return the girders to the fabricating shop. Then the whole process that has already been gone through before has to take place again. What a waste!

Design

There is a relationship between value and quality. The process of achieving value in projects was covered in Part 6, Section 3. In its simplest form, the relationship between value and quality is shown in Figure 8-12.

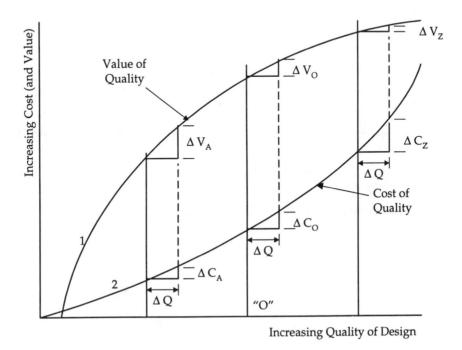

Figure 8-12: Quality and Value Relationship

In Figure 8-12, the horizontal axis relates to the quality of design, which would be determined by the quality characteristics for the item or the element being evaluated. The vertical axis shows the cost (and the value) of the item or element being evaluated. What the Figure shows is that curve 1 is the value of quality and curve 2 is the cost of quality. The "value" curve is concave downwards and the "cost" curve is concave upwards. They are both positive curves — in other words, they increase from bottom left to top right; when the quality of design increases, both the cost of quality and the value of quality increase.

Furthermore, the Figure tells us that, for an incremental increase in the quality of design, ΔQ, the incremental cost of quality can be greater than the incremental increase in the value of quality. In other words, if you look at scenario A you will see that the increase in cost ΔC_A is less than the increase in value ΔV_A. If you now look at scenario Z you will see that the increase in cost ΔC_Z is greater than the increase in value ΔV_Z for a similar incremental increase in the quality of design as A. Somewhere between A and Z, the incremental cost of quality and the incremental value of quality of an incremental increase in quality of design is the same; that is, ΔV_O is equal to ΔC_O. This is shown by line "O" and it is referred to as the optimum level of "quality of design". In summary:

- below the optimum level of design quality, each mu spent on quality will provide more than an mu worth of value;

- above the optimum level of design quality each mu spent on quality will provide less than an mu worth of value.

The concept is fairly simple to understand, but remember that there are other parameters, such as the number of units to be produced, that can affect the final selection of the quality of design.

Conformance

To control quality costs money. There are two elements to the cost of quality control:

- the cost of skilled labour, equipment, material, methods and supervision to produce quality output;

- the costs of monitoring and verifying the quality of output and of correcting or replacing defective work.

These elements are shown graphically in Figure 8-13.

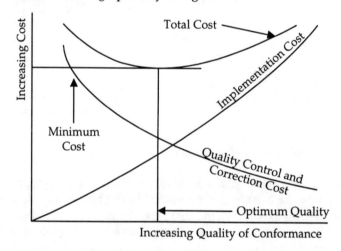

Figure 8-13: Quality of Conformance

The information shown in Figure 8-13 is also provided in Figure 8-10, which shows the relationship between the cost of mistakes and the cost of reducing the number of mistakes. To optimise conformance costs for a given quality of design, we have to minimise the sum of the direct implementation costs and the quality control costs. This summation is shown by the upper curve in Figure 8-13.

Organisation for QA

The Principal Parties

Quality is viewed differently by the different parties involved in a project. What do the owner, the designer, the contractor and the regulating agency each want? The following helps to understand the differences in their objectives:

- owners want to maximise the quality characteristics associated with the intended function of a project;

- designers want a level of quality that will assure satisfactory performance of the facility without undue cost overruns;

- contractors will be interested in satisfying the specifications at minimum direct cost;

- regulatory agencies will set quality standards for characteristics that may not be directly related to the primary function of the project and without any concern for the cost effect.

One of the most important tasks of the project manager is to set quality standards that will satisfy the regulatory agencies and provide an economical quality–cost performance in keeping with the owner's objectives.

Typical Organisations

Within certain industries, it is normal to find quality assurance separated from the production activities. Sometimes the quality assurance is carried out by a separate organisation; this is especially true for conformance-oriented quality control activities.

In traditional, competitively bid public works and private works contracts, the quality control is the primary responsibility of the resident engineer or, if the project is small, the clerk of works. Requirements for project cost and time control, as well as the quality of the project, are the major responsibilities of the contractor.

In other types of contract, such as design-and-build, the quality assurance is likely to be carried out by the design-build contractor, but organisationally separate from them. The idea of such a system is to create an independent, objective group that is free to apply controls without interference or censure from the operating organisation.

In management-type contracts, the management contractor, the implementation manager or the project manager provides effective third party quality of design and inspection services that assure the control quality of conformance. Experience has shown that this provides a high level of effectiveness not found in most alternative forms of contract.

Tasks, Responsibilities and Procedures

The methods used in planning the project tasks, which have already been examined, are equally applicable to planning quality assurance. It is therefore no surprise that for quality assurance planning the WBS, OBS and RAM are all needed to develop properly a plan: what needs to be done, who is going to do it and who else will check, inspect, approve, etc.

Some of the Tools of Quality

There are many tools (Bicheno, 1994) that can be used in the search for quality improvement. Whether the project is providing goods or a service, the project team member will find them equally valid.

Flow charts and process charts are used during the quality planning process. Process charts list every step in the manufacture of a product or the delivery of a service. Special symbols are used to indicate such things as:

◯   "operation"

▢   "inspection"

⇨   "move"

𝖣   "delay"

▽   "storage"

The chart documents the process completely and helps to identify wasteful actions. It is recommended that the process chart should be drawn using the standard symbols. Should time be a critical aspect of the process being charted, then a time scale can be added. Figure 8-14 shows a typical process chart.

In the service sector, process charts can be made more effective by dividing the chart into two halves, with one half showing the actions that are entirely internal and the other half showing the actions where there is a direct interaction with external entities. So, for example, the process chart of an aircraft being made ready for take-off can be shown in a left-side chart, the booking-in of passengers can be shown on the right-side chart. The two halves together would show the complete sequence of events covering "the pre take-off process".

A flow chart is similar to a process chart and is often used when decisions are involved. Flow charts have their own set of symbols; see Part 6, in particular, Figure 6-2, for an example of a flow chart.

Whether using a process chart or a flow chart, these charts are best assembled using a team approach, preferably with the primary stakeholders or core project team members. These charts are a first step in systematically documenting the nature of quality problems and defects.

Once the process charts have been used to list and classify problems, Pareto analysis, as described in Section 2 of Part 6, can then be applied to help recognise the small number of problem types that account for a large percentage of the total number of problems that occur. It is often found that this equates to "80/20" — that is, 80 per cent of all problems are due to 20 per cent of all the types of problem that occur (typically the range can be roughly between 90/10 and 70/30). It makes good sense, as Juran states, to tackle the most pressing problems first — the vital few. Once the Pareto analysis has helped to identify the most serious problems, the responsible team can begin to explore the possible causes and their solutions.

Details of	☑ Old ☐ New Method	Chart Symbol	Distance in feet	Time in mins.	Notes
Invoice received, date stamped					By mail clerk
To mail clerk			20		
On first payable clerk's desk				1/2	
Purchase order attached					
To cost accountant			25		
On cost accountant's desk				1/2	
Coded to appropriate job					
To first payable clerk's desk			25		
On first payable clerk's desk				1/2	
Copies made					
Original to project manager			110		
On project manager's desk				3	
Examined & approved by project manager					
To second payable clerk's desk			90		
On payable clerk's desk				1/2	
Vendor number & due date added; extensions checked					
Data keyed to magnetic tape					
INVOICE PAID					
To file clerk's desk			30		
On file clerk's desk				2	
Invoice filed					

Figure 8-14: Process Chart
Source: Dilworth (1992)

The cause and effect diagram, otherwise known as the Ishikawa or fishbone diagram, is then used to brainstorm possible contributing causes of a particular problem or defect (effect). This type of diagram is described in Part 1, Section 1 (see Figure 1-3). The most pressing "effect" demonstrated by the Pareto diagram becomes the spine of the "fishbone" and the causes are constructed on the diagram, arranged in a hierarchy, by one person reflecting the ideas of the contributing team.

The histogram has much in common with the Pareto diagram. The histogram is used to show graphically the relative number of causes (events) as bars measured against frequency. A typical histogram and its connection with Pareto's analysis is illustrated in Figure 6-12, in Part 6, Section 3. The decreasing frequency histogram is therefore a tool that can help in identifying causes that require further investigation. Having identified the most significant causes, the next step is to find out how these causes can be eliminated.

Run diagrams and correlation diagrams are used to explore relationships between events and time and between problems and causes. Run diagrams are simply graphs that show the trends plotted against time. Typical types of run diagram are shown in Figure 8-15. Figure (a) shows defects plotted against time — in this diagram, higher defect rates are shown to occur between noon and midnight. In Figure (b), dimensional variation in units or batches can be plotted at the time they are measured — the diagram shows that there tends to be greater variation in "manufactured" units/batches between midnight and noon (in the am period).

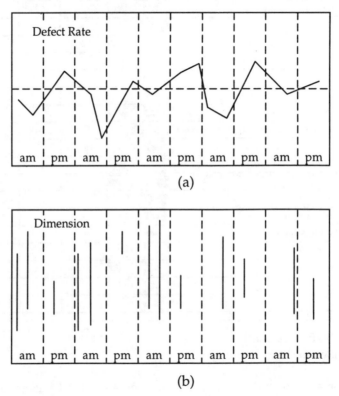

Figure 8-15: Typical Run Diagrams

Correlation diagrams (see Figures 4-20 and 4-21 in Part 4, Section 4) are used to plot one variable — usually level of defects — against some other experimental variable in order to find the real factors that make a difference in eliminating problems or causes.

Another form of diagram is referred to as stratification, which simply means splitting the data into groups and plotting the results on graphs. Usually, data can be separated by operator, machine, material, time, batch, customer, location, etc. Sometimes a stratification approach will yield patterns which are hidden, or are not obvious, in correlation diagrams.

Run diagrams, correlation diagrams and stratification have the effect of identifying what is called *special effects*. Special effects are events or defects which cannot be explained by natural variation of a process. Control of natural variation requires the use of a more sophisticated tool called SPC (statistical process control). SPC is undertaken through the use of charts on which performance of a process is plotted. The reader is referred to other specialist texts (Gitlow et al., 1987) for an insight into the importance of SPC as a means of achieving good quality by prevention rather than detection.

There are many other tools which are now part of the quality process and should be added to the set of tools described within this sub-Section. These tools include:

- affinity diagram

- interrelationship diagram

- tree diagram

- matrix analysis

- contingency chart

- critical path analysis.

Although this book describes many of these tools, the reader is referred to Shigeru Mizuno's book (1988) for a comprehensive explanation of what he refers to as "new" tools.

SECTION 5: COMMUNICATIONS AND CONFIGURATION MANAGEMENT

Contents

- Aims and Objectives
- Configuration Management
- Change Orders
- Meetings and Reporting

Aims and Objectives

The aims and objectives of Section 5 are to:

- Define what is meant by configuration management;
- Design and use a change order process;
- Recognise the importance of effective meeting procedures;
- Present useful tips for good reporting.

Configuration Management

Configuration management concentrates on the management of technology by identifying and controlling the functional and physical design characteristics of a system and its support documentation (Shtub et al., 1994). Simply put, this means that the configuration management process must first describe what needs to be achieved and then positively control all changes during the period(s) of developing the project deliverables. The mission of configuration management is to support concurrent engineering (see Part 6, Section 1), but it should be seen as a necessary element of the project management process whether or not concurrent engineering is adopted. The purpose of configuration management is to warn the project manager and the project team as soon as the integrity and security of their project are jeopardised.

Configuration management, in conjunction with quality assurance, creates a management framework that ensures the integrity of the design and engineering documentation through all project phases. Phil Crosby refers to "zero defects" or getting *it* right first time — nothing less than perfect quality has to be the aim (see the previous Section). This implies that we understand what "it" is. Configuration management is the discipline to define, communicate, and control the "it". In each phase of a project's life-cycle, a baseline is prepared which defines the procedures for handling proposed changes. The baselines (and the phases) are:

- functional (conception phase);
- allocated (definition phase);

- product (implementation/completion phases).

The *functional* baseline contains technical data regarding functional characteristics and integration aspects, design constraints, imposed operational constraints and other considerations. The *allocated* baseline contains performance specifications which will guide the development of the project and its subprojects. The *product* baseline includes information on the project as built and provides commissioning, operating and maintenance manuals. In addition to these three baselines other baselines are frequently needed when the project is complicated.

To function properly, the configuration management process has to perform certain tasks, namely:

- definition;

- communication;

- control;

- incorporation.

It is not possible to manage effectively something that cannot be *defined*. In the case of projects the *something* is(are) the deliverable(s), the culmination of each phase of a project. To define the "somethings" means defining (1) the variables that compose the configuration of these entities, and (2) the stakeholders that control these variables. This can be achieved by creating a matrix of variables and stakeholders for each deliverable; the RAM is a good basis for the development of such a matrix.

Communication is vital to effective configuration management. When a variable is changed it must be communicated to all the affected stakeholders in the project. Communication takes many forms, from computerised data to specifications, drawings, part lists, written instructions, etc. Communication presumes awareness and understanding of and access to that which is being communicated. In other words, you must know something is being communicated, you must have access to this communication, and you must be able to understand what is being communicated.

It is necessary to identify the media through which the configuration entities are communicated. For example, drawings, specifications, bills of materials, purchase order forms, quality assurance forms, etc. are different media through which information needed to explain an entity's configuration, or changes to it, is communicated.

Typically, changes are communicated at two points in time; before an event and after an event. Communication before the event enables the schedule and cost effects to be known before making the change; this is a form of proactive control. When the communication is after the event, the change has already been made. After-the-event communication is the more costly and disruptive.

Change is a necessary part of any project. Without an effective change control process, a project is literally *out of control*. Change control transforms change from an "engineering" or technical environment to a business decision. Many changes would not be incorporated if their effects on costs and schedules and on the potential return on investment (ROI) were analysed properly. Because of the importance of this process, the control of change should not be handled by an entity that is outside the normal project structure. To be effective, change control must be part of project management's role.

Experience shows that some change requests are unnecessary and inappropriate. Project managers must screen all requests for change. Such screening should identify the source and the reason for the change request. The source of the change request can usually be categorised as coming from customers, engineering, materials or manufacturing. The reason for the change request should also be categorised. Reasons for change requests can indicate the importance of a request as well as serve as a check on change costs.

Incorporation is the implementation of the corrective action specified by an approved change request, and it is just as important as the design of the corrective action. Many organisations assume that a change will be implemented automatically, and they stop tracking the change after it has been approved. They thus fail to follow through to ensure that the responsible functions "do what they are supposed to do".

The project manager's role is to make certain that planning is taking place, that through good organisation there is good communications, and that relations between all in the project organisation are good. The project manager is not directly involved in the day-to-day activities but should plan to be an observer by sitting in on the progress/co-ordination meetings to assess how the project and the associated implementation work are developing.

Change Orders

A change control system defines the procedures by which the project scope may be changed. It includes the paperwork, tracking systems, and approval levels necessary for authorising changes. The inputs to scope change control include the WBS, progress reports, change requests and the scope management plan. A scope change is any modification to the agreed-upon project scope as defined by the approved WBS. Scope changes may or may not require adjustments to cost, time, quality, or other project objectives.

Most scope changes are the result of:

- an external event (e.g. a change in government regulations).

- an error or omission in defining the product (e.g. failure to include a required feature in the design of a product).

- a value-adding change (e.g. an environmental project is able to reduce costs by taking advantage of technology that was not available when the scope was originally defined).

Scope changes are fed back through the planning process; technical documents and the project plan are updated as needed, and stakeholders are notified as appropriate.

Changes on projects, from a practical viewpoint, are inevitable and must be allowed for by establishing a procedure for handling them. When the design team or contractor starts work, ideally there will be agreement on the scope of work; any deviation from this scope will constitute a change. The management of change means that no change is made to the scope of work before the change has been reviewed and approved. No effort — people effort or other associated resource effort — should be expended on the change until the corresponding approval and authorisation, to introduce the change to the project, has been given.

It has been found that most changes to a project come from the owner's organisation. Other sources include changes necessitated by erroneous assumptions or misleading/conflicting specifications or stipulations, by changed conditions, or by *force majeure*. Everyone on the project has the responsibility for early identification of change. As soon as a potential change is observed, a project change notice should be written which alerts the project manager and triggers the project change-management process. A typical sample report form is shown in Figure 8-16 (Hamilton, 1997).

PROJECT TREND REPORT	Owner	Order No.	
	Project	System No.	
Originator	Date	Originating Dept.	Trend No.

Description of Change

Reason for Change

Owner Request ☐	Design Development ☐	Construction Req't ☐
Cost Reduction ☐	Schedule Improvement ☐	Safety Req't ☐
Regulatory Agency ☐	Other ☐	☐

Cost Effect

Services			Changes to Equipment and Material		
Disciplines	Man Hrs	Evaluated Date Units	PO or Contract No.	Description	Cost
Architectural					
Electrical					
Mechanical					
Instrumentation					
Construction					
Procurement					
Other			Total Equipment & Materials incl. Installation £		
Total			Total Cost to Project £		

Effect on the Schedule	Project Completion
	Intermediate Activity

Project Approvals

Project Engineer	Accepted	Rejected	Date
Project Manager	Accepted	Rejected	Date

Action Requested	☐ Action Taken	Name	Units	Date
Client Approval	☐ Change Notice sent to Owner			
Forecast Change: Costs	☐ Requisition for Forecast Change Completed			
: Manhours	☐ Manhour Records Updated			
Re-submit	☐			
Other	☐			

Figure 8-16: Sample Project Trend Report

Any change can be requested by someone in either the owner's organisation or in the contractor's organisation — or, in fact, from any of the stakeholders of the project. Every change must be defined, evaluated, and costed, as in Figure 8-16. Every change has the potential of affecting the time schedule and/or the budget cost. Proper assessment of its effect must be made. Based on this information, the proposed change is approved and authorised as stipulated by the provisions of the contract. Then a formal change order is promptly issued (Hamilton, 1997). An example of a typical change order notice is shown as Figure 8-17. No work on the change should be started until all approvals have been granted as contained within the change order.

PROJECT CHANGE NOTICE	Client	Order No.	
	Project	System No.	
Change Notice No.	Change in Scope	Yes ☐	No ☐
Related Trend Report No.	Originating Dept.		

Description of Change

Reason for Change

Instructions Received	From	Date
	How	By

Effect on Schedule
Design
Procurement
Construction

Estimated Effect on Cost		Remarks
Design	£	
Procurement	£	
Construction	£	
Total	£	

The following changes have been incurred to date and are an extra cost for the project £
Additional Remarks

	Name	Title	Date	Remarks
Prepared by				
Approval		Project Manager		
Client Approval				

Figure 8-17: Sample Change Order Notice

The project manager's job on any project is to a large extent the management of change. Only those changes that are absolutely necessary should be approved. The project manager must attempt to minimise the cost, schedule disruption, and any significant problems with the attitudes and perceptions of those working on the project.

An approved change has to be introduced into the budget estimate as soon as it has been accepted as a planned project cost, and the summary estimate and detailed estimates adjusted accordingly. Any effect of such changes on the project's time schedule needs to be incorporated.

Corrective Action

When controlling projects, priority has to be given to those activities or work packages that are on the critical path and behind schedule. The task of the project team is to devise plans for corrective action to return activities or packages of work to acceptable performances.

The purpose of a continuous monitoring approach is to provide opportunities for timely correction of real or anticipated adverse effects on the project's schedule or budget. Some problems found in the projects' environment occur repeatedly. The different types of problem that are often found include the following:

- information not available;

- over-optimistic target date;

- adverse quantity trends;

- mistakes, errors and omissions.

Information Not Available

Often, a very easy excuse for not performing is that the necessary data, information or documentation has not been received.

People usually have two reactions if they don't get information when it is needed. Both are detrimental to the project manager's efforts to run an efficient project. Some people abdicate responsibility if they do not have all the information needed to do the work. This causes schedules to slip. Others tend to "invent" the information they need, taking into account their prejudices, perceptions and bits and pieces of information that are available to them.

Definite responsibility is needed for inputting and/or generating the information required for all aspects of the project. This is one of the reasons why the RAM is so important; it identifies who is to do what!

Over-optimistic Target Dates

Very often the time required to undertake a specific activity or work package is underestimated. Underestimating is likely to have an effect on both schedule and budget. A new and better estimate has to be made and the effect on the following activities or work packages determined — not to mention the overall effect on the project.

For activities on the critical path, a delay in their completion will be a very serious matter because, such a delay will have the effect of delaying the whole project. A good guideline worth remembering is as follows:

If a project is over 40 per cent complete, over budget, and behind schedule, there can be little optimism in continuing without a major effort to change the remaining execution plan. If this is the case, the project team may tend to justify overruns by reference to the "peculiar difficulties" presented by "this project". The project is likely to be unsuccessful if very stringent and possibly unorthodox measures are not introduced urgently. Corrective action at the very least must be to redouble efforts to improve productivity and reduce spending wherever possible without further eroding the chances of completing the project successfully.

Adverse Quantity Trends

Early material takeoffs may bring up evidence of an under-estimated quantity. The project budget may be sensitive to errors in quantity estimates. An overall evaluation is called for to determine the effect of the actual design on the budget. Re-design is one alternative that must be considered. An offsetting estimate is sometimes possible. More frequently, a general trend of underestimating is likely to be discovered.

Mistakes, Errors and Omissions

Even with many of the calculations computerised and an aggressive checking procedure, errors are possible. If an individual has been directed to proceed with work based on assumed data, there could be complications in completing the scheduled work on time and within the budget if the data turns out to be erroneous. Where critical path activities are involved, more serious consequences may arise.

Meetings and Reporting

Project Monitoring

To provide timely and effective control-related decision-making, the project must be tracked and observed systematically. This requires setting up a monitoring function. There are two activities that comprise project monitoring:

- data collection;
- information reporting.

Data Collection

During the first stage of the control process, while the performance standards are being set, a system of data collection and information reporting needs to be established. Typical data sources include materials, purchasing invoices, staff/worker time sheets, change notices, etc. Data for monitoring the project must be directly related to the project.

The information collected during the project for control purposes serves as the basis for taking many of the most important project decisions. The information must be right, not only in the sense of being correct, but also that it is appropriate information and that it is used properly. The degree of accuracy required is dependent upon what the information will be used for and the time urgency for the data. For project control purposes, knowing today that an item will cost about a half-million mu rather than a quarter-million mu is more important than finding out eight weeks from now that it will cost exactly 502,340.50 mu.

Only a few years ago, one of the biggest problems faced by project managers was the length of time that it took to get meaningful information on the status of their project. The selection and use of an adequate computerised information system is now within the reach of all but the smallest organisations.

A manual approach to cost control could well be appropriate for all small projects and/or small companies. Generally speaking, if a small firm has experience in dealing with repetitive projects, then a manual system will suffice.

PCs (personal computers) are well suited to remote locations and small projects, and they provide the ultimate in personal productivity, to the extent that the required project management tools can be put into the hands of each member of the project team. There are now many standardised software packages, such as spreadsheets, databases, etc. that can be used to gather data and support cost control.

The minicomputer is the bridge between PCs and the mainframe, providing decentralised data processing for large jobs, multiple workstations and the ability to run more than one job at a time. The mainframe computer utilises the most expensive hardware and software and offers decentralised data handling and support and faster processing. Remote job entry, while requiring a communication hook-up, allows for multiple interaction between functions and locations on projects. You are likely to find that computerisation and cost control on most of today's projects go hand-in-hand.

Information Reporting

The monitoring function must ensure that all stakeholders receive reports in sufficient detail and frequency to enable them to identify problems while they are small and take corrective action. It must guarantee that significant deviations from the plan — variances — will be highlighted.

The timing of measurement and reporting, be it daily, weekly, or monthly, is important. Data can be collected periodically or topically and reported periodically or by exception. The distinction is crucial to the effectiveness of the monitoring function. As a minimum, reports should coincide with significant project milestones and be available in sufficient time to permit problems to be spotted while they are still minor.

Status reports are needed to provide the project's management with such information as:

- accomplishment/progress/problems;
- the baseline scope, schedule and estimate;
- a listing and explanation of variances;
- plans for the next period;
- progress curves and reforecasting.

It is necessary to emphasise exception reporting in the status reports. In other words, management need to be made aware of major areas of variances to allow the project's management to concentrate its efforts on those areas.

A typical status report schedule and progress curve chart are shown in Figure 8-18.

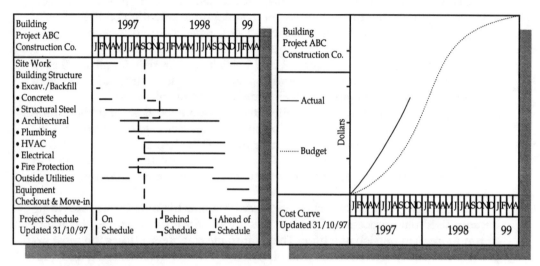

Figure 8-18: Illustrations of Status Report Charts

Reports are generally written, but they can be given by means of oral presentations or using multi-media (video, tape, CD-ROM, etc.) methods.

Collectively, status reports should furnish an accurate history of the project from beginning to end. Status reports are invaluable for informing and for helping to make decisions on corrective action, and they are extremely useful to have when planning similar projects for the future.

Communications technology is changing almost daily. Many companies associated with projects use electronic mail or e-mail for correspondence and reports. It is much easier to transmit information to the project stakeholders using these systems.

Computer programs have the capability of producing information in advance. This is a tremendous advantage for the project team. If they have a difficult decision to make and need to look at options, it is worth examining "what if" scenarios which will provide nearly instantaneous solutions.

Site refers to the location of the project's implementation. Site co-ordination meetings are normally arranged by the prime contractor and are the main opportunity for the various project participants engaged in implementation to discuss progress achieved, to forecast their planned activities within the next period and to highlight problems being, or likely to be, encountered before the next co-ordination meeting.

Other project meetings called by the project manager will deal with such matters as work progress and difficulties being encountered by the contractors or subcontractors.

Reporting

Status reports deal with factual material about on-site conditions, progress and productivity, as well as actual and anticipated problems. The status reports, which go to the project manager, must be completed and issued on schedule in order to be integrated with the project manager's report to the owner.

Reporting levels and the type of detail that is usually provided at each level are shown in Figure 8-19.

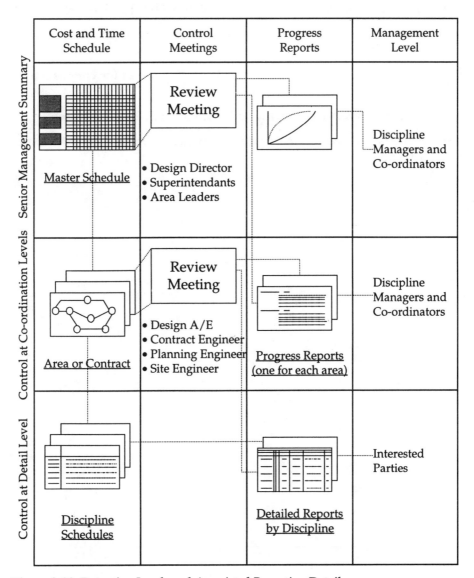

Figure 8-19: Reporting Levels and Associated Reporting Detail

The frequency with which the reports are issued is an indication as to what they should contain. The ten most important topics to be covered in a status report are:

- progress of the work compared with that planned;
- unfavourable variances in job progress;

- cost status of project work compared to the plan;

- unfavourable variances in job cost;

- status of material and equipment relative to promised deliveries;

- status of subcontractors' work and relations with subcontractors;

- current status of labour relations and any problems or anticipated labour relations problems;

- listing of the safety statistics for the latest period and the cumulative statistics for the job;

- significant variances in quality and how they have been addressed;

- photographs showing progress at the project's location since the issue of the last report.

SECTION 6: COMPLETING THE PROJECT

Contents

- Aims and Objectives
- Termination Process
- Commissioning the Facility
- Project Completion
- Summary of Key Points
- References

Aims and Objectives

The aims and objectives of Section 6 are to:

- Explain the ways in which a project can be terminated;
- Define the key elements of the commissioning process;
- Explain the importance of project completion and feedback.

Termination Process

The termination of a project rarely has much impact on technical success or failure, but it has a great deal to do with residual attitudes — in other words, does it please the owner (client), senior management of the performing organisation, and the project team? At termination, the exhilaration of discovery is past. Problems have been solved, steered around, just about "lived with", or ignored. Implementation plans have been carried out. The project's owner is either, at one extreme, delighted, at the other extreme, furious — or just about satisfied, if they view the project as neither a disaster nor a total success. Senior management and the project team have the capacity to view the project in the same way.

There are varieties of termination. A project can be said to be terminated when work on the substance of the project has ceased or slowed to the point that further progress on the project is no longer possible. Termination also occurs when a project has been postponed indefinitely or when resources have been deployed to other projects. There are three fundamental ways in which projects can be closed-out: extinction, inclusion, and integration (Meredith and Mantel, 1995).

In termination by *extinction*, the project is stopped. It may be that the project has been totally successful and achieved all its targets. Conversely, the project may have been stopped because it has been superseded by internal factors, such as the discovery that the project will cost too much or take too long. Termination may occur because external factors, such as the emergence of cheaper and better alternatives, are available from competitors. Other examples are termination by environmental factors, failed test of new drugs, failure of some sub-system or component.

Termination by *inclusion* relates to a project that is terminated by institutionalising it as part of the parent organisation. Good examples of this type of termination can be found within the process industry. Providing the project is a success, it is not uncommon for the project resources simply to be transferred to the new facility which is considered to be a new division or new entity within the corporate or operational structure.

Termination by *integration* is perhaps the most common and complex way of dealing with successful projects. The resources are distributed among the elements of the parent organisation. The output of the project becomes an integral part of the operating systems of the parent organisation.

Success-related factors in projects vary for different industries. The factors which create project failure, and hence can present reasons for termination, are many and varied. The factors and their relative importance are peculiar to the industry, the project type, and possibly to the performing organisation. There are four fundamental generic reasons why projects fail:

1) a project form of organisation was not appropriate,

2) there is insufficient support from top management,

3) the wrong person was selected as project manager,

4) there was poor or incompetent planning.

The performing organisation needs to understand the reasons for using the adopted project type of organisational structure and more particularly when it is inappropriate to use such a structure.

Each project, and its project manager, need a "godfather" in top management who, when the situation requires it, will back the project when it is in need of resources. Projects invariably develop requirements for resources that were not originally identified or allocated. If the project is not to suffer resourcing arguments between the functional managers and the project manager, the godfather is needed as a referee and to look favourably on the requirements of the project.

A common problem in resourcing projects is to appoint a project manager who has excellent technical skills but is weak in people management or who has inadequate training in the project management process and associated techniques.

In the rush to get on with the project, it is common to find that competent planning is neglected or discarded through the mistaken belief that what is more important is to make progress with the substance of the project. Such action usually means that crisis management becomes a way of life as difficulties and problems are compounded and the project slowly gets further and further behind and the overall cost becomes more and more above the anticipated budget.

Commissioning the Facility

The commissioning stage consists of the following elements: inspection and testing, acceptance, facility turnover, and initial operation. The commissioning stage has to be dealt with, from a planning viewpoint, in the same way as other project stages. Prior to this stage, a detailed plan needs to be developed that will fully cover the tasks that are likely to be contained within the four elements specified.

Inspection and Testing

Throughout the implementation process the acceptance and testing of certain works is a part of the substance of the project. For instance, the installation of buried pipework is inspected and tested as it is laid and completed. So inspection and testing should not be seen as end-of-job activities; they can happen at any time throughout the implementation period.

During inspection and testing of some elements of the project, it might be necessary to obtain implementation assistance from specialists and manufacturers. Tests on major equipment items, such as furnaces, compressors, large pumps, etc. should be conducted in the presence of experts. Where possible, the owner's operating and maintenance personnel should also be in attendance.

Safety is a very important consideration during any sort of testing. For instance, where an element or component of a project is subjected to what is called hydrostatic pressure testing, this can be extremely dangerous. The commissioning plan should indicate the individual who is responsible for safety of the personnel and the facility. This individual has to review and approve testing plans and procedures.

Acceptance

Acceptance of the facility by the owner is an extremely important occurrence because of the significant legal implications. In other words, the day prior to acceptance, responsibility for the project belongs with the contractor even though the owner may have paid out the full, or close to the full, amount of the project cost to the contractor. As soon as acceptance is assigned to the owner, the owner is responsible for what is now known as the facility. So once the owner takes over the facility, the care, custody and control of what had been the project passes to the owner. The owner is now responsible for insurance, safety, security, maintenance, and housekeeping.

Another significant aspect of the acceptance event is that the owner's operational and maintenance personnel have witnessed the inspection and testing of the facility, and they have agreed that the work has been done in accordance with the contracts, drawings and specifications. It is the contractor's responsibility to correct any elements of the system that are noted as being defective or deficient and that were not in accordance with predetermined requirements.

Facility Turnover

With the facility now in the hands of the owner, the start-up process is the responsibility of the owner's operational and maintenance personnel. The contractor is likely to be involved in related and subsequent activities, particularly on matters that the owner's personnel find are in need of further work. An example is the adjustment of doors that are not closing or locking correctly. Another example is the adjustment of the seals of a water pump which are found to be leaking.

The start-up of the facility is normally carried out on a sub-system by sub-system basis rather than all at once. As the start-up can take time, appropriate calendar time should be made available in the detailed before-the-event planning. The first step in facility turnover is the written notification by the contractor that the project plant (equipment) is completed and is ready for owner acceptance. All of the formalities of plant start-up should be checked and completed in accordance with the contract(s).

Initial Operation

This element of commissioning refers to the first real operation of the facility. For example, if the facility is an industrial development, then the design feedstocks into the facility and the processing of these feedstocks into the specified end products for which the facility was designed have to be witnessed. Another example of a different type of facility and its initial operation is an IT system for a business. For this facility, it is necessary to witness, check and review the first use of the IT facility when it is operated by the user staff and, if appropriate, their customers.

Project Completion

Assume that the project has been completed and officially handed over to the owner. That is not the end of the project. Not yet! What ends the project is an activity, or a set of activities, that are referred to as project "closeout". The elements that are included within close-out are:

- subcontract close-out;

- purchase order close out;

- financial close-out;

- warranties;

- demobilisation;

- close-out report.

The project close-out can be much less interesting than everything that went before, but it is nevertheless an essential aspect of project management and has to be undertaken. Until these activities have been carried out, the project cannot be declared completed, and a project not properly closed loses much of its value in providing feedback for the planning of future projects.

Close-out should be undertaken promptly at the end of a project and before all, or most, of the key personnel who possess the project knowledge are assigned to their next project.

Contract/Subcontract Close-out

All contracts require checking to ensure that all work has been completed and that all changes or omissions have been properly documented. All variations that have not already been dealt with and settled, have to be negotiated and, where necessary, compensation agreed. Any tasks that are found to be incomplete should be finished or an acknowledgement given in writing that absolves the responsible party from any further action; any monetary difference also needs to be resolved.

Purchase Order Close-out

All purchase orders need to be reviewed against the received deliverables; the position on returnables and assessed charges or credits need to be actioned. Included within this review is the need to check all records that cover fabrication, testing, erection, spare parts, maintenance recommendations, vendor drawings, etc. — whatever happens to be the make-up of a project.

Financial Close-out

Financial audits need to be carried out on all contracts and purchase orders, and this information compared with what had been anticipated. A review of the major differences, whether they are extra costs or savings, should be identified for all the principal tasks or elements of the implementation work.

Warranties

The programme that provides the owner with guarantees on such matters as building and equipment operation needs to be implemented and handed over to the owner's group responsible for the operation of the facility.

Demobilisation

Temporary structures used by the project team, such as portable buildings, scaffolding, implementation equipment, stores and stored materials, etc. all need to be transported off-site.

Clearing up the implementation location in compliance with the contractual provisions is a necessary component of project close-out.

Close-out Report

It is expected that the owner's project manager will prepare the close-out report. However, there are times when the contractor's implementation manager will also prepare a report; the data and information used are likely to be common to both. These reports are normally for internal use and for senior management within the respective organisations to observe and learn about the life and performance of this particular project.

Close-out reports should contain summaries of the completed works, information on staffing and worker levels, the on-site organisation, the project time schedule, the costs, quality of work, major problems encountered, how they were handled, etc., etc. Much of what is contained in a review of the contracts and purchase orders and the financial close-out, would be contained in these reports. Extensive use is usually made of graphical presentations. Specially selected implementation photographs would also be included to show work conditions and general progress.

It is normal to conclude the close-out report (the one by the project manager) with recommendations for handling future work of this type, or, if appropriate, work of any nature. It is essential that the lessons learned from today's completed project are feedback to be used for the benefit of tomorrow's projects.

Summary of Key Points

- The planning and scheduling of the implementation and completion work are based on conformance with the overall scope of work and the contractor's proposed methods of carrying out the work. The broad assumptions that were made previously in addressing the implementation period and the implementation works are now replaced with detailed method statements, detailed plans, time schedules and other information that will displace the broad assumptions.

- The project management team has a very important part to play during the implementation of the project, which of course is driven by the contractors and their support team. The project team's responsibilities are to maintain the "big picture" view of the project and ensure that there is a balanced judgement in meeting the project targets of performance (scope and quality), time of completion and cost at completion.

- From the overall plan for the implementation works, the contractor needs to undertake monthly planning and weekly or daily planning as a way of keeping the project's implementation work on schedule. Implementation planning needs to be more comprehensive and detailed simply because of the "many people, many tasks" syndrome.

- Every contractor and/or subcontractor has the right to expect that they can perform the work that falls within their responsibility in an efficient manner. From time to time, there inevitably will be situations that develop when the implementation work will involve problems. The simple answers for getting over many of these types of problem are excellent planning and good communications.

- The control of project work can be expressed as "those measures that are necessary to make sure that the expected happens". Control with respect to time schedule, cost and performance (the triple constraints) is fundamental in achieving project success. The control activities in any project must be supported by the entire project team.

- Projects cannot be controlled unless they are properly planned, and projects cannot be planned unless there is a clear knowledge of the owner's requirements and the project objectives. Time drives projects, and for this reason, networked scheduled plans that are time-based are used. Cost does not drive projects; cost is an outcome of time expended.

- The levels of control on a project differ according to the project management organisation and its procedures, but classically there are four levels of control in a project: summary, co-ordination, detail, and task. Projects are controlled at the second level of scheduled plan — the co-ordination level.

- It is often necessary to measure the actual performance of a project and compare it to what was scheduled at an earlier date, usually at project commencement. The earned value approach is used for this purpose. Earned value compares the budgeted cost of work scheduled, BCWS, with the two other variables of interest, BCWP and ACWP.

- Performance against budget is a comparison of the singular actions "what I did" against "what I paid for". If "what I did" is greater than "what I paid for", it means that I am under budget. Conversely if "what I did" is less than "what I paid for", then I am over budget.

- An updated schedule provides an important record of the project status at a specific time. A network regularly updated to show the effect of changes, errors or delays can be used to determine and allocate responsibility.

- Progress payments, which are paid periodically to the contractor during the implementation of a project, are based on the amount of work accomplished to date and can be shown as a cash-flow profile that would be the contractors' anticipated earnings. This information can be used by the owner as the basis for planning the project finances and the weekly (monthly) outgoings; the implementation cost being one of those outgoings.

- Network schedules can play an important part in implementation delay claims. Delays can be identified, defined, and explained by schedules. By recalculating (or rerunning through a computer) the schedule with the delays, the effect of the delays on the project completion date can be shown and the effect of future delays can be previewed.

- Quality is defined as "the totality of characteristics of an entity that bear on its ability to satisfy stated or implied need". A critical aspect of quality management in the project context is the necessity to turn implied needs into stated needs through project scope management.

- The field of quality management has been strongly influenced by such people as Deming, Juran, Crosby, Feigenbaum, Ishikawa, Garvin, Shingo, and Taguchi.

- One of the most important tasks of the project manager is to set quality standards that will satisfy the regulatory agencies and will provide an economical quality–cost performance in keeping with the owner's objectives.

- The configuration management process first must describe what needs to be achieved and then positively control all changes during the period(s) of developing the project deliverables.

- Communication is vital to effective configuration management. When a variable is changed it must be communicated to all the affected stakeholders in the project. Communication takes many forms, from computerised data to specifications, drawings, part lists, written instructions, etc. Communication presumes awareness and understanding of and access to that which is being communicated.

- A change control system defines the procedures by which the project scope may be changed. It includes the paperwork, tracking systems, and approval levels necessary for authorising changes.

- To provide timely and effective control-related decision-making, the project must be tracked and observed systematically. This requires setting up a monitoring function. The two activities that comprise project monitoring are data collection and information reporting.

- A project can be said to be terminated when work on the substance of the project has ceased or slowed to the point that further progress on the project is no longer possible. Termination also occurs when a project is postponed indefinitely or when resources are deployed to other projects.

- The commissioning stage consists of the following elements: inspection and testing, acceptance, facility turnover, and initial operation. The commissioning stage has to be dealt with, from a planning viewpoint, in the same way as other project stages. Prior to this stage a detailed plan needs to be developed that will fully cover the tasks that are likely to be contained within the four elements specified.

- Project close-out is an essential aspect of project management. Until the related activities have been completed, the project cannot be declared completed. A project not properly closed loses much of its value in providing feedback for the planning of future projects.

References

References used in the development of Part 8:

Bicheno, John (1994), *The Quality 50*, Picsie Books.

Crosby, Phil (1989), *Let's Talk Quality*, McGraw-Hill.

Dilworth, James (1992), *Operations Management*, McGraw-Hill.

Feigenbaum, Armand (1991), *Total Quality Control*, 3rd edition, McGraw-Hill.

Gitlow, Howard and Shelley (1987), *The Deming Guide to Quality and Competitive Position*, Prentice Hall.

Hamilton, Albert (1997), *The Projects Approach — PM Diploma Course Module*, University of Limerick.

Hamilton, Albert and Thomas, Monica (1997), *Planning, Scheduling and Control — PM Diploma Course Module*, University of Limerick.

Humphreys, Kenneth K. (1991), *Jelen's Cost and Optimization Engineering*, 3rd Edition, McGraw-Hill Inc.

Ishikawa, Kaoru (1985), *What is Total Quality Control? The Japanese Way*, Prentice-Hall.

Juran, Joseph J. (1979), *Quality Control Handbook*, 3rd edition, McGraw-Hill.

Meredith, Jack R. and Mantel, Samuel J. (1995), *Project Management, A Managerial Approach*, 3rd Edition, John Wiley & Sons.

Mizuno, Shigeru (1988), *Management for Quality Improvement: The 7 New QC Tools*, Productivity Press.

Nicholas, John M. (1990), *Managing Business & Engineering Projects — Concepts and Implementation*, Prentice-Hall International Editions.

Project Management Institute (1996), *A Guide to the Project Management Body of Knowledge (PMBOK)*, PMI Publications.

Shtub, Avraham, Bard, Jonathan F. and Globerson, Shlomo (1994), *Project Management: Engineering, Technology and Implementation*, Prentice-Hall Inc.

GLOSSARY

This glossary relates to terms that are used within the projects' environment. Most of the glossary content can be found within this book.

The glossary is not intended to be comprehensive. For a more specialised coverage of words and terms, the following Standards should be consulted:

- BS 4335: 1987 (Glossary of terms used in project network techniques)

- BS 7000: Part 10: 1995 (Glossary of terms used in design management)

- BS EN ISO 8402: 1995 (Quality management and quality assurance vocabulary)

abscissa

the horizontal axis of a graph. Also used to denote the first number in an ordered pair of numbers (co-ordinates).

activity

a series of tasks performed over a period of time.

activity description

the description given to an activity that normally indicates the activity's scope of work.

activity duration

the time period needed to complete an individual activity.

activity-on-arrow

a form of network diagram that uses arrowed lines to represent activities and nodes to represent events. The tail of the line is the start of the activity and the arrow (head) is the finish of the activity.

activity-on-node

a form of network diagram that uses nodes or boxes to represent activities and arrowed lines to show dependencies between activities.

ACWP

this means the "actual cost of work performed" and is the total actual cost of the work that has been undertaken up to some defined point during the project's overall duration.

aggregate

the sum or total of a collection.

algorithm

a systematic procedure for carrying out a computation; any method of computing; step-by-step procedure.

analogy

a form of reasoning in which it is concluded that if things are alike in some respects they are probably alike in other respects.

Aristotle

a great Greek philosopher who laid the foundation for most of the branches of science and philosophy known today.

array

an orderly arrangement of objects in rows and columns.

arrow

a symbol that is used to show activity and direction.

arrow diagram

an activity-on-arrow diagram that is drawn to scale so that it relates to a time calendar.

average

a single number representing a set of numbers. Is given by t divided by n, where t is the total and n is the number of items.

BAC

this means "budget at completion" and is the estimated total cost of a project when completed.

backward pass

the term used when calculating late start and late finish dates of activities within a network diagram.

bar chart

otherwise called Gantt chart. It is one of the graphic displays used to show a scheduled plan of activities.

baseline

the original scheduled plan with approved changes that provides the current basis for project control.

BCWP

this means "budgeted cost of work performed" and is the summated budget estimates of all work carried out to the end of a defined period.

BCWS

this means "budgeted cost of work scheduled" and is the summated estimate for all activities scheduled to be performed during a given period.

bell-shaped curve

the normal distribution curve.

boundary

a line that separates a system from its outer environment.

budget estimate

an estimate of the cost of a project or an element of a project.

calendar

a method of measuring and recording time, especially in cycles of a year, including the arrangement of days into weeks and of weeks into months.

calendar unit

also referred to as time unit. It is the smallest unit of time used in scheduling a project plan.

CBS

this means "cost breakdown structure" and is the result of combining the WBS, the OBS, and the code of accounts to create an array of costed activity that can be aggregated into work packages, project packages, program packages, etc.

change control

a methodology for identifying and controlling any type of project change.

code of accounts

a numbering system that is specific to each project, identifying the activities within a WBS.

compound interest

interest paid not only on the principal but also on the interest which has been added to the principal.

concurrency

is the act of more than one activity happening or taking place at the same time.

concurrent engineering

an approach that calls for many of the project activities to be undertaken at the same time. Normally this refers to multi-design activities and multi-production activities happening at the same time.

contingency

a provision made when planning a project to mitigate against schedule and/or cost risk.

contract

a binding agreement between a buyer and a seller requiring the seller to provide goods or services and the buyer to pay for such goods or services.

control

the process of comparing actual performance with what had been predicted, through the provision of a scheduled plan, and taking whatever corrective action may be necessary.

control charts

a type of graph that usually has upper and lower limits plotted against time. The chart is used for showing the variance in a variable when plotted over time.

cost budgeting

allocating the project cost estimate to project packages or elements of the project.

cost control

the process of controlling changes to the project budget.

cost-slope

the simplified relationship between an activity's cost and duration obtained by determining the effect on cost of an elemental decrease (or increase) in the activity's duration.

CPI

this means "cost performance index", a ratio that is obtained by dividing BCWP by ACWP.

CPM

this stands for "critical path method", a method of network analysis used to predict the duration of a project. CPM utilises discrete values for activity durations and focuses on the FS (finish to start) type of dependency between activities.

crashing

otherwise known as least-cost scheduling. The process of analysing the project cost – project duration relationship to determine the least duration, the least cost, and all options between.

criteria

otherwise referred to as attributes, they are standards that are used in judging something.

criteria weighting matrix

a device for comparing and ranking qualitative attributes (or criteria).

critical activity

any activity whose early start and finish dates are the same as the late start and finish dates. It is normal to find such activities on the project's critical path.

critical path

the path or paths within an analysed network which, being the longest path(s) determines the earliest completion of the project.

CV

this means "cost variance" and is calculated by subtracting ACWP from BCWP. A positive value of CV indicates that the project is below budget.

cycle

an interval of time in which some regular events take place.

dangle

an activity within a network where either the preceding or succeeding dependencies are missing and hence it is not linked to either preceding or succeeding activities.

data

facts or information often arranged in charts or graphs to show the relationship between them.

DCFR

this stands for "discounted cash flow return", a means of economic evaluation that takes into account the time value of money and reduces cash flows to a present value.

DCP

this stands for "definitive control plan" and is the deliverable from the design stage which includes a refined PMP, project record system, and risk management plan.

deliverable

a measurable, tangible outcome that concludes a project phase or a project.

dependency

the logic relationship between two activities which shows the activity that precedes, the activity that succeeds, or the activity that is concurrent.

dependent variable

in the function $y = 3x$, the value of y (dependent variable) is determined by the value of x.

depreciation

loss in value of goods or property, or a decrease in the value of money.

deviation, standard

the most widely used measure of the variability of a distribution.

DFP

this stands for "detailed firm plan" and is the deliverable at the end of the procurement stage.

difference

the amount by which one quantity or number is greater or less than another.

discrete

separate or distinct. The opposite of discrete is continuous.

distribution curve

a graph derived from a frequency distribution.

divergence

the property of not being convergent.

dummy

used in the AOA (activity on arrow) diagrams to complete the logic relationship between two or more activities where such relationship(s) cannot be satisfied by means of a regular activity.

duration

the number of time periods that is estimated are needed to complete an activity or other project task.

duration compression

the process through which an activity's duration can be shortened through the use of increased work periods, increased resources, etc.

EAC

this stands for "estimate at completion" and refers to the cost when the associated work has been completed.

EF

this stands for "early finish" and is found during a forward pass by adding an activity's duration to the activity's early start date.

effort

the number of person-hours (or days) needed or expended to complete, or partially complete, an activity or a project consisting of a number of activities.

EMV

this stands for "expected monetary value", which is synonymous with *expected value* (EV), and is the summation of the products of the probability of an outcome and the financial result of the same outcome.

ES

this stands for "early start" and is found during a forward pass by determining the latest date of EF of all preceding activities.

estimate

by its nature an estimate is an imprecise assessment of a likely quantifiable element (time, cost, etc.).

ETC

this stands for "estimated time to completion" and at any project reporting date is the forecasted time when the project will be completed.

EV

see *EMV*.

evaluation matrix

an evaluation matrix includes criteria that affect an element of a project and develops a weighting system that shows the response of various alternative solutions (properties and/or costs) against the criteria.

event

any work action that doesn't require time. Start and finish events are a feature of AOA diagrams.

exception reporting

document that includes only major variations to what had been planned.

FF

this stands for a "finish to finish" relationship between two activities; see *dependency*.

finish date

a calendar date when an activity will be or has been completed.

float

the amount of time that an activity may be delayed without delaying subsequent activities or the project finish date. Also referred to as *total float* or *slack*.

formula

a rule expressed as an equation.

forward pass

the term used when calculating early start and early finish dates of activities within a network diagram.

free float

the amount of time that an activity can be delayed without delaying the ES of any succeeding activity.

frequency distribution

a table showing how often each event or measurement occurred.

FS

this stands for a "finish to start" relationship between two activities; see *dependency*.

functional

a type of organisational structure.

game theory

a branch of mathematics concerned with, among other things, probability; see *Monte Carlo Analysis*.

initiation

the first of the five steps of project management process, the other steps being plan, execute, control, and close.

lag

a delay between the end of a preceding activity and the start of a succeeding activity.

LCC

this stands for "life cycle cost" and is fully inclusive of initial cost, operation cost, maintenance cost, salvage cost, and other associated costs.

lead

an overlap between the end of a preceding activity and the start of a succeeding activity.

levelling

usually refers to the attempt to create a uniform resource over a specific time period.

LF

this stands for "late finish" and is found during a backward pass by determining the earliest date of LS of all succeeding activities.

link

usually refers to the logic relationships (dependencies) between activities.

logic diagram

part of the planning process and the outcome of the WBS, OBS, and RAM. The logic diagram consists of activities, shown as boxes, and the dependencies, shown as arrowed lines.

logic relationship

see *dependency*.

LS

this stands for "late start" and is found during a backward pass by subtracting an activity's duration from the activity's late finish date.

matrix

any form of table which compares two variables. Also refers to a type of organisational structure.

milestone

a significant intermediate or end event that usually refers to the achievement of deliverables.

monitoring

the connection between the processes of execution and control; the analysis and reporting of actual performance as compared to predicted.

Monte Carlo Analysis

a mathematical technique using random numbers which are combined many times to provide a distribution of outcomes.

mu

monetary unit(s).

network

a schematic display of activities complete with dependencies and activity durations; a further development of a logic diagram.

network analysis

the process of mathematical calculations which will provide the early and late start and finish dates for all uncompleted activities.

node

a start or finish of an activity denoted by a circle in AOA diagrams. Also refers to the activity box in the AON diagram. Can also refer to the junction where a number of relational activities come together.

non-critical activity

an activity that is not critical and therefore contains float or slack.

OBS

this means "organisation breakdown structure" and is the means used to present the various parties involved in performing the project and linking the parties to the principal work items.

parameter

an arbitrary constant; a variable in an algebraic expression that temporarily assumes the properties of a constant.

parametric estimating

using a statistical relationship between historical data and other variables to calculate an estimate.

Pareto diagram

a histogram, usually shown as a decreasing histogram, which shows how many results were generated by each identified cause.

path

a set of sequentially connected activities in a network diagram.

PDM

this stands for "precedence diagramming method", a network diagramming technique which uses AON and can include SS, FS, FF, and SF dependencies.

percent complete

an estimate, expressed as a percent, of the amount of work completed on an activity or group of activities.

PERT

this stands for "program evaluation review technique".

PERT diagram

an event-oriented network which uses the AOA technique and a statistical approach to determine activity durations and the project's duration.

phase

a part of a project's life cycle; the number of phases being determined, inter-alia, by the type of project.

PMBOK

this stands for "project management body of knowledge" and is the inclusive term that describes the sum of knowledge within the profession of project management as defined by the Project Management Institute.

predecessor

an activity or activities that come immediately before the activity under consideration.

probability

the likelihood of occurrence. The ratio of the number of chances by which an event may happen (or not happen) to the sum of chances of both happening and not happening.

programme

a group of related projects managed in a co-ordinated and integrated way.

project

an impermanent endeavour which, with uncertainty, utilises resources to create a unique product, facility or service.

project charter

a document issued by top management that provides the project manager with the authority to use organisational resources for undertaking project activities.

project life cycle

a sequence of phases which divide the overall project period to allow better control and identification of phase deliverables.

QA

this stands for "quality assurance" and is the process of evaluating overall project performance on a regular basis.

RAM

this means "responsibility and accountability matrix" which links the WBS and the OBS into a matrix array and assigns responsibility to the individual.

resources

the people, equipment, materials, money, etc. that can be used to perform project activities.

resource levelling

a form of resource management that seeks to create a more uniform use of resources than provided by an initial schedule-driven allocation.

RFP

this stands for "request for a proposal" and is a document invitation that solicits proposals for a product or a service.

risk event

the precise description of what might happen to the detriment of the project.

risk probability

the degree to which the risk event is likely to occur.

S-curve

the name given to a graphical display between two variables that produces an S shape relationship; classically reflects the relationship between cumulative project estimated cost when plotted against project time period.

scheduled plan

the outcome of analysing a plan and setting the activities against a date (time) calendar.

scope

the totality of what is included in the products and services of a project.

slack

see *float*.

solicitation

obtaining quotations, bids, offers, or proposals as appropriate.

SOW

this stands for "scope of works" and is a narrative description of products or services to be supplied under contract.

SPI

this stands for "schedule performance index", a ratio that is obtained by dividing the BCWP by the BCWS.

SS

this stands for "start to start" relationship between two activities; see *dependency*.

successor activity

an activity or activities that come immediately after the activity under consideration.

SV

this stands for "schedule variance" and is calculated by subtracting BCWS from BCWP. A positive value of SV indicates that the project is ahead of schedule.

synthesis

the combination of elements into a whole.

task

see *activity*.

tolerance

the allowable error in a given measurement.

total float

see *float*.

TQM

a common approach to implementing a quality improvement program within an organisation.

tu

time unit(s).

uncertainty

the possibility that events may occur which will impact the project either favourably or unfavourably. Uncertainty gives rise to both opportunity and risk.

variable

a letter or other place-holder in a mathematical expression.

Venn, John

an English mathematician (1834–1923) who worked with statistics, probability and logic, and whose name is given to the Venn diagram.

WBS

this stands for "work breakdown structure" and relates to the structure (can be a listing) of project elements grouped into deliverable-oriented products and services.

work package

a deliverable at the lowest level of the WBS. A work package is likely to be divided into activities and tasks.

INDEX

Note: Figures are indicated by italic page numbers